LANDSCAPE

PATTERN, PERCEPTION AND PROCESS

LANDSCAPE

PATTERN, PERCEPTION AND PROCESS

SIMON BELL

First published 1999 by E & FN Spon
11 New Fetter Lane, London EC4P 4EE

Simultaneously published in the USA and Canada
by Routledge
29 West 35th Street, New York, NY 10001

E & FN Spon is an imprint of the Taylor & Francis Group

© 1999 Simon Bell

Typeset in Sabon by Elaine Dick, Stockbridge, Edinburgh
Printed and bound in Great Britain by T. J. International Ltd,
Padstow Cornwall

British Library Cataloguing in Publication Data
A catalogue record for this book is available from the British Library

Library of Congress Cataloging in Publication Data
Bell, Simon
    Landscape: Pattern, Perception and Process / Simon Bell.
        p. cm.
    Includes bibliographical references and index.
    1. Ecological landscape design. 2. Landscape assessment.
    3. Regional planning–Environmental aspects. I. Title.
    SB472.45.B46 1999
    712´.2–dc21   98-41656

ISBN 0-419-20340-0

CONTENTS

ACKNOWLEDGEMENTS

This book emerged over a long period of time and I am grateful to the many collegues, friends and aquaintances who have helped me test and clarify the ideas and structure as they developed. A special debt of gratitude goes to Duncan Campbell for his intensive efforts at helping me get the ideas and their expression clarified and comprehensible. His forthright editing of the first draft and his subsequent comments enabled me to achieve what I hope is a worthy result. Caroline Mallinder, my editor at Spon, displayed endless patience as the book evolved and grew. Valuable material was provided to me by Steven Warnock and I was permitted to use examples from British Columbia by Norm Bilodeau and Marvin Eng of the provincial Ministry of Forests. Helpful unpublished material was provided by Peter Gunter of the University of North Texas. Permission to use photographs and artwork was given by the Forestry Commission, Countryside Commission, Patricia MacDonald, James Ogilvie and Richard Kyle. Ideas were bounced off Dean Apostol, Nancy Diaz, Roland Gustaffson, Minna Komulainen, John McLoughlin, Tim Yarnell, Nick Shepherd, Gareth Price, Graham Pyatt, Chris Quine, and others too numerous to mention individually. Elaine Dick made a fine job of the design and my wife Jacquie word processed the initial drafts.

Thank you all.

PREFACE

I have been privileged to be able to travel widely and to work or visit many landscapes, ranging from the most urban to the most wild, and from those where human influences go back many thousands of years to those where settlement has been relatively recent. I have also had many opportunities to study much recent research into landscapes and their processes and the scientific and philosophical background to their perceptions. This wide ranging study has enabled me to develop the extensive links between so many natural and cultural phenomena that became the synthesis presented here. I have also observed at first hand many of the problems that human mismanagement of the landscape cause and firmly believe that there is a middle road between laissez faire development and outright protection. Readers may detect a bias to the geographical spread of examples cited here. This is because they are all ones I am personally acquainted with and I hope this gives them more immediacy. The vast majority of the photographs were taken by me and these also reflect the experiences I have brought to the book. Many of the case studies presented here reflect ongoing projects with which I have had a direct connection, so that the theoretical material is supported by examples that demonstrate its validity. I have been excited by the possibilities I have encountered during my researches and I believe that there are hopeful signs that we are at last understanding how we relate to the world around us and using that understanding to manage natural and cultural resources better and more sustainably. There is still a long way to go and I would like to think that this book is a modest contribution to the journey. I hope you enjoy the book as much as I have enjoyed the process of developing and writing it.

Simon Bell FICFor, MLI
Dunbar

INTRODUCTION

The View from Scarth Nick

It is late summer and I stand at the edge of the escarpment above a narrow valley called Scarth Nick, in the Cleveland Hills of North Yorkshire, in the north of England. The weather is bright and sunny with a little haze and the purple bloom of heather on the moorland behind me is just fading.

This scene used to be my home, for I was brought up on the farm that lies on the scarp slope below me. However, it is some 20 years since I lived here. My infrequent visits have allowed me to see the changes more clearly, whilst I have widened my experience of life and landscape during my extensive travel and work around the world. What once I saw with the eye of an active participant, I now see as a passive observer.

With that eye and also with my ears, nose and tactile senses, I can deduce that many threads have been woven together to form the somewhat worn tapestry of landscape spread out beneath me. There is the geology, jurassic and triassic sedimentary rocks of shale, sandstone and, deeper down, limestone. There are the effects of earth movements and erosion that have produced the escarpment, rising to 1000 feet (300 metres) and more above sea level, gently dipping southwards. Glaciation has also left its mark, eroding a meltwater channel through the scarp, leaving boulder clay deposits on the lower slopes and, on the plain below, the bed of a former lake dammed by ice.

The view from the escarpment of the Cleveland Hills at Scarth Nick in Yorkshire, England. The landscape is the result of the interaction of human and natural processes over several thousand years. The patterns of landform, cultivation, woodland and settlement reflect the forces of sedimentation, uplift, glaciation, ecological colonization and succession together with many generations of people who have lived there continuously.

Vegetation has been altered by countless generations of farmers, including my family. Woodland still clings to the steepest parts. Heather colonizes the exhausted sandy soils, where the forest was cleared by grazing animals in the Bronze Age and is still grazed by the hardy Swaledale sheep. On the skyline behind me I can make out the subtle outline of a kerbed cairn, one of a series of burial mounds constructed by those Bronze Age farmers 3500 years ago. Mixed farming of cattle rearing and arable crops occupies the lower slopes and the plain below, much as it has always done: the rigg and furrow patterns from mediaeval ploughs in some of the fields provide that evidence. A few, more modern crops are also present, such as oilseed rape, partly introduced to take advantage of European Union financial incentives. Villages can also be seen, across the plain and tucked into the foot of the hill. Their names reflect the Anglo-Saxon and Viking settlers, some recalling features in the landscape, such as Whorlton, named after a round shaped hill ('Weraltune' in old English), or after their founders, such as Swainby, probably after a man called Sveyn. As well as the villages, there are farms, a Norman castle and a church reflecting the mediaeval period. Few remains of the Celtic or Romano-British occupants persist in place names or are visible, although they are probably present somewhere under the soil.

More recent elements are an old drove road, seen as a pair of deeply eroded parallel tracks leading up to the valley of the meltwater channel and once used to drive cattle to markets before the railways developed. Across the valley of the meltwater channel and along its sides are the weathered and overgrown remains of sandstone quarries. These provided material for the houses and farm buildings erected at the time when many rural settlements were rebuilt during the 18th and 19th centuries and for the stone field walls, where parts of the moorland were once reclaimed to pasture. Shale tips record where ironstone was mined in the 19th and 20th centuries to fuel the steel industry on the river Tees, some 10 miles away, and jet was extracted to provide fashion jewellery in the Victorian period. One of these mines was dug by my great grandfather in the 1870s.

Also visible are modern elements: electricity pylons, large industrial farm buildings, houses built of brick and motor roads from which a distant and continuous hum of traffic can be heard. All are part of the landscape to which my family and I have also contributed. Hence my feelings towards the place are important to me, feelings affected by my cultural background, wider experiences, education and the emotional attachment of home.

Some of the most recent elements jar the eye, but otherwise everything seems to belong there, to be an integral part of the landscape that has evolved over thousands of years, as the countless and largely unnamed generations have passed through. It is a landscape defined by the limits of visibility, by the distinctive patterns that are readily discernible and by the processes that have taken place over the millennia. It is a self-organized landscape, at no time dependent on a plan or design, that has grown out of the land, determined only by the limitations imposed by climate, ecology, technology and slowly changing human perceptions. What does an understanding of these patterns and processes tell us and is there anything to be gained from an approach to planning, design and management based upon them?

The Importance of Patterns

Consciously or unconsciously we seek order out of chaos. We tend to look for patterns which seem to make sense in the knowledge that we have about our world, as well as being aesthetically satisfying in the relationship of each part to the whole.

Humans have been making patterns from time immemorial, as decoration, as symbols or for religious purposes. Some patterns can be connected with certain cultures whilst others are more universal. People, by their settlements, fields, roads, village layouts and towns have subconsciously evolved the landscape to suit their purposes, although they may not have been fully aware of the patterns being created.

Pattern recognition is important to help us understand and relate to the world around us. We can develop a language of description and analysis to communicate relationships between different patterns, the processes that change the landscape and our aesthetic and emotional responses to them. How we perceive and understand patterns also depends very much on what we are looking for and why. For example, a cultural geographer, a farmer, a forester, a physical planner, an ecologist, an explorer or an army general are likely to describe the pattern of a landscape, based on their own knowledge, experiences and what it provides for them. However, whilst they are all describing the same landscape, containing patterns made from the same components, each person may perceive them rather differently. It is often helpful to compare such descriptions to see what can be deduced from them. If there are some fundamental components and arrangements common to each description then such factors are likely to have a degree of significance. They may be valued for their importance in explaining the pattern, in controlling processes and function, or in giving distinctiveness and a sense of unity to the area. As such they might be used elsewhere, as patterns, in the sense of templates or models, especially for restoring damaged landscapes and for planning and designing landscape change.

The Relevance of Pattern Analysis

The world is a very complicated place and it is difficult to keep up with its constant change. The more we discover, the less we seem to know or understand. It is no longer possible to be a 'renaissance man' and to retain a complete grasp of a wide range of disciplines. Gone are the days of the 18th century American polymaths Benjamin Franklin or Thomas Jefferson, who produced original research in physics, practised architecture, writing, running estates or businesses, studying philosophy and practising law, based on the latest knowledge and thinking of their time. Studying the world and managing various facets of it has now become the task of a large and ever increasing number of specialists.

For example, to study the earth, there are geologists concerned with its structure, the rocks, plate tectonics and vulcanism. Geomorphologists study erosion, landforms, and the changing shape of the earth's surface. Ecologists consider how wildlife survives and interacts with its habitats. Cultural geographers, planners and urban designers work with the demands of people and their interaction with the land and its arrangement. Farmers and foresters try to use and develop natural resources, in a way that can be sustained for use by future generations. Each look for the patterns and processes that help them to understand their interests. At present, despite many countries in the world accepting the principles of sustainable development, there still seems to be a reluctance to consider all the interactions and relationships between the elements of the whole system. Perhaps this holistic approach just seems too complicated to handle or there is a fear of becoming trapped in detail, in quantities of facts, or too much analysis. There may be concern that benefits are too difficult to define in such a way that research or other funds can be attracted. The contrary view is that multi- and inter-disciplinary studies can yield large dividends and that specialists from a wide variety of disciplines who jointly consider a broad range of issues and their integration can make a significant contribution to the effective implementation of sustainable development.

From my own perspective, as a forester and landscape architect, travelling around the world and meeting people working in many of the disciplines described above, there does seem to be a relationship between every process or facet of activity in the world and the patterns created by them. If we can understand these relationships, I believe we can achieve a unity of thought and action between the physical, biological, cultural and aesthetic components of the landscape. However, at the detailed level, where most people are working, it is often difficult to see the larger picture. One approach is to cut across the narrow compartments of disciplines with a broader connection, allowing bigger problems to be solved at the appropriate scale, then cascade down to solve smaller, more detailed problems within the framework of the larger context.

There are several factors to be bear in mind when reading this book:

1. The world is forever changing: it always has and it always will.

Sometimes these changes are so slow or so infrequent that we do not perceive them. It is those that we experience personally that affect us most and influence our perceptions of the world. Although we may be inclined to preserve or protect species, habitats, buildings or landscapes of perceived value, this may be of no avail because of the inevitability of change at some point.

2. People have affected most places in the world, to a greater or lesser degree, during the whole of human existence. As we are an integral component of the world, its future manifestations will continue to combine natural and human effects. Hence, we cannot absolve our responsibilities to manage landscapes or to preserve so-called wild areas untouched; neither should we be egotistical and arrogant in our approach, assuming we can control the whole world, changing it to suit only our narrow interests.

3. Society is forever changing. People's demands and expectations, fashionable causes and tolerance to change alter over very short time spans. Political imperatives drive actions. It is difficult, amid such rapid fluctuations, to find secure foundations on which to base action. They are present in nature, in the slower pace of geology and the cycling of nutrients, in the gradual succession of generations of forest trees and the self-organizing patterns of sensitive human use.

4. The changing world is neither chaotic nor totally unpredictable. In fact, we can predict events over short time periods within a defined range of possibilities, of which all could happen, but some are more likely than others. This gives us more flexibility in the possibilities for action, yet at the same time places prudent limits on their achievement and our reliance on technological solutions.

5. There is a strong hierarchical structure to most natural and human patterns and processes, so that broad solutions for large scale problems can often be repeated in detail to yield similar solutions for smaller scale problems. As our knowledge expands, we can develop flexible, adaptive plans for the changing landscape. Robust solutions, that stand the test of time will also depend upon the understanding of this knowledge by local communities assisted by specialists.

In the so-called 'developed world', our increasingly urban perspective has tended to insulate and isolate us from our surroundings. Most of us see the world as passive observers, safe in our homes, cars and laboratories, through the lenses of our cameras and camcorders, or through the intermediary of TV or cinema screens. At the same time, many people find a powerful attraction in natural or wild places because they give deep aesthetic experiences of sublimity and beauty, or perhaps that return to a pre-Eden innocence which enable us to transcend, for a moment at least, the pressures of our daily lives.

As we have become removed from direct interaction with the landscape, we have taken our destiny into our own hands. We have used the powerful tools of science to split the atom and to engineer the gene. We have no idea where this might lead, as it has the potential to alter irreversibly the fate of the world and evolution. The safeguards are not yet given proper consideration in the scramble to discover more secrets. Pandora's Box was opened a long time ago and the repercussions of some of our technology and of ozone depletion, global warming, pollution and desertification are now becoming apparent.

However, there is also a realization that technology does not have all the answers and sometimes it causes more problems than it solves. The folly of trying to control the forces of nature became evident during the 1993 Mississippi and 1997 Red River floods in the USA. These were exacerbated, because failure of the complex flood defences caused worse flooding than allowing these rivers to follow more natural courses. However, technology is invaluable for its ability to model and compare various environmental scenarios, using computers with sophisticated systems.

Geographic information systems, virtual reality and other specialist software permit increasing amounts of data to be analysed effectively. Patterns have become easier to interpret and processes easier to test than was the case a few years ago.

My proposition is that, by using the templates of nature and culture, we can attempt to make new parts to restore lost or damaged areas. By working with natural processes we may be able to restore functioning to moribund ecosystems. This is not idle thought or vain speculation. Techniques and processes already exist to do this and are developing fast.

I believe the time is now right for such a reappraisal. Our recently developed ability to see the earth's surface and to measure various aspects from space, by satellite, is providing an enormous stimulus. We can now see large areas in fine resolution and measure temperature, chemical constituents and changes in land use easily and quickly. This helps to monitor the rate and extent of changes, so that natural and human induced catastrophes or inappropriate land uses can be identified quickly and strategies for repair developed. Our understanding of ecology at the broad or 'landscape' scale has increased over the last decade, allowing the consideration of larger scale ecological processes. More radical, perhaps, has been the rapid development of 'chaos theory', with its focus on complexity, probabilistic models of intricate systems and fractal geometry.

Hence this book commences with an introduction to patterns, leading to their perception and our aesthetic response. This is followed by an exploration of the patterns and processes of nature and culture, starting with those creating the basic structure of the terrestrial surface, and adding ecological layers and cultural dimensions. Means of analysing patterns will lead to an assessment of their implications for the planning, design and management of many types of landscape. This is extensively illustrated.

The Origins of this Book

How did this book come about? In 1988 the late Dame Sylvia Crowe, an eminent British landscape architect, produced her last book, together with Mary Mitchell, called *The Pattern of Landscape*. This comprised a photo essay exploring the patterns of the landscape, some of the processes that formed them and the responses people make to these patterns. Since then I have travelled widely in the world and worked in situations where an understanding of patterns, processes and perceptions was all important. This included working in multi-disciplinary teams and learning about the interactions of different areas of expertise. This inspired me to write this book as a way of supplementing Sylvia Crowe's work and by exploring key components in greater depth, to provide a useful and practical guide for designers and managers.

Other elements which have helped in this task include Ian McHarg's *Design With Nature*, which my generation of designers used as a major text and was a key influence on landscape design and planning in the USA and elsewhere, especially during the 1970s. This book considered the wide range of processes at work in the landscape and their effect on design which, at that time, was suffering from an over optimistic reliance on technology.

The work of American forest ecologists Jerry Franklin, Larry Harris, Chris Maser and David Perry concerned with the effects of industrial forestry practices advocates managing them more closely with natural patterns and processes. This is having a profound effect on the way many foresters now think, and the integration of the requirements of forest ecosystems with goals of forest management is now being implemented.

The development of landscape ecology, which espouses a number of explanations for landscape structure and process at large scales has also been well timed. The work of American landscape ecologists Richard Forman and Michel Godron galvanized a number of us to consider the implications for design and management of landscapes.

The use of ecological classifications systems that help to relate plant communities to landscape patterns are tremendous aids to the development of concepts in this book. Examples are the Biogeoclimatic Ecosystem Classification developed by Klinka, Krajina and their colleagues in Canada, and the National Vegetation Classification assembled by John Rodwell and his team in Great Britain. These permit vegetation and landscape patterns to be analysed at various vertically integrated scales that can also be related to a number of processes at work in the environment.

The long development of cultural landscapes is of great importance, especially in Europe. The idea of assessing and categorizing areas into landscape character types, for use in policy and strategic planning, was resurrected during the late 1980s and early 1990s. This took advantage of computer analysis, new information and the understanding of landscape history, presented by W. G. Hoskins and Oliver Rackham, the work of the British landscape planner Steven Warnock, and impetus given by various countryside agencies in Great Britain. These techniques have matured so that there are now some useful tools for landscape planning and management. Some of these can integrate ecological and cultural patterns, such as the recent work of Scottish Natural Heritage, using biogeographical and landscape data.

How we perceive patterns physiologically and psychologically is now more widely understood thanks to the work of David Marr and J. J. Gibson in Great Britain and the USA amongst others. The aesthetic response to landscape, and its importance, has also recently been updated and extended by philosophers such as Arnold Berleant, Peter Gunter and Cheryl Foster from the USA. This has given a sounder basis for explaining the importance of aesthetics in our lives and the ways in which this dimension can be incorporated into the design and management of landscapes.

The way in which creativity occurs and the thought processes we adopt when deciding on courses of action have also been studied. Without a wider understanding of this aspect it would be difficult to take full advantage of the stimulation I hope this book provides. In Great Britain, Margaret Boden and David Perkins have made progress in understanding how creativity operates, whilst the late Hans Eysenck has contributed towards identifying creative people.

Finally, there has been the recent interest in nature's patterns. From the work of Peter Stevens in the USA during the 1970s to Ian Stewart in Great Britain in the 1990s, the fundamental natural order in the world has been shown in all its beauty. This has been followed by the development of chaos theory by a range of people, but presented so well in popular form by James Gleick. I became very excited once I grasped the implications of this because it seemed at one stroke the difficulties of scale resolution, the dynamics of the landscape and the problems of uncertainty were given an integrated framework. As soon as I started looking at our environment with my awareness raised in this way, I saw it in a new light. Chaos became order, but not in a way I had understood it before.

I am indebted to geographers, ecologists, designers, historians, psychologists, philosophers and many others for the insights it has been my privilege to gain. Therefore, as well as stimulating debate and giving designers and managers an updated tool kit, I hope the integration of ideas I am presenting will help to bring a wide range of disciplines together. I hope it will trigger the kind of inter-disciplinary engagement that I advocate.

This book is not meant to be a complete examination of each topic, so readers should not be disappointed if they feel that their subject is treated somewhat superficially. This broad study also has an element of selectivity, as I have chosen to refer to places with which I am personally familiar. I hope that this first hand knowledge will enliven the account and make it more meaningful.

It also meant that I could illustrate it with examples from first hand knowledge. Other works cover the deeper, narrower fields of knowledge and the Bibliography should give guidance on obtaining further information to supplement the issues presented here.

I have set myself a formidable task. I may not succeed completely, but I hope that readers will gain a clearer picture of the interactions and interdependencies of pattern and process in the landscape and how we might use this to work with nature, to design through natural and human patterns and to restore a degree of harmony and balance to damaged places. At the very least, I hope the book will stimulate further thinking and discussion on these matters.

CHAPTER ONE

WHAT ARE PATTERNS?

Patterns are all Around Us

When we study the world around us we realize that it is not a random collection of objects that have arrived at their position by chance. Patterns are everywhere, and it is by recognizing them that we can orientate ourselves, try to make sense of the world and predict the way that certain actions might occur. Without the ability to perceive patterns, the human race would not have been as successful in coping with a wide range of circumstances and occupying a significant proportion of the world's climatic zones.

Not only are we observers and users of patterns but we are also pattern creators, both unconsciously in our everyday behaviour and consciously as planners and designers. Often we gain our aesthetic pleasure from associating patterns with meanings; especially patterns possessing strong qualities of structure. When patterns are no longer evident or cannot be predicted we may become disorientated and worried. The failure to perceive order and structure in an unknown city can upset a visitor in the same way that an apparently homogeneous forest can be completely confusing to an unobservant wanderer.

Patterns are evident at a very wide range of scales from the molecular structure of DNA, at the microscopic level, to the spirals of galaxies in the universe. On the other hand, an examination of patterns reveals a surprisingly narrow range of pattern archetypes that occur everywhere. This applies both to natural patterns and to those produced by people over the millennia, although it could be argued that many people simply copied their ideas from nature.

A major challenge is to understand the processes that create such a wide occurrence of a limited number of patterns and their interrelationships.

How is it possible for a spiral to be the same form as a galaxy, caused by complex interactions of gravitational forces operating over millions of light years, a tropical storm a hundred miles across that absorbs its heat energy from the ocean and the spiral shell of a snail a few centimetres in diameter responding to growth hormones? The answer lies in the fundamental numerical relationships which represent their essence, such as gradients of energy and the way material fills space economically. Numbers provide a common link and go a long way to explain the eloquence and beauty found in such forms. The human construction of a spiral staircase incorporates exactly the same numerical relationships of angles and proportions as are found in the DNA helix, the snail shell or the branches of a fir tree.

Whilst the perception of the abstract beauty of these universal patterns is real, we need to be aware that it is not sufficient to admire them solely because they exist. In recent years there has been a series of books celebrating natural patterns, using stunning photographs. These often compare and connect very different classes of object, because they have the same superficial appearance.

However, beneath each of the patterns lie the processes which created them. There is a complex interdependency between the processes of a wide range of patterns. Some processes possess feedback systems, others are hierarchically related in scale. Some operate over different cycles of time, where the patterns created by one process become the starting point for another. The new science of complexity and of self-organized systems can be difficult to understand because their mathematics are complicated. I have tried to keep explanations as relevant and as simple as possible.

What are Patterns?

The dictionary offers various definitions of 'pattern', each of which is relevant to the subject of this book:

- an arrangement of repeated or corresponding parts, decorative motifs etc
- a decorative design
- a style
- a plan or diagram used as a guide in making something
- a standard way of moving or acting
- a model worthy of imitation
- a representative sample

a

b

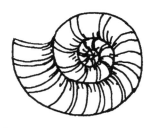

c

Three examples of natural patterns which occur at a wide range of scales.

a) A spiral galaxy some millions of light years in diameter, formed as the forces responsible for the formation of stars cause them to be thrown outwards.

b) The spiralling pattern formed as heat energy in the atmosphere intensifies the vortex of wind and cloud to form a hurricane some hundreds of miles in diameter.

c) The spiral shape of a snail shell is the natural pattern formed as the animal grows.

An arrangement of repeated or corresponding parts, decorative motifs etc. The repetition of similar parts can be seen everywhere, in field patterns, in city layouts and architecture, in mountain peaks, or in ripple marks on sand. Decorative motifs have been used for many thousands of years. This is an important aspect of the definition, since it demonstrates how, in the main, we attempt to make sense of our surroundings or use patterns to create order. Both approaches involve seeking order, not chaos.

A decorative design. One of our most powerful urges is to make ourselves and our surroundings attractive through the use of decoration. There could be many varieties: realistic or abstract, traditional or modern, timeless or ephemeral. Often there are strong relationships between decorative patterns created by humans and those found in the natural world.

A style. One of the myths about design is that it is concerned solely with visual appearance which is subject to the whims of fashion. Certainly there are styles that are short lived in their popularity, but there are also enduring ones that have stood the test of time. It is the latter that are of most interest.

A plan or a diagram used as a guide in making something. All through history people have borrowed patterns and used them to make materials, products, buildings and landscapes. The source of these patterns can be determined by many factors, but there are two main ones: nature and human creativity. It is the connection between these two, the use of nature's patterns as a guide for landscape restoration and the means of creativity that are central themes in this book.

A standard way of moving or acting. Patterns can be dynamic; people, animals, water and wind can all move according to standard patterns, determined by physical forces, the environment, social structures or economic imperatives. Principles can be determined for some, others are uncertain or occur within a range of probabilities.

A model worthy of imitation. This can reveal fascinating possibilities, whether as a model of economic or political structures or as a model of natural structures and processes that fit a particular place and time. One of the purposes of this book is to examine how far some models can be used in space, over time and between different scales.

A representative sample. We can often learn by looking at samples of ecosystems or settlement patterns, and extrapolating the application of these patterns to other places. Representative samples of natural habitats have been adopted as the basis for many land protection strategies, such as those recommended for retention by the World Commission on Environment and Development (The Brundtland Report, Anon, 1987).

Towards an Understanding of Patterns in an Uncertain World

The processes at work in the world produce landscapes where everything is in a constantly dynamic state. The competition for resources, the interaction of organisms with each other and with inorganic, physical processes, the cycles of carbon, nitrogen and water, together with a wide range of weathering and erosion activities, combine to drive the engine of the biosphere fuelled by the energy of the sun and of nuclear reactions deep in the earth. Out of this endlessly shifting cycle of growth and decay, a myriad of patterns is apparent, evolving at various rates into an uncertain future. Humans are part of this world and contribute to the patterns and processes to varying degrees.

This uncertainty is an important concept, as experience indicates that everything is determined by possibilities and probabilities: the likelihood of a fire burning a forest, of an avalanche burying some animals, of a volcano erupting and covering an area with hot ash or a hard winter killing a late hatched brood of baby birds. Some of the events that alter the evolution of landscape are more predictable than others, in the sense that they are significantly more likely than unlikely to occur. Some are unexpected, only because we have not experienced them before. Others follow regular, or nearly regular cycles. Few are completely random.

The perception and understanding of the patterns to be explored in this book depend on two factors. Firstly, it is our perception, as human beings with an average lifespan of three score years and ten, based on around 5000 years of civilization. Secondly, our perception is partly determined by the acuteness of the various senses we possess, our physical size relative to our surroundings and our position in the world when we experience it. Until recently (since the advent of balloons, aircraft and manned spacecraft), we could only see the earth from ground level. The maximum range of visibility was only possible from a high point, perhaps looking down from a hill top. Our views from lower elevations such as a valley, looking horizontally or upwards were more limited. Therefore we are naturally conditioned to relate to the scale of a scene visible from a single point, if we are stationary, or a series of points, if we are moving. We are also limited by the focusing ability of our eyes and the limits to the lateral view imposed by the horizon, atmospheric haze, the curvature of the earth's surface or intervening landforms and objects. We obtain a three dimensional view looking forwards as a result of our stereo vision, originally suited to hunters of high intellect but limited physical strength, who needed sharp eyes for the clear detection of still and moving prey over long distances.

However, since we can now see the world at a much larger scale from space or aircraft (p.233, Fig. 1) and by contrast can also focus on

From the air we can gain views and appreciate the presence of patterns that are not obvious at ground level. The grid pattern seen here is typical of the way the landscape of North America has been divided up. The sense of this grid can be partly deduced at ground level from the straightness of the roads and the right angled junctions.

its minute structure through microscopes, our sense of pattern and structure is immensely enhanced. Readers will notice I have used sets of illustrations throughout the book that give a view of patterns both from the air and from ground level. Sometimes these are different views of the same landscapes giving us a range of perspectives to consider. Interestingly, some mediaeval artists made attempts to visualize 'bird's eye' views of landscapes and designs, to imagine how they would look from the air even though they knew they would never see the view. They realized that seeing the bigger picture aided their understanding and that of their viewers.

Whilst the external appearance of the earth has been known reasonably accurately for centuries and depicted on globes, the patterns showing vegetation zones, river basins and coastlines have been relatively crudely portrayed. Now, from orbiting spacecraft, we can obtain accurate views of the largest useful scale of pattern that can be perceived: the continental level. From this altitude, especially from the higher orbits or the more distant scene once obtained from moon trips, it is possible to observe the gradual change from one vegetation type to another, and to identify zones of transition that are subtly graded to express the changes determined by altitude and latitude, drainage, rainfall, temperature and humidity. Modern space technology, such as remote sensing cameras, also allows these patterns to be observed at successively larger magnifications, until the current maximum resolution of a few metres is reached (p.233, Fig. 2).

This small scale pattern shows the distribution of specialized plants growing in damper places amongst a coastal sand dune system. The microsite variations of moisture and the way blown sand is collected by the plants results in a dynamic interaction of patterns and process. The collected sand creates drier places better suited to the plant growth. Water can wash sand out from between plants and remove them as the cycles of drier or damper conditions vary the balances between these processes.

At the other extreme, a botanist with a magnifying glass might be observing a cluster of small plants distributed across an area of coastal sand dunes. On closer examination denser patterns can be seen here, bare areas there, gradual transitions from one to another and fingers of denser clusters extending into more open areas. At length it is possible to observe that the distribution is correlated with areas of dune that are wetter or drier than others and that the small, fragile plants survive and grow according to their tolerances for one or the other, expressed at a very fine scale.

Many of these patterns are not the result of human design or planning. They are self-organized and occur in similar types, forms and distribution at a range of scales from very large to very small; it is very difficult to measure them because of the effect of this scale variability. The classic example, often cited in the literature, is the measurement of a length of British coastline, such as part of the outer Hebridean island of Harris. Following the line on maps of 1:625,000, 1:250,000, 1:50,000, and 1:10,000 scales and then walking it, following the high water mark, will give progressively increasing lengths. The actual length only exists in terms of the scale chosen, becoming infinite when measured at the molecular level.

One of the starting points for an understanding of patterns is the numerical relationships which underlie them. The major numerical systems of interest are the various forms of geometry used to describe the multi-dimensional world. Simple patterns such as the Fibonacci series (explained below) stand out because they are found to occur in a wide range of situations.

Apart from measurement there are other ways to describe the properties of these patterns. One of the links, developed in later chapters, concerns our aesthetic response to many of these patterns and one method of description is to use the design vocabulary developed in

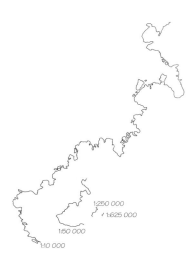

These illustrations of the coastline of the Hebridean island of Harris show how the length of a section increases with the scale of measurement. From 1:625 000 to 1:10 000 the length increases dramatically and would continue to do so with measurements at even larger scale.

my earlier book *Elements of Visual Design in the Landscape*. I believe that many of the terms used in that book have a direct relevance to the properties of natural or cultural patterns, such as position and orientation, shape, interval, texture and density, colour, visual force, interlock, enclosure, rhythm, balance, scale and proportion, asymmetry, hierarchy, transformation, similarity and continuity. Using them we can determine the precise balance between the tendency towards chaos (or a superabundance of diversity) and the self-organizing, unifying trends inherent in dynamic, open systems in evolution.

We can also describe patterns by the processes that give rise to them and to the functions they perform. The changes from unstable high energy to stable low energy states, processes of weathering, erosion, transport, deposition, cycling, capture, release, growth, seed dispersal and so on, all directly or indirectly affect the patterns that emerge at any time. Such is the range of variables in play, that the evolution of landscape ought to be extremely unpredictable. In that we recognize that there is an infinite range of detailed outcomes, we are unlike earlier generations of scientists who held a more deterministic view. However the principles of probability suggest there are usually a limited number of the likeliest outcomes within a range of natural variability, restricted by time, space, location and scale.

The American architect Louis Sullivan famously said, 'form follows function', but in landscape, the relationship is far more complex. If we substitute 'pattern' for form and use 'process' as an alternative to function, we can say that sequentially 'pattern follows process'. But 'process can also follow pattern'. That is, some patterns are created by some processes, but other processes are limited or directed by other patterns. This can be in the form of a positive or negative feedback loop, or it can be more direct (positive feedback is when a process increases its own intensity, for example, when a fire draws in oxygen its burns more furiously, which draws yet more oxygen into the system to make the fire even more intense; negative feedback occurs when a system is self-limiting, for example when an insect population expands until it runs out of food, which causes it to decline).

As intelligent organisms endeavouring to understand the world around us, so we may survive and prosper, we need to deduce its patterns. Most of us wish to see order and not chaos. Disorder can be disorientating and usually does not enable us to function to the best of our capacity or to fully utilize our environment. We use all our senses to analyse our surroundings, particularly sight, which fulfils 87% of our sensory perception. Our brains process, catalogue and try to make sense of this information. Often we may see a scene that is similar to another one. If our brain connects the two, we may tend to ascribe the same characteristic to the new scene. We are sometimes misled in this desire to seek order from chaos because we may not have all the knowledge needed to recognize the true pattern and so may arrive at the wrong conclusions.

A classic example of this misunderstanding is how we have tried to comprehend the universe over the centuries. On the basis of observation, all the stars seemed to be points of light arranged on the inside of a sphere. Patterns were observed and given names after the gods or heroes of the time. One set was ascribed power over the lives of people - the signs of the zodiac. Now we know, from astronomical observations using telescopes, that these patterns are not real arrangements. For a start, the stars have moved in their relative positions and continue to do so. Secondly, they are not arranged on a curving plane, but occupy three dimensional positions in an expanding space, often many light years apart. Thirdly, some 'stars' are actually galaxies containing billions of stars themselves.

As patterns interact with processes we must be sure that the patterns we seek to use are real and can be objectively measured or described in some way.

Geometric Principles

Manifestations of early geometry can be seen in buildings and in decorative patterns around the world created by bygone cultures from at least 15,000 years ago (see Chapter Seven). Geometry, as a science (Classical Greek *geo*, earth, *metry*, measure) in its original form, was practised by ancient Egyptian surveyors, who marked out field boundaries, irrigation ditches and later temple and palace layouts using sighting rods, triangulation, distance measures and stretched ropes for setting out perfectly straight lines.

It is thought the first theorems were developed by a number of unknown Greek philosophers. Thales of Miletus, working around 600 BC, used to be credited with the work, but this is doubted nowadays. Pythagoras of Samos is well known for his theorem about right angled triangles and he also attempted to explain the universe numerically by counting numbers represented as geometric shapes. Some numbers were triangular (1, 3, 6, 10, 15) whilst others were square (1, 4, 9, 16). Magnitudes, that is measures of quantities unable to be described by counting numbers, were represented by the lengths of segments of lines composing the geometric shapes. These segments led to the concept of algebraic formulae or equations.

Plato the ancient Greek philospher and his pupil Aristotle emphasized the use of geometry and the principles of logical reasoning. Regular polyhedrons (the tetrahedron, octahedron, dodecahedron etc) sometimes known as *Platonic solids* were used by Plato in his attempts to explain the scientific phenomena of the universe. It was Plato's mathematics, taught in his Academy, that was put into a logical structure, along with the work of a number of other early mathematicians, by Euclid.

Euclidian geometry is based on the concept of three dimensions expressed as points (no dimension, only position), line (one dimension), plane (two dimensions) and solids or voids (volumes, three dimensions). This is the traditional way of describing or reducing the world about us into its constituent parts. This system can work well, especially when other related branches of geometry are included in the general spatial concepts. However, it also has serious limitations.

For some 2000 years Euclidian geometry was assumed to be the only correct form, but in the 19th and 20th centuries other types have emerged. The main differences between them lie in the properties of lines and especially of parallel lines. In spherical geometry, which is the spatial relationship of points on a sphere, it is impossible to have parallel lines of the same length. However, it is possible to have more than one line between the same two points such as from pole to pole. Both these features are not found in Euclidian geometry.

The description or location of points on a sphere or conic by the use of co-ordinates was first recorded by the Greek Apollonius of Perga around 225 BC and further developed by Oresme in the 14th century and René Descartes the French philosopher (1596–1650). As a result of Descartes' work, they are known as 'Cartesian co-ordinates' and are used in the study of many types of geometry. They form an integral part of Descartes' work on scientific theory and have had a major impact on human perceptions. As a consequence, they have created a range of patterns and imposed these on the world, such as the land survey grid pattern of the USA that covers most of the land (see Chapter Seven).

Another type of geometry worth mentioning is *affine geometry*, which is relevant to calculations and perceptions of perspective. Here, parallel lines apparently converge to a single point on the horizon line. Our understanding of the world changed greatly when artists started to use perspective and calculated the changes to the apparent size of objects over varying distances.

Finally, *topology* is the study of lines that correspond to linear continua or curves. This includes identifying different line shapes that can pass through a pattern of points arranged two dimensionally on a plane or three dimensionally in space. Topology can also involve distortion in shapes, similar to sketching a pattern on the surface of a balloon, where distances between parts of the pattern change as it is filled with gas, but the relative positions of these parts stay the same. This kind of distortion and spatial relationship has influenced views on the character of, for example, the expanding universe.

The 1970s saw the maturation of an evolving mathematical theory that is radically different from the Euclidian and Cartesian geometries described previously. This is known a 'fractal' geometry, a term coined in 1975 by the mathematician Benoit Mandelbrot (from the Latin origins *frangere*, to break, and *fractus*, irregular and fragmented). The idea of fractal dimensions (though not the name) was first put forward in 1919 by Felix Hausdorff, a German mathematician, who looked at the small scale structure of mathematical shapes, and it was further developed by the Russian mathematician Besicivitch.

The central feature of fractal geometry describes objects or patterns that are *self-similar* at a range of scales or magnifications, or *scale-symmetric*. Literally, this means that the small parts of such objects are exactly similar to their larger or their smaller appearance, when magnified or reduced. This is consistently repeated at ever larger or ever smaller scales on into infinity. They also differ from Euclidian shapes by being devoid of the smoothness associated with Euclidian lines, planes and volumes. Mandelbrot studied turbulent phenomena and the scale-dependent measurements of the British coastline already mentioned.

Some mathematical forms such as the 'Cantor bar' or 'Koch curve' are fractally perfect, being repeated indefinitely until the object contains an infinitely large number of infinitely small identical parts. However, fractals are not solely mathematical phenomena and need not be completely self-similar or scale-symmetric as described above. In fact natural fractals are extremely common in the world, to the extent that Euclidian geometry can be considered the exception rather than the rule. The main characteristics of natural fractals arise when sets of probabilities occur amongst the processes that create the patterns. As such there are upper and lower limits to the ranges of occurrence of each fractal set. Above and below that range shapes may be 'conventionally' Euclidian or be rough and irregular but not truly fractal, or they may display a different type of fractal structure. This is typical of many landform patterns (see Chapter Five). There are further complications where one fractal pattern occupies a space created by another, different fractal structure. This is the more common natural situation and may help to explain much of the diversity and beauty of nature.

Euclidian spatial dimensions are 1, 2 or 3, that is described in whole numbers or integers. We are familiar with this concept, for example, when we speak of an object having 3 dimensions. Fractal dimensions are expressed as fractions themselves. The fractal dimension describes or indicates the extent to which the fractal pattern or object fills the space it occupies. Linear fractal structures would have a dimension between 0 and 1, structures situated on a plane have dimensions between 1 and 2 and those occupying a volume of space have dimensions between 2 and 3. A dimension of 1.2 would describe a structure of lines that barely began to spread into a plane whilst 1.8 would probably be a convoluted structure of multiple lines that almost became a plane.

If it is true that Euclidian and Cartesian geometries are simplifications created by the human mind to deal with complex patterns in the absence of mathematical tools, this has many important implications for design. Until now almost all designed human constructions and planned changes to the landscape have been based on Euclidian geometry. This has tended to oversimplify what nature had already provided (see Chapter Seven). Fractal geometry can be used to understand more fully the structure of the world and to extend the creative possibilities open to designers.

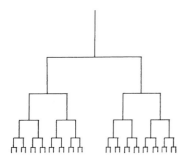

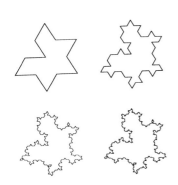

The 'Cantor bar' and 'Koch curve' are mathematically perfect fractal patterns. Each smaller section is a perfect repetition of the preceding larger one. This self-similarity at each descending scale could theoretically continue until the pattern contains an infinitely large number of infinitely small parts.

Review of Pattern Analysis Methods

Pattern analysis has been divided between topological explorations and classifications of a wide range of natural phenomena, usually complete objects or single systems, whose patterns are similar, and the examination of landscapes comprised of complexes of patterns. The next section reviews some examples as an introduction to the issues referred to in later chapters of the book.

In 1974 Peter Stevens, an American, published a book entitled *Patterns in Nature*. This remains a fascinating and enlightening approach to describing and cataloguing various categories of patterns found in the natural world. More recently the British mathematician Ian Stewart has studied *Nature's Numbers*. Much of Stevens' analysis is based on observation of examples of patterns and linkage is made to some of the processes that create them. However, his book just predated the formal birth of fractal geometry by Mandelbrot and the subsequent development of chaos theory, so it is still rooted in Euclidian geometry. This limits the analysis, but many of the categories remain valid and are worth summarizing as a useful starting point. Stewart has examined numerical phenomena and their role as determinants of form.

Stevens identified some basic types of pattern as the result of topological studies of lines joining a pattern of dots. He came to the conclusion that despite the tremendous variety existing in the world, there are limitations to the possible range of patterns, mainly due to the restrictions imposed by spatial dimensions. Although there is variety in, say, the leaves of the same tree, the degree of similarity is greater than the degree of difference. This is a key conclusion and emphasizes the subsequent importance of similarity in pattern recognition processes. It also reminds us that plant form, for example, is determined by a balance between the instructions provided by the genetic code and the laws of physics or chemistry.

The basic patterns in nature identified by Stevens are:

1. Spirals
2. Meanders
3. Branches
4. Explosions

These patterns vary in the total length required by each to fill the available space. Spirals are short in the total length used to fill the space but this is done extremely circuitously. Explosions are very short in distance from centre to perimeter of space but are extremely long in total length. Meanders and branches are somewhere in between.

There are four geometric characteristics that can be used to describe these:

1. Uniformity
2. Space filling
3. Overall length
4. Directness

The spiral is very uniform, entirely fills a two dimensional space, is short in length and very indirect. The meander is not so uniform (in fact it can be very turbulent or chaotic), fills the space completely and is indirect. Branching patterns are less uniform, fully fill a space, but not with equal density, and are relatively direct. One variety with regular triple junctions has the shortest total distance of all the patterns. Explosions are uniform in the constant angle between lines, but they cannot fill all of the space to the same density (they are denser at the centre than the perimeter) and are extremely direct.

The patterns described so far are simple, two dimensional versions and do not reveal any hierarchies in pattern structure. The type of pattern occurring depends on the process involved and to that end, pattern follows process.

Pattern type is also determined by flow dynamics, such as turbulence or eddies, now closely associated with chaos theory, which also develops structures such as spiralling or meandering forms. These are always similar but not identical; they are stationary in position, whilst constantly introducing and disposing of new material. Examples of such turbulence patterns are water flowing behind a rock in a river, or the pattern of turbulent water behind a ship. These patterns are easy to observe in liquid. Other flows are of stresses or energy, not directly visible, but inferred by indirect evidence such as stress fractures in wood, sand dunes produced by the wind or the structure of bones, evolved to respond to stresses, whilst minimizing the use of materials.

This pattern of eddying currents is the wake of a moving ship. The turbulence is chaotic yet it produces strongly ordered patterns. There is a tendency for the spiralling vortices seen here to be paired. This spontaneous self-organization into ordered patterns by a turbulent medium is one of the hallmarks of systems studied by chaos theory.

Spirals

Spiral forms result from growth or deformation, when one part of a surface or object grows or expands faster than another. The uncurling of a spiral is the reverse of this, such as when the inner cells of a spiral bracken frond divide faster than the outer ones. Control of spiral growth is easy using a gradient of energy, stress or stimulant across the object, such as a plant growth substance.

Spirals come in various forms depending on the relationship between the length of the radius extension and the angle it makes with the positive directional axis. If the radius extension is arithmetically proportional to the angle the spiral is *Archimedean*, if not, or if geometrically proportionate, it becomes a *logarithmic* spiral. René Descartes first described the logarithmic spiral in 1638. Examples of it can be seen in nautilus shells, sunflower floret patterns and many other places. These are all two dimensional types. There are also *parabolic* and *hyperbolic* spirals.

 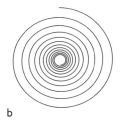 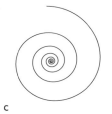

a   b   c

Spirals are the first basic type of pattern:

a) A spiral formed by joining a pattern of points based on Peter Stevens' theory.

b) A simple or Euclidian spiral.

c) A logarithmic spiral.

Spirals also relate closely to the *Fibonacci* series of numbers and the rule of proportion called the *Golden Section*. The Fibonacci series, named after the Italian mathematician Leonardo Fibonacci, who invented it in 1200, is a number pattern where each consecutive number is made from the addition of the previous two. The majority of plants have a number of petals taken from this series and the petals (or florets in a larger flower) tend to be arranged as spirals. If we take a giant sunflower, the pattern of the florets is composed of a number of intersecting spirals, some going clockwise and some anti-clockwise. The number of these spirals can be found consecutively in the Fibonacci series, for example 8 in one direction and 13 in the other. In this way the spiral pattern is also symmetry breaking (see below). The nature of consecutive Fibonacci numbers when the smaller is divided by the larger is close to (and gets closer the bigger the number pairs) 0.618034, which is the Golden Section number (for example, used by ancient Greek architects in setting harmonious proportions to temples). This, multiplied by 360 degrees, gives an angle of 137.5 degrees, which is the angle of divergence of successive leaves or branches around a plant stem. This angle is often called the *Golden Angle*.

An analysis of the florets of a flower of the daisy family shows a pattern of logarithmic spirals forming out of the centre. This reflects the growth pattern within the plant and an effective means of organizing and maintaining the gradually expanding florets into a tight pattern.

Helixes are three dimensional spirals,

a) shows a helix which maintains the same radius as it turns.

b) shows a helix expanding logarithmically.

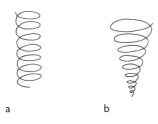

a   b

The pattern of growth of these fir trees shows a logarithmic helix. The gradual spiralling of each branch around the trunk enables an efficient distribution of needles in order to receive as much light as possible.

A helix is a three dimensional spiral and like the two dimensional forms it can be Archimedean or logarithmic. An example of the former is a vine tendril wrapping around a twig, whilst many conifer trees grow in the form of logarithmic helixes, their branches winding around the stem at angles of approximately 137.5 degrees.

Spirals occur frequently in nature, because they represent an efficient method of filling space using a single element. The processes that lead to spirals or helixes are, however, quite varied. An important process is regular spurts of growth related to seasonal or other periodic impulses. The chambered nautilus grows according to lunar cycles, whilst some trees, such as many conifers, exhibiting a helical form, grow a set of branches and leading shoot extensions once a season and turn their branch whorls around the stem in order to expose as much leaf area as possible to the light. Other processes that lead to spiral patterns are the movement of materials in a confined space, so that a vortex occurs when centrifugal forces are applied or a smooth continuous line is produced on the surface of a rotating object.

Meanders

Meanders are related to spirals in several key attributes, although their resulting patterns are quite different. A spiral can result from growth impulses acting in one direction, whereas if these switch direction periodically then a meander can result, weaving back and forth. Oscillations produce wave like forms; for example, the muscles along a snake's body or cat's tail may tense and relax alternately, causing their characteristic sinuous movement. A more random or variable meander can double back on itself in order to fill space more completely.

If a line is curved as described above it is a meander, but a plane can be subjected to the same kinds of force to become a wavy surface or a pattern of ripple marks. Rock strata can be folded so that in cross section they display meandering structures. The processes producing these can be:

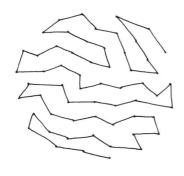

The meander is the second pattern type created by joining dots.

A meandering river. This example, from British Columbia in Canada, is continuously changing its path within the confines of a broad, glaciated valley. Previous meanders can be seen highlighted by vegetation patterns.

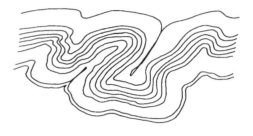

- Lines of flow in a substance, such as water or wind. The patterns can be produced within the material or be reflected in the shape it gives to another material such as sand, in ripple marks or dunes.

- Flows of energy, as in the rippling of muscles described above.

- Opposing forces acting to compress a material in one direction so that the space to be occupied contracts in one dimension, such as folded rocks.

A section through folded rock strata shows a meandering pattern as lateral pressures forced the rocks to buckle.

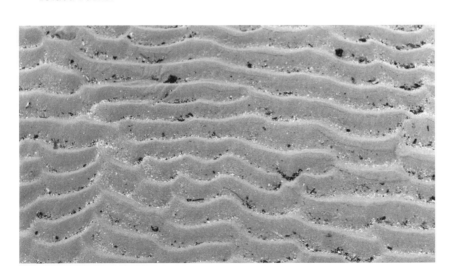

Ripple marks in sand form a pattern of meanders or waves that directly reflect the movement of the water flowing over them.

• Opposing forces competing with each other along a common boundary where their relative strengths vary; for example, where a forest edge meets a bog and each tries to spread into the other. The irregular line often shows a meandering pattern (see Chapter Six).

Branching

Branching patterns occur whenever a number of flows start from a set of initial points, whether moving in a random direction or restricted by a substrate, such as a surface tilted in one direction. Collision between some of the flows and their incorporation into a combined flow is inevitable at some point and keeps occurring, even though the number of individual flows get successively smaller, until a single flow results. This happens in river systems leading to a definite hierarchy of flow (1st, 2nd etc) until the last and highest order is the single flow. The 1st order streams are the smallest, first flows. Each subsequent flow formed from the combination of two lesser ones becomes a higher order.

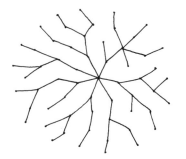

Branching is the third basic pattern formed by joining dots.

The volume of water in each order is a factor of the number of preceding orders and of collisions. In simple bifurcated branching, it is double the preceding two orders. This is always a feature of branching patterns that either arise from a process (flow) or a structure. The length of higher order streams also tends to be greater than that of lower order ones. The shape of the drainage basin tends to vary in a similar fashion, being longer (elongated) for larger systems than smaller ones. The range of alternative network patterns possible with any form of branching is finite, depending on the number of 1st order elements to start with.

The elegance of natural branching patterns is greater than that of artificially created ones because of variations in the angle of branching, using the principle of 'least work'. This involves the ease with which fluid flows from one branch into another (in either direction); this is affected by the flow along narrow conduits, which produce proportionately greater friction than larger conduits. Hence the type of branching pattern depends on the relationship between branch size and the angle of branching. For the smallest streams, into or out of the main stream, branch angle approaches 90 degrees.

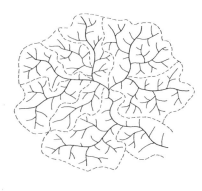

The branching pattern of a river drainage system. Main branches separate secondary systems from the main one. All parts of the land area are accessed by the pattern which balances total length with the directness with which the water from the furthermost areas can reach the end of the system.

Where river branching occurs in roughly two dimensions (or between 2 and 3 in terms of fractal geometry), trees branch in three dimensions. The position of branches can display more variety as a result. During the 15th century, the famous Italian artist and inventor Leonardo da Vinci observed that 'the branching of plants are found in two different positions: either opposite to each other, or not opposite. If opposite to each other, the centre stem is not bent; if they are not opposite, the centre stem is bent.' The volumes of all the first order branches are the same as the last order 'trunk', but the total cross sectional area of the smaller ones is greater, to allow for the increased friction of fluid flow. This partly explains why higher order branches tend to be longer as noted above, volume being a function of cross sectional area multiplied by length. There may be differences to this feature in rivers, where topography and the effect of gravity may increase the available energy to counterbalance the frictional effect.

However, there are differences in the organization of branching patterns between rivers and trees. Rivers are self-organized systems. The location of their branches, the point at which they occur and the angles formed, are determined by interaction of factors such as landform (which changes during erosion and so feeds back to the river structure), geology, obstructions to flow and the effects climate has on water availability in different parts of the collection zone. There is no code as to how flow is arranged, so that flow characteristics and branching pattern are expressed as the outcome of the processes involved.

In trees, the genetic codes for each species produce pattern templates, which are then subjected to the laws of physics and chemistry to yield the branching pattern. These, in turn, are affected by environmental forces which give variability to the overall structure. A major environmental factor is light. The tree seeks to put all of its leaves at the outer extremity of the crown to maximize the efficiency of its light collection for photosynthesis. As the tree grows and the crown expands, leaves and branches left inside it die; thus the genetically perfect branching pattern observed in a young tree is drastically altered in the interests of greater efficiency in the assimilation of light. The direction of light, shade, competition for light with other trees, wind and insect or fungal attacks all cause the tree to change its pattern or shape. Even so, different individuals of the same species tend to resemble each other, despite exposure to a range of environmental variables.

Tree branches. The pattern and shape of the smallest twigs reflects that of the biggest branches in a typically fractal fashion.

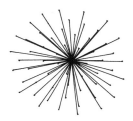

The explosion is the fourth type of basic pattern by which dots can be joined up. It creates the most direct pattern but it is also greatest in total length.

The splash made by a drop of liquid bursting on impact with a surface. This is typical of an explosion when bays and promontories form spontaneously.

The explosion pattern of a seed head of a plant of the Umbellifrae family. The florets and seeds are equally distributed on small stems which all arise from a single point.

The patterns made by a spreading agent such as a fire.

a) The small area with a slightly wavy edge as the fire starts.

b) The pattern of promontories and bays as the fire develops and spreads equally in all directions.

c) The pattern is modified as the wind increases the spread in one direction.

Explosions

This variety of basic pattern is very easy to identify and understand. The term refers to all patterns, where the structure or the distribution of material radiates outwards from a central point or area. It consists of direct paths from the centre to every outlying part, so that the density of the pattern diminishes with distance. A pattern caused by the impact of stone on sand or a meteorite shows this reduction in density as do some types of volcanic cones (see Chapter Five). Any movement out from a centre will tend to show some of these characteristics.

Splashes of liquid demonstrate a general circular shape with protruding promontories in a fairly regular pattern. As the splash increases in size the promontories extend and become more linear. The spacing results from the existence of one promontory, which tends to preclude the development of another immediately next to it, usually because of a lack of material. Hence, smaller sized patterns tend to be regular whereas larger ones, with more material, can become increasingly irregular. This is the case where a forest fire spreads out from a centre as well as other expanding, spreading agents such as wind, insect outbreaks and colonizing patches of plants. Such characteristics may also mark a change in nature, from local scale Euclidian geometry, to larger scale fractal geometry, where it has been noted that perfect scale similarity is not always possible.

Packing and Cracking

Stevens also described some other patterns that concern non-linear objects occupying space, which did not fall into his four basic types. The linear elements described so far create simple patterns that assume properties of two or three dimensions. Alternatively, they can reflect the complex patterns of fractals when simple Euclidian models of geometry are inapplicable. The same conditions apply to planar surfaces or volumes (both open and solid) such as packing objects together to fill space or the constriction of a homogeneous material in a fixed space and, conversely, the stretching of a homogeneous material as space expands.

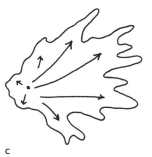

a   b   c

Whichever scenario applies, some common factors have been observed between all of them:

- 120 degree, 3 way joints are very common in the packing, cracking and splitting of elastic materials such as shrinking mud, cooling lava, as well as in tree crowns and honeycomb cells.

- 90 degree joints are more common in non-elastic materials such as fracturing solid rock.

Such surfaces or volumes are frequently best described in terms of fractal geometry. They look the same at decreasing scales, especially cracks, which vary in width from large to small in keeping with successive scale reductions.

a

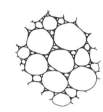

b

Two characteristic patterns.

a) Where an elastic material such as mud shrinks and cracks and

b) Where objects such as stones or bubbles pack tightly together.

The characteristic cracking pattern as peat dries out and shrinks. Smaller cracks between the larger ones repeat the pattern at a smaller scale and produce a fractal structure.

The columnar formation in basalt rocks, formed when the cooling molten rock shrank. The equal rate of shrinkage produced the evenly sized columns.

Mosaic Landscapes

Whilst many of the basic pattern types described above can be applied to large scale landscapes there are also many examples where this fails or else the occurence is restricted to certain scales. For example, unlike meanders, the spiral is not found in vegetation patterns; rivers obviously show branching and meandering; explosions can be seen in the spreading patterns of forest fires or volcanoes.

Landscapes are not usually so clear in their patterns, because they comprise many layers of components. Often the identification of the essence of patterns needs a careful search because they are intricately woven together, due to the interaction of all the processes at work. For example, it is possible to consider landscapes as complexes of networks and mosaics. The networks are patterns of linear features, such as the meandering and branching systems that run through and between the elements which produce the mosaics. The American landscape ecologist Richard Forman has recently explored the characteristics of mosaic landscapes in some detail. It is useful to summarize some of the relevant aspects of his work to complete this initial introduction to the characteristics of patterns that will provide the basis for deeper explorations of the genesis and properties of landscape patterns in later chapters.

Mosaic patterns can be found over a very wide range of spatial scales, from the submicroscopic in the soil, to the whole planet, where continents and archipelagos form a mosaic. Human perception of mosaic patterns ranges from a few to some hundreds of miles/kilometres, based on experience of our daily lives or when travelling around. On the other hand continents yield mosaic patterns

A large scale mosaic pattern across a landscape. This example is the pattern of rock, bog forest, lakes (frozen) and rivers (frozen) in Labrador, Canada. The water areas lie in depressions formed by glacial erosion and deposition. They are different in shape and size, yet they contain similar features which give a sense of unity to the pattern. The river shows a strongly developed meandering pattern.

A small scale mosaic pattern of lichen growing on a rock. There is repetition of the growth pattern of each patch of lichen as they expand and intersect each other.

of up to thousands of square miles/kilometres. Thus we can identify a series of mosaic patterns formed by the aggregation of individual plants, stones, water bodies, structures, fields and so on, which can be aggregated to give a larger mosaic. An hierarchy exists from the individual elements that form communities, which, in turn, aggregate to form habitats and ecosystems or land uses. These, when aggregated, form landscapes that are compounds of regions, which are sub-divisions of continents or oceans; whilst all are part of the biosphere.

The size of each stage of the hierarchy can vary greatly, depending on the individual elements (small plants or big trees), the variability of the substrate (very variable intertidal zone or broad rolling steppe) and the climatic variation (very variable in British Columbia, in Canada or homogeneous in the River Amazon basin in South America). This hierarchical structure is useful, because different types of planning, management or design apply at different scales.

Mosaics arise because of energy inputs into the biosphere. If the earth's surface was a closed system with no energy input or loss, it would become amorphous or structureless (entropic, according to the second law of thermodynamics). However, because energy is received from the sun or nuclear reactions in the earth at variable rates, the system is unevenly dynamic. There is constant flux as energy moves around the system. This produces earth movements, climatic fluctuations and interacts with spontaneous genetic mutation; this is another factor producing variability in living organisms which is also an integral part of the biosphere. Thus the mosaic patterns of the world are spatially, structurally, compositionally and temporally heterogeneous at all the scales described above.

Heterogeneity can be expressed in two ways. Some landscapes are composed of gradients that change gradually from one structural or compositional type across the land. It is difficult to detect a pattern in these types, because there are no edges (this is a feature dependent on our perceptual abilities - see Chapter Two). Such landscapes are fairly rare, being mostly moist tropical forests or sometimes temperate rain forests. Gradients also depend on the scale of observation. At the continental scale there is a major mosaic pattern, but at the regional or landscape scales, the pattern is perceived as a gradient.

The second type of heterogeneity is where the patterns are defined by distinct boundaries with varying degrees of contrast between them. These boundaries may be defined by structure or composition of rock, soil, vegetation, water or human changes and constructions and the patterns of their movements. Hence, there is a limited range of patterns that can be found in mosaics, some of which fall into the categories considered earlier in the chapter.

However, Forman expands and develops some of the classifications and patterns formed by aggregation or mixes of elements. The mosaic patterns are determined by mechanisms whose characteristics are instrumental in defining the possible range of types. There are three of these:

- Heterogeneity of the substrate beneath the land mosaic, such as landform, moisture, soil structure and nutrients. This heterogeneity is itself dependent on the processes of geology and geomorphology interacting with the climate. This will be examined in depth in Chapter Five.

- The effect of natural disturbances to the vegetation that colonized and grew on the variable substrate. Natural fires, wind, sandstorms, insect pests or fungal diseases change structure, composition and affect rates and directions of natural succession of vegetation. The range of ecosystem processes and their relationship to substrate heterogeneity will be covered in Chapter Six.

A large scale mosaic pattern of patches of different vegetation in northwest Washington State, USA - fields containing different crops and forest of different types. The mosaic also contains networks of linear features such as roads and rivers running through it. The rectilinear pattern discerned here is that of the American survey grid.

- Human activity ranging from manipulation to clearance of vegetation, erection of structures, modification of landforms and interference with the climate and genetic composition of plants or animals. Chapter Seven will examine the patterns created by such actions.

Thus, the form of the landscape is the result of the forces or processes at work: 'form is the diagram of force' according to Forman, or, as we could say, the pattern is the diagram of process.

Within the hierarchical structure, there is a degree of vertical integration with feedback between levels and connections and between individual landscape mosaics and their constituent elements, by means of energy flows (direct in the case of heat or indirect in animal or human activities). These flows are dependent on and, in turn, affect the patterns of the mosaics; thus they change over time and at different rates. The dynamics of the feedback systems are usually negative, that is they act as regulatory mechanisms to dampen the degree of variability within a natural range. Occasionally positive feedback occurs destabilizing the system until a higher level limitation is reached.

As mosaics are composed of elements with defined edges or junctions, another of the ways to characterize them is by the structure and shape of the boundaries between them. The following list categorizes some of the basic features.

- The shape of the edge, whether geometric (Euclidian) or organic (fractal)
- The hardness or softness of the edge
- The contrast of composition
- The contrast of structure

Straight or rectilinear shaped edges are usually caused by human activity. Organic shapes can be of natural or human origin. They can vary in the degree of convolution or multi-scale structure, both aspects of their fractal characteristics. For example, fields are usually rectilinear, whilst forest fires always produce convoluted shapes.

The hardness or softness of edges is also an indication of their origin: abrupt, severe edges are mostly the result of human activity, whilst gradual, softer edges, sometimes known as ecotones, are more typically natural; for example, a hard forest edge caused by cutting or its natural, softer edge against a bog.

The degree of contrast of the composition is indicative of the range of heterogeneity in the landscape or a part of it. There may be a complete contrast, as between land and sea, or a slight contrast, as between oak/hazel and oak/birch woodland.

The contrast of structure may also be high or low. A field next to a woodland shows a high contrast, whilst a mature woodland next to a middle aged one shows lower contrast.

All these classes again relate to the processes causing them, their

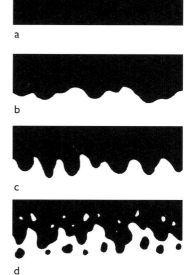

a

b

c

d

Characteristics of edges:

a) A straight, hard edge.

b) A slightly wavy edge.

c) An edge characterized by bays and promontories that describe a meandering pattern.

d) A diffuse, broken edge.

(After Forman, 1995)

origin (natural or human), the substrate character and climatic variations. Some key characteristics of edges will be explored in Chapter Six.

Patterns of movement can also be observed in edges, because none are static: in many cases they advance or retreat over different time scales. Advancing forest edges of straight character are usually associated with human activity such as forest cutting, whereas natural edges advance in promontories and lobes, forming meandering lines and thus accounting for some of the characteristics of shape considered previously.

Edges or boundaries define the shapes of areas or patches in mosaic landscapes. Forman categorizes shape by its degree of convolution and elongation, as being two independent variables applicable to natural and artificial shapes. He also concurs with earlier observations that some shapes are rarely found naturally at the landscape level, such as spirals, hourglass or dumbbell shapes, hexagons, straight sides or wave shapes.

The most regular types of shape result from explosive forces acting in multiple directions and of equal strength; these are found in volcanic cones, ice polygons or mud cracks, where there is little substrate variability to affect the force. Elongation of a shape is usually associated with a degree of direction in its origin, such as wind, erosion or transport (either in the same or opposite direction); for example, sand dunes aligned at right angles to the wind or drumlins aligned in the same direction as ice flow.

Corridors, those linear elements along which various types of flows (energy, liquid, animals) take place, also have characteristic patterns. Meanders and branching are obvious ones already considered; braiding is another. Straightness is also a factor linked to artificial origins. Corridor width variations are usually related to the major linear shape patterns and can often be described as fractal in a similar way as for natural edges and patches.

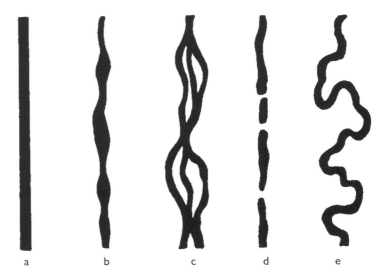

Characteristics of corridors:

a) A simple line.

b) A corridor of varied width.

c) A braided corridor.

d) A broken, discontinuous corridor.

e) A meandering corridor.

(After Forman, 1995)

a   b   c   d   e

A further view is that patterns derived from the aggregations of mosaic elements, particularly corridors connecting patches, fall into a number of limited categories. This view is held by Margot Cantwell, from Canada, and described by Forman using diagrams of lines and circles as a shorthand way of describing patterns. Spiders, necklaces, 'graph cells', candelabra and 'rigid cells' are the main types.

The Patterns of Chaos

The developing understanding of the range of patterns which can evolve from the application of small initial variations of the same processes has led to new insights about nature and the world. Chaotic behaviour seems to follow deterministic principles, but at the same time appears to be extremely irregular. However, it is not the complex, patternless behaviour that it seems. In fact, the development of the theory of chaos has revealed a misunderstanding of the way cause and effect operate during natural processes, and the patterns they produce. Irregular effects on process and pattern can be mistaken for randomness, but belie a deep order. The reason for this misunderstanding lies in the assumption that simple causes lead to simple effects and conversely, that complicated, multivariate causes produce complex effects. Now we know that simple causes can produce complicated effects, processes and patterns.

This suggests that we have little hope of understanding the more intricate results of complex causes, but simple observation indicates that it is not correct. As we look around us, the world is full of repeated patterns, of perceived order, and not chaos (in the usual meaning of the term). Paradoxically, these patterns are the large scale simplifications that emerge from the complex interaction of large numbers of different causes or elements.

For example, in a river system, there are a wide range of geological structures as possible substrates, with innumerable possibilities of shape to start with. The climatic conditions producing rain can vary enormously, along with the vegetation growing on the landscape producing evapotranspiration. The numbers of interactions of all these possible variations is huge and the numbers of possible patterns ought to be limitless. This is true of minor detail - which stream goes where and how it erodes a particular piece of rock - but at the larger scale, it produces a pattern that is remarkably similar to all other drainage systems. In chaos theory, the gradual coalescence of a number of different patterns into a single pattern caused by changes to the initial conditions is said to be caused by a *strange attractor*. The branching pattern of drainage can be considered the result of one of these.

Patterns Created by People

The final section in the survey of patterns reviews briefly the type of patterns that have been produced by people over the millennia.

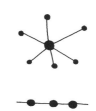

a

b

c

d

e

Examples of graph theory patterns:

a) A spider.

b) A necklace.

c) A graph cell.

d) A candelabra.

e) A rigid cell.

(After Forman, 1995)

Humans are the only species consciously to design objects and patterns using creative skills and imagination.

It is believed that the earliest toolmakers were prehuman hominids, such as *Homo erectus*, some 420,000 or more years ago. Constructing artifacts provides one of the first opportunities to create something from a preconceived idea, using highly developed cognitive and conceptual skills. Many of the earliest flint tools are functional as well as beautiful. Thus, our sense of awareness is part of our genetic inheritence and has evolved to contribute to our intellect today.

Decorative patterns of an abstract or stylized nature have been found wherever humans have lived, from the earliest paleolithic times onwards. When settled communities developed in the neolithic period and stone structures began to be erected the first planned or designed landscapes came into existence. Significantly, the earliest patterns and over time, those proven to be continuously popular, seem to be ones that are extremely similar to the kinds of basic natural patterns explored in the earlier part of this chapter. In a fascinating study of 8000 years of ornament, Eva Wilson, of the British Museum in London, England, has classified these motifs or patterns into a limited number of types. Some types are extremely wide ranging and others very specific and deeply symbolic. Why such patterns are so universal is difficult to explain. Perhaps they are easy to copy or to create in simple carvings on clay pots or have important symbolic meaning.

Scrolls, spirals and meanders are amongst the earliest patterns, found on pottery, carved on stones as part of burial structures, incised or engraved on weapons, painted on plaster and carved in turf. The spiral can exist in its own right or be compounded into multiples, be linked to create meanders or become almost plant like. It can be curvilinear and flowing or geometric and stiff.

Ancient patterns carved on stones built into the neolithic tomb at Newgrange in Ireland. Spirals, concentric circles or curves and zig-zag shapes are patterns found from ancient times to the present.

Animals and plants occur, often stylized into intertwining, branching, meandering or spiralling forms. Some of these are highly symbolic. Animals dominate the art of nomadic peoples, whereas plants are more common in settled agricultural areas. Amongst the most complex and diverse are the interlocking, meandering stylized animals found in Celtic and Anglo-Saxon art. The same ideas, although expressed differently, are found in the art of the native coastal peoples of British Columbia in Canada.

It is tempting to read into many of these patterns, a degree of symbolism that may never have existed. Spirals occur in nature, meanders in rivers - do these signify life forces when used as decoration or are they merely attractive as patterns? We will never know for certain, but it is significant, in our quest for patterns, that so many natural ones have a strong attraction to us. It may be easier for us to recognize such patterns, to gain aesthetic satisfaction from them or to sense a deeper meaning or symbolism in them.

In many of the earliest landscape designs, some of these patterns were repeated using vegetation. In gardens, the layout of plants often became a larger version of decoration or embroidery. The knot garden or the grand patterns created, during the late 17th century, by André Le Nôtre at Versailles in France, repeat the interlocking forms, spirals, meanders and other similar themes, sometimes curved, sometimes geometric in their execution. At their most extreme concept, these symbolize human domination over nature, order out of chaos, symmetry and control over the world.

a

b

c

Examples of spirals used in decoration from various ancient cultures. (After Wilson, 1994)

a) Scroll motifs found on objects from the late Scandinavian Bronze Age.

b) A panel from a stamp seal from Anatolia (c1600 BC).

c) A design from jewellery from the royal graves at Mycenae (1550-1500 BC).

The knot garden at Hampton Court Palace near London, England. Hedges are used to create abstract patterns designed to be viewed from windows in the upper floors of the palace.

Celtic spirals from a bronze disc from Lagore, Ireland (7th-8th century AD).

Another major pattern that has been repeatedly used since early civilizations is the grid. Planned or designed landscapes have been laid out according to right-angled grids. The Roman architect Vitruvius described the layout of the ideal city based on the grid, while the majority of the land ownership pattern of the USA is divided into a grid. Forest cuttings have appeared like chequerboards on hillsides and ecological experiments have been set out in repeated squares. This pattern represents an elegant order to be overlaid on unruly nature. Its effects continue to be significant in many landscapes.

Summary and Conclusions

At the close of this first chapter I have introduced a number of concepts: the notion of patterns in the landscape; uncertainty in the predictability of pattern generation and the present ability of humans to perceive patterns on a previously impossible scale; the relationship of patterns to our developing understanding of geometry; pattern analysis and classification; the role of processes in pattern creation and the creation of patterns by people.

We can conclude from this, that many disciplines should be integrated in order to interpret fully the range of patterns, their originating processes and our perception of them. Although disciplines such as geology, ecology, cultural geography, psychology or philosophy are immersed in a deep but narrow consideration of a subject, the requirement for this study is a summary of the essential aspects of each in order to present a clear picture of their interrelationships with the processes and patterns that are created.

Now that the existence and importance of patterns, processes and perceptions has been established it is appropriate to develop the perceptual and aesthetic aspects further. Then a picture of our world can be constructed, starting with the underlying structure of the earth and the processes that give rise to its landform patterns. Over this will be laid the patterns produced by ecological processes, followed by the cultural patterns determined by human use. Once the basic building blocks have been established, we will analyse the patterns. The emphasis will remain at the 'landscape scale' of the land mosaic level we have discussed in this chapter.

CHAPTER TWO

THE PERCEPTION OF PATTERNS

Introduction

In the first chapter we explored the concept of patterns in the landscape and the way they are intimately connected to the processes that created them. The discussions were primarily concerned with applying objectivity to the description of patterns, a task that will be explored more deeply in Chapters Five to Seven. This is necessary to provide a firm base to explore the ways that we perceive and respond to these patterns in an aesthetic sense, and how this might help us create new patterns by design. Thus, both pattern analysis and design necessitate an understanding of how human perception works, how it influences our opinions and feelings, and therefore, how we understand and relate to the patterns and processes explored in this book.

The Senses and Their Use in Perception

It has been traditional amongst aestheticians and philosophers to divide the senses into those dealing with distance and those for nearness or the proximal. Sight and hearing are the distance senses, although smell can sometimes be involved. These have also been identified, since the time of the 18th century German philosopher Immanuel Kant (see Chapter Three) as the aesthetic senses, because they allow us to reflect on a scene, art object or music from a distance. In this book we are more concerned with the perceptions and aesthetics of nature and our environment than of art.

Sight uses light energy to detect shapes, textures, colours, intensities of light and movement, together with aspects of spatial dimensions such as distance and depth. Sight is a particularly important sense for humans to which we have become evolutionarily adapted. It has also become one of the main ways in which we think and use the 'mind's eye' to picture creative ideas, like we use our real eyes to picture our environment.

Hearing uses the energy of sound waves which we apprehend as noise, or as specific patterns of pitch (high to low notes), order, rhythm, beat, timbre (the quality or character of the sound) and other distinct sets of patterns, which may be identified as unique, such as the sound of running water or the voice of a person well known to us. The distance we can hear depends on the loudness and pitch of the sound. Our ears, being spaced apart, enable us to hear in stereo and gain some spatial assessment of the world around us. We can use hearing to reinforce the information provided by sight.

Smell uses the nose to detect small amounts of chemicals borne on the air and is one of the more primitive senses in terms of its evolutionary development. It is also immediate in its effect and very powerful at triggering the retrieval of complete memory sequences, from apparently simple odour combinations. Smells can carry significant distances when the chemicals are borne on the wind. Taste depends on putting substances into our mouths. We can taste four sensations: sweet, sour, salt and bitter. When taste and smell are combined flavour is obtained. We mainly use taste for food, but we can sometimes use it for other purposes.

Touch or tactile sensations are much wider in their scope than is often imagined. With the basic sense of touch we use mechanical energy to feel shape, texture and pressure. Using other sensory cells in our skin, we can also feel temperature, humidity and pain. Our body movements tell us about direction, elevation and the degree of resistance offered by surfaces underfoot. These senses can be grouped together under the general heading of kinaesthetic, meaning perceived through movement. They are all proximal in their application, that is we detect stimuli from them directly.

All these senses are rarely used in isolation. Usually they are interconnected and this is important in giving us a complete picture of our environment. However, some are stronger or more important than others under different circumstances. When walking through a forest we use sight to guide us through and admire the trees and light; we listen to the sounds of the wind in the trees or the birdsong; we taste berries that we pick and feel the warmth or coolness of a glade or dense grove, the pressure of the breeze, the softness of the forest floor underfoot and pain when a thorn pricks us. We take all of these sensations together and connect them to form a complete picture. If we sit on a cliff overlooking a broad panorama we can only use tactile and taste senses close to us, so that smell, sound and especially vision become proportionately more important as the scene moves further away, until we rely completely on vision. Thus when the term 'landscape' is used in the sense of a 'prospect of scenery', the visual impression is by far the most important for perception and the corresponding aesthetic response. In Chapter Three, there are also important distinctions to be made between the landscape as scenery and the environment as a multisensory engagement.

However, some human senses are naturally more strongly developed than others. Our evolution as a species in the savannah landscapes of what is now East Africa, resulted in our bipedal, upright posture, binocular frontal vision and high degree of intelligence. This also led to the pre-eminence of sight as the major sense used in the perception of our environment.

Our intelligence has given us highly developed mental abilities to appraise the world about us, with the process of perception followed by representation, memory and reasoning. These faculties rely upon information received over increasing distances, because it is often the remoter parts of our environment that interest us most. Thus, the distance senses allow us to be removed from the direct impact of a landscape or event, not in order to contemplate it in some detached philosophical way, but to form a rational judgement about a situation without having to react spontaneously to other sensory stimulation. This derives from our early evolutionary success as hunters, which was due to our well developed intellect and not the brute force, speed or sharp teeth needed in situations that require an immediate reflex action. Hence we can interpret a scene, analyse its characteristics, refer to past experience and form a plan of action if needed.

The amount of information and knowledge we obtain depends on the variety and degree of contrast of the sensory data that we receive and the extent to which we can differentiate them: that is, detect patterns. All the senses are able to do this to varying degrees, but not all can be used directly as for thought and reasoning. We can experience smells and tastes in great abundance, but we cannot think in them. Touch can be used to reinforce vision but as a proximal sense it is of limited use in the wider world except for unsighted people. We can hear and appreciate patterns of pitch and rhythm that stimulate our imagination but we cannot think in sound. In music we have a stimulating medium for creativity, but it is more limited for perception of the wider world. Using sight we can organize shapes, colours, textures, movements and other contributors to pattern perception and we can also imagine what the unseen parts are like. Rudolf Arnheim, a German psychologist, has developed a theory of visual thinking and its implications for creativity.

Language is the main use of sound, but we tend to convert words into images before we can make full use of them. Sight, by comparison, not only permits a much greater variety of information to be received, but it leads directly to the means by which we think and express ourselves. In this respect, the sensory input about the world is much more than mechanical reception of data, later processed by the brain as a separate activity. For example, at the same time as we perceive the world, we also project our subjective feelings and preconceptions onto it. This is why concepts such as 'landscape' or 'wilderness' are as much states of mind as they are physical entities; this has major implications for aesthetics and for the meaning of the term *environment* (see Chapter Three).

The eye may in some respects be constructed and act like a camera, but, being directly connected to the brain, it also interacts with the mental processes that use it. Most of us rely so much on a constant flow of sensory information that if deprived of it, perhaps by being shut in an empty, dark and soundless room for a period, the mind starts to supply images to fill the void. The extreme results of this are hallucinations. Hence, it is clear that perception is not just the passive reception of information.

Blind people are excluded from the perception of the world available to the sighted. However, they compensate by developing the other senses, especially touch, to much greater degrees than most people. Similar compensations occur for those who cannot hear or speak. The extent to which the 'mind's eye' exists for blind people, especially those blind from birth, is difficult for sighted people to appreciate.

The rest of this chapter will concentrate on vision, because it is so important, as a perception and a thinking medium for most people. In order to understand visual perception, we must know something of the physiology and psychology of the mechanisms involved. Recent research is uncovering much about the detailed processes of image formation and the way in which the brain cells build up an image of the world. An extremely helpful synthesis has been written by the British team of Vicki Bruce, Patrick Green and Mark Georgeson, from which much of the following discussion is sourced.

Light as the Medium of Visual Perception

Light is a form of electromagnetic radiation (which extends from invisible X rays through a narrow range of visible light to radio waves). The spectrum of visible light is divided into the perceived colours of the rainbow, each within its own range of wavelengths. Some animals have a visible range extending to ultra violet, others can see light, but cannot detect colour.

It is convenient to think of light in the form of rays varying in wavelength (colour) and intensity. The light is altered when it passes through a medium. For example, it undergoes some absorption on passing through air or water; *photons*, the units of light energy, collide with particles of matter, yield their energy to them and so disappear.

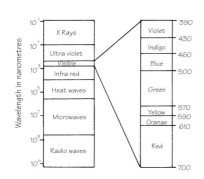

The electromagnetic spectrum, showing that part visible to the human eye.

Some wavelengths, such as the longer ones in the orange and red part of the visible spectrum, are absorbed more readily than others. This partly accounts for the blue appearance of the sky, water and more distant parts of the landscape.

Light is diffracted as it passes through a medium such as air. The particles are scattered when they strike matter and are deflected by it. This accounts for the overall brightness of the sky (ambient light) because of the diffraction caused by the atmosphere. Blueness in the sky is also partly caused by this phenomenon, as longer wavelength light in the red range of the spectrum is diffracted more, so that additional short wave light in the blue range is received.

When light strikes an opaque surface some of it is absorbed and some reflected. The reflected light gives an object colour. Different surfaces absorb and reflect different combinations of wavelength. A yellow/green leaf absorbs more blue and red light, whilst a blue/green leaf absorbs more yellow, orange and red and reflects more blue in its colour. Surfaces are rarely smooth and so tend not to reflect light evenly. This varied, reflective pattern contributes to the appearance of surface texture, whilst the quantity of light reflected yields information about shadow and depth.

Thus, light is emitted in different degrees from a range of objects and surfaces; it varies in colour and brightness and is affected by the medium through which it travels. The precise quantities and qualities of the light received by an observer vary, depending on the position. The eyes look in a particular direction from a specific location, and so receive a unique combination of light. The totality of all the light received from all directions is known as the *optic array*. General perceptual rules apply to this, as we normally recognize upwards as being lighter and downwards as darker. The intensity of the sunlight relative to the position of the horizon gives information on the time of

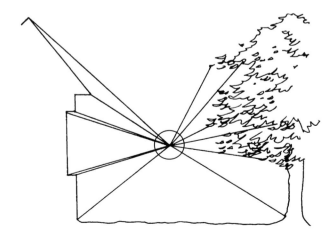

The concept of the optic array: all the light of varying wavelengths and intensities reaching a single point. This gives the observer a unique combination at the moment of perception. (After Bruce et al., 1994)

day. Surfaces orientated at 90 degrees towards the light are brightest, those facing away are darker, so giving information about three dimensional space in the absence of stereoscopic vision or over distances where stereoscopic vision is weaker. Changes in the optic array denote movement, either of the observer or of parts of the scene under observation such as animals, vehicles, clouds or water. The detection of movement is an important aspect of perception.

This brief discussion indicates that the eyes receive light as a pattern of intensities and colours. From this the brain has to construct a meaningful image, where reality can be tested or validated against information provided by the other senses and in part by the experiences gained from using the image. We work on the assumption that what we see is reality, so that we can be fooled by visual tricks such as *trompe l'oeil* illusory effects, where truth is only validated if we use senses other than vision.

The Physiology of Visual Perception

The eyes are the sense organs used to capture information from the optic array. Several different models of eyes have evolved. The human version is a single chambered eye like those of all vertebrates and some invertebrates. It consists of a chamber with an aperture through which light enters. The light is focused by a lens onto the rear wall, the *retina*, to form an inverted image of the scene being viewed. The amount of light entering is partly controlled by the aperture or *iris* and the image is detected by a layer of specialist receptors lining the retina cells. These cells can be of two types according to their shape - rods and cones. They detect light by absorbing it to different degrees, using a special photosensitive pigment contained in each cell. As the pigment absorbs light its molecular structure changes, producing a stream of enzymatic chemical reactions causing a degree of *hyperpolarization* (where the interior of a nerve cell becomes more negatively charged than the exterior) in the cell membrane to trigger a response in the connecting nerve cells proportional to the intensity of light (in the rods) and the wavelengths of the spectrum (in the cones) received. As all of the retinal cells sample the image every few milliseconds, the signals from each cell vary over time and across the retina. Thus a map is built up of the scene, according to the light characteristics received by each rod or cone (p. 233, Fig. 3).

To function properly the eye must be able to form as sharp an image as possible focused on the retina. The efficiency of the resolution of an image, or the *acuity* of the eye, is governed by this ability. There is a limit at which we cease to be able to differentiate variation in a pattern. At this point the eye perceives a single, uniform field of average brightness. This acuity is measured as a visual angle relative to the eye. This means that objects close to us yield more detail than those further away, because of the relative size of the object to the visual

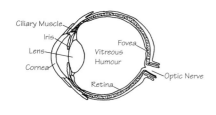

A section through the human eye showing the mechanism for collecting information about the scene being viewed.

angle. This can be seen in the dot patterns used to print newspaper photographs: at a distance we see uniform tones whereas close up we see varied dot sizes and spaces. This means that we perceive different levels of resolution over different distances; hence for distant scenes, general structures and features dominate, whereas at close ranges more detailed aspects stand out. There is a grading of detail over distance that has implications for landscape pattern recognition and the perception of space (see discussions of J. J. Gibson's approach later in the chapter).

The normal focus of the human eye is usually effective for a range of 6 metres/20 feet to 'infinity'. We can also see well between 6m and a few centimetres because of the ability of the lens of the eye to change shape (accommodate) and thus maintain the sharpness of the image on the retina. This degree of accommodation is particularly useful in primates and humans, who are adapted to manipulate objects at close quarters as well as wanting a view of broad and distant panoramas.

The eye has to cope with a wide range of light intensities that affect the efficiency of the transformation of images into photoelectric stimuli. This is because the retina has to cope with a fluctuating rate of photon (light energy) reception in order to maintain a steady image. At very low light intensities it may not be possible to maintain an image, if the average rate of photon reception is so low that for nearly half of the time there are too few photons to trigger a response in the retinal cells. The eye adjusts to this by using the two types of pigment cells in the retina.

The rods contain more pigment than the cones, which increases the chance of photon absorption at low light intensities. However, the rods are not sensitive to colour, so that in low light intensities the image received by the eye tends to become increasingly monochrome. Human eyes contain about 7 million cones and 120 million rods. Because we are awake and use our eyes more during daylight, the efficiency of the smaller number of cones is enhanced by being closely grouped. If they were too widely spaced the acuity of colour daylight vision would be too low. The cone area, the fovea, which is slightly depressed in shape, therefore provides high acuity under high intensity light conditions, whilst the large number of rods, whose images are pooled, provide high sensitivity vision in darker or dimmer conditions.

In the human eye the iris does not control the amount of light entering the eye as much as it does in other animals. Instead, the retinal cells can adjust their sensitivity to a wide range of light intensities, although, at any one time, only a narrow section of the full range can be used. This accounts for the phenomonen of not seeing detail on shady sides of objects in bright light, because our eyes adapt to the brightness and so reduce their sensitivity to the darker range.

The eyes sample the optic array by looking in different directions and focusing on various objects. The human eyes are arranged frontally and are binocular. This increases the quality of vision and achieves greater acuity because of the greater overlap of the images received by the two eyes. This process of stereopsis also provides three dimensional vision. However, to be sure that we can see around us, we must move our eyes, our heads and frequently our bodies to look at greater areas, or position ourselves so that information from behind is not needed (seeing a prospect from a safe refuge, leading to an alternative theory of landscape preferences advanced by the British geographer Jay Appleton, see Chapter Three).

The eyes sample the optic array by means of jumps or *saccades* between *fixation points*. The fixation is the short time (a few milliseconds) needed to gain an image of part of the array. Saccades and fixes happen several times a second. Once an area of the array is fixed, pursuit, either of a moving object or of a static object by a moving observer, can be achieved to keep it in view. The eye with the fovea focused on an object, can see it in high acuity, whilst the rest of the image, the peripheral scene, is of lower acuity. The constant saccades and fixes by the eye thus sample more of the optic array at high speed to build up an overall image of high acuity.

Colour vision is achieved by the cone cells in the retina, which are sensitive to different wavelengths of light. The human eye possesses three varieties which are sensitive to the blue, red and green ranges of the spectrum. Birds have four types so they may be able to differentiate a wider range of colours, where we see only one. They may also have cells receptive to the ultraviolet wavelength.

Visual perception is not just about detecting light, which is merely the means for seeing the objects, surfaces and movement making up the landscape and its patterns. The purpose of the eye is to collect information about the world that is useful to us. Therefore, we look actively and selectively or passively, depending on the circumstances at a particular time. Thus our aesthetic involvement can be varied between engagement with the environment in terms of extracting a wide range of useful sensory information and the contemplative or non-specific gaze, where no utilitarian objective is involved in the perception.

The primary processing of the retinal image commences with the mechanisms for transmitting the electrical signal, triggered by light to the *ganglia*, a type of nerve cell, whose axons (see below) make up the optic nerve, located behind the retina. There are various, partly understood, means by which the nerve response threshold is triggered and how the input of each cell is aggregated and compared to extract a coherent image. In higher mammals there is some evidence of simplification in the retinal processing, perhaps to allow more complex interpretation to proceed in the brain. This may be because our reactions are only partly spontaneous to the perceived image, compared with less intelligent animals. We may wish to add the other sensory information to complete or reinforce the images, before deciding whether to act on them or not.

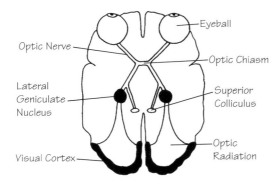

The layout of the image processing parts of the human brain. Information from the two pictures presented by each eye is exchanged at the optic chiasm and the processes of image recognition take place in the LGNs.
(After Bruce et al., 1994)

The cell *axons* (the linear parts of nerve cells that act like electrical wiring in the brain) extend from the eyes into an area of the mid brain called the *optic rectium*. The pattern of the axons that make up the optic nerve is the same as that in rods and cones of the retina, so that the image proceeds along them positioned in the same way and with the same proportions, as seen in the view by the observer. This is maintained in the rectium, where the cells are arranged in layers called retinoptic maps. Most of the ganglion cells then continue to the two *lateral geniculate nuclei* (LGN) located in an upper section of the brain called the *thalamus*, where they terminate in synapses (where the ends of two cells nearly touch and where electrical activity in one affects the other). The two LGN also contain layered cells arranged in retinoptic maps. The cells in the LGN vary in the way they handle the information from the retina. Some cells transmit wavelength (and thus colour), others intensity. The balance of these functions and the threshold at which they become active, play a further part in the process of perception. On the way to the LGNs the nerve cells from right and left eyes meet in the middle at the *optic chiasm* where information from each side of the visual field is transmitted to the other side of the brain. Thus the two left halves of the visual field go to the left LGN and vice versa for the right halves. Beyond the LGN the visual information proceeds to the visual cortex, an area at the rear of the brain where the visual image is processed and integrated.

This represents the present limit of knowledge about the cellular level of image processing and more research will no doubt reveal further understanding.

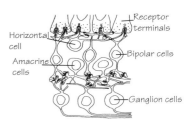

A section through the retinal cells shows how the information they collect is sent on to the brain along the optic nerve.

The Psychology of Visual Perception

We know from the previous discussion that the eyes receive light of varying intensity and wavelength as an image on the retina, which is transmitted into the processing areas of the brain as a spatially related pattern. The brain has to interpret and make sense of that pattern and use the results to inform us how and where to look next.

As previously outlined, human eyes have evolved as aids to survival. As a result we indulge in perception that is purposeful and selective. We need to understand the way the landscape is assembled, we seek out and notice change and movement and we apply meaning, where we wish to engage with our surroundings and feel part of the world we inhabit. We tend not to notice things that do not concern us. To that extent our view is subjective. Thus we have to disentangle the multitude of light patterns into something we regard as the reality of the scene and about which we can, with experience, predict certain cause and effect relationships.

The first things we are able to detect and classify are the edges defined by varying light intensities. These begin the process of shape and pattern definition. Shape (two dimensions) and form (three dimensions) are highly significant variables that provide two of the major building blocks of pattern comprehension. One issue is to determine which edges belong to which shapes and thus to separate out the elements of the scene. This comprehension is not helped by the variations in light and shade intensity, which can be subtle where two objects meet or distinct within the confines of one object, thus making the correct identification of edges and their relation to objects more difficult. In addition, changes in viewer position, relative to the light source, will yield a completely different set of edges from the same set of elements or objects. Since this apparently causes us few problems, there must be an efficient mechanism to achieve the first breakdown of the scene into its basic elements.

In the absence of biological models or a clearer understanding of the cellular level processes, psychologists, in particular David Marr, from Great Britain, have devised their own models or algorithms to deduce the processes of perception that allow us to make sense of a scene.

A scene in Waterton Lakes National Park, Alberta, Canada. How does the brain work out which bits belong where?

One of these is the concept of the *primal sketch*, the first transformation of the retinal image into a derivative that describes the detailed features of that image. This sketch has to be able to define the edges of the image from the light intensity and to compute their significance and general associations with different elements of the scene.

This sketch is synthesized from three derivatives. The first is based on the steepness of gradients of light intensity across the image. However, there is a risk that certain threshold levels will be used to detect such edges and hence much detail from less well defined, less steep gradients could be lost. Thus a system of filters has been postulated, giving a somewhat hierarchical structure to the primal sketch. For example the detection of main edges is followed by less well defined ones and so on until we cease to notice any differences. In this model the filtered image does not solely yield defined linear edges, but also contains segments made up of 'bars', 'terminations' and 'blobs', each of varying strength and possibly detected by special cells in the brain. These have to be spatially organized and related in order for the primal sketch to be meaningful.

The use of the term sketch above has similarities with the notion of an artist making the first basic outlines of a scene. The first task is to identify the main structural elements arising from the edges: skylines, shorelines, tree outlines, building outlines and so on. Then the finer details are added and shading is used to define the character of the edges of particular elements. In a way an artist is subconsciously repeating the psychological processes of perception, according to the theory described previously, and recording them on a sketchpad rather than in the memory. This analogy may also be related to our active, directed vision when observing a scene for a particular purpose.

A 'primal sketch' of the photograph on page 48 produced by a computer program where the main edges are identified due to their contrast. This provides the first structure according to David Marr's theories of visual perception.

The second derivation of the primal sketch is based on the variations in light intensity that yield not only distinct, step like edges, but also patterns of graduated change or *luminescence valleys*. The sketch process batches these at the extremes of darkness and light in order to define them. A computer based algorithm, which can produce a very similar outline sketch to that of a human draughtsperson described above, helps to validate this model.

The third route to the primal sketch is concerned with variations in energy intensity in different parts of the image and the way this triggers responses by several types of cell at various thresholds. This uses concepts of *signal processing* similar to the way radio signals are received; the strongest signals occur where intensity variations are more extreme. This model may also account for 'mach banding', the apparent change in luminescence where two colours meet.

The organization of the line segments, bars, linear termination and blobs is complicated by our tendency to fill in gaps to complete lines and create shapes, often when none are present. It is possible that the brain cells seeking linear terminations are suppressed, when many of the segments of lines are long enough to overlap each other. This overlap causes interactions between the types of cells that are adapted to seek contours which describe continuous surfaces or shapes. Thus we are predisposed by our brain cell structure to perceive complete shapes in the absence of comprehensive information or when presented with illusory information.

In the theory presented so far, the retinal image has been reduced to its basic elements: a set of edges, contours and energy variations across the scene. It is important to know which are linked and how they are combined into more complex images. As well as edges (lines) and blobs (points) we see surfaces (planes) and three dimensional objects

An image derived from the photograph on page 48, used to identify the changes in intensity as ranges of value rather than single edges. This image processing is thought by David Marr to play a part in our perceptive processes.

(volumes). Early concepts centred on ideas of *association*, of linking like with like, or with simpler images combining to form more complex ones. These concepts do not explain shape and order (the way elements are organized to form structures) when these elements overlay any existing associations.

Gestalt Psychology

One of the most influential set of theories to explain how more complex images are created from the identification of edges and contours in the primal sketch is known generally as *gestalt* psychology. 'Gestalt' means, in German, both *shape* and the *character of the shape*. A number of German psychologists, notably Wolfgang Kohler, developed ideas about how we determine shape, together with a range of other spatial cues, in order to discern order in the images presented to us.

The first of these spatial cues is commonly referred to as *figure and ground* where the object or 'thing' being identified stands out as a separate entity or 'figure' from the rest of the scene, or at least its immediate surroundings. The perception of a figure can depend on its shape, its colour, texture and position in relation to the background when viewed in three dimensions. In addition, there are several other 'gestalt laws of organization', which are all spatially based. *Proximity* or *nearness* of visual elements causes them to be perceived as a discrete group, especially when they are similar in shape, colour, texture, direction or position. In addition, the *common fate* of such elements, in terms of how they move in a recognizable pattern, can also help to distinguish their character. Amongst these laws are *continuity* of patterns, such as the position of elements in a line which can be read at a sweep, or closure where there is enough evidence to suggest a shape, from elements partly enclosing space.

My earlier work *Elements of Visual Design in the Landscape* described a number of design principles and included all these laws under the general heading of *spatial cues*; they are of great use when composing designs that are inherently unified. The notion of unity in a scene, where all the organizational elements are separate yet embedded in a whole, so that 'the whole is greater than the sum of the parts' is not only a major objective of design but is also a vital component in the gestalt approach. This enables us to make sense of the scene we perceive and is a key characteristic of many of the patterns to be discussed in future chapters. It is also fundamental to the sense of beauty in a landscape or design and so has an important aesthetic dimension.

The gestaltists seek the most elegant or simplest solutions in this spatial organization. In abstract forms or man-made geometry this may be possible, but such Euclidean geometry does not exist in more natural scenes (see Chapter One). Hence, we must ask whether it is possible to

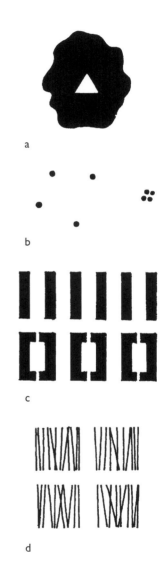

In gestalt psychology the immediate perception of a) figure and ground; b) nearness; c) closure; d) similarity are keys to perception. They also form an important set of principles used in visual design to help in unifying the elements or objects or the arrangement of objects in their surroundings.
(After Bell, 1993)

apply gestalt laws in more complex circumstances. It may be easier to demonstrate them in simpler, abstract worlds or where observers have more time and reject some options, when assessing the structure of more complex scenes. To some extent it may also explain why humans have constantly tended to produce simple patterns when changing their environment and so make it easier to comprehend their structure and to render them more predictable.

More recent approaches have developed gestalt ideas further, introducing the concept of *goodness of shape*, in which first impressions of apparently two dimensional but rather complex, multiangular shapes become easier to understand as three dimensional ones. This concept developed so that, hierarchically, we may see the bigger picture before breaking it down into constituent parts, so coping with the complexity problem.

Seeking to discover why the gestalt laws work we can proceed in two ways: by looking at circumstances where figures do not stand out from the ground, and, secondly, by using means of detection that are easier to analyse as alternatives or surrogates for the little understood human or animal brain (such as artificial intelligence).

Camouflage is the technique used by many animals and by military organizations to hide themselves or objects from predators or enemies. This is achieved by developing colour schemes or other markings that visually disrupt their shape and blend it into the ground. This prevents the gestalt laws from coming into effect, because the perceptive mechanisms cannot separate figure from ground (p. 234, Fig. 4).

Artificial intelligence, where computers are developed to 'think' for themselves, is developing quickly. Its use to test the laws has advantages, because some aspects of the processes can be explored. For example as perception is not spontaneous and requires some processes, discovering these should help us understand their significance. One of the problems with the gestalt laws is that they are only descriptive, irrespective of how well that description reflects reality or seems to work on the basis of empirical evidence.

In the primal sketch concept described previously such elements as edges, line segments, bars, blobs and terminations were identified. The artificial *process model* looks for these and tries to segregate them from all the other competing line segments, terminations and so on. To do this a higher order organization, which sees a simpler pattern, has been postulated, by which the developing structure is tidied up, joined and completed. In addition, the spatial cues of similarity, proximity and closure could also be brought in to give further organization. Using artificial intelligence to describe a line, the mechanism would identify a termination to start the line, followed by a series of line segments of varying length, proximity and similar orientation, eventually concluding with a final termination. If done at several scales of resolution, this could yield a fairly convincing percept, built up from the basic elements provided by the primal sketch. Other cues could also be mobilized such as lighting direction, orientation, texture and so forth.

As mentioned already, our perception is not a random sampling of the visual array, like an automatic video camera recording activities in a street. We use saccades and fixations to register pattern and we search for our visual objective. When we see a new scene for the first time, we may look for something in particular or contemplate and understand its structure or just enjoy its beauty. Whatever the motive, exploration may be prompted by certain features, perhaps those with highly defined edges or prominent contrasts. Once such a feature is noted, we are likely to explore less easily comprehensible areas with a further series of saccades and fixations, so building up the primal sketch and simultaneously reinforcing the first tentative pattern comprehension. When a scene has little or no apparent structure, we are likely to be confused and frustrated: the eye will roam fruitlessly, seeking interest and points of connection, from one fixation to the next, without much success.

Tracking Eyeball Movements

We can validate this continous assessment or feedback process of perception, by tracking the eyeball movements in relation to various scenes containing different structures and features. With an observer's head clamped in a frame, the eye movements over a series of projected photographic slides can be tracked by low intensity lasers, as they move from a registered point. The saccades and fixes will show how the attention of the eye is first caught by certain features and drawn to explore them further, perhaps as a result of some aspects of the image, such as its direction, position or visual force (an observed tendency for the eye to follow certain lines or edges in a scene in a particular direction). The feedback with the conscious brain will direct further exploration, perhaps fixing on certain parts of the scene in order to select more detail. This may depend on the objective of the viewer.

Active Perception

There is evidence that different people will look at the same scene but perceive different shapes and patterns depending on their knowledge, experience, culture and so on; this further reinforces the theory that active, selective and intelligent perception is normal, as opposed to passive sampling. The greater the involvement by the observer in the landscape the greater the degree of intelligent perception and active visual thinking that occurs.

In many instances intelligent perception acts as a filter to determine what is worth seeing and comprehending in an otherwise confusing scene. Looking for a well known face in a large crowd involves having the image as a template, so that key features are sought from all the possible faces present. As soon as the template is seen, the selective cognition takes place, thus saving the great effort of scanning each face separately. This phenomenon always happens and explains why different people see different things in the same scene: to some extent, they are preconditioned to look for patterns they can recognize, although the brain probably does not retain templates as immutable objects, since memories are thought to lie in specific neural networks.

Perception of Depth and Movement

So far we have considered the world as if it were two dimensional. However, humans with binocular vision are well adapted to see three dimensions, so that perception of depth is a major aid in discerning structures and patterns. This type of perception is made possible, in part, by *stereopsis*. Although the idea of the eye as a camera is to some extent valid, we have two eyes that look at the same scene, but from slightly different positions. Because of this, the two images must somehow be associated simultaneously in the brain and in so doing the perception of depth occurs. Stereoscopic binocular vision, giving this kind of perception, must be an extremely valuable evolutionary trait because, by losing the 360 degree view available to many animals with eyes on the side of their head, we obtain poorer warning of predators. Advantages include better judgement of distance allowing calculation of the interception path of prey when hunting, the arrival of a predator or, in the case of early primates and humans, better ability at hitting prey with stones or spears, and ease of manipulating or manufacturing tools at close quarters.

Stereopsis is most effective at short distances. This is because the greater disparity between closer images received by each eye, when combined in the brain, gives a greater sense of depth. In addition to stereopsis the effect of *accommodation* of the eye in order to focus, helps to give depth cues. We can only focus on certain parts of the scene at once, with other areas appearing blurred. Another minor contributor is *convergence*, where the eyes have to incline inwards to greater degrees over shorter focal distances.

People with one eye can perceive depth, as can those animals with no stereoscopic vision. Other major cues to depth perception include the effect of perspective, where the apparent size of objects diminishes over distances at a constant rate. In order to be accurate, this requires some objects that provide the relative measures. In empty landscapes, devoid of objects of known dimension, our judgement of depth can be severely flawed. The effect of light and shade also suggests depth. We are conditioned to see light cast from above, so that convex forms have shade underneath them and concave ones shade inside the upper section. Landscapes in the distance can appear flat, if viewed with the sun behind the observer, but when lit from the side they assume a greater depth. Atmospheric perspective, where succeeding parts of the landscape appear bluer with increasing distance, due to increased diffraction of light, can also help. Finally, the sense of some objects being behind others and partly hidden aids depth perception.

Depth perception is also facilitated when the observer is moving or an object is moving relative to the observer. This uses the rules of *parallax*, where near objects appear to move or pass by faster than more distant ones. We see this when looking out of a train window; we see the telephone poles and track edge fence posts rush past us, trees in the middle distance march sedately by, yet a mountain in the far distance seems to stay in one place for a long time.

Gibson's Theory of Optic Flow and Affordance

So far the psychology of perception has been based on the processing and comprehension of the optic array, starting with the retinal image. The active, evaluating and reflective nature of perception has also been noted. Unfortunately, the techniques employed to develop and test theories based on processing of image formation by the retina have tended to use simple Euclidean geometry, often viewing abstract patterns under static conditions. In the real world, humans and animals use perception to gain information of practical use in relation to the location and size of the individual and the purpose for which the information is sought. We rarely see objects without a background that is three dimensional and composed of surfaces, which have their own qualities of texture, colour, density, form, orientation and so on. This perception of surfaces at varying distances is important, because it gives a framework for the space being viewed.

Thus depth perceived from the stereoscopic image of an isolated object also includes the qualities of the surface it sits upon, such as the gradual change to texture in terms of the proportionately decreasing size and interval of the elements that comprise the surface (perhaps gravel or tiles) with increasing depth. The scale of the landscape is relative to the known size of the observer and their location, whereas the proportion of a person seems to be the same whether they are close or far from us, despite the decreasing size of the retinal image. Thus we perceive variable information yet relate this to constant characteristics in a landscape such as the consistently receding ground surface or the position of the horizon relative to the observer. This is how we are able to perceive distance and three dimensions in a computer generated terrain model using a grid of lines: the textured surface produced continuously recedes, but at different rates so that we see flat areas as receding faster than sloping or vertical areas. Objects stand out, because their surface texture does not recede in the same way as the background.

This view differs from the theory based on the analysis of the retinal image and has been called the *ecological* approach. This term is not the misrepresentation it first appears, because it treats visual perception as part of the necessary interaction between organisms and their

A low level aerial view across a forest. Our sense of space and detection of distance is due to the way the surface textures recede from us, reducing in scale at a fairly constant rate. As we fly over this scene the movement over features relative to ourselves, or optic flow, helps us to establish our position in the air as used by James J. Gibson.

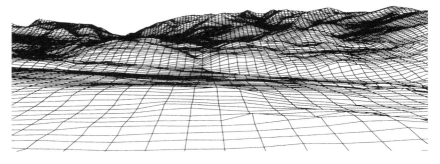

A digital terrain model (DTM) produced from topographic height information by a computer is depicted as a regular grid. We sense three dimensions in this image because we perceive the receding scale of the grid cells into the 'distance'. We also see steeper or flatter parts and curves as we read the apparent cell angles.

environments. The landscape is viewed in relation to the viewpoint of a normal, mobile observer, who is actively evaluating a moving optic array with respect to the information it might yield and not passively sampling a static optic array. This theory, developed by the American psychologist James J. Gibson, has some connection with the gestaltists in one important aspect: that we view the world in terms of what various parts *afford* us in a utilitarian sense. For example, apples are to eat, a road is for driving along, a forest is for obtaining timber, for taking a stroll or for a wildlife habitat (the forest implications have been used in some British landscape preference research carried out by Professor Terence R. Lee).

In many ways this approach only differs from that described earlier in terms of the added means of depth perception available to us. The more philosophical differences relate to the perception of movement and its vital importance to the whole system of perception. We constantly move our eyes, our heads, our bodies, our positions and elevations and do this to build up a picture of the relationships amongst the surfaces and objects we are looking at. One way we can tell a photograph from the real world is when we move our head the landscape in the photograph stays the same, whereas the relative positions of objects in the real landscape change even if we shut one eye and then look out of the other. Conversely, we can be fooled into feeling motion when a film containing plenty of movement, is shown on a large format or a wrap around screen that completely fills our field of view.

As in parallax, the automatically changing optic array follows some criteria that maintain the spatial relationships amongst the elements of a perceived scene. As we move into a landscape the scene flows towards us and past us, whilst constantly maintaining a correlation between the changing optic array and our spatial position. This *optic flow* defines direction; for example, when in a stationary train we can be fooled into feeling we are moving by another train passing in the opposite direction. Optic flow is the mechanism by which we can judge distance and speed and so drive a car, fly a plane or shoot at a moving target. We make all these judgements as a continuous perception.

In Gibson's theory, the perception of motion through our sensing of the changing optic array is considered to be a basic or primitive aspect of vision. In Marr's explanation of perception using the retinal image model, a creature with a simple eye can detect movement by the light being interrupted and so either follow possible food or escape an enemy. Other creatures use the changes in light intensity to move into shade away from light or vice versa, thus using this simple means of movement to determine a direction from a primitive optic flow.

In the same way that a number of the gestalt laws can be translated into terms used as design principles to describe a coherent pattern, so can the 'Gibsonian' variables of texture, density and colour applicable to surfaces. For example, many of the patterns in landscape can be defined by the correlations between different textures at different

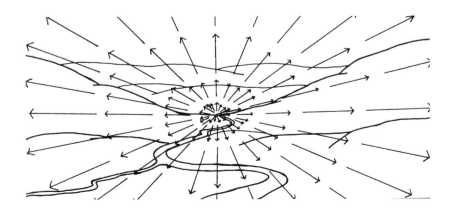

A diagram showing optic flow as we move through a landscape.

scales: some of the computer techniques for pattern analysis use this. The drawback of these concepts is their dependency on scale. When we perceive a scene we already account for this by interpreting pattern graduations as changes of scale or as distance indicators.

The Gibsonian view of perception is most useful for animals and humans living and moving about the environment for various purposes. Navigation between and interception of other moving objects is a major part of this existence. In contrast, the design process has traditionally viewed the landscape as a static scene from fixed viewpoints, comprising the spatial relationship of several parts to the whole. The techniques available to designers - plans, perspectives and models - are also fixed and often contrived representations of spaces. Although this accords with the gestalt approach discussed earlier, methods for incorporating movement into the design process will be considered in Chapter Seven.

Processes of Pattern Recognition

Whether we subscribe to the psychological, gestaltian or Gibsonian views, the perception of patterns depends on two aspects: recognition of objects and their interrelationships. It is the relationships that are the key determinant for the pattern of a landscape. In visual design it is convenient to subdivide its principles into three parts: the identification of objects into basic elements, according to their dominant dimensions (points, lines, planes, volumes); the descriptors of these objects in terms of variables such as position, shape, colour, texture; and the way these objects are organized into a pattern, using spatial, structural and ordering principles. We can apply this vocabulary with suitable description for each variable or organizing principle. For example, shape can be categorized into geometric or organic, regular or irregular, rounded or angular and so on. These are objective descriptions and are not susceptible to influence from preconceived attitudes by the observer.

Many of the qualities of pattern recognition can also be analysed in terms of the gestalt properties, the development of the primal sketch or by optic flow. As such they are *cognitively impenetrable*, that is they cannot be influenced by beliefs or expectations. This leads to a means for connecting, objectively, the visually perceived environment with the geographic and ecological patterns which will be described and analysed in Chapters Four to Seven.

However, this picture is insufficient if we need experience in the act of perception. One theory of object and pattern recognition relies on the matching of perceived objects to 'catalogues' of stored descriptions of objects that we have already seen in the pattern. It is a compelling theory: that we recognize people because we compare their features (and voices and smells) with catalogues of people and find a match. Hence, we can understand how we find problems in recognizing people

A sketch of the Waterton Lakes landscape that interprets the features considered important in depicting its character, reinforcing the point that we think visually. The sketch concentrates on lines used to describe the shapes and textures, the planes and volumes that make up the scene. Some of these lines draw the eye to concentrate on the highly fractal upper parts of the focal mountain. Areas of light and shade tell us about the depth and three dimensional nature of the landform.

who have changed in some ways but not others, or where our aquaintanceship was not long enough to build a good memory for the catalogue. We could apply this theory to other objects, places or whole landscapes. However, if we use such a catalogue of descriptions, we are at risk of arriving at value-laden conclusions about an object, because of its past experiences in our memory. Equally we can be faced with an object or scene for which we have no experience, no description in the catalogue, and therefore we cannot come to terms with it that way.

In part, the role of the memory may be the efficient storage of information that is easily retrievable, perhaps if the memory is considered as a pattern of activity within the brain. A particular memory is retrieved by a cue triggering a pattern within the entire range of connections that make up the memory potential. Thus, from a small part of a known pattern the rest can be reconstructed; this is called *content addressable* and forms part of the *connectionist model*. This obviates the need for a catalogue of symbols or images that have to be searched through one by one, although there remains the problem of failing to recognize a friend, where the pattern triggered by one known part of the person's features does not fit the image that is currently perceived. Conversely, we are able to cope in the world, because the frequent use of some patterns found in the connections of activity in the brain, reinforces and updates the memory. For example, this is experienced when we gradually become familiar with a new area over a period of time, so building up the brain's activity pattern, or where we adjust to sudden changes in a well known scene and update the memory.

The context of such patterns, such as the relationships of objects to each other and to their settings also becomes embedded in the activity pattern within the brain. Thus, when we see a unified scene, where all the parts relate to the whole, it is possible that we can more easily make a pattern of connections, as these are more readily activated in the brain. This makes some patterns fit together better and might explain why some patterns offer greater aesthetic appreciation than others.

The connectionist model is sometimes considered similar to the catalogue theories, with the same shortcomings. Nevertheless, it not only provides a mechanism for recording patterns and identifying objects possessing similar characteristics, but also offers an opportunity for learning from our experiences and for constructing 'object centred', rather than 'viewer centred' images. These points are all important within the context of this book because we are concerned with the objective analysis of the perceived patterns from the viewer-as-user point of view.

This connectionist theory of recognition does not negate the psychological theories of perception and is useful for implementing some of the results. In fact, the development of the apprehension of objects or scenes as symbols, out of the initial activity pattern, may be due to the order in which these percepts occur. Repeatedly perceived patterns may be subsequently imbued with symbolic associations, meanings or sense of place.

From the basic process of visual perception and recognition of objects or patterns, we can conceive they may have some relationship with the cultural context in which they and the observer exist. This relates to some of the fundamental points made earlier in this chapter, concerning the active part of perception. We look at a scene with a purpose in mind: to enjoy a natural prospect, to find a route through it, to evaluate it as a good place to live or to build a factory. This affects where we look, how we look and what visual cues we seek out, such as easy walking places, good house sites, level ground or water supply. Thus, some people will see some objects and patterns and not others; yet all may believe that they perceive the reality of the scene in objective terms.

The brain visualizes what it might be like to be in the scene or to change it, perhaps by building that factory. From this point it is a logical and easy step to think visually at the same time as we carry out the act of perception. This is not merely pattern recognition, but the kind of reasoning that infers values to some parts of the scene or seeks creative possibilities. It is the reasoning that can project the scene 'as exists' to 'what might be'.

One primary use of perception is to create models that explain the underlying order of the percept. Hence, we use pattern recognition to abstract from the sensory data, a simplified and powerful image (symbol, metaphor) that somehow is the distillate of everything we perceive. We use images to describe or visualize abstract concepts, such as liberty or justice (woman with torch, woman with scales) and we tend to reduce the landscape into an impression that satisfies our need for generalities, which can be related to many of the preconceived ideas we possess. This is one reason for the classification and analysis of patterns presented in Chapters Four to Seven. In order to be able to apply a general theory we have to abstract from the circumstances of a case, to recognize the *particular* pattern as belonging to a class of patterns.

This is echoed in the various theories used to try to explain human preferences for various kinds of landscape (see Chapter Three), particularly the most desirable components of human habitat. If, as Appleton believes, a large degree of biological heredity affects how we perceive and value certain objects and patterns in the landscape, there is also likely to be considerable generalization into archetypes of human habitat components. Visual thinking and the interpretation of the world around us, can easily lead to the identification of potential in a landscape as a place to live. Many of the similarities in the patterns of cultural landscapes, such as the 'ancient countryside' of Great Britain can be accounted for, partly, by colonizing people perceiving the same potential in a site and creating a landscape that offered as near optimum 'habitat' conditions as possible (see Chapter Seven). It may also account for the persistence of some of these patterns over time. What is less evident from this explanation is the great differences in consciously designed landscapes and the varying tastes and fashions over the years.

Summary and Conclusions

This chapter has been included to demonstrate that our understanding of the physical, ecological or cultural processes that result in the kinds of patterns to be described in Chapters Four to Seven, must be placed in the context of how we perceive the world. We experience it as real, three dimensional space, filled with surfaces and objects arranged in various patterns. The mechanisms of perception, especially visual perception, enable us to capture information and form percepts about the world that help our survival.

We have concentrated on visual perception for two reasons. Firstly it is the sense that provides the greatest amount of information, especially about more distant scenes; secondly it is the sense in which we think. Hence, our perception is active, directed and purposeful, with immediate feedback as we carry out that activity. The other senses are important adjuncts to sight, supplementing our perception, adding different dimensions to it and reinforcing or confirming visual perception. Sight impaired people have to adopt and refine their remaining senses to develop as full a perception as possible.

The mechanisms of sight, the structure of the eye, the way it receives light and its limitations, define what can be seen. The way the brain processes the information and constructs images from it defines what we see in the world and how we see it. The cognitive processes and the structure of the memory are used to identify and classify objects and patterns into a coherent, meaningful, understandable picture. Our visual thinking processes use this picture as the basis for a wide range of analytical and creative purposes, ascribing values and meanings to it and constructing symbols from it. We are also able to create a percept that is object oriented, relating more to what is perceived, rather than viewer oriented, relating more to our subjective values, and to use this more flexibly.

Marr's work on the physiology and psychology of perception and the theory of the primal sketch helps us understand how we build the picture of our environment. The analogous use of artificial intelligence helps to determine how this may occur. We will have to wait until more knowledge of the brain's functioning is gained, before a complete understanding can be achieved. However, the perceptual task is clearly that of constructing patterns, comprehending the perceived relationships amongst the objects, surfaces, lines and contrasts, which are evident from the optic array presented to the eyes and brain.

The gestalt approach is interesting for its practical applicability and because it relates so well to many of the empirically derived principles of visual design. Thus the detection and creation of patterns can be linked in terms of the spatial cues presented by the gestaltists. The power of some of the basic pattern types discussed in Chapter One may also be associated with the application of the gestalt laws.

The Gibsonian view of perception, with its emphasis on movement and affordance in our use of the landscape, clearly relates this subject to how we directly experience the environment and find our way through it. Allied to the theories on landscape as a human habitat that concentrates on our genetically programmed needs in the landscape, we have a useful means of linking perception with aesthetics and ultimately with design.

In the next chapter we will discuss aesthetics and consider how the perception mechanisms examined here intersect with our responses to the environment around us. This will be included in an examination in some detail, of the range of patterns and processes found in the world that is described in Chapters Five to Seven.

CHAPTER THREE

THE AESTHETICS
OF THE LANDSCAPE

Introduction

The subject of aesthetics is frequently misunderstood. It is often taken to refer to the sensory pleasure gained from contemplating works of art in a detached or academic way. It has associations with an elite culture, accessible only to those who have learned to appreciate it. The aesthetics of landscape has often been linked with carefully designed pleasure grounds or artfully constructed vistas, where the scene recreates a landscape painting, thus relating the perceptual sensation once more to fine art. The beauty of nature is also part of the traditional realm of aesthetics; in recent times this has become associated with the myth of a pure world, untouched by human activity. Wilderness is its most extreme manifestation.

As a result of the association of landscape aesthetics with fine art and natural beauty, the landscape has tended to be treated as a separate object. This has segregated it from everyday life and it is often treated as an optional extra or irritating constraint to the utilitarian demands made of the same scene.

In this chapter, we will explore a different set of connections between the basic mechanisms of our sensory perception and the environment, described by the American philosopher Arnold Berleant, as 'the field of everyday human action', which also has an aesthetic dimension. We will examine some recent theories, relating aesthetics to various aspects of the natural and cultural world, that could form the basis of a fresh approach to design. The discussion will include philosophical and psychological aspects.

The Nature of Aesthetics

Aesthetics is usually associated with the nature, meaning and appreciation of the arts, such as the fine arts of painting and sculpture, together with music, drama, dance and possibly architecture (although the latter is complicated, because buildings usually have utilitarian functions which art, as described here, does not). The decorative arts may be used to embellish useful objects or give them a pleasing appearance; they can be highly susceptible to the whims of fashion and omitted if the cost seems too high for 'optional extras'.

The term aesthetic comes from the Classical Greek words *aisthanesthai*, to perceive, and *aistheta*, things perceived. Thus, as we saw in Chapter Two, perception is at the heart of the way we understand our environment and in this chapter we will see that it is also central to our sense of beauty and the pleasure we obtain from our environment. Aesthetics is basic to human nature.

The term *landscape* carries many connotations, in an interchangeable way, between a piece of land, as seen from a viewpoint, or a painting of the same place. There is cause for confusion, especially as some of the designed parks and gardens in Great Britain and Europe, laid out within the early landscape gardening period of the 18th century, were meant to be viewed as living paintings or were even constructed as real life copies of actual paintings.

Hence, when allusion is made to the non-utility of art, this refers to the practical use to which it can be put. For example, a painting or sculpture cannot be eaten or worn. Nevertheless, the purpose of art is open to debate and this illumines some of the issues concerning the aesthetics of the environment. For example, some people believe that art should give pleasure through the contemplation of a beautiful painting by a famous master; to others, it should convey emotion and meaning, although not necessarily being attractive to behold. The philosophy of this argument about aesthetics masks the importance of the perceptual character at its core. We need to express the meaning of aesthetics in perceptual terms and relate this in a practical way to our everyday experience of the environment around us. In this context, the term aesthetics refers to the perceptual and sensuous features of the landscape we experience. All the senses are at work, although, for practical design purposes, sight may receive more attention. However, the perceptual aspect cannot ignore the ability of art to communicate and stir emotions. Although nature is not art, can it be properly appreciated without some appraisal of these non-perceptual aspects? The arguments for and against this will be rehearsed later because they lead to different conclusions and their implications for designers and managers are significant.

A designed landscape where the scene has been laid out to portray a painting of an imaginary classical scene.

Environment and Landscape

Arnold Berleant has examined the meaning of the term environment in ways that are very pertinent to our deliberations. We are used to experiencing the dichotomy of ourselves as separate entities from the world around us, *the environment*. Thus, the concept of the word environment carries certain philosophical assumptions about all of these aspects - self, experience and the world. If we consider the term environment to be mainly synonymous with the natural world, we tend to forget there is very little left and, for most of the time, we inhabit and experience places with little naturalness. Even when we think of environment more generally as 'our surroundings' we tend to give it a concept or image, which converts it into some kind of object that cannot easily be grasped or classified. This Cartesian separation between self and surroundings is a recent phenomenon and is especially powerful in western culture such as that of Europe or North America.

Alternatively, we can consider a more integrated approach in which we and our surroundings are united to form an interdependent whole. We are a part of our surroundings and our perceptions, as discussed in Chapter Two, are the means by which, through our behaviour and actions, we exchange information with our surroundings and act on them, resulting in the dynamic, cultural landscape to be described in Chapter Seven. We should no longer refer to 'the environment', because the inclusion of the definite article implies separation from ourselves.

The other major problem with the idea of the environment separate from ourselves is that we tend to regard it as a thing or opponent, to be conquered or tamed, especially when unruly forces of flood, fire, earthquake and storm conspire to destroy our own works, usually perceived as more important. The lack of understanding of landscape processes and the increasingly cultural, but unnatural character of our surroundings also demonstrate this. This separation, not only from the forces of nature, but also from lower animals, is partly what defines us as humans. This dualism is part of our cultural inheritance, but the obverse is that everything is a part of the same whole, that the natural and human worlds are all part of the same continuum. As soon as we accept this notion, we take the responsibility, as Berleant sees it, of the very human role of drawing distinctions, setting standards, assessing values and choosing actions. All these occur within the context of this total or holistic world and cannot be implemented by adopting the external position of an impartial observer. This also reinforces our distinction as human beings and avoids regarding ourselves as merely another animal in an impersonal web of life.

Therefore, environment, according to Berleant's argument, is everything: nature, culture and ourselves in an interconnected system. As a consequence all participants, all processes, all human activities that make up the world have to be taken seriously. We must act with respect and humility, as opposed to the arrogance and disdain frequently given to 'our' environment. This raises another point: as we extend the meaning of environment, we also enlarge the domain of aesthetics. We experience the aesthetic dimension of all environments, from the apparently unspoilt, natural beauty of a national park to the commercial landscape of shopping malls and derelict industry. Everything and every experience yields an aesthetic dimension; all impinge on our sensory perception and as that perception is immediate our reactions are very quick.

However, this book uses the term landscape, rather than environment. As a concept, 'landscape' has a utility and a flexibility that is easier to understand as an everyday reality than is 'environment'. Hence, we need to refine the definition of landscape, because of the many connotations it holds. In the sense that environment includes everything, the landscape becomes that part of environment, which is the field of our present actions. Landscape is the part of environment that we can engage with at a given time, so linking it to the original use of the word and its modern embedding within environment.

Landscape can also be understood in terms of the scale of area over which our actions take place, in a similar sense to the ecological use of the term, as will be discussed in Chapter Six. We experience this wide arena composed of different elements and structures during our daily lives. This links well with the Gibsonian approach to perception and affordance we examined in Chapter Two. In many ways, therefore, landscape is that part of the environment that is the human habitat, perceived and understood by us through the medium of our perceptions. We cannot escape it and it must not be treated as an optional extra nor solely as a place to visit on special occasions. It has a powerful effect on the quality of our lives and should not be left to experts or market forces. This awareness has many implications for planners, designers and managers of landscape. There is a direct link here, between the patterns and processes that make up the land, our perceptions of them, and our constant aesthetic engagement that converts the physical dimension of land into the perceptual one of landscape.

What is an Aesthetic Experience?

In her thesis *Aesthetics and the Natural Environment* Cheryl Foster, an American philosopher, has explored in depth the components of an aesthetic experience. Some of her arguments are summarized here. Throughout our lives we constantly use our senses to perceive the landscape of which we are a part. Some aspects of this perception yield distinct sensations. For example, we find beauty in some scenes and ugliness in others. Some places seem to be composed of parts that fit well together and are unified, whilst other places are apparently disjointed and difficult to understand. Is this aesthetic experience dependent solely on the perceptual factors involved at the time of perception or are other, non-perceptual factors involved, such as cultural conditions, scientific knowledge or pre-ordained conceptual patterns? Or do we, through perception, gain the initial aesthetic experience and then use non-perceptual factors to put it in context?

These questions involve two schools of thought. If we accept the various elements that influence our preferences (and hence our judgements in relation to value or quality), such as history, culture, social class, personality and the use of the landscape, do we obscure what is meant by aesthetics? The 'integrationists' (such as the aesthetic philosophers Mary Carmen Rose, Allan Carlson and Duane Willard from the USA and Canada) support the first question and hold the view that most perceptual qualities are integral, interdependent and occur simultaneously in people.

The 'perceptual view' of aesthetics in the second question, supported by F.E. Sparshott and May Warnock, disagrees with the integrationist position by emphasizing that aesthetic aspects lead to pleasure or displeasure arising from the perceived scene or object at the time of perception. These positive or negative values are only dependent on the way the scene or object appears to the observer. The judgement, according to this view, is not dependent on knowing the history or cultural framework of a scene or object, but is based solely on how it looks, sounds or feels. Our perception stops at the perceptual surface and this defines the limits of the initial aesthetic judgement.

Relating intellectual, non-perceptual factors to the scene or object afterwards is a different matter and it is then that history, culture, experience and so on can help in further appreciation and understanding. This is the crucial point where an understanding and appreciation of the origin and dynamics of patterns in the landscape enters the equation. It is the raised awareness of the structure and processes of the perceived landscape that illuminates the relationship between the aesthetic response and the changing scene; this is also one of the differences between environmental or landscape aesthetics and that of fine art, in that landscape is continuously changing so that its influence is always different.

Yuriko Saito, an aesthetician working in the USA, identifies a more specific quality arising from the interaction of sensory elements with social aspects. This is the experience of a sense of place; this can often be a powerful aesthetic dimension, but may only be manifest with some degree of knowledge. This knowledge and the social aspects enhance the aesthetic awareness from the initial sensory apprehension into something with meaning as well as value.

Cheryl Foster considers that the perceptual viewpoint exposes the weakness of the interdependent viewpoint of the integrationists, because their focus on conceptual and non-perceptual issues diminishes the impact of the appearance. The appearance, especially the aesthetic component of landscape, is attached to a physical entity of which we are a part. Our perceptions adhere to this entity and give it an appearance. Sparshott and Warnock also insist on the specificity of aesthetics as a concept, which has to be separated from interdependence with other social and cultural factors. If we can identify these other factors, because they are more readily defined, we should be able to do the same with aesthetics as a field of endeavour in its own right. Then aesthetics can interact with other factors in a much more influential way.

This approach has advantages, because it is clear that aesthetic values can be attributed to landscapes, especially utilitarian ones, in the same way as any other values. Some landscapes, such as national parks, are set aside primarily for their aesthetic value, although their main aims are often complicated, because they include other values, such as preservation of nature. This reinforces the case for aesthetics to be treated fairly and separately alongside all the other issues.

A further weakness of the interdependent view of the integrationists is that if our aesthetic response is conditioned by factors such as knowledge and familiarity, we are likely to find new scenes difficult to appreciate. We frequently tend to recognize familiar patterns, and possibly prefer certain landscapes, because of our prejudices. However, new scenes of which we have no prior knowledge or cultural reference are also stimulating and contain an aesthetic dimension.

Nevertheless, the perceptual thesis presented thus far is not straightforward. According to Berleant, although comprehending the landscape is a necessary precondition for a subsequent multisensory, aesthetic experience, it is not only comprehension that prompts aesthetic awareness. The perceptual realm is also engaged in ways that enhance and intensify aesthetic awareness. In the appreciation of landscape, there is deliberate attention paid to its component features within the overall setting of our engagement. This is compatible with the gestalt notions discussed in Chapter Two about making sense of the perceived scene, but extends them to include judgement. As discussed in our exploration of perception, we do not comprehend our surroundings in a passive way, but actively search out and direct our entire sensory apparatus so that it accepts and interprets sensuous qualities. It follows that this must be a continuous process when we are awake; thus, the landscape can be regarded as a constant source of aesthetic experience. By the same argument, our whole environment is a perceptual system with which we are in constant engagement.

If we accept that the concept of constant aesthetic engagement is correct, it is of concern that it has been so often overlooked and frequently ignored. For large areas of activity in the landscape, aesthetics is treated merely as an overlay to our everyday activities. Aesthetics is frequently regarded as an optional extra in commercial development and experiencing the aesthetics of a landscape, particularly its natural components, is relegated to a special activity to be consumed as an alternative to other pastimes or theme parks. Visits to national parks and other scenic places ration the vivid, satisfying aesthetic experience we could have every day. Moreover, this experience is frequently complicated by the explanations displayed at viewpoint information boards, which often overlook aesthetic aspects in favour of natural history. Set piece vistas and specially laid out scenic routes separate the viewer from the environment, whilst the experience is filtered by the camera or video lens or car windows. Aesthetics may be ignored, because of ignorance, a perception that function is more important, or perhaps due to discomfort felt by many people when 'esoteric' subjects are raised. Part of the solution might be to include aesthetic awareness as a serious subject in school, higher and further education curricula and to separate it from an exclusive association with art.

Increasingly we view landscape through the medium of a camera, camcorder or even the windows of vehicles. This separates us from direct sensory engagement.

Without perhaps realizing it, there is a tendency to expect and accept a dull mediocrity in our everyday surroundings. We have to make a special effort to see natural beauty and refresh ourselves. Many people do not or cannot make the effort and so are progressively alienated from their environments. Aesthetic sensitivity becomes moribund and a cycle of lack of care establishes itself. This need not be so if aesthetics is recognized as a vital aspect of a full life and treated with the same importance as the profit motive.

A further reason for the disregard of aesthetic value in the landscape may be the division between natural landscapes and human altered or cultural ones. We know experience of natural or naturalistic landscapes has a number of positive psychological benefits, but concentrating on this misses much of the diversity and beauty of the cultural landscapes we inhabit. In Europe, where there is a longer history of landscape development, there is less distinction between nature and culture, Indeed, many people refer to cultural landscapes as being natural without any concern for the inherent paradox. In the USA, nature, in its apparently pristine state, can be experienced, in stark contrast with loose planning regulations that have led to fast growing and frequently ugly urban and suburban sprawls. Here, the aesthetics of environment is much more dichotomized, engendering a range of attitudes and values like the purity of nature versus the impurity of human landscapes.

A similar high aesthetic value can be obtained from good quality cultural landscapes of long inhabited countryside and city, as from most natural places. It is a different kind of aesthetics, revelling in the whole sensory engagement. Examination of the characteristics of a number of these places can identify those sensory qualities that yield the aesthetic experience; these can be linked with some of the universal properties of patterns, such as spirals and meanders. An understanding of the role of these patterns could improve the design and management of the inhabited world, as we shall see in Chapter Seven.

Experiencing the aesthetics of landscape is open to everyone and requires no prior knowledge of the landscape. Our subsequent assessment is always affected by social and cultural concepts, which can focus on distinct qualities and help set the aesthetic experience in a personal and cultural context. We, therefore, gain an immediate aesthetic experience when we perceive the landscape; this deepens when we have knowledge of its origins and can appreciate it for its natural or cultural characteristics.

Pleasure as a Part of the Aesthetic Experience

Setting aside the aesthetics of art and focusing on the aesthetics of landscape, we can examine the role of pleasure. If we wish to protect, manage or create landscapes that enrich our lives, we need to recognize that enrichment occurs to a large degree by providing pleasure. Sensory immersion in a landscape can yield different degrees of pleasure or displeasure. Strong emotions may be aroused when we experience particularly beautiful environments. For a short while, we may be stimulated to forget personal concerns or become transfixed by the vastness of a scene that takes our breath away, and even fall into a sort of trance. The converse occurs in the face of devastated landscapes, of slums and polluted, derelict industrialized and degraded areas. In surroundings of sheer ugliness many people learn to ignore aesthetic sensibilities and this fosters a dulled response or emotional inertia to the spread of more ugliness.

The range from the most beautiful landscapes to the most ugly, includes those where the scene invokes a neutral response. In many ways this is the most meaningless landscape of all. When faced with ugliness, we may feel impelled to do something about it, but the spiritless, bland landscapes tend to leave us enervated and passionless. These tend to be most numerous in light industrial and commercial suburbs, industrial agricultural areas and transport corridors. We can be demoralized by endless repetitions of unimposing houses, green spaces, warehouses or factories, featureless crops and dull roadsides. Nevertheless the landscapes of streets, gardens, parks and transport routes should all be capable of giving aesthetic pleasure.

In both the USA and Great Britain this neutral sprawl of settlement has insidiously spread over many places. Its consequences are a loss of much of the distinctiveness of the older rural landscapes with their variety of materials, diverse sensuous surface and unity of pattern. Bland landscapes are also the result of negligence in planning, design and management, coupled with a demand for cheap, short term solutions. They are the most challenging to change, because it is hard to justify spending resources on places that are not obviously ugly and degraded.

A landscape of sprawl, where economic forces have created somewhere bland and spiritless, where we are likely to become aesthetically demoralized.

Hence, a landscape with less powerful qualities will invoke a sustained aesthetic response of lesser pleasure or displeasure. As noted above, due to the mediocre quality of much of our surroundings, this level of response is likely to occur in the majority of situations for most of the time. Attractive surroundings, whether at work, home or any other part of our landscape, contribute to making life palatable. However, we do become accustomed to the same scenes, despite their attractiveness and so variety is necessary both in kind and degree. Ideally, this should be obtained by having plenty of variety within easy reach of where people live or work; occasional visits to special places may also be needed to provoke a jaded palate.

Beauty and the Sublime

At the high quality end of the aesthetic spectrum, lies the twin consideration of beauty and the sublime in landscape. In the 18th century, much intellectual energy was expended developing these concepts, by the Irish philosopher Edmund Burke, among others, describing their attributes and differences. As concepts, they significantly influenced the direction of landscape gardening and design, especially the picturesque tradition, and became fundamental aspects of landscape appreciation up to present times. They were also fundamental criteria in the founding of national parks in many countries.

An esoteric debate over the distinction between the beautiful and the sublime might seem irrelevant nowadays, with other environmental issues at the forefront of concerns. However, it is worth reappraising the factors from which these concepts are derived, for it is here that psychological indices of landscape preferences, philosophical considerations and designers' guiding principles intersect. This intersection will help our understanding of what people prefer, why they prefer it, and how designers can create everyday landscapes that give pleasure.

Cheryl Foster's thesis reappraised the work of two German philosophers, which still has a major influence on the way we consider the beautiful and the sublime: Immanuel Kant (late 18th century) and Arthur Schopenhauer (early 19th century). They differed in many respects but also presented similarities.

Foster describes how Kant spoke of free beauty, where the judgement that a scene is beautiful does not depend on concepts determining the nature of that judgement, and dependent beauty, which does depend on such concepts.

Schopenhauer drew a distinction between the presence or absence of 'will', which can be interpreted as our self-conscious interest in objects. Any notion of practical interest in what we perceive 'falsifies' the way in which we perceive it. However, if during the act of perception of beauty, our mental or physical state requires no control or personal investment of interest in a scene, we are in the right frame of mind to achieve a pure aesthetic experience. This leads to a state where the observer and the scene or landscape being perceived are no longer separated and a respite from the usual world of the will or choice is achieved. In many ways, this bears out Berleant's insistence on the lack of a dualism between humans and environment in the aesthetic realm: during a free aesthetic experience the observer and world become one. Also, for Schopenhauer, there is a great sense of beauty to be obtained if the scene expresses what he calls the 'idea', which we can interpret as its essence, or perhaps its spirit of place (*Genius loci*).

According to Foster, Schopenhauer sees beauty in a landscape when a diversity of objects are found together, when they are clearly separated and distinct, but at the same time 'exhibit themselves in a fitting association and succession.' This definition is applied primarily to the natural world, but there need be no conflict extending it to many aspects of cultural or designed landscapes (p. 234, Fig. 5). This concept also accords with the three objectives of good visual design expressed in the author's earlier book *Elements of Visual Design in the Landscape*, namely diversity, unity (the fitting association and succession), and the expression of spirit of place, or *Genius loci*. This demonstrates the developing link between the subjective perception of beauty and a rational description of its characteristics, which can be universally experienced. There is also a direct link, through the use of design terminology, from the analysis of aesthetic characteristics to creative design solutions that respect and build on that character (see Chapters Four to Seven).

Foster quotes Schopenhauer as saying that, 'nature's beauty in particular compels our attention and has an effect on even the most apathetic of observers.' Here, he differs from Kant, who held that only men of genius could experience beauty. Foster also quotes Schopenhauer as claiming that 'the man tormented by passions, want or care, is so suddenly revived, cheered and comforted by a single, free glance into nature' and is moved 'in a marvellous way by its forms.' Many people today would still support that view.

Foster concludes her reading of Schopenhauer on beauty by stating that 'in order to attend to the form and processes of nature we need to engage in a sensuous apprehension of the environment around us.' This appreciation involves being aware of ourselves, while ignoring the feelings normally associated with self-consciousness.

A sublime experience occurs when our senses are swamped by the magnitude of a landscape that is difficult to comprehend and suggests limitlessness. The imagination and capacity for judgement are also overwhelmed by this impression, in a similar way to trying to comprehend the notion of the infinity of the universe. Our reason can conceive totality, whilst our imagination finds great difficulty in doing so. This is usually the initial feeling experienced by many people on first visiting the Himalayan mountains in Nepal, the Grand Canyon in

The Niagara Falls in Canada are a prime example of a sublime landscape. We sense danger without the physical presence of it. Hence when we perceive the huge natural forms and the power of natural processes we tend to feel small and humble. This releases emotions which allow us to escape our preoccupation for a time.

the USA, Niagara Falls in Canada, or seeing a view over an apparently limitless desert or forest. We tend to feel very small, humble and helpless in the face of the scale of these scenes or the awesome power of processes such as volcanoes, glaciers or hurricanes. The feeling of *potential*, but not *actual*, danger gives the experience an extra sharpness, such as might be felt when looking over the parapet into the depths of the Grand Canyon.

Foster usefully summarized the ways that Kant differentiated between the beautiful and the sublime in terms of their similarities and differences.

The similarities are:

- Both are pleasing.
- Both involve judgement based solely on reflection, not on logic or common sense.
- Both provide pleasure from the presentation of an immediate insight
- Both demonstrate an accord between our imagination and conceptual faculties.
- Both exist as unique judgements.
- Both are universally valid for all observers.

The differences are:

- The completeness and unity of the form of the scene produces beauty, whereas formlessness, or a form with the appearance of formlessness due to its complexity and incomprehensibility, is a hallmark of the sublime.

- In both we are presented with indeterminate concepts, but that for beauty is one of understanding, whilst for the sublime it is of reason.
- Beauty is more concerned with quality, the sublime with quantity.
- In beauty our emotions tend to be directed to the furtherance of life, whereas with the sublime, after the initial sense of pleasure, our energies are checked as a more powerful emotion surges through us, one that is intensely sensuous and not wanting to be given delight by the scene.

The most important distinction between the two is that in beauty we can comprehend the entire scene and find it pleasurable; hence we are prepared to cherish it. With the sublime, because we fail to comprehend it entirely, we respect it when we try to do so. The stimulation it provides can be due to a sense of fear, but not the presence of it. This response may not be pleasurable.

Thus, those scenes that possess unity, diversity, respond to the sense of place and are comprehensible as complete patterns are likely to be deemed beautiful. We may not be so powerfully stimulated by them as we are by the sublime, but they can give us intense pleasure.

Our response to beauty can occur quite spontaneously when the right ingredients are present. The scene can be mainly natural or be cultural or designed. Order and diversity are necessary: these are found in many places, but not always with the key ingredient of a relationship to spirit of place. Many of the uninteresting landscapes that are not recognizably ugly, have order in the sense of repetition, but lack diversity and spirit of place. As recognized by Stephen Kaplan, an American researcher, there is frequently a wide consensus about what are mainly beautiful landscapes; the point that may be debated is where they cease to be beautiful and descend into ordinariness or blandness.

The sublime occurs when we are more emotionally engaged with large scale complex scenes, when we feel small in relation to them and experience a degree of fear. We may find this emotion too powerful to encounter every day, but it remains an important and valuable one to restore our sense of perspective (literally) and to free us from awareness of ourselves and the insistence of the will (as defined by Schopenhauer). Natural landscapes are more consistently able to yield sublime experiences, because of the complexity of patterns and processes. However, large scale human created scenes, such as the view over a city from the top of a skyscraper or the atmosphere within a massive gothic cathedral, may also evoke it.

The sublime experience is one which may also provide a route to aesthetic appreciation that takes account of the human size in relation to the natural and in some cases the cultural or designed landscape.

A question arises as to whether the deeper understanding of natural processes and patterns diminishes the sense of the sublime. This may be so, if we adhere to the integrationist approach, as many of the chances to perceive beauty and to experience the sublime would be lost, because of the need for prior knowledge. This would not be so if we prefer the perceptual approach.

Finally, it is worth noting that many landscapes, especially those chosen as national parks, contain both beauty and the sublime. In this case there needs to be a means of acknowledging the two components in order that planning, design and management do not overlook the less powerful of the two.

The Aesthetic Theory of Alfred North Whitehead

Peter Gunter, an American philosopher, has developed the links between a metaphysical theory of environment and aesthetics postulated by the early 20th century British philosopher and mathematician Alfred North Whitehead. This theory presents some useful ideas that may have been overlooked, because Whitehead often uses complicated and ambiguous terms which make his work difficult to understand for many people.

Metaphysics is a part of philosophy that investigates the essence and relationships of living things (being) and of reasoning (knowing). Whitehead's metaphysics and his philosophy of nature extend both terms into a wider application, that in some cases includes non-living things. Whitehead refers to living things as organisms, and the way they observe and reason about their environment as prehensions (as in apprehend or comprehend).

All aspects of an organism's prehensions merge into what Whitehead calls concrescences, meaning coherence, or coming together. Thus organisms like ourselves can be said to exist as a fusion of their character and the sum of all their prehensions, or interactions with their environment and other organisms.

This concept has obvious links with Berleant's self-environment continuum discussed earlier, and helps explain how aesthetics assumes importance in our everyday lives.

Whitehead then develops this metaphysical concept into an aesthetic theory. He sees us existing in our environment as living organisms among other organisms, undertaking prehensions. The sense of beauty is gained as a result of positive prehensions and ugliness is due to negative ones. This leads to his recognition of two forms of beauty, a *major* and a *minor*. The absence of discord or painful clash amongst the prehensions (and presumably the absence of a negative concrescence) or the absence of 'mutual inhibition' gives the minor form. We may liken this to the basic level of unity in a landscape, of a lower end of attractiveness where there is no obvious discordance or imbalance, but where our senses are not significantly aroused.

The major form requires the existence of the minor form before it can occur, and builds on this. It involves one or more contrasts between the factors of perception, which provoke an intensity of feeling. This increases the intensities of the basic component feelings, so there is a positive feedback that further increases the overall intensity of the experience. There are two characteristics of the landscape that provoke these intensive feelings. The first Whitehead calls *massiveness* or the presence of a variety of detail with effective contrast. Massiveness includes diversity or complexity, but does so at a range of scales. This can be likened to the fractal patterns that were introduced in Chapter One and possibly helps explain their extraordinary aesthetic qualities. The second characteristic is called *intensity proper*, meaning comparative magnitude (or scale), without reference to the variety of detail that gives massiveness. Intensity proper could be linked with the magnitude that induces a sublime experience. Where massiveness and intensity proper occur together, it is conceivable that a form of order or unity would exist.

We have already explored the variety of patterns in nature and culture. Those which we find the most beautiful or attractive should, according to Whitehead's theory, contain massiveness and intensity proper. Before examining some examples, we need to assess how the idea of prehension and aesthetics is invoked. When we seek to comprehend a landscape, we may use our eyes to look at it, some parts distant, others close up; we also feel the solidity of the earth beneath our feet and can touch nearby surfaces. As we do this we are taking aspects from this landscape and incorporating them, using the mechanisms of perception, into part of ourselves both mentally and physically. We thus also gain affordances, in Gibsonian terms, by the incorporation of these prehensions into an organism (ourselves) and we maintain our place in the self-environment continuum as defined by Berleant.

The minor form of beauty, 'the absence of painful clash, the absence of vulgarity' ensures that the component parts of our perceptual experience do not inhibit one another and prevent the feedback of intensity. Any landscape we habitually experience should possess this. It can be found: in the unified, self-organized, yet undistinguished woodland mosaic; in the rural scene, where traditional architecture and well managed land present an ordered and homely yet ordinary working landscape; or the pleasant market town where solid, provincial houses and a gradually evolved layout relax the senses. Discordant elements, such as a badly designed area of felling in the wood that introduces a disharmonious shape, colour and texture, a suburban bungalow development built on farmland, or garish fast food outlets in the market town, would all inhibit the minor form of beauty. These are obvious examples; there are many more subtle ones, including traffic noise, light pollution at night, advertisement hoardings, parked cars, litter, vandalism and so on.

The major form of beauty is also present in many landscapes. The Grand Canyon possesses massiveness in the contrasting variety of detail of its fractally eroded landforms, vegetation, light and shade and rock colours. It also has intensity proper in its comparative magnitude when taken as a whole, without reference to qualitative variety (see Chapter Five).

We may also consider a plantation of pine trees, where all the trees are the same age, planted in rows, without understorey, yet tall and cylindrical of trunk. Here is comparative scale, but little or no qualitative variety; thus it has intensity proper but lacks massiveness. In contrast, a natural or semi-natural pine forest has a range of ages and sizes of trees of varying species, together with undergrowth and wildlife. Each tree has a different form, some twisted, some branching, some straight. This kind of forest has massiveness as well as intensity proper and is a definite possessor of the major form of beauty (see Chapter Six).

The city of Venice in Italy possesses massiveness in full measure. The massiveness is a function of the contrasts: water, sky, buildings; spatial contrasts within the canal and street layout, variety in the building styles, colours and forms; variety in the textures of materials and the sounds along the streets or canals. The characteristics of each contributes to the massiveness of the whole. It also has intensity proper, as the comparative magnitude of the whole city is a significant element, irrespective of its variety (see Chapter Seven).

The culmination of massiveness and intensity proper in the greatest degree is referred to by Whitehead as *strength*; in some ways it is similar to the strength of character that distinguishes the most attractive landscapes, possessing a strong sense of place, from ordinary landscapes. The Grand Canyon, the natural pine forest and Venice all possess strength and exhibit the major form of beauty.

The Grand Canal in Venice, Italy. When moving about this city either by boat or on foot we are aware of a complete sensory engagement which produces a diverse aesthetic experience. This is related to the structure of spaces we move through and the characteristics of the building facades as well as the abundance of sounds and smells. The kinaesthetic senses are fully engaged on the water as well as in the twisting and turning streets and the way our bodies respond as we are drawn to the range of sensory stimuli.

There are also circumstances where hierarchical contrasts contribute to strength. The city of Edinburgh in Scotland, at its core consists of the old and the new towns. The old town, organic and self-organized on the volcanic/glacial landform is massive, with a huge variety of individual components. The new town possesses less variety, in the repeated use of classical architectural details, but it has powerful intensity proper, because of the scale of its magnitude (its large extent). Together, the old and new towns form an even greater contrast and put massiveness and intensity proper in a perceptually dynamic relationship, thus giving the city centre its tremendous strength (see Chapter Seven for a more detailed analysis of the urban landscape of Edinburgh).

The Alcazar in Seville in Spain, laid out as a palace and gardens from the 10th century onwards, is an example of a designed landscape. The style is a blend of Moorish and baroque architecture known as *mudejar*. The overall layout requires the visitor to explore the pattern of internal and external spaces, ranging from rooms to courtyards to garden, in order to understand its concept. All the senses are engaged. There is water for temperature variation, tactile sensation and sound. Scents of orange and other blossoms fill the air. The kinaesthetic senses are also fully engaged as the visitor walks on different surfaces, up and down steps, round corners and occasionally ducking under low arches.

There is massiveness in the overall layout of each space and an hierarchical layering of detail from the contrasts of spaces and their character down to the fine detail of carving on plasterwork and the designs on tiles. There is also a strong sense of mystery and this enables the landscape to appear bigger than it is and so convey intensity proper. The totality of all the contrasts (spatial, stylistic, textural,

Part of the garden of the Alcazar, Seville, Spain. The enclosing walls and variety of vegetation produce a full sensory experience. The design in all parts contains 'massiveness' in Whitehead's terms.

Left: inside the courts of the buildings in the Alcazar in Seville, Spain, one is greeted by another smaller scale scene of massiveness, where the great variety of detail relates from the entire Alcazar down to the finest detail of decoration on the plaster work

Right: the detail of the plaster carving provides the final layer of the extraordinary aesthetic experience provided by the Alcazar. The finest detail within the carving can be appreciated as much as the overall structure and layout, endorsing not only Whitehead's theory but also the qualities of coherence, diversity and mystery identified by Kaplan.

colours, light/shade, internal/external, architectural/horticultural and so on) gives enormous strength to the composition. This always encourages a long stay, while the ability of the landscape to induce a calm, reflective state, is truly marvellous. The gardens descend from a lineage of Moorish paradise gardens and it is easy to understand the meaning of the term by visiting this place. It exhibits Whitehead's major form of beauty in full measure.

Whitehead's scenario of beauty is invoked by positive contrasts, so a problem might arise if the otherwise beautiful natural scene has discordant natural elements within it such as trees blown down or burnt areas. However, these can only be considered discordant, if obsolescent knowledge of nature's processes is applied. Beauty arises from regeneration, and massiveness can only develop from the processes that change the simple pioneer stands into the complex structural and spatial pattern of the fully developed forest. Even if these factors are seen as negative, they can provide the extra sense of raw, vibrant life that translates the merely pretty into a form of mature beauty, whose strength arises in part from the reality of nature.

From the initial consideration of what constitutes an aesthetic experience we have moved to be able to define more precisely, albeit in metaphysical terms, what characteristics can determine beauty and the sublime. In the discussion on the importance of post-perceptual knowledge, we saw that the aesthetic experience can be deepened if we know more about the landscape. In the appreciation of nature it would seem logical that there should be some direct links between aesthetics and ecology, as suggested in the example of the natural pine forest described earlier.

Ecology and Aesthetics

The famous American conservationist of the early 20th century, Aldo Leopold, attempted to develop ecological aesthetics that could transform the way people change the landscape. This was based on his land ethic, where Leopold claimed that 'A thing is right when it tends to preserve the integrity, stability and beauty of the biotic community. It is wrong when it tends otherwise' (Leopold 1981, pp. 224-5). Paul Gobster, an American researcher, writing about Leopold's ecological aesthetic theory, believes that this change in focus broadens our ideas of the aesthetic experience, expanding it from the essentially visual, and immediate pleasure gaining process, to one that uses all our senses and our intellect. This includes aspects of the non-perceptual in aesthetics, about which reservations were discussed earlier, which stem from the basic differences between the scenic aesthetics of contemplation, the type of experience often traditionally associated with nature or the landscape (the perceptual approach), and that of prior knowledge about the landscape and its ecological robustness (the integrationist approach). However, this is not a problem as long as we recognize the order in which the parts of an aesthetic experience occur. We can enjoy a beautiful landscape all the more if we also know it is ecologically healthy, but this is not absolutely essential for the perception of the initial aesthetic experience.

Since Leopold's theory comes from an ecologist, not an aesthetician it throws new light on aesthetics, for as Gobster argues, the landscape we observe can become more comprehensible as our focus widens to include more complex layers of ecology. The dramatic scene continues to give pleasure either in the Kantian mode or in terms of complete sensory engagement; nevertheless, the greater degree of exploration and appreciation of the dynamics of natural change leads ultimately to a deeper satisfaction and elucidation of the spirit of the place. This is exemplified by indicators of aesthetic/ecological health, such as the range of wildlife species present.

This theme is continuing the idea of more detailed examination of the environment and our capacity for conserving its particular qualities. Leopold also said, 'Our ability to perceive quality in nature begins, as in art, with the pretty. It expands through successive stages of the beautiful to values yet uncaptured by language' (Leopold 1981, p. 96). This is an essential link with Whitehead. Aesthetics begins with the pretty (the minor form of beauty) which leads to the major form of beauty and the strengths of the ecologically healthy landscape, expressed in its massiveness and intensity proper.

This connects the natural and cultural patterns and processes with a most rewarding vein for aesthetic exploration. The link completes the circle from the structure of the landscape to our basic perceptions of it; if we are able to make sense and orientate ourselves in the landscape, whilst appreciating the process involved, this can lead to the highest aesthetic experience. This can also yield fresh experiences every time we engage with the landscape.

The Individual Versus Universal Appreciation

The cliché 'beauty is in the eye of the beholder' is, as many clichés are, a self-evident truth. For many, it means that everyone perceives a different quality in a landscape and that some find a thing beautiful that others find ugly. This may be so if the perception and appreciation involves the will and an interest in the scene under perception. A logger may not find a logged mountainside ugly, whereas a committed environmentalist may well do so.

However, we each possess the same sensory faculties and, apart from those who are impaired, have the same access to the perceptual surfaces, sounds, smells, tastes and kinaesthetic responses. We all have brains with similar mechanisms able to process and interpret the basic perception and to find order, pattern, structure and sense in the world. With a few exceptions, designers have been able to create landscapes that the majority of people find attractive or beautiful; it tends to be a minority, who claim to see beauty in some universally decried scene.

Thus, we can postulate that there is frequently a high degree of universality in the acceptance of a sense of beauty or sublimity when people are presented with certain landscapes and that personal preferences, cultural overlays and practical involvement are all applied post-perception, to yield the nuances of moral or ethical standpoints that are commonly encountered. It is important for designers to challenge these reported perceptions and to identify the universality so that, rather than accept the lowest common denominator for beauty and sublimity, they expose and reject all superficial appreciation and false ethical positions, based on unsound knowledge.

Measuring Aesthetic Appreciation and Preferences for Landscape

How do we discover the characteristics and their strength of any universally accepted model for landscape beauty and sublimity, when there is such a tremendous range of examples? Traditional studies have been based on psychological models, similar to the experiments used to determine the validity of the gestalt laws. Some of these studies seek to elicit statistically valid measurements of preferences, using randomly selected observers who look at a number of photographs of different landscapes or landscape design proposals and score their attractiveness.

These studies were not aimed at identifying beauty or sublimity, but sought to elicit aesthetic preferences for certain scenes. There has been a division in these approaches between those based on correlations between the presence or absence of objective, measurable physical factors in the scene and those using cognitive factors of comprehension in relation to the observer. Many of the objective methods measure variables in a scene and develop complex, mathematical formulae to uncover their statistical relationships and the degrees of preference expressed by the sample of observers. Frequently, these studies measure the quantities or percentages of occurrence of different features such as trees, hills or water and their measurable attributes like size, steepness of slopes and so on. The resulting analyses often demonstrate that relationships between these factors exist, but are extremely difficult to quantify or use in the proof of previous theories, because of the problem of disentangling the degrees of significance amongst a range of dependent variables. The objective techniques can also be criticized, because of the lack of a theoretical foundation; this results in the selection of features that are easily measurable or readily identifiable, rather than those believed to be significant.

The second type of approach is to elicit preference scores and relate them to the cognitive aspects of the perception of the scene such as coherence, complexity and degree of mystery. These studies have been used to test previously developed theories that a relationship between cognitive aspects already existed. Such approaches also need methods for measuring or describing characteristics relevant to the cognition of landscape quality, to enable meaningful correlation, as it is ultimately the physical composition of elements and their organization in the landscape that produce the cognitive characteristics.

Instead of asking observers to score preferences, some studies also used expert opinion and numerical marking to build up scores, not of preference, but of value. For example, the 'Fines' system developed in the late 1960s gave mountains high value scores and plains low ones; the adding up of positive and negative scores associated with the component features was deemed to give an 'objective' valuation. Value in itself may be valid information, but such studies do not help to assess why such scenes are valued. They are also based either on expert judgement, or on potentially superficial public assessment.

Recent approaches to preference research are developing in two directions. One technique aims to test the effect of different aesthetic characteristics by using a series of photographs that have been altered to depict various different versions of the same landscape. Modern computer graphic technology enables a number of scenes to be shown, with complete control of one or more independent variables. For example, preference studies concerned with forest landscapes test preferences for geometric or natural shapes (plantations or felled areas); these variables can be tested with less risk to statistical significance, than using the results from other unknown factors in a scene. Observers then rate the scenes on a scale, enabling the relative importance of the variables to be determined. The main problem with this approach is combining all variables and ranking their cumulative or relative effects. This method has been used recently in Great Britain

Examples of two images used to test public preferences for landscapes and landscape change. These were used to ask people which type of shape used in forest felling looked better. Everything about the two images is the same except the factor under test so that preferences can be directly attributed to the different characteristics of the concept or principle under test.

Straight Edges to Forest Boundary

Contoured Edges to Forest Boundary

to test forestry design principles, which were empirically developed, and to validate assumptions about public preferences made by professional designers.

The second recent development is the use of interview techniques, where aspects of a scene, or a real landscape, as experienced by observer and interviewer, are discussed using open ended questions, to identify the factors that the observer feels are important. The statistical analysis of such interviews can be difficult, but the repeated emergence of significant characteristics in a landscape, as experienced by a number of observers, can suggest conclusions that establish a standard as well as showing the range over which the preferences are distributed.

A number of these recent preference studies have explored the links between landscapes that not only provide a pleasurable aesthetic experience of beauty, but also fulfil a function. The question may be asked: in what terms do I prefer this scene over that one? As a place to live? As a place for a picnic? As a place to see wildlife? This brings more than perceptual values into play and uses the landscape, not only as the setting, but also as an integral part of the overall experience. Such an approach opens up several issues. Firstly, there is the place of non-perceptual factors in aesthetics. Secondly, there is the aspect of engagement with the landscape as opposed to contemplation, and the link to Gibson's affordances in our perception. Thirdly, there is the utilitarian component to the preference equation, which may confuse matters (Schopenhauer's will).

The most successful of these studies can give us useful information about many of the characteristics that signify why some landscapes are more preferred than others. These can also indicate the extent to which such preferences are universal in statistical terms, by measuring the distribution of these preferences around a mean related to a particular human population and its attributes. Stephen Kaplan has worked in the field for many years and has shown that cognitive features common to nearly all highly rated landscapes can be summarized as:

- Coherence: the ability to see and comprehend the pattern inherent in a scene (the opposite of chaos)

- Complexity: the range of different elements in an object or scene which provides sensory stimulation

- Mystery: the aspects of a scene that cannot be comprehended all at once.

We will return to these factors later in the chapter, because they are also very similar to ones derived from approaches, such as those of Whitehead.

Aesthetics: Integration of Perception and Knowledge

If we subscribe to the perceptual school, that adds knowledge, conceptual factors and the social and cultural background of the observer into the equation *after* the initial perception, what happens to that first sense of beauty or sublimity? This is an important question, because it relates closely to the links I am advocating between all forms of patterns and our aesthetic appreciation that could yield practical tools for designers and managers.

There are two options here. Firstly, we may, like Kant, after the initial perception, be disappointed to discover that what was believed to be natural turns out to be artificial. Alternatively, the revelation of a different origin from that expected may lead to a change in appreciation, but not necessarily disillusionment.

Some integrationists, as well as insisting that the perceptual act involves prior knowledge, demand purity in the natural qualities of a scene that must be objectively measurable to be appreciated as natural beauty or sublimity. This position is difficult to sustain when most of the landscape is to varying degrees, a cultural one; it is further affected by the preponderance of wrongly perceived notions about nature. If we can accept that most landscapes lie along a continuum of natural to cultural, it is easier to refer to 'natural' scenes in a wider, more pragmatic sense. However, this approach must be overseen by an ethical stance, such as the rejection of naturalness for apparently attractive lakes, which turn out to be highly polluted lagoons, or curious land forms that are dangerous mining waste.

Difficulties arise if we assert, as do some committed environmentalists in the USA, that everything natural is by definition beautiful, and that everything man-made, after Christopher Columbus discovered America in 1492, is ugly or dishonest. The problem is not just the extreme illogicality of the assertion, but the frequently

This landscape in the Scottish Highlands will be considered natural and beautiful by many people. However, it is partly the result of deforestation, depopulation, overgrazing sheep and deer management. Thus, according to the integrationist view, because it is a 'degraded' scene we should not find it beautiful once we find the truth about it.

inaccurate understanding of what is natural. This is a particular problem in forestry management. The dynamic pattern/process system that drives forest ecology (see Chapter Six) and changes landscapes through agencies like fire is not widely understood; people still subscribe to the outdated concept of the stable climax forest. Others are willing to accept natural events as beautiful, whilst decrying similar changes created by humans as unnatural and therefore ugly. The dilemma facing managers is that, paradoxically, the same people may applaud ideas of ecosystem management based on natural processes.

Another misconception concerns the ancient countryside of England; it is commonly agreed to be beautiful and because it was created by farming, it was erroneously assumed that continuation of farming, of any type, would automatically ensure the maintenance of that beauty. It has been recognized that these landscapes depend on traditional methods of farming to maintain their appearance and financial assistance is now given to farmers to continue these practices.

If we accept that post-perceptual judgement may invoke a different, but not necessarily less pleasurable response, we may avoid problems arising from strict adherence to the notion that only natural manifestations can be beautiful or subliming; this will enable us to concentrate on those characteristics of a landscape that produce qualities leading to an experience of beauty or the sublime.

Characteristics and Qualities in the Landscape

Andrew Brennan emphasized that we are part of the natural world as well as the cultural one. He developed a notion of *ecological humanism*, underlining his belief that if we live nearer the ecological reality of the world, our lives will be more rewarding and fulfilled. What we are comes, partly, from where we are. Thus, the identity of place strongly influences our views as individuals and those of the communities in which we live. It is important to comprehend the world as a total environment, rather than a mass of single isolated objects (coherence). Hence, a link between ethics and aesthetics can be made by understanding the environmental characteristics. This requires the ability to identify the link between the characteristics of the whole (unity) in relation to the sum of the characteristics of the parts.

Schopenhauer believed that the connection between parts offers a beauty far exceeding the beauty of the parts themselves. Whitehead defined characteristics such as massiveness, intensity proper and strength in terms of a minor and major form of beauty. Designers, such as landscape architects, seek to synthesize the parts into a unified whole and use a range of techniques to achieve this. A link is now needed between the aesthetic description of environmental characteristics, both physical and perceptual, the qualities they yield (subjective, value laden, aesthetic) and the application of that description to practical design. Many of the perception and preference studies have sought to identify this link; it emerges in the intertwining of the philosophical strands developed by aestheticians with the empirically derived principles employed by designers. The key to establishing this link is a common vocabulary to describe the issues involved.

From our exploration of perception, we have already established that environmental aesthetics is not simply the successive perception of different objects, but how we comprehend the pattern of the entire scene as a coherent or unified whole. In design terms, this is the result of the spatial characteristics of the scene such as a nearness, enclosure, interlock, similarity and figure and ground (remember their role in the gestalt laws), the structural components of scale, proportion, balance and tension and the ordering components of hierarchy, transformation and symmetry. Other factors also work together, such as the shape, colours, textures, positions, orientation and visual forces, which give compatibility, contrast and coherence to a scene or design. Thus, the characteristics inherent in the scene combine to produce the aesthetic qualities perceived by the observer, such as coherence, complexity, mystery or spirit of place.

In most environments, other variables can influence the scene, such as the effect of decay, growth or the variety of weather and lighting conditions. These add temporal variation to the landscape, enabling it to produce a large number of differently perceived environments: new entities possessing new coherences, new complexities and new senses of mystery, however familiar we are with a particular place.

Emotions generated by landscapes are the subjective, qualitative aspects such as openness, agoraphobia, wildness, bleakness, intimacy, claustrophobia, serenity, calmness and so on. Each is achieved due to the interactions of various characteristics. The emotions felt are personal, although many may also be universal. For example, openness is due to a lack of enclosure, a large scale in proportion to the space and the textures of the surfaces, whilst intimacy is the product of strong enclosure, small scale (in relation to our size) and small size of the constituent parts.

Thus, we can say that a landscape is constructed from a number of constituent parts, each possessing describable characteristics, as does the whole scene, where the parts act in combination. The sense of place or the emotions provoked by the landscape are qualities experienced by the observer, but depend ultimately on the characteristics possessed by the landscape.

To express environmental aesthetics simply, it can be said that the overall sense of beauty or sublimity depends more on the characteristics of the whole than its parts. A strongly unified landscape may contain some discordant elements that are not dominant enough to upset the overall effect. This explanation has some use, but does not allow us fully to explain the difference between beauty/sublimity and ugliness. Some of the techniques to be described in later chapters do not attempt this, electing instead to describe character and leave the valuation of beauty or sublimity to one of the psychometric tools mentioned earlier. Landscape criticism, as a discursive method similar to art criticism, may provide a route, where the relationships between characteristics and qualities are discussed, and referenced by other examples. However, this criticism does not assert whether something is beautiful or sublime, but seeks to define, in a more informed way, why and how this arises. The presence of the sublime, defined by the great scale of the landscape, and the power of the forces at work, is easier to identify and analyse. The presence of beauty, alongside or within a sublime scene, may be overlooked, if the characteristics are not fully recognized.

The question follows as to whether the starting point is the pleasure gained from the beautiful or sublime scene or whether it is pleasure that ultimately defines it as beautiful or subliming. The terms were defined by Kant and can be linked, as we have seen, to the qualities of coherence, complexity and mystery. In this way, pleasure could be gained, not only in the appearance of a scene, but also from an understanding of the factors that make it beautiful or sublime. Logically, this means we could gain pleasure from understanding landscapes that are not beautiful or sublime, even though we do not find them attractive. This could be construed as being more of an intellectual pleasure in the understanding of the landscape, than pleasure in the landscape itself. It echoes the integrationist view, but means that we can find several levels of pleasure in the landscape, from the initial, perceptual response, to a deeper, more considered or reflective appreciation. We may also consider the ecological, aesthetic view of Aldo Leopold to be amongst these latter appreciations.

The ability to define and describe the characteristics and qualities of the landscape also requires knowledge of the vocabulary described previously. Many people are inherently sensitive and gain pleasure from the way the landscape fits together, but lack the means of articulating it. One solution is to rely on the expert critic to articulate the beauty on their behalf, another is to inform, educate or help people to become articulate themselves. This is what the author attempted to do in *Elements of Visual Design in the Landscape* as far as visual perception was concerned. Experience of training professionals to use the principles in this book in other fields, such as forestry or ecology, has shown that the level of aesthetic appreciation can be raised. This replaced the generally perceived subjectivity of aesthetics and its dismissal, as superficial and irrelevant, by a more informed and rational description of the characteristics of landscapes that present varying degrees of unity, diversity and contribution to the spirit of place or the obverse.

This 'democratic' approach reduces the chances for aesthetic elitism to develop and the occurrence of different perceptions between 'experts' and 'lay' people.

The Aesthetics of Engagement

Earlier in this chapter we discussed landscape in terms of 'the field of everyday human action' and aesthetic experience as the constant engagement with the environment using all our senses throughout our lives. Berleant has explored the ways in which we perceive space, either from outside or within, and concludes that, by setting aside physical models of space in favour of a phenomenological approach, space becomes not a 'neutral and objective medium, but one continuous with the act of perception.' It is shaped by the observer and is inseparable from this unique and individual action. This relates to the Gibsonian way of perceiving space as we move through it (see Chapter Two). There is a distinction between panoramic and participatory landscapes. The panoramic landscape of highway rest stops, overlooks and viewpoints, so beloved of national park authorities, presents the view from a cliff top towards a scene, distant and separated from the observer, where sight is the only sense used to perceive it. The participatory landscape requires the use of all the senses to develop a spatial continuity with the observer. Whereas the viewer of the panorama is likely to be a disinterested observer, contemplating the scene for its beauty or sublimity, our everyday lives are of the participatory kind, where we engage with our environment. There is also a connection with some of the patterns identified in Chapter One. We will discuss these in future chapters, together with the analytical approaches to the experience of landscape proposed earlier in this chapter. In this section, ways of developing an engagement with different types of landscapes will be explored. The aim is to understand how we can reconnect people to the landscape in a more positive way, building on the understanding of aesthetics gained so far.

Engagement with Natural Environments

At its best, the contemplative mode that can be engendered when we engage with nature or wild surroundings, and the sense of beauty or the sublime that helps to leave our cares behind, is more than a detached Kantian contemplation; it can be the fullest expression of complete engagement, responding to a higher level of environmental beauty. Wandering the trails of Yosemite National Park in the USA, the Cairngorm Mountains in Scotland, or any other place at the more natural end of the nature-culture continuum, away from the liveliness and stresses of the city streets, can put many of us in a benign frame of mind. Our motives are different and our sensory awareness becomes attuned to different wavelengths.

Engagement with the natural world can put many of us in harmony with the cycles and rhythms of life, such as the changing seasons, the tides or animal and plant life cycles. Cheryl Foster discusses this theme and quotes Guy Sircello, another American researcher, who thinks alienation is the great malaise of our century, linking it with a lack of interest in beauty so that we can almost feel as strangers in our own environment.

This alienation, paradoxically, occurs at a time when natural imagery is a powerful influence on the style of life to which many people aspire. Concern about the environment is very great, but this is frequently misplaced or misdirected through ignorance of the dynamics of the natural world or the realities of rural life; this is due to a lack of contact or engagement with our environment. The car borne visitation to a national park or other scenic area, as already mentioned, tends to filter the experience as a detached perception, wholly visual and based on the distant panorama.

This scene from Yosemite National Park, USA, is a natural one. When hiking through such a landscape we engage all our senses. We see the patterns of landform and forest, hear the wind and birds, feel the warmth of the sun, the path underfoot and smell the tree resin. This engagement envelopes us.

At a conference on the aesthetics of the forest held in Finland in 1996, Cheryl Foster described how she led a group of urban students into a forested area - about as natural as it is possible to find in Rhode Island or New Jersey in the USA - and observed (as a piece of research) their reaction. From an initial phase of busyness, chatter and intellectual concerns, the enveloping qualities of the forest, the rhythm of walking and the complete sensory immersion gradually took over. The initial bubbling thoughts calmed down and the aesthetic experience began. By the end of the walk, physical tiredness and mental calmness had superceded the muscular tension and mental activity of the indoor and sedentary urban environment. There are lessons here for all of us. Forests provide a special, enveloping environment, which easily engages all the senses and where the absence of cultural layers and other humans, helps the manifestation of the aesthetic experience.

Andrew Brennan takes this a step further, asserting that because we are a part of the natural world, we require contact with it to become fulfilled human beings. He links our identification with nature as the first step towards an environmental ethic. In as much as ethics and aesthetics go hand in hand, like the link between truth and beauty, it is illogical to recognize the direct benefit of our engagement with nature and then ignore its care as much as we do.

Arnold Berleant, in trying to define how nature differs from art in aesthetic terms, concludes that we need an 'aesthetic that bases our appreciative response on the awareness, selection and understanding of the order by which natural forces have produced the objects we admire.' This takes us back to the search for coherence, complexity and mystery inherent in beautiful landscapes and manifested in nature, as well as the deeper engagement described here.

This should help us to develop an appropriate ethical position for the environment, perhaps based on Leopold's land ethic. We also need a greater understanding of the patterns and processes that produce beautiful landscapes. Later chapters will provide us with the tools with which to achieve this.

Engagement with Everyday Cultural Environments

The majority of the self-organized landscapes of countryside, village, winding lane, ancient town or city have the qualities of coherence, complexity and mystery. They score highly in most perception and preference studies, when compared with planned, geometric and simpler examples. They are also participatory landscapes *par excellence*, by encouraging entry and exploration. The means of describing such places cannot be restricted to the visual, as it can for the panoramic landscape. Berleant recognized the engaging qualities of winding paths, curving roads fitted to the landform and the diversity of an urban square that is complete only when containing people. These are living landscapes as well as landscapes for living, so our pleasure

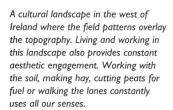

A cultural landscape in the west of Ireland where the field patterns overlay the topography. Living and working in this landscape also provides constant aesthetic engagement. Working with the soil, making hay, cutting peats for fuel or walking the lanes constantly uses all our senses.

comes partly from discovering them, from the mental maps we make, the affordances they provide, the landmarks we use and the sensory stimulation, which is effortless. Even routine activities in such places yield constant delight, because of the ever changing scene, of seasons, light, weather, people, sounds, smells and so on. These environments also have that spirit of place, which makes them special and unique in ways that industrialized landscapes can never be.

The qualities of coherence, complexity and mystery are to be found in certain recurrent features in any landscape. The winding paths and streets of participatory landscapes encourage exploration to achieve a full sense of their coherence, although we can sense there is a pattern to be discovered. Geometric or grid layouts are too predictable; we can see along the street or path, so there is no mystery. Our full kinaesthetic, sensuous enjoyment is also further stimulated as we follow winding streets or lanes, climb steps, dip in and out of sun and shade, and turn and twist our bodies in the process. Straight, gridded streets do not provide any of this, nor do they possess massiveness according to the Whitehead model, only intensity proper. Hence we can use the concept of the aesthetic of engagement and full participation in a landscape to help define the characteristics that give us pleasure.

The character of the spaces found in participatory landscapes possess an hierarchy, a fractal quality of subdivision into various sizes and proportions; a varying sense of enclosure and openness, all defined by edges and zones of transition. This gives the complexity of spatial structure, massiveness, and also its strong coherence, as following our exploration the unity of the pattern is also comprehensible. These aspects of self-organized patterns also appeal to the intellect. Wandering the streets of Venice in Italy or Prague in the Czech Republic is rewarding, because it takes time for these places to unfold their characteristics and for us to comprehend the pattern. Using a map to explore such places is frequently a hindrance, because we are forced to orientate ourselves by its planimetric pattern. These cities were not

This woodland path leads us into the landsape. It provides a strong sense of mystery and invites our complete sensory engagement in an enclosed world where we can be shut off from the surrounding city.

laid out according to a plan and so it is difficult to reduce them to one. By contrast, a gridded layout is understood in a few moments and navigation becomes a question of counting streets across and along the blocks. There may be a variation if the city is built on a hill or if there are other lanes, plazas or spaces adjoining the grid, but again the layout is intellectual and not organic; it appeals to the sense of control and order, but does not stimulate participatory engagement.

As in the perceptual nature of aesthetics already discussed, the aesthetics of engagement does not require previous knowledge of the landscape before it can be appreciated. Much of the pleasure gained from exploring Venice or the Cotswold Hills in England is through the discovery and understanding gained as a result of that exploration. Knowing the history of development, whether the houses are genuine or reconstructions, or the problems facing the city structure or rural economy of either place is unnecessary in the first instance. The sensuous, aesthetic pleasure that engagement brings can be spoiled by too much reading of guidebooks, being steered towards certain sights, instead of letting mystery be the guide. It may add to our appreciation and make us keen to help conserve the city or countryside, but this does not prevent us from perceiving the complexity, making sense of the pattern or feeling the mystery of either place.

As we explore our world, even our everyday surroundings, we develop our own mental maps and affordances, because we bring to the engagement our social, cultural and utilitarian background and values. However, this does not diminish our aesthetic experience, which enriches and gives meaning and purpose to our lives. Arguably, we are as much the product of our social and aesthetic interactions with our whole environment, as we are genetically unique individuals. Unless we engage with our environment socially and aesthetically, we may miss opportunities to enhance our contribution in the workplace and in our personal lives; adopting an integrated and holistic position should minimize this effect.

Summary and Conclusions

This chapter has been a rather selective excursion into the field of aesthetic philosophy in an effort to understand, in greater depth, our perception, understanding and response to the landscape patterns to be described in subsequent chapters. We have explored the recent works of a number of aestheticians who have studied the aesthetics of environment. Several major themes emerged from this.

Firstly, there is the nature of aesthetics and the idea that the aesthetics of environment is different from that of art, although there are relationships. Aesthetics is about experiencing the perceptual and sensuous features of the landscape or environment, using all of our senses.

Secondly, there is the definition of environment and the idea, developed by Arnold Berleant, that we and the environment are not separate, but are part of an interdependent whole that includes nature. We took landscape to mean the visual field, as well as the field of present human action, engaged by all the senses. Each of us has a landscape with many personal affordances.

Thirdly, we considered the nature of an aesthetic experience. We discussed whether it is purely perceptual or dependent on non-perceptual factors. We explored the ideas of Cheryl Foster and others and concluded that the experience, although subsequently informed and affected by non-perceptual factors is essentially a perceptual one. This distinction turns out to be an important one, because it gives aesthetics the right to be treated seriously as a major factor in our lives. Finally in this section, we came to the view that cultural landscapes have aesthetic values as well as natural ones.

Fourthly, we discussed the role of pleasure as part of the aesthetic experience. We explored the emotional stimulation and pleasure or displeasure gained through our perception and recognized that different landscapes evoke this in different degrees. We concluded that the pleasures associated with beautiful or sublime landscapes are of a special order and have particular value.

Fifthly, we turned to the unique aesthetic theory of Alfred North Whitehead. We considered his metaphysics of 'organism' and 'prehension' and the aesthetics it invoked. The concepts of 'massiveness' and 'intensity proper' were reviewed, with the roles of the 'minor' and 'major' forms of beauty. Applying this theory to examples, yielded further enlightenment in our search for the link between beauty and the characteristics of the environment or landscape.

Sixthly, we briefly considered tentative links between healthy ecosystems and aesthetics, postulated by Aldo Leopold. These provide connections between perception, beauty and natural landscape patterns and processes.

Seventhly, we tried to determine whether all appreciation is individual and personal, or whether there are universal experiences. We reviewed some of the psychological research studies that try to discover these things. There are no hard and fast conclusions, but together coherence, complexity and mystery seem to be fairly universally valid factors that produce definite preferences.

Eighthly, and in light of the earlier discussion on non-perceptual factors in aesthetics, we reviewed the knowledge and prejudices we possess and the role of post-perceptual information and understanding. In this context, changes in perception may affect the later aesthetic experience.

Ninthly, we considered the relationship between characteristics of the landscape and the aesthetic qualities these invoke. This is important, because it enables a direct link to be made between aesthetics and the tasks of planners, designers and managers, who need to be able to know the aesthetic effects of their alteration of the landscape. This link was established by the use of the vocabulary of design principles.

Finally, we returned to the deeper exploration of Berleant's aesthetics of engagement as the main means of approaching a meaningful and useful application of aesthetics. This proved to be extremely fruitful, linking with the Gibsonian view of affordance and the universal properties of preferred landscapes described above. The achievement of a sense of beauty or the sublime is possible as are more common yet aesthetically valuable experiences. After this we looked in detail at engagement with nature in terms of the special qualities we can achieve in our experiences; this emphasized the value of nature in our lives when compared with the alienation all too commonly found. The problems of and opportunities for engagement with cultural landscapes were then considered.

We can conclude from these ten themes that aesthetics is an all embracing, multi-sensory engagement with our environment within which we are a natural component. Where the emotional content of beauty or the sublime is high, the aesthetic experience can be an intense one, giving a valuable and necessary mental stimulus. It can also be a more ordinary, everyday sense of pleasure in our surroundings, which is greatest when the landscape is coherent, complex and has some mystery. There is a strong correlation between the pleasure derived from these characteristics and the need to understand and orientate ourselves in the environment we engage with, and its range of affordances. There is a further connection between the qualities of unity, diversity and sense of place and the universal preferences for coherence, complexity and mystery. In the aesthetic theory of Whitehead we found that massiveness, or diversity of contrasts, coupled with intensity proper, or comparative magnitude without reference to qualitative variety, produced a strength of character in landscapes.

These themes can be synthesized in order to orientate ourselves, make sense of and find beauty and the sublime in our environment. To facilitate this the landscape should contain the following qualities:

Diversity/complexity in terms of complexity expressed as multi-layered, multi-scaled elements contrasting with one another. This is a characteristic of all self-organized landscapes (to varying degrees) and of all healthy ecosystems. Simple, less diverse environments may either possess diversity at another spatial scale or have been simplified as a result of management or other human alteration or design. Subsequent chapters will develop an understanding of self-organized landscapes and healthy ecosystems.

Coherence in terms of an ordered structure that we can understand, and where comprehension of the whole is more significant than the individual parts. As we shall establish in the following chapters, this is a feature of all natural or cultural, self-organized, planned or designed landscapes. Unity and conformity are synonymous with this characteristic. However, these are often absent from landscapes where *ad hoc* economically driven change takes place.

Spirit of Place where the landscape has a special quality of uniqueness that is identifiable. All self-organized patterns and the better designed landscapes are the unique expression of all the processes at a given point in time, which yields this quality. It is sometimes known as *Genius loci* when it is especially intense and associated with landscapes capable of producing sensations of beauty or sublimity.

Mystery in the sense when the landscape has coherence, it cannot all be perceived at once. This invites us to explore such landscapes and spend more time learning about them. The organic, self-organized natural or cultural landscapes possess this in full measure, whereas it tends to be absent in the simplified, planned examples.

Multiple Scales where there is an hierarchy or range of scales to the landscape pattern in relation to the human size. This is the aspect of comparative magnitude and it provides a framework for complexity, gives stimulation of the same diversity close at hand or far away and reflects many of the characteristics of self-organized, naturally fractal patterns, particularly those found in nature and described in Chapter One.

Strength is the overall mixing of factors 1 to 5 which reinforce each other and enhance their individual qualities. When all are present in quantity, the aesthetic result is as powerful as possible.

Attainment of these qualities should be the measure of success for any change to a landscape; they usually occur at a maximum amount within the natural range of variability provided by the climate, landform and ecology. At this point, we are in a position to develop a deeper understanding of the opportunities presented by design to enable solutions that meet aesthetic as well as practical and economic criteria. This will be the subject of the next chapter; it will set the scene for the remainder of the book, where an understanding of the characteristics and processes of the various landform, ecosystem and human patterns, as well as their analysis and design application, will give us a firm basis for future planning, design and management.

DESIGN FOR LANDSCAPES

Introduction

The last chapter concluded with a summary of the key qualities most often to be associated with landscapes of a high aesthetic value. We also noted that these qualities should be incorporated into design concepts. This is no easy task. It requires an understanding of the process of design, central to which is creativity. One of the aims of this book is to foster a multi-disciplinary approach to managing landscape change. Of the disciplines that are currently involved in landscape planning and land management, the one with most training in design is landscape architecture. Landscape architects are likely to be most familiar and comfortable with many of the aesthetic concepts discussed in the previous chapter. They normally work with other disciplines when undertaking most of their projects. However, the place of design and the need for designers is not always well understood. It will be valuable to summarize what landscape designers have to offer and to clear up some misconceptions about this profession.

The Place of Landscape Design and Designers

When we use the word 'landscape' it is conceivable that many people will think of nature or beautiful scenery. Some connections may be made with landscape art and paintings by English artists, like Constable and Turner, or the photography of Ansell Adams in the USA. Sublime or picturesque scenes of mountains, waterfalls, arcadian landscapes or attractive rural life may dominate. The word 'landscape' itself is so interconnected with scenery and paintings of scenery that aesthetic considerations between the two can be confused, thus associating the concept too closely with art. Hence, there has been a preoccupation with distant vistas to be viewed in a contemplative mode, which we sought to overcome in the previous chapter. There is a significant history of landscape and nature appreciation culminating in the various national park movements in the 19th and 20th centuries and it is no surprise that most national parks contain scenery of this description. Some cultural scenes of attractive farmland and villages may also be included, especially in Europe.

Ask people what a landscape architect does and the answers are not usually enlightening. Landscape gardening may be offered, where plants are composed into pleasing and harmonious scenes; perhaps city parks will be mentioned, maybe attempts to screen unsightly developments, or possibly the layout of recreation facilities. As James Corner, an American landscape architect puts it 'our innocent citizen may... conclude that landscape architects... will make things appear to fit together, to put things in place, screening out the undesirable while preserving and framing the scenic moment.'

There is a long history of landscape design and a tradition underlying this profession, albeit poorly known by members of the public. The profession can look back many centuries to see examples of consciously designed and ordered landscapes. The earliest of these were associated with religious precincts, temples and ritual landscapes, where processions and large scale ceremonies took place. The great temple complexes of Egypt in the fourth to first millenia BC, or Mexico in the 13th to 15th centuries AD, the third millenium BC landscape around Stonehenge in England or the Athenian Acropolis of the 3rd century BC in Greece were clearly laid out to impress people with their scale, order, magnificence and, in many cases, beauty. They demonstrated both temporal and spiritual power.

Gardens too have a long history associated with all civilizations, but especially those of arid or semi-arid climates, where irrigated man-made oases were greatly valued by the people of high status in Persia or Mesopotamia in the third to first millenia BC, India in the 16th century or Aztec Mexico of the 14th century AD. As idealized forms of nature and symbolic representations of paradise, gardens have continued to be both public and private expressions of our long relationship with nature. At Versailles and other great French chateaux, in the 17th and 18th centuries, the epitome of the human manipulation of vegetation was achieved. The complex and ornate plantings reflected the prevailing philosophy of René Descartes, who was influential in his views about order, geometry and human power over nature. Designs symbolized the temporal power of Louis XIV, the 'Sun King'. André Le Nôtre is the first great exponent of this type of landscape design and one of the progenitors of a profession, still closely associated with parks and gardens.

The English contribution reflected a different tradition and was manifested in a diverse set of styles. The French and Dutch formality in design introduced during the Restoration period, after Charles the Second came to the throne, and by King William of Orange in the late 17th century, was eventually replaced some fifty years later by the style commonly associated with the names of William Kent, Lancelot 'Capability' Brown and Humphry Repton. This created idealized, arcadian scenes reminiscent of or based on landscape paintings. Vistas were composed, designed to be seen from specific viewpoints and containing architectural features such as Greek temples that related to classical notions of beauty and harmony, as well as Athenian democracy translated as English liberty. Such landscapes also combined elements of the traditional wood pasture of ancient deer parks (see Chapter Seven) and newly improved agricultural practices that often resulted in planned countryside. Thus, an harmonious combination of country sports, economic improvement, aesthetic pleasure and English libertarianism was possible in one scene.

The discovery of the picturesque and the appreciation of the sublime, marked a departure from the self-conscious beauty of the arcadian park. Landscape design began to include elements such as mountains or rocks, not directly part of the park or garden and often some distance away. Footpaths or carriage drives were laid out to obtain picturesque and dramatic qualities, where a sense of the sublime could be experienced. This initiated the vogue for wild, natural scenery that culminated in the ethos of the National Park movement in the USA in the late 19th century and the efforts of the International Union for the Conservation of Nature (IUCN) in Europe after the Second World War. The predominance of dramatic mountains and other wild and sublime scenery in the selection of such places, stems directly from the picturesque movement. At the same time the dichotomy between so-called natural and cultural landscapes developed, as did the relative values to be placed on these.

As the urbanization of Great Britain, Europe and parts of North America advanced, the provision and design of parks in their urban form became a necessity for the health and well being of all social classes, not merely the privilege of the wealthy country gentry. The pioneering American landscape designers Frederick Law Olmsted and Calvert Vaux imported the English 'naturalistic' style into America during the 19th century and their finest work, such as Central Park in New York, is testament not only to the designer's skill, but also to the persistent attraction of this concept to the thousands of people who still visit these parks every day.

Whether in the urban scene or wilder landscapes, the concept of the

A well designed park: one of the major accomplishments of landscape architects is the ability to design and build landscapes where pleasurable aesthetic experiences can be gained. It is probably one of the few places that many ordinary people would recognize as the work of landscape architects.

'park', providing respite from the everyday experiences, has important implications for aesthetics. Landscape preference research consistently finds that the quasi-natural landscape style is still preferred by many people. It is also the greatest contribution so far made by professional people, now called landscape architects. The park can be regarded as an object of design with a defined and significant purpose; this enables people to obtain an aesthetic experience of great value and importance for their everyday lives, in the case of the urban park, and to protect nature and provide aesthetic, moral and spiritual experiences in wilder parks.

The other major field where landscape architects have operated is in urban and suburban developments of all kinds. Here the emphasis has been on reducing detrimental impacts of housing, roads, factories and retail premises and, where possible, of beautifying them using earthworks, paving, plants, water and sometimes art. This is the realm of achieving the minor form of beauty (in Whiteheadian terms) by mitigation of negative effects and occasionally achieving the major form by creative design. The canvas for this activity is the populated landscape of everyday life; unfortunately the application of landscape design practices and techniques is not universal. Those modern cities, highways or housing areas where good design has been successful, demonstrate that development need not be detrimental. Furthermore, places designed for everyday life, that include diverse opportunities for aesthetic engagement, can be as rewarding as the highly prized national parks or wilderness areas.

A smaller corps of landscape designers have become involved with large engineering projects, extractive industries, forestry and agriculture where there are chances not only to mitigate aesthetic degradation but also to create new stimulating landscapes that fit into the dynamic setting of natural and cultural patterns and processes at a larger scale.

As yet the potential of this latter issue is unfulfilled and this offers one of the greatest challenges for design at the present time. Later chapters will explore some of these opportunities.

Modern landscape architects are trained to be more than park designers. They study a wide range of subjects in order to develop skills of multi-disciplinary working and an holistic, integrated approach. They seek to achieve the best balance between beauty and function, always with due respect to landscape character, its sensitivity and carrying capacity. They span the worlds of art and science, integrating analysis with creativity.

Thus the history of design is a fine, but limited one. The challenge now is to develop ways of incorporating the multi-dimensional, multi-layered, participatory concept of landscape, as suggested in the previous chapter, into planning, design and management of a wide range of landscapes. The traditional process of design needs to be reviewed and the role and nature of creativity expanded. The new paradigm for designers lies in harnessing creativity to the deep analysis now possible without overlooking the realities of the dynamic landscape.

Design Methods and Practice

Landscape design endeavours to reconcile the capacity of the physical and perceptual landscape, to meet a range of human needs at a given time. In order to be sustainable, any reconciliation must also ensure that landscape quality is maintained for future generations and their options for action are not inhibited.

Setting Objectives

One of the first steps in the usual process of drawing up any design or plan, is to define the objectives of the project. These may be wide ranging or limited, depending on the project, the scale and type of the landscape and the clientele involved. One end of the scale may be a small garden, owned by an individual, whilst the other may be a substantial tract of land owned by a national government or a large commercial organization. Large numbers of stakeholders increase the potential for conflicts before objectives can be agreed. In the case of natural resource development, such as timber or mineral extraction, the stakeholders may include local residents who may support or oppose the development, the developer, regulatory authorities and non-governmental organizations.

There are two, complimentary, ways of determining the correct balance of objectives for a range of stakeholder interests. The first is to wait until analysis is complete, so that the deeper understanding of the landscape, its dynamic character, evolution and limitations, is able to help the client or client group assess its capacity to accept change. In some circumstances, the hierarchical structure of the landscape can be used, so that the broad analysis for an extensive area can be used to determine the appropriate balance of objectives for a smaller part of that area. Thus, top level planning can steer the establishment of compatible lower level objectives further down the hierarchy. The Hazelton Mountain (McCully/Date Creek) analysis, to be described in Chapter Six, used this approach to determine the objectives relevant to different landscape character areas; it also described the landscape conditions best suited to achieving these objectives over time. In this way, the design of the individual character areas is strongly influenced by the top level plan.

The second means of determining objectives is to work with the client or client group to identify and list all the values they place on the landscape and/or wish it to yield. The list can be presented with or without priorities. Identifying the values is insufficient, unless there are some indicators for assessing the success of achieving them by the designer or design team. Such indicators may be quantitative or qualitative. For example, to maintain or enhance the aesthetic value of a landscape may be an objective. The designer needs to know what specific aspects or places have value and how aesthetic qualities such as coherence, complexity and mystery are manifested in the landscape.

At this stage there should be no preconceptions about how far these objectives can be met; once the analysis stage has been completed, the

A table showing a very practical method of setting out design objectives. Filling in a table like this can be a good task for community groups who wish to take more control over their own landscape. It helps the professional to develop the design brief and to engage with the community to explore the potential conflicts between competing objectives.

VALUE	OBJECTIVE	MEASURE OF SUCCESS
WATER	• To maintain and enhance water quantity over time.	Levels of pollutants will decline over time. Fish will recolonize the river. River levels will remain higher than at present as abstraction is reduced. Peak flows will be reduced as drainage is restored to a more natural condition.
ENVIRONMENT	• To restore degraded parts of the environment. • To maintain or enhance the good quality parts of the environment.	Polluted and derelict areas will gradually disappear as restoration proceeds. Sources of pollution will be gradually eliminated. Good quality parts of the environment will be protected from development and pollution.
LANDSCAPE	• To protect attractive parts of the landscape. • To improve the unattractive parts of the landscape.	The attractive areas will be protected from development. Trees will be preserved and managed. Restoration of degraded areas will fit into the landscape character of the area. Sites with special aesthetic qualities will be protected.
RECREATION	• To provide for a wide range of active and passive recreational activities.	Recreation will be planned to meet the needs of the local community. The carrying capacity of the landscape will not be exceeded. Uses will be zoned to avoid conflicts between uses or uses and the environment.
NATURE CONSERVATION	• To conserve existing habitats and species. • To improve the nature conservation value of the area.	Special sites will be assessed and protected. Sites that are degraded will be restored. New habitats will be created to link existing ones together and expand the total amount of habitat.
INDUSTRY	• To provide the infrastructure and quality environment to attract new industry to the area.	A new and improved communications network will be developed. Sites for new factories will be laid out in attractive settings. Derelict old industry will be demolished and sites restored for reuse.

objectives can be reviewed, and the client or client group appraised of any difficulties. Even so, how far the original objectives can be achieved, or which ones are the most difficult, will not become known until the design concept or option has been developed.

When setting objectives it is important to be as imaginative as possible and avoid the crude zoning of any landscape to overcome conflicts amongst the identified values, which may prove to be erroneous as understanding of the landscape character advances. Thus, what are initially perceived as mutually exclusive choices, such as either preserving a 'pristine' natural scene or developing it in some way, may not be so, if open minds are maintained and creative planning and design are used to the full; if a creative and practical option can be identified, all can benefit.

Survey or Inventory

The collection of basic landscape information is an important step, because high calibre analysis and design depends on good quality basic survey or inventory. Depending on the landscape, layers of information should be assembled, starting with geology and landform, hydrological and ecological information and human influences. Each of these will be explored in depth in the next three chapters and their analysis considered, before looking at applications for design.

Analysis

The analysis phase follows the collection of inventory information and is intended to build up a detailed appraisal of the landscape. The analysis is used to develop an understanding of the patterns, perceptions and processes inherent in the landscape under consideration. It will be rarely the case that it leads directly to the design solution. In particular, it is important not to reduce the analysis to a set of constraints, which are then dealt with separately. This is the weakness of sieve mapping approaches, where layers of constraining site factors are built up leading to crude solutions, which leave unconstrained areas free to be developed. Of course, sieve mapping can be used in more sophisticated ways but, essentially, it is not fully integrative.

Solutions determined by constraining legal factors present similar shortcomings, where following a set of rules severely constrains the scope for creativity by the designer. Many civil engineering solutions have been arrived at by applying sets of rules, as have various spatial systems, for example, optimization models based on computer programs for timber harvest planning. The design of highways is based on minimum carriageway widths, radii of curves, sight lines, gradients and other factors, which minimize the scope for creative solutions based on the landscape character.

A good starting point to avoid such problems is the discussion of aesthetics in the last chapter, from which a means of analysing the character of the landscape can be developed. It is during analysis that we begin to recognize the inextricable connections between the physical characteristics of the landscape and our responses to them. These responses involve our full sensory engagement, although, for purposes of design, there is a strong concentration on the visually perceived character. Once we understand the landscape as a whole we are better able to examine its parts.

In the last chapter, we examined the relationship between the characteristics of the landscape and the qualities it invokes, such as coherence, complexity and mystery. If we wish to manage or alter landscapes yet retain these key qualities, we need firstly, to know what characteristics and qualities exist at present, and secondly, to try and predict if the proposed changes will maintain or enhance them. Thus, we need techniques of analysis and modelling. Some of these can be simple, others more sophisticated. Some will be reviewed later in the chapter.

Analysis of Aesthetic Factors

A pragmatic approach is to describe the aesthetic qualities of landscape using a combination of emotional responses and visual descriptions related to its characteristics, so as to identify the main contributors to its pattern. The more subjective descriptions concentrate on the aesthetic qualities and can include simple scales such as wild to tame, comfortable to bleak, quiet to busy and so on. Such measures are difficult to calibrate or quantify, and it is not easy to train people in their assessment. However, two sets of characteristics that lead directly to these qualities are more amenable to objective assessment and reduction of surveyor bias. These are the visual contributors to landscape character and the sensory contributors to an emotional response.

The *visual landscape character analysis* uses a well developed vocabulary such as that presented in *Elements of Visual Design in the Landscape*, to describe factual aspects of the scene, experienced by observers or surveyors travelling around it. Qualities such as diversity and the degree of unity are two of the main outcomes of this analysis.

Diversity can be difficult to define, because its effects are more complex. Diversity provides interest, sensory stimulation and distinction among and between different landscapes. It is also subject to the law of diminishing returns when additional variety becomes busy, then overstimulating and finally overwhelming. Frequently, the point at which diversity starts to be overendowed, equates with the breakdown of unity. On the other hand, inadequate diversity is boring or understimulating, although, depending on the scale of the landscape, it may be natural.

Unity is the sense that all parts of the composition or landscape comprise a complete whole. Key contributors to unity are the repetition of similar shapes, textures, colours and rhythms, all of which give a sense of continuity to an area. Spatial factors such as enclosure (by trees, hedges, woods, buildings), proximity or nearness of elements in repeated sequences, are also significant. Visual structure is given by the scale of the landscape in relation to the human figure, the proportion of different elements and their balance. If there is an understandable hierarchy of patterns, this also strengthens the sense of unity of parts within a whole. These are all related to the psychological aspects of pattern recognition, such as the gestalt approach, discussed in Chapter Two.

Some of the most characteristic, persistent and memorable patterns in the landscape also tend to possess strong unity. The intact ancient landscapes, populated by traditional buildings in nucleated settlements (to be discussed in Chapter Seven) possess inherently strong unity; this is provided by field shapes (similar but not identical), long established building forms and materials, in various combinations, and their textures and colours, which also blend with those around them. Spatial enclosure is frequently important and the scale of the landscape this provides is of a small, often intimate quality.

The grid landscapes of North America (see Chapter Seven) also possess unity, with the repeated, continuous pattern of squares. Where the settlement is carved from forest, a more organic pattern is often superimposed, leading to complementary unity (where contrasts help to reinforce the overall pattern rather than disrupt it). Such unity can be defined easily, but the landscape may not always produce a positive aesthetic response because of a lack of diversity or sense of place. However, all landscapes with a definable and distinctive character also exhibit a strong sense of unity.

The same can be said of many natural landscapes, especially where the landform presents strongly defined patterns or where basic patterns, such as meanders and branches, are present. Vegetation patterns, being frequently closely related to the underlying landform, also show characteristic patterns. These will be explored in Chapters Five and Six.

The method of recording the landscape character is to describe it in words and pictures using the visual vocabulary alluded to above. Photographs or sketches can be used. The benefit of sketches is that they can focus on key components that are deemed to characterize the landscape.

Assessing the aesthetic characteristics for the other senses is more difficult, although written descriptions can be valuable. Techniques to record the order in which stimuli occur, and their strength, include the use of video cameras and tape recorders taken into the landscape by observers or surveyors. More sophisticated methods include recording electrical responses on the skin and eye pupil dilation, to try to measure subconscious responses, which are objectively correlated to the verbal descriptions.

A scene in the Austrian Alps. The aesthetic qualities found in this landscape depend on the characteristics of landform shape, scale, texture and colour; the contrast in shapes between mountain, intermediate hill and foreground plain; the complementary contrasts of textures and colours of vegetation; the hierarchy of topographic shape and scale; the diversity and unity of the organization of the landscape components especially the natural and cultural elements; and the Genius loci inherent in an alpine scene such as this.

It is important to assess and define the distinctive character of an area, as this forms a basis for determining its patterns and aesthetic qualities, as well as for any future evaluation. Distinctive features may include many of the matchless archeological and historic remains as well as unique landforms, vegetation communities, traditional farming practices or building materials. These may be quite localized, so that each village may have its individual distinctiveness in terms of a church, castle, old inn, ancient tree, village green or manor house. The distinctive features should be listed and recorded on a map. Clusters of some features, perhaps ancient earthworks, burial mounds, stands of trees, series of waterfalls or rock formations may be especially powerful indicators of a special character or spirit of place (*Genius loci*).

This analysis should be completed for every landscape, regardless of other layers of survey and analysis. It is the common connector, allowing us to bridge the physical with the perceptual landscape.

Design Synthesis

The next stage of design is to move from the analytical phase to the creative. This is where the factual and perceptual analysis is used to define, together with the objectives, the conceptual space for searching for possible creative solutions. It requires the application of the techniques described earlier in the chapter. A large number of solutions may present themselves. Deciding which of them is the best option requires evaluation against the objectives and the analysis. It is helpful if some indicators are available of how objectives will be met or standards achieved. This step is often considered the most difficult and the least logical, because of the often mysterious way that solutions present themselves, sometimes seeming to come 'out of the blue'.

Creativity as Part of the Design Process

What is Creativity?

All new ideas, concepts and designs emerge through a process of creativity. At face value this is an inexplicable event, the sudden 'creative leap' when an idea appears, seemingly, out of nowhere. Often the person responsible for the idea or concept is not consciously aware of how it happened. At one extreme, this is seen as divine inspiration or intuition or, at the other, rationalized, as merely a novel combination of old ideas, where the surprise at the idea arises from the improbability of the combination.

According to British psychologist Margaret Boden, an idea, in order to be counted as creative, whether a novel combination or an inspiration, must have value in some way. This may be, for example, a possible solution to a difficult problem, a work of art that moves the observer or a beautiful design that fulfills a disparate set of objectives.

A number of creative solutions are the result of unusual combinations, but many are not, because they have not occurred before and also could not have done so. These can be considered as more original and therefore they are the truly creative ideas. Boden classified ideas as creative in two ways: psychologically creative, when a person has an idea for the first time, and historically creative, when the same idea has never occurred before. Thus all creative ideas are new to someone, but not all are **completely** new. In most landscape design projects, a novel combination of old ideas is usually acceptable, because of the constraints placed upon the range of possible solutions. However, there are also cases where the solution to a design problem has to be completely new. Such design concepts can be accepted as creative, only when they present usable and thus, valuable solutions to a given problem.

According to the definition, creative ideas, if they are not combinations of old ideas appearing either randomly or at the lower end of the range of probabilities, must seem unattainable by the normal mental processing mechanisms employed in any subject area. Hence, is there some special process for the creation of original ideas that could change the search for a solution or concept from a laborious trawl through innumerable possibilities to a transformation of the sum of those possibilities into something else entirely?

The Process of Creativity

As a way of trying to understand creativity, psychologists have pursued the notion that we explore and, possibly, transform an imaginary space in our minds, called a conceptual space. This space is defined by our understanding of the organizing principles, rules and practical constraints that define a range of possibilities for dealing with an issue, such as options for a design solution. When considering a landscape

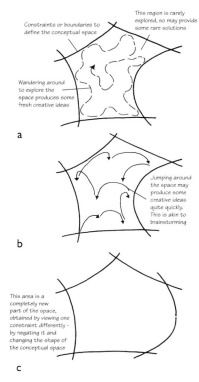

Constraints or boundaries to define the conceptual space

This region is rarely explored, so may provide some rare solutions

Wandering around to explore the space produces some fresh creative ideas

a

Jumping around the space may produce some creative ideas quite quickly. This is akin to brainstorming

b

This area is a completely new part of the space, obtained by viewing one constraint differently - by negating it and changing the shape of the conceptual space

c

A diagram of a conceptual space, with spatial variations within which creative searches take place. a) shows the search by wandering around; b) searches by jumping around; c) shows a change in the nature of the conceptual space itself.

design problem, the organizing principles of composition, the analysis of the landscape and the practical constraints define this conceptual space. Initially, the quest for a solution is a search in this space. The designer attempts to understand and map the structure and pathways of this space and explores them. From this exploration may arise the unusual and rarely encountered combination of ideas.

However, in the truly creative mode, it is the way in which the conceptual space is altered, that provides the uniquely original design concept or solution. Such changes may be made before the limitations of the whole conceptual space have been tested. For example, they may be minor changes, involving the opening of an unexplored region or a major change, such as a transformation of the structure of the conceptual space.

The notion of conceptual space exposes the difference between the options generated by a computer based modelling programme and human creativity. The computer model is only able to work within the conceptual space defined by the program rules and the limits on the data. This type of program seeks to identify possible solutions from a range of variables at a high speed and relies on this to achieve a result. The computer may come up with the improbable, optimum combination and may seem to do the same job more time-efficiently than the designer, but this is a deception. Transformations of the conceptual space are currently beyond computer models and so true creativity remains a human attribute.

Thus the steps humans undertake when attempting to find creative solutions are to identify, map, explore and transform conceptual spaces. As landscape design is primarily a spatial and temporal process, it is important that the conceptual space is not confused with the real, physical space where the design is to be applied, although any emerging concept obviously has a spatial dimension. The design concept may be a kind of spatially defined expression of the transformed conceptual space. Although the eventual design solution may not resemble this physically, it will still remain true to the essence of the ideas derived from the exploration of conceptual space.

David Perkins, another British psychologist, has developed the idea of conceptual space into the notion of a 'Klondike space' after the problems of prospecting for gold in a land of few clues. This designated landscape or space is a 'problem space' where the creative process tries to find a new solution that lies beyond the limitations of the rules that initially defined the space. He has identified four basic problems that are present in creative systems and need to be solved by the creative person.

1. Rarity: valuable solutions are sparsely distributed in a large area of possibilities, because of the virtually infinite recombinations or configurations of past elements, many of which are not viable as solutions.

2. Isolation: the places in the conceptual space where valuable solutions are to be found can be widely separated and unconnected, so that to find them is very difficult. One option may not lead easily to the discovery of another.

3. Oasis: when solutions have been found in one place, it is hard to leave them to try elsewhere. Hence, the first idea may become the eventual solution, which might be sub-optimal.

4. Plateau: many parts of the conceptual space, being similar, give no clues as to the direction in which fruitful or fruitless explorations may lie.

Each of these problems causes inertia and tends to prevent the creative search. Rarity makes search a long task, isolation means solutions lie in out of the way places, an oasis tempts the searcher to stay in an area of promise, whether this is productive or not, and the plateau creates the frustration of not knowing which direction to follow. How are these overcome?

Designers who are successful at developing creative solutions are not content to wander about aimlessly, but try to maximize the probabilities of success by managing the process. There are several points on a spectrum of chance for creativity, from sheer chance to safe bet, with a reasonable balance lying around the techniques of systemized chance and fair bet. Using systemized chance, the designer searches for and examines a number of options that fall within a range defined by some target characteristics. This reduces the time needed for

a) A diagram of a 'Klondike space'. (After Perkins, 1994)

b) A Klondike space formed from the overlap of the conceptual spaces of a range of people, perhaps representing different disciplines in a team. The creative process becomes much more difficult and the range of solutions appears to lie within a narrow field. It is the talented creative person's role to see a larger, different conceptual space arising from the synthesis of all the spaces shown here.

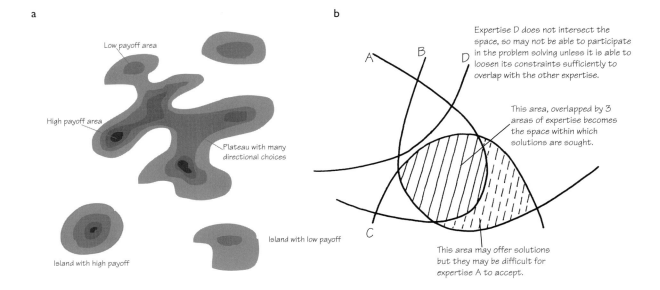

a

Low payoff area

High payoff area

Plateau with many directional choices

Island with high payoff

Island with low payoff

b

A   B   D

Expertise D does not intersect the space, so may not be able to participate in the problem solving unless it is able to loosen its constraints sufficiently to overlap with the other expertise.

This area, overlapped by 3 areas of expertise becomes the space within which solutions are sought.

C

This area may offer solutions but they may be difficult for expertise A to accept.

search and once some promise is spotted it can be followed up. Using the fair bet approach, the designer floats a few concepts and refines them, in the expectation that one or another will do the job. Using such approaches the problems raised by Perkins can be overcome.

- **Rarity** can be overcome by the use of quick conceptualized sketches to identify a range of possible solutions.

- **Isolation** is solved partly by chance leaps about the space and landing in distant places; and partly by cultivated chance, where the mind is prepared to see solutions from wherever they spring, rather than following the path of logic towards a deterministic solution. Another way is to identify connections between isolated areas, by spotting common traits from unusual positions. This is where breaking the rules or transforming the space can be useful.

- **Oasis** is solved by knowing that it happens and deliberately moving to other parts of the space to obtain a different perspective.

- **Plateaux** can be overcome by jumping around or trawling, using systemized chance.

Hence, some techniques, such as brain storming and multi-disciplinary teamwork, can be used to generate ideas and to focus on the most promising possibilities; they can also harness the different viewpoints of various team members. However, truly creative solutions, those that transform the possibilities, are achieved by creative people with particular qualities. This does not mean only artists, architects or designers with a training in creative design, but can also include people working in any field. It is possible that human minds have evolved to aid creativity, so that some minds may be more adapted to occupying and exploiting conceptual problem spaces than others. The spatial, visual thinking skills (popularly associated with the right side of the brain) are likely to be particularly useful, especially in landscape design.

Characteristics of Creativity in People

Creative people are acknowledged as those who produce new or unique ideas, insights, inventions, designs or art works, which are perceived as valuable (in whatever terms) by experts. These products should also be appropriate to the time in which they are produced and for the circumstances where they are needed. This is important for landscape design, where the solution has to be fitted into an existing area, and its conditions, as well as being acceptable to a wide range of interests.

Hans Eysenck, the late British psychologist, studied the traits for creativity shown by successful, creative people, and suggested that, whilst intelligence is needed, there is a trait of great productivity in the generation of ideas, which is partly independent of intelligence. Among the many findings in relation to creative personalities, there is a preference for seeking complexity over simplicity. This preference has been found to correlate with the personalities who demonstrate a high degree of originality and creativity. Complexity, as we have seen throughout the book, is a feature of the world and of dynamic systems.

Hence, willingness to seek or accept complexity seems to be a significant requirement for the attainment of original solutions. The desire for simple solutions has produced many mistakes, as will be demonstrated. However, some elegant solutions may appear simple, whilst comprising highly unified but complex elements or interactions.

The major variables affecting the achievement of creativity can be divided into three categories: cognitive, environmental and personality.

Cognitive variables are those of intelligence, knowledge, technical skills and special talents. These are generally selected for and taught at colleges of further education or universities and by experience at work.

Environmental variables include politico-religious, cultural, socio-economic and educational factors, They provide the setting and the framework within which design takes place. Since the landscape is an amalgam of many of them the designer needs to be aware of their influence and importance.

Personality variables include personal motivation, confidence, non-conformity and the trait of creativity. These may be the most important, because they can influence the selection of people with these qualities for any team assembled to solve complex design problems.

Creativity Within the Context of Self-Organized Landscapes

Within the self-organized, dynamic landscape we encountered in Chapter One, and will study in more depth in the next three chapters, there are many solutions and possibilities, which analysis alone will not identify; this underlines the need for creativity of a high order. In many ways, an appreciation of the characteristics of landscape patterns and processes and modes of perception, enable us to define, together with the design objectives, the conceptual space we should explore. Creative design is exciting and fulfilling and should be embraced as greater than the identification of spaces left over from the overlap of constraints, simple pastiche of existing features or slavish restoration of historical circumstances. It is about exploring the conceptual space of possibilities and using creative and original thinking to seek out the unique and special solution.

In this way the dynamic processes of landscape can be continued as defined by natural evolution and society's changing perceptions and demands, while the design is grounded firmly in the accumulated knowledge of how the landscape works.

Modelling the Past, Present and Future Landscape

Computer models are used increasingly to handle complex interactions of data collected at various scales. While they cannot substitute for human creativity, models can be extremely helpful for evaluating the results of creative design, in terms of how well a design option can meet a wide range of objectives over time. Their development is proceeding very quickly and needs to be directed, so that they fit into the design process and perform their function properly.

Some models are aspatial, dealing with a variety of data that are geographically unrelated to their original source locations. Others use samples taken randomly or systematically at defined map scales so that a spatial dimension is retained, but modelling can only be achieved at a coarse definition. These two types are best used for covering large areas or more global influences. True spatial analysis and modelling uses data that is referenced geographically ('georeferenced'), in one of two ways, and these form the basis of geographic information systems or GIS.

GIS provide the basic means of collecting, recording and managing georeferenced data in a number of layers, which can then be combined or overlaid in specific ways to answer various questions. The two varieties introduced here have their strengths and weaknesses.

The methods of using polygons, lines and points to represent different features with area, length and position, are known as vector systems, because the lines, used to define edges, have a starting position and a direction or vector. Each spatially referenced object can normally be linked directly to a database, which records whatever attributes have been collected. When different layers are overlaid, such as geology, soil and vegetation, polygons can be combined or split to produce new layers, which answer various queries asked of the system.

The pixel or raster based systems use a different approach altogether. Here the information is ascribed to each pixel (or 'picture element') that makes up the whole pattern as seen on a computer screen. This is also how television pictures are created. For mapping purposes, a pixel size is defined as a square of certain dimensions used in the same way. The smaller such squares are, the more refined the maps and analysis can be. The advantage of raster systems is that new patterns can be produced that are not limited by the pre-ordained polygon boundaries of the vector system. However, the scale of resolution of both is limited by the size of the smallest recorded features.

Modelling incorporates the use of GIS data, together with assumptions and decision rules about processes at work over time, to produce possible patterns in the landscape, either in the past or in the future. The calibre of the results of modelling depends on the quality of the initial information and the validity of the assumptions used to set the starting conditions. One of the main difficulties with environmental

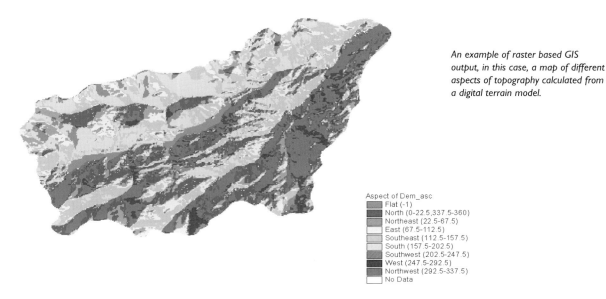

An example of raster based GIS output, in this case, a map of different aspects of topography calculated from a digital terrain model.

Aspect of Dem_asc
- Flat (-1)
- North (0-22.5,337.5-360)
- Northeast (22.5-67.5)
- East (67.5-112.5)
- Southeast (112.5-157.5)
- South (157.5-202.5)
- Southwest (202.5-247.5)
- West (247.5-292.5)
- Northwest (292.5-337.5)
- No Data

modelling is that the results can be highly unpredictable, because we know relatively little about many of the natural systems.

Computer Based Analysis of Landscape Character

To aid analysis of landscape character, it is possible to start with GIS based layers and then use a sorting program to identify patterns, where elements are consistently associated. An example of this (used for a number of sorting and classification purposes in natural science) is a program called TWINSPAN. It takes features and looks for pairings, according to a hierarchy of attributes. Early examples, for large scale landscape assessment at low resolution, used sample kilometre or quarter kilometre squares in order to limit the amount of information needed. These samples were then interpolated by computer to provide a complete picture. Sometimes the computer could not produce a clear pattern, so some professional landscape assistance at setting criteria for the resolution was needed. The maps were of a series of squares and so they looked unnatural. Manual smoothing of the boundaries was necessary.

A good example of a regional landscape character analysis using TWINSPAN was carried out, as a pilot project, by the English Countryside Commission (an agency responsible for Government policy on the countryside) for the southwest peninsular of England (Cornwall, Devon, Somerset, Dorset and Avon counties). A number of layers of attributes were prepared by kilometre square (using geology, soil, elevation, slope, drainage, settlement, field patterns, crops etc). TWINSPAN linked these together, and after several runs of the program, formed reasonably clear patterns for the area (p.235, Fig. 6). These were then used as the basis for public perception studies and can be used to identify areas of high landscape value or to develop guidelines for management (see Chapter Seven for a discussion of landscape assessment).

Modelling Dynamic Systems

The development of chaos theory arose partly as a response to attempts to model complex, non-linear dynamic systems, such as the weather. It was discovered that a very small change to the initial conditions produced very large differences in the behaviour of the models as they ran over time. Some chaologists (as some researchers in chaos theory are called) have created whole worlds on computers, where such unpredictable self-organization spontaneously occurs. This warns us of the difficulties of modelling the multi-variate processes of the natural world without placing limits of probability on the results. This type of model can provide much information about the way dynamic systems operate, but is less useful for evaluating designs. However, one possibility is to combine a degree of stochasticity (randomness within defined ranges of probability) to test the outcomes of some ecosystem models over time; here a design directs the scale, type and rate of change for most of a landscape, but leaves room for natural processes to occur alongside.

One of the most effective ways to use a dynamic model is by developing a set of decision rules by which it operates. An example would be following an analysis of the landscape ecology of an area, as will be demonstrated in Chapter Six. The initial conditions of the system are the landscape structure and composition, defined in a database and spatially recorded on GIS. The range of successional paths provides one set of rules, with some variations that test or develop alternatives. Disturbance events could then be added, occurring in the range of frequencies and obeying rules of their scale, duration and intensity. These rules would be given probabilities for success of a disturbance initiation, linked to the landscape structure, topography, aspect, moisture regime and other environmental variables.

After setting the initial conditions, the model would be allowed to run and the developing pattern sampled at regular intervals to see what transpired. The evolving vegetation structure can be tested at suitable intervals, using analysis of indicators of ecological functioning, such as degree of connectivity or fragmentation, seral stage distribution or mean patch size. This kind of modelling can also produce statistics for other outputs, such as amounts of timber, water, breeding sites for rare birds and so on. However, because it is dependant on the initial conditions, the resulting patterns are to a great extent limited to development from those conditions. When we examined the role of design earlier, we noted the importance of the creative step to move from the analysis towards the development of options for the desired future condition for the landscape. Hence without the creative step the type of modelling described above is rather limited in its scope.

Nonetheless, some modellers might argue if the persistent testing of options against the range of desirables wanted by society is continued over time, then sooner or later the precise dynamic result will emerge. They might also argue that high powered computers enable such testing of alternatives. However, what such arguments miss is the inability of analytical systems to generate completely different scenarios from the existing patterns, due to the constraints of the initial conditions. Therefore, the alternative use of modelling is to refine the best means to secure a desired future condition that has been identified using a different, more creative, synthesizing process (as opposed to analysis only) and to test the ways in which the vegetation structure performs during the process.

An example of a computer program that can be used to test the outcome of a landscape pattern prepared by design is called 'Habscapes'. This can assess how well a mosaic landscape (such as defined according to Richard Forman) fulfils the habitat potential for a carefully chosen range of key species (sometimes refered to as *guilds*). As well as the presence or absence of a satisfactory landscape structure, this computer program can include features such as size, shape or proximity, set to certain threshold values. At the time of writing, the program could deal with the habitat and fauna of Pacific west coast forests in the USA, but needed complex database assembly before being ready for use in other areas. This kind of modelling holds great potential, because it provides more than a neutral descriptor of measurable factors regardless of their significance; it can show aspects of the quality of the landscape for the key species.

Another example of modelling, related to human perceptions of the landscape, is determining where different degrees of 'tranquillity', or a sense of peace and quiet, are present in a landscape, either before or after design. This is an attempt to measure and model the degree to which the perceived intrusion of noise, artificial light and certain visible objects reduces our sense of comfort, calmness and general positive sensory responses. It is based on GIS maps of features with measurable effects that affect tranquillity, such as the known distances over which sound can be heard, light observed and so on. It has been used at a regional and local scale in England to assess the changes to the countryside over a number of years. Maps can be produced showing a four or five point scale of tranquillity. The following factors are included:

- At the required scale, the main travel routes are noted together with figures for traffic flows. The lesser routes can be included for local assessments. The effect of noise over distance moderated by landform is plotted as it radiates outwards from the road, conveniently shown as steps, using an established decay function (reduction in loudness over distance) that is built into the GIS program.

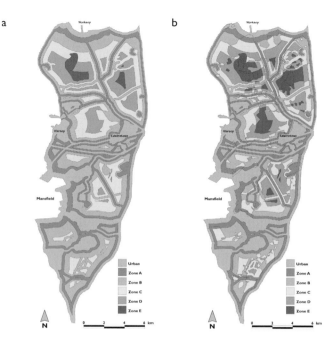

Maps of Sherwood Forest, Great Britain, showing different degrees of tranquillity. a) is 'basic' tranquillity whilst b) shows the effect of woodland which tends to increase the sense of tranquillity. (reproduced by permission of the Forestry commission)

- Air traffic routes and approaches to airports can be plotted with numbers of flights and the noise spread, marked out in similar fashion to the roads.

- Railways are subject to the same rules as road and air routes. Visual intrusion of urban influences depend on the perceived effect of certain structures. Large transmission pylons and cables, microwave transmitters, wind turbines, chimneys, factories, smoke or steam plumes, and other dominating structures have effects that are widespread but which diminish over distance.

- Street lighting, especially the orange glow from sodium lamps, penetrates darkness over a wide area directly and by reflection from clouds. This also diminishes over distance.

- Smells from factories, roads, intensive farms or sewage works affect areas, depending on the wind and seasons, but their general extent can be plotted.

Statistics of the factors and accepted formulae for measuring their effects are widely available and each type can be plotted on maps to show the cumulative effect of each layer of intrusion. Tranquillity is expressed as a percentage of all effects and can range from 100% in their complete absence to 0% in their total presence. Examples for all England show a drastic diminishing of tranquil areas between the

1960s and 1970s. In Sherwood Forest, the tranquillity map developed by the late Simon Rendel, a British landscape architect, includes 'without trees' and 'with trees' options. This can be used to model the effect of different planting on tranquillity, with the aim of increasing it by strategic placing of areas of trees. GIS is ideal for handling this type of information.

The outputs of these models are also developing: the production of statistics and especially, the visualization of the landscape in quasi-realistic terms. Three dimensional terrain models, overlain with thematic maps or computer generated vegetation, can provide much more realistic and accessible results. These can be used to evaluate the aesthetic results of the processes as well as the physical outputs. Virtual reality tools are being developed that allow us to drive or fly through the modelled landscape in 'real time'. These will evolve very quickly, including use on basic computers and provide more effective, interactive tools to demonstrate results to the uninitiated or 'lay' people. Such tools have great potential use in planning projects where public involvement in decision making is important (p. 235, Fig. 7).

Summary and Conclusions

This chapter has introduced some of the practical tools and methods available for developing a better understanding of the land, its structures, patterns and processes. This understanding provides a firm base for the description, analysis and design potential of a wide range of natural and cultural patterns to be covered in Chapters Five to Seven.

The analysis of patterns and their accompanying processes can be facilitated by following the logical order set out in the next three chapters of the book: the landform, then the ecosystem and finally the cultural patterns. This order also helps identify where correlations between these layers are strong or weak and so demonstrates the range of patterns from the most persistent or constrained to the most transient or least constrained; these correlations may provide opportunities for the planning and design of sustainable landscape development.

It is important to be objective in the analysis of a pattern and its process and to use good scientific methods wherever possible. However, it is also important to recognize that judgement has a significant role, because the recognition of patterns often requires a synthesis of the many layers and factors revealed by the various analytical techniques.

It is clear that a range of techniques should be employed in landscape pattern analysis, but it is also helpful to present the results in ways that make comparison as easy as possible. The use of consistent scales, precise terminology and the ability to integrate databases are all crucial, when a variety of disciplines are involved in the complete analysis.

The scale of resolution is important, because the hierarchical scale is dependent on self-similar qualities of patterns and the feedback loops with processes that affect them. This needs to be recognized in any classification or data capture system. Fine scale resolution can always be aggregated to a coarser scale pattern, but not the reverse. Therefore, the type of data and the lowest grain of sample should be very carefully considered at the outset of every analysis.

It is always important to remember why any analysis is being conducted. The method of analysis, the correct type and resolution of data, and the means of presentation, depend on the purpose for which it is being prepared. Many of the indices of patterns are neutral and only serve to illuminate the picture if they are meaningful. They cannot be used, unless a special database is assembled and this requires the reasons for analysis to be carefully considered. All modelling tools are only as good as the data used to fuel them. It is not always possible to gather perfect data sets, so that circumspection must be applied to all results. However, uncertainty can be balanced by the knowledge that natural or cultural processes are not precise and that wide ranges of probabilities exist, within which the answers may lie.

Finally, it is worth noting that objectivity and judgement are not confined to the physical world. When we explored psychology, philosophy and aesthetics, we were still influenced by the laws of physics and biology, reason, judgement and logic. Readers, most comfortable with tangible rocks, plants, animals and houses, should reflect that they also apply perceptual systems, aesthetic judgement and cultural norms to their own environments. The beauty of elegant geometrical constructions, fractal patterns, healthy ecosystems or self-organized ancient landscapes can be appreciated by all, whether we are knowledgeable about them or not. In order to use our intellectual capacities to the full, it is important that we do not ignore the 'creative right side' of the brain as it balances the 'analytical left side' and vice versa.

CHAPTER FIVE

LANDFORM PATTERNS

Introduction

The structure and processes of landform supply the basic underlying layer or substrate upon which all terrestrial life and human activities rely. Landform interacts directly with climate to maintain a continuously dynamic state. However, the rates of change are so slow that for most ecological processes, or considerations for human use, it supplies a stable framework and sets limits or boundary conditions. Areas of ancient shield rocks, where erosion is extremely slow, possess extremely stable geologies. There are places in which dramatic landform processes occur reasonably frequently, notably in regions with active volcanoes.

The Structure of the Earth's Crust

The pattern of all land and the dynamics of all landform creation are derived from the structure and processes at work in the earth's crust. Our understanding of the crustal structure is based on the existence and continued movement of a complete system of plates of solid rocks covering the earth. These structural or tectonic plates 'float' on the molten rocks or *magma* beneath them. They move as a result of new material welling up at some plate junctions causing them to spread apart and by subduction at other junctions where one plate slides beneath another and returns to molten magma.

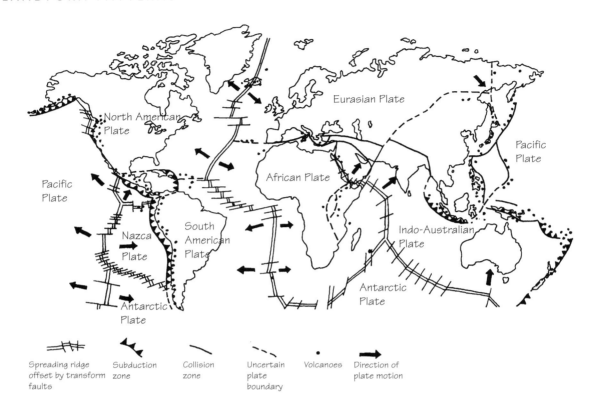

Spreading ridge
offset by transform
faults

Subduction
zone

Collision
zone

Uncertain
plate
boundary

Volcanoes

Direction of
plate motion

A map showing the structure of the tectonic plates that form the earth's crust. The pattern of volcanoes can be seen to coincide mainly with subduction zones where plates are drawn down into the mantle beneath the crust. This structure creates the major patterns of landform and hence determines the possibilities for human use. The crustal plates are examples of cracking patterns.

The pattern of these plates is not regular. Some plates are very large, others are quite small. They have drifted over the earth's surface for billions of years so that continents possess rocks formed from erosion and sedimentation that took place a very long time ago and in a different climate from that found today. Rocks once at the bottom of the sea have been uplifted to become dry land while, elsewhere, land has sunk to become covered by sea.

The pattern of plates determines the location of most of the volcanic regions of the earth, the areas of mountain building, the places where stable ancient shield rocks dominate and the zone of earthquakes. Apart from the shield areas, the other regions mentioned are present at places where tension and compression forces acting at plate junctions are released. These areas are where the most active landform processes occur, but even those operate at very slow rates.

The basic processes which give the land its form are: vulcanism, where magma from beneath the earth's crust is forced to the surface as a volcano or into the subsurface layers as an intrusion; weathering and erosion, where rock is disintegrated by various agencies and transported to be deposited elsewhere; uplift, where earth movements raise, fall, bend or break pieces of the crust. These processes occur to different degrees in different places.

Vulcanism

Volcanoes are distributed in a pattern. They occur mainly at junctions between the earth's tectonic plates, where the movement of one plate beneath another increases heat energy through friction and the pressures created are released by volcanic eruption. Others occur at hot spots in the magma beneath the crust and produce isolated volcanic features. These hot spots remain fairly stationary but as the plates move over them new volcanoes form. Yet others are located where tectonic plates are spreading apart and new molten material wells to the surface.

A chain of volcanoes related to the junction of tectonic plates extends all the way up the range of mountains which lie inland from the Pacific Ocean in western North America. The Cascade Range extends from California northwards to British Columbia. At intervals along its length a procession of volcanoes occur, some active, some dormant. The mountains in which these volcanoes lie are raised like wrinkles as the coast is pushed sideways by the subducting action of the Pacific plate. The volcanoes erupt at various undetermined intervals to relieve the stress this causes.

A map showing the distribution pattern of the volcanoes forming the chain of the Cascade Mountains of the Pacific Northwest of the USA and Canada.

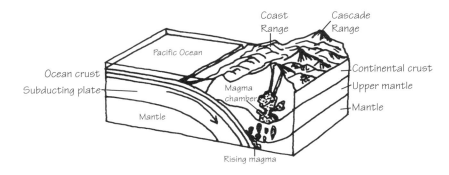

A section through the subduction zone of the tectonic plates that produced the Cascade Range. The melting rock of the plate descending into the mantle produces magma which wells up towards the surface, the pressure being released by the volcanoes. The lateral pressure also produces the Coast Mountain Range.

A view showing (left to right) Mount Rainier, Mount St. Helens and Mount Adams. The three volcanoes rise above the lower elevation areas composed of lava flows, some recent and some old. They are each examples of 'explosion' patterns.

The simple, almost perfect, conical form of a cinder cone, an example of the explosion pattern described by Peter Stevens. This is Mount Edziza in British Columbia, Canada.

The classic volcano shape is a cone, a solid volume of regular, almost symmetrical appearance. This occurs because material emerges from a central point or vent and may be equally distributed all around it. The accumulation of material is densest closest to the vent causing the cone to accumulate. Mount Edziza, a recently formed cinder cone in British Columbia has an almost perfectly conical shape. This is a good example of an explosion pattern as described by Peter Stevens.

The Cascade volcanoes are all examples of more complex stratovolcanoes. These are built up over long periods where each eruption contributes more lava flow or ashes to the height of the mountain, although material may also be lost during the initial stages of an eruption. Lava flows down the side of the volcano following the lines of least resistance, perhaps using channels or hollows lying between previous lava flows or valleys of soft material eroded away by streams. Some of these volcanoes are massive structures and have lost their perfect conical form in favour of an irregular or fractal structure. Their high elevation is cold enough for glaciers to exist, so these volcanoes are also being eroded at the same time as they are being built up.

At the smaller scale, there are patterns created by the cooling of lava flowing from the volcano or vent. In British Columbia the Nis'gaa lava beds are very recent (300 years old) and show a solidified flow pattern complete with ripples or waves. At the Craters of the Moon National Monument in Idaho, one type of lava (pahoehoe or rope lava) can be seen with a wrinkled, wavy surface caused by the thickening consistency (low viscosity) of the cooling lava at the surface flowing more slowly than the hotter lava of higher viscosity beneath. The patterns of repeated curving waves are interesting, because they show the direction of the lava flow and aid appreciation of the process.

The pattern of pahoehoe lava. The surface of the molten lava flow cooled and became less viscous before that beneath and set into this wave pattern, recording the direction of the flow as it did so. Craters of the Moon National Monument, Idaho, USA.

Where lava cools more slowly it can develop larger crystalline structures. Basaltic columns, roughly hexagonal in cross section can be seen in many places, especially the Giant's Causeway in County Antrim, Northern Ireland. These are prime examples of the pattern caused by shrinking and cracking of an elastic material. The hexagonal shape is not perfect, but the prevalence of the 120 degree joints is typical of this pattern and accords with Stevens' observation of cracking patterns in elastic materials.

Where vulcanism produces new rocks and landforms on the surface of the land, igneous rocks also form beneath or within the crust. Intrusions of molten rock into the layers of sedimentary rock may create linear shaped features, where cracks were forced open and filled, or massive lumps of fine grained rock with a large crystalline structure. These may be exposed by later erosion which, being hard, they often resist. The massive granitic landforms of Dartmoor, Exmoor and

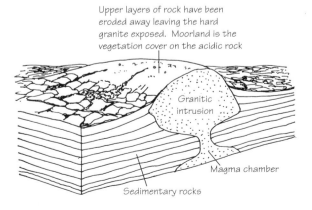

Upper layers of rock have been eroded away leaving the hard granite exposed. Moorland is the vegetation cover on the acidic rock

Granitic intrusion

Magma chamber

Sedimentary rocks

A diagrammatic section through an igneous intrusion such as Dartmoor in Devon, England. A large granite mass or pluton was forced into and through the sedimentary rock. The upper layers were later eroded leaving the solid, dome-like landform which is more resistant to erosion.

Bodmin Moor in Devon and Cornwall in the southwest peninsular of England are examples of these igneous intrusions. They also lack joints or other internal structures, so that weathering and erosion tend not to produce easily defined patterns.

The patterns of vulcanism range from the large distribution of volcanoes related to crustal plate subduction zones, to the structure of the volcanic cones, lava flows and internal rock structure. Apart from the irregular distribution pattern, the other structures all conform to one of the basic pattern types observed by Peter Stevens and explained in Chapter One: explosions, meanders (ripples) and cracking. Aesthetically, the simpler but large scale forms of volcanic cones present a strong contrast with their more irregular surroundings, while the fractal qualities found in the lava flows and other structures provide examples of naturally massive structures. This contrast gives the landscape a sense of strength, in Whiteheadian terms, while the forces of nature expressed by eruptions are a major source of the sublime.

Mountain Building

Since earliest Precambrian times, the sediments from long erosion of the land have accumulated as deep deposits in depressions of the crust formed by their weight. These sediments may be uplifted gradually or quickly (in geological time scale), by movements of the tectonic plates to form new land masses, often of great elevation. Limestone, sandstones, and other hard sedimentary rocks have been uplifted, folded or faulted to create mountains. For example, the world's tallest mountains are presently located at the junctions of plates or other areas related to plate movements. The Himalayas are rising because of the Indian plate moving north eastwards, colliding into and buckling the Asian plate. The basic mountain structures have many patterns within them.

The layering of the sedimentary rocks that once lay horizontally, may be tilted, curved, folded over or faulted and fractured. These movements are due to compressive or tensile stresses applied to the rocks. When folding occurs, the underlying structure shows strongly curving or meandering patterns in cross section. This structure and the relative strengths and weaknesses of the different rocks will affect the subsequent actions of weathering and erosion.

A cross section of the Jura Mountains of France and Switzerland shows the inner structure of folding and faulting which raised the range. Subsequent erosion exploited the jointing and faulting to produce the present mountains. The characteristic meandering pattern can be seen in the strata.

The greatest erosion occurs in the highest mountains because of the greater potential energy and the stronger effect of gravity. The lower temperatures at high elevations also lead to the right conditions for erosional forces like glaciation to occur. Very often the action of these forces will tend to follow the lines of least resistance in the underlying structure such as layers of weaker rock. The Rocky Mountains in western North America are recently elevated examples, still weathering and eroding under the influence of glaciation. Many are composed of limestone, a hard rock, arranged in layers, but also folded and faulted. The resulting forms are irregular and massive with definite directional patterns to them. Their complex form is the result of their internal structure (meanders) overlaid by the pattern of erosion (branching patterns of directional flowing forces such as glaciation) and is strongly fractal.

In contrast, older mountains, such as the eastern American Appalachian or Scottish Caledonian ranges, are ancient rounded stumps of once tall mountains. They tend to be composed of ancient igneous rocks exposed by long periods of erosion. They are not now tall enough for glaciers to form - their last major erosion phase was during the last continental glaciation, which lasted from 30,000 to 10,000 years ago.

In addition to raising sedimentary rocks, the earth forces of pressure and heat may change or metamorphose such rocks into new types, not so obviously layered, but with different internal structures. These rocks may be harder than the original sedimentary ones and result in landforms that retain an extremely angular, jagged appearance following their subsequent erosion. The Purcell Mountains of British Columbia are examples of these, whilst some of the older Caledonian ranges still exhibit irregular forms that have persisted through the ice ages.

Part of the Purcell range of mountains of British Columbia, Canada. Formed from metamorphic rock they have been eroded to produce an extremely broken, jagged structure.

The appearance of mountains provides examples of massive structures also displaying intensity proper, in Whiteheadian terms, so that they possess strength. This is linked to their fractal structure caused by erosion. It is typical for a similar set of forms to be found within a single mountain range, a repetition of the pattern that helps develop a sense of unity. The complex fractal structures also give diversity to the landform and contribute to a sense of mystery. Finally, it is huge landforms that often present a sense of the sublime. Mountains were not appreciated for their beauty until the picturesque movement and Edmund Burke's work on the sublime. Now they are among the most valued types of landscape and are found in parks all over the world.

Moulding the Land

The processes of erosion sculpt the earth into the landforms that provide the substrate for life and the complex structures we find so aesthetically attractive. Weathering, the effect of water solution, freeze/thaw action, chemical solution by acidic water dissolving limestone and some organic agents like plant rooting, gradually works pieces of rock free. The transporting agents of wind, water and ice then move the material away. The transporting agents also wear the rock down, for example, by the abrasive effects of rock or sand carried by them, by air pressure or water pressure of waves in cavities.

There are two main categories of landform created by weathering and erosion: erosive structures and depositional structures.

Erosive Structures

These are the remains of the rock during erosion. Based on Peter Steven's descriptions, the types of patterns created by each of the three main erosional agents are mainly branching, meandering and packing/cracking. Fractal structures are extremely common.

Wind

Wind erosion happens when light particles of material are rolled, bounced or lifted by the wind as it travels across the landscape, sometimes at great speed (such as a sandstorm) and hit exposed rock, gradually wearing it down. Sand composed of hard quartz particles is very effective at doing this.

The landforms created by wind are rounded and smoothed. Weaker strata within layers of rock will erode more easily and can create strikingly sculpted and eery shapes, like human figures or monsters. This type of erosion occurs in deserts, but the resulting landforms can still be seen where former deserts are no longer subject to these forces.

Examples of rocks eroded by wind and the abrasive effects of blown sand. The softer layers in the sedimentary rocks have been exploited and eroded more than the harder portions.

An example is Brimham Rocks in Yorkshire, England where wind eroded landforms present a scene of great curiosity.

Water

Water in its liquid state erodes in three ways:

- Wave action by the sea or large lakes along shore and coastlines
- Running water in rivers or streams
- Water dissolving limestone

Coastline Patterns. Wave action creates the coastlines with their highly complex fractal structures of cliffs, caves, stacks and wave cut platforms. The composition of the rock, whether soft and easily eroded or hard and resistant, or the manner and direction of its bedding, partly determine the pattern of the coastline and the character of its structures. Tilted bedding of larger rocks of different types and strengths may result in a series of ridges containing rock pools, whilst horizontal bedding can lead to vertical cliffs. Weaknesses in some layers leads to undercutting and collapse, leaving stronger sections, which are then eroded further.

The pressure of water and air in the waves thrown against cliffs helps to erode concave sections into caves. The intervening convex sections can become promontories and are eventually eroded away by the expansion of erosion in the caves. Lower strata may erode leaving higher sections intact leading to arches or natural bridges that subsequently collapse leaving a rock tower or stack out at sea. The coastal edge thus describes a series of meandering shapes while the development of bays and promontories relates to aspects of explosion patterns and their outward spread.

All this leads to the highly fractal nature of coastlines with many microhabitats between high and low water for marine wildlife to use. The diversity displayed by the range of sizes of coastal structures and the habitats created by the different rock types and evolving structures make these some of the most aesthetically attractive landscapes. Their

A typical eroded coastline showing a highly indented pattern of bays, promontories, caves, a sea arch and stacks. The fractal character can be observed here. West Coast of Vancouver Island, British Columbia, Canada.

wildness, the force of the elements (wind, waves, tides, storms) also make it a dynamic landscape. Artists have always been drawn to coastal landscapes. Even in heavily urbanized areas, coasts give an immediate sense of wildness and closeness to wilful and uncontrolled nature so that sublime emotions can be felt. The power of the forces at work are so great that attempts to control them with artificial defences usually fail, unless they respond dynamically to the patterns of erosion.

Rivers and Streams. The landforms above sea level provide the first substrate upon which rain or snow falls and melts. The flow of this water both follows a pattern and creates one, a classic example of the unity of pattern and process.

An example of the fractal qualities of heavily branched drainage patterns can be clearly demonstrated in 'badland' landscapes such as those in South Dakota or Arizona in the USA. These consist of deep deposits of fine grained material blown there by the wind (loess) in arid conditions and eroded during the infrequent but powerful rain storms. The weak, clay like structure of the deposits is extremely erodable during such events, and different sizes of landforms appear very similar and regularly structured because of the equality of the distribution of rainfall over the area. Thus the fractal structure is highly developed in the landform pattern. The complexity of eroded landforms combines with the unique colouring of different bands of clay to produce exquisite sculptural landscapes, although they are demanding to live in or travel over: hence the name 'badlands'. In addition, the periodic disturbance of the clay and the harsh growing conditions of the climate make plant colonization a slow process, leaving the bare landforms in their primal state.

The force of water as an erosion agent depends on its quantity and the velocity with which it flows. Geographers have described river systems as juvenile, mature and senile, meaning that the upper reaches have high, youthful energy whilst lower stretches are slower and less dynamic. It is the upper areas that are most erosive because the energy of gravity is greatest even though the total volume of water is smaller.

Whilst some rivers develop a simple pattern of parallel streams, it is most common to find a complex branching pattern. This branching may resemble that of a tree, hence it is referred to as *dendritic* (from the Greek *dendros*, meaning a tree). The pattern has a highly developed structure. There is a strong hierarchy of minor streams to major rivers as the smaller elements coalesce to form bigger ones. The hierarchy can also be seen in the pattern of water catchment basins and the aggregation of basins into larger drainage systems. The dendritic branching pattern is one of the most commonly encountered of the four basic patterns identified by Peter Stevens (see Chapter One).

If each stream leads to an increasingly important stream at every junction, the resulting landform, typified by V shaped valleys, is similarly hierarchical. Small ridges between minor streams are parts of bigger ridges between catchments and this is repeated up to the main mountain or hill ranges that direct complete river systems. The solid volume of the hills or mountains is almost perfectly matched by the open volumes of the valleys, so that on contour maps, valleys can look like ridges and vice versa. This hierarchy makes the landform three dimensionally fractal and has important implications for distribution of vegetation, use by animals and humans, as well as for human

Part of the Badlands of the Painted Desert National Monument, Arizona, USA. The highly dissected structure produced by water erosion shows a complex branching pattern and a highly developed fractal structure.

perception. The repetition of the pattern at varying scales gives a very powerful aid to pattern recognition and to the overall sense of continuity and unity of the landscape. The variety of pattern creates high ecological and visual diversity and also provides a major framework within which other natural pattern processes can work.

Dendritic river systems are most developed where glaciation has not affected the landscape so that continuous water erosion has taken place. Tropical areas often show this pattern best, although the dense vegetation can reduce some of the erosive power of heavy rain.

The dendritic pattern can be altered where the erodability of the rock varies due to different strata being composed of rocks of different strengths. Hard layers can lead to waterfall formation, whilst in other places the V shaped valley may take on a more step-like appearance. The underlying rock structure thus interacts with the erosion pattern to produce a more complex result.

Mature rivers are those in the middle stretches. The mature stages combine the erosive characteristics of the juvenile stages with the deposition of the senile stages. The river often erodes a wider valley with a flatter floor and takes up a meandering shape.

The Skeena River in British Columbia, Canada. This is a well developed, meandering river confined to a distinct valley, originally cut by glaciers. The limitations placed by the valley cause the river to maintain a very active character. Braided streams, gravel shoals and eroding bluffs keep the river structure unstable. The gravel shoals show a repeated, typical shape, reflecting the flow of the water.

The meander is another of the basic forms of nature, and is similar to branching patterns in the balance of total length and space filling properties. It has a definite character: its sinuous form is a natural line that is often to be found in scenes people find aesthetically attractive. It is akin to the 'serpentine line of beauty' of early landscape designers, such as William Kent who worked in England in the 18th century.

The meanders progressively work their way down the valley, eroding the lower parts of the outside of bends and depositing material on the slower moving inner parts. River meanders all show the same relationship, where the frequency and extent of the meander loop is proportionate to the width of the river. Rivers rarely run straight for more than ten times their width, the radius of bends is usually 2-3 times the width and the wavelength (the distance between the same points on adjacent meanders) around 7-10 times the width. In the mature phase of a river the space available for the meander pattern is often limited by the landform (pattern having an effect on process).

Where a valley is already defined and uplift of the earth's crust then takes place, the river cannot find a new route. The uplift raises the height of the river thus giving it greater energy. It responds by eroding faster, creating an incised valley or in extreme cases a canyon or gorge. This can be seen in the breathtaking splendour of the Grand Canyon in Arizona, USA, where the uplifting earth caused the Colorado River to incise through innumerable horizontal strata of rock.

The movement of meanders and the flow of currents within them are closely related. The spiralling nature of the current is responsible for eroding material in one place and its deposition in another and drives the downward movement of the meander pattern.

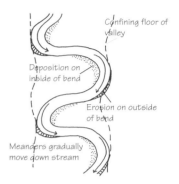

The Grand Canyon in Arizona, USA, is a highly dissected, fractally patterned landscape. The broad stepping pattern is the result of the erosion of rock strata of different hardness whilst the lateral fretting is the result of secondary erosion leading to the accumulation of talus fans.

In terms of pattern, the Colorado River already displayed a meandering route, which it preserved as it cut downwards. Harder strata resisted or slowed erosion, resulting in more vertical cliffs and ledges upon which eroded material built up. Eventually these collapsed and formed buttresses at the base of the cliffs. Along the side walls irregular indentations occur at roughly similar intervals. These side valleys each have a deposit of rock debris or talus of conical form at their mouth so that a system of buttressed walls and sloping debris fans has been created, which is repeated many times.

Once again, this exhibits classical fractal geometry of repeated structures at varying scales, producing a strong sense of unity expressed by the continuity and similarity of forms, rhythmically spaced at related or repeated intervals both horizontally and vertically. The whole structure of this landform is thus a direct expression of process on pattern.

The pattern also demonstrates massiveness (or presence of variety of detail with effective contrast) and intensity proper (or comparative magnitude), both qualities discussed in Chapter Three in relation to the aesthetic theories of Alfred North Whitehead. Thus the landscape of the Grand Canyon possesses strength. Finally the views from the edge of the canyon can induce a sensation of the sublime in an observer; that emotion felt in the presence of vast landscapes, where there is also the sense of danger and the feeling that we are insignificant beings when compared to the forces of nature.

Limestone Topography

The third type of landform is created by acidic water dissolving limestone. This scenery, called karst after a location in Croatia, includes many underground structures such as caves or tunnels whose roofs occasionally collapse to produce gorges such as the Cheddar Gorge in Somerset, England.

On the surface of the rock this chemical effect results in an expanse of fissures, which then enlarge to form wide cracks. Known as clints and grykes or limestone pavement it can produce a variety of complex microclimates. One well known example is the Burren in County Clare, Ireland, where the rock structure has influenced the land use and landscape over many centuries.

The Burren (from the Irish word for a stony place) is a landscape of around 250 square kilometres dominated by bare limestone of thicknesses up to 780 metres. The rock occurs in horizontal or slightly dished layers, much as it was formed in warm shallow seas during the Carboniferous era 340 million years ago. The layers represent various phases of deposition and many of them are exposed as a series of terraces stepping up and down the dome shaped landform. The landform shape was exposed by erosion, in particular ice movement, which removed the last vestiges of accumulated shale overlays. Clay layers remain to the southwest, where its edge coincides with a major

line of potholes in the limestone. Thus the present upper layer of the limestone is the final layer of rock deposited during Carboniferous times.

The limestone is not only layered horizontally, it is also jointed vertically, broken by linear cracks in very close parallel arrangements. Once exposed to the atmosphere, weathering by water solution quickly begins to erode and open these cracks, excavating them into gullies and eventually the deep narrow crevices called grykes. As the weathering proceeds, the sides of the crevices become undulating and erode into bays and promontories; the irregular shape becomes exaggerated and occurs at different sizes so that a highly fractal surface pattern develops. The weathering may also selectively attack some of the limestone layers to create lateral grooves on the walls of the crevices. Eventually the upper layers of rock are completely cut through and become detached leaving a rubble accumulation on the surface. The pattern of weathering is multi-scaled, ranging from the major joints, which may run for hundreds of metres, to the fine detail of crevice sculpting, some few centimetres across.

The landscape of the Burren, a limestone area in County Clare, Ireland. The rounded, ice eroded landforms of bare rock, pale grey in colour, rise above green valleys.

The detailed eroded, fractal pattern of the limestone pavement. Acidic water solution exploiting cracks in the limestone has produced this complex, interdigitated structure.

Some of the higher hill tops were exposed above later glaciation (called nunataks) for part of the time, and received no drift, remaining bare and covered with rock fragments to this day. The glaciers in the valleys produced steeper slopes or scarps up to the line where the summits were exposed. Hence the eroded and weathered surface of the Burren was once mostly overlaid by glacial material and colonized by vegetation. Early farmers' flocks browsed and overgrazed the sparse cover allowing the thin drift deposits to wash away and expose the limestone to weathering. In summary, rainwater erosion of rock tends to produce rounded sculpture whereas the sea creates sharper, more angular shapes.

Ice

Ice has been the major force for erosion in large parts of higher latitudes over the last 2-5 million years, ending 10,000 years ago (the Pleistocene Epoch). It continues to erode high mountains and some lands such as Iceland, Greenland and Antarctica. The erosive power of ice is very great, ranging from the widespread effects of continental ice sheets, many hundreds of metres thick to major and minor valley glaciers, gouging out large valleys as well as eroding rock surfaces at the small scale.

An aerial view of the mountains of Greenland, showing typical erosional landforms. U shaped valleys, the knife edge ridges where the bowl-shaped corries cut back to one another and pyramidal peaks produce the angular and concave patterns.

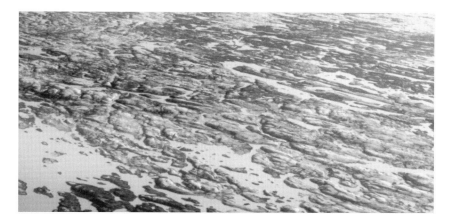

An aerial view of part of the Canadian tundra shows a distinct directional pattern, the result of the movement of continental ice sheets. The ridge and valley pattern is partly erosional and partly depositional. Some of the ridges are drumlins, composed of ground up rock and boulders dumped by the ice.

At a grand scale, the interaction of ice sheet movement across the ancient Precambrian rocks of the vast Canadian Shield left behind an undulating topography. From 36,000 feet/11,076 metres high, travelling in a transcontinental airliner, the view shows a definite grain or directional pattern to large areas of this tundra, land where the subsoil remains permanently frozen. The pattern partly reflects the directional flow of the ice and the underlying rock structure, where weaknesses have been exploited by the ice. This erosive landform also contains depositional patterns of drumlins (linear deposits of eroded material). This extensive pattern has had a major effect on the drainage pattern and microclimate affecting vegetation distribution.

In order to see the way in which the process of glaciation works under different conditions, such as latitude, elevation and aspect, it is useful to examine an area where all of these variables can be observed. Such a place is the Cascade Mountains running from California northwards to British Columbia which were discussed earlier in relation to landform creation.

The Cascade Mountains contain many peaks high enough to accumulate sufficient snow to compress into a hard packed form that eventually turns into granular ice, under the pressure of its own weight, and starts to flow downhill under gravity. For example, Mount Rainier supports twenty six glaciers, each of which is the source of a major river in the region. The glaciers can easily erode the less consolidated material of these stratovolcanoes.

The pattern of glaciation varies with latitude and aspect, well illustrated in the position of the firn line, the elevation on a glacier where snow accumulates in rates equal to those of ablation (dispersing and melting) and above which snow builds up to force a glacier to flow. The summit (10,457 feet/3217 m) of Lassen Peak in California only supports a few snow patches through the summer, compared with Mount St Helens, some 800 feet/246 m lower but 370 miles further north, where the summit remains capped with snow all year round, supporting five glaciers.

A view towards the glaciers on Mount Rainier in Washington State, USA. The glaciers carve down into the material of this stratovolcano releasing debris washed down the valley. The eroded structure may become the route down which lava flows if and when the volcano erupts again.

The zone below the firn line is where snow melt is greater than its accumulation. Glaciers flowing beneath this line gradually melt away, their snouts advancing or retreating according to fluctuations in the climate. These effects are known as ablation, and the zone where this starts increases in altitude with decreasing latitude ranging from 9,000 feet/2769 metres for Mount Shasta in California, to 3500 feet/1077 metres on Mount Rainier further north. This is because the lower sun angle in northern latitudes produces less solar energy to melt the ice.

Thus, on the shady northern faces of mountains in the northern hemisphere glaciers have tended to persist longer and extend further downhill. The firn line locally descends, and with greater net snow accumulation, the glaciers erode more deeply. This often results in north facing slopes being more significantly eroded and containing more corries (small bowl shaped valleys or hollows) than south facing slopes, with corresponding effects on subsequent depositional landforms and vegetation patterns. This pattern is most clearly observed on an isolated conical peak such as a large volcano.

The eroded landforms produced by glaciation are typically angular and jagged, such as the pyramidal shaped peaks, where several corrie glaciers have eroded all sides of a mountain, the nunataks exposed above ice sheets and subject to weathering from freezing action, or the knife edged ridges called aretes.

Glaciated valleys are usually characterized by a U shaped cross section, compared with the V shape of rivers. Side valleys of former tributaries may be cut off and left hanging above the new deeper, straighter valley; spurs that lay between the tributaries of former winding valleys of river origin may also be cut off or truncated when the valley glaciers straighten out the valley. Steep cliffs also occur on the near vertical sides of some valleys where the spurs have been cut off.

There is an interesting relationship between the pattern of erosion landform produced by glaciation and the underlying geology. Rock types tend to leave either more rounded or more angular landforms, depending on the ease with which they can be eroded. Rocks with many joints (cracks or fissures) can be gouged out by the ice more easily than rocks with fewer joints and tend to develop more broken, angular shapes. Very hard rocks, such as the massive structureless igneous intrusions, resist erosion compared with the surrounding sedimentary rocks and may end up more rounded in shape.

A good example of the different landforms created by these effects can be found in the Cuillin Mountains on the Isle of Skye in Scotland. Here there are two distinct igneous geologies, the so-called Red Cuillin, composed of hard gabbro, and the Black Cuillin, made of softer basalt. The Red Cuillins are characterized by simple, rounded, convex forms whereas the Black Cuillins are angular, jagged and composed of concave forms arising from the abundance of corries.

The Great Glen in Scotland was formed by glaciers exploiting a weakness in the earth's crust, a major fault line. Thus, ice gouges and erodes at scales ranging from the largest fractures to the smallest rock jointing. The striations or scratches on the sides of rocks along the direction of ice movement are miniature versions of the Great Glen or the grain across the Canadian tundra.

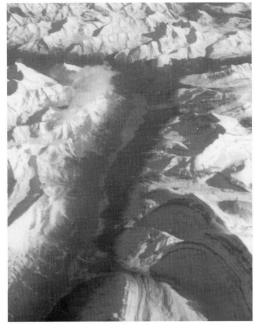

An aerial view of glaciated topography in the Rocky Mountains of Alberta, Canada. The distinctively U shaped valley is now colonized by forest. Also visible are numerous corries, knife edge ridges or aretes and pyramidal peaks.

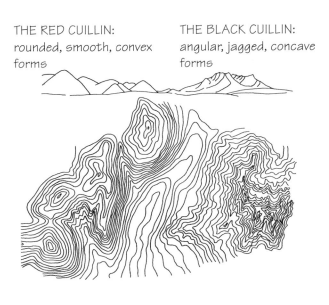

THE RED CUILLIN: rounded, smooth, convex forms

THE BLACK CUILLIN: angular, jagged, concave forms

A diagrammatic sketch and topographic map of the Cuillins on the Isle of Skye in Scotland. The convex, smooth, rounded forms of the harder gabbro Red Cuillin contrast with the convex, angular jagged forms of the softer, basaltic Black Cuillin.

Other types of distinct ground patterns can be created during glacial periods in areas subject to intense cold or permafrost in the soil. This patterned ground appears as polygons or circles and persists long after the tundra conditions have disappeared. It results from repeated freezing and thawing of the upper surface zone, in permafrost conditions, during winter and summer seasons. This causes a heaving of the surface which gradually moves larger boulders or rocks outwards leaving finer sediments inside.

On flatter ground a pattern of rough circles or polygons results, reflecting the close packing type of pattern phenomena. On slopes the effect of gravity converts polygons into stripes, terraces or steps. These persist where they are not covered by vegetation or deep soil. A fine example occurs in Oregon in the USA, in the east area of the Cascade Range and in parts of the Columbia River Gorge. The close packed polygons are evident on flatter or gently sloping areas whilst the striped effect is more distinct on steeper slopes. The drier climate has inhibited the growth of vegetation on these features thus preventing them from being covered by soil and enabling them to be seen to this day.

The type of geometry exhibited by all these landforms is fractal. The repetition of form at decreasing scales and the interlocking landform structures can only be explained or described in this way. Also characteristic is the complexity of directions, where continental scale movements were overlaid by localized reactions to earlier drainage patterns, fault lines, rock structures and aspect variation.

We can see the landform patterns where they are not covered by vegetation. The edges are strongly defined, making it easy to perceive the structure and form the primal sketch, as we saw in Chapter Two. Our aesthetic response to some of the glaciated landforms can be one of the sublime where we feel powerless in the face of such forces as glaciers. Many landforms possess massiveness and intensity proper, in Whiteheadian terms, combining strength with unity as described in the section on mountain building.

Patterned ground occurring in an area up above the Columbia Gorge in Washington State, USA. On the slopes the characteristic polygonal shapes have become more irregular under the force of gravity. The coarser, rocky patches remain unvegetated. These are examples of close packing pattern.

Depositional structures

The same agents that erode landforms are responsible for depositing the eroded material elsewhere. A huge amount finds its way into the sea or into lakes, but much also remains on land to create new landforms, some stable and some unstable or temporary.

Wind

The main depositional landforms created by wind action are sand dunes. These are semi-permanent features and need several conditions to be fulfilled in order to occur:

- Wind tending to blow persistently in one direction
- Wind speeds high enough to blow sand
- An area where sand can be amassed in sufficient quantities

Normally sand dunes are associated with deserts, typically the Sahara or Arabian deserts, but they can occur anywhere the conditions are met, such as along coasts, where the sea washes up sand that can be blown on shore or inland when dry.

The size of sand particles is critical to enable them to be blown. Small sizes tend to stick, retain moisture or form a smooth surface of low friction and are difficult to disperse. Larger sizes are too heavy to be picked up by the wind. The normal size is 0.1 - 0.5 mm (0.004 - 0.02 inch) in diameter. They move either as dust clouds suspended in the air or by bouncing along (saltation). Dune areas can be of one or a combination of six basic patterns:

- Parallel linear (seifs)
- Parallel wavy/crescentic
- Isolated crescentic (barchans)
- Star or radial
- Parabolic or U shaped
- Sheets or stringers

The pattern of dunes and their progress in waves depend on the characteristics of wind such as direction, strength and persistence, as well as the type of ground surface and the amount of sand. Radial dunes do not move much because of the constantly changing wind direction that creates their form. Barchans occur where sand supply is limited. Parabolic dunes occur in slightly moister conditions, where the side arm becomes anchored by vegetation, but the central part keeps moving.

The general wave form of dunes is consistent with one of the basic pattern types - that of meanders/waves, which are seen so frequently in nature. Dune formation is a classic example of pattern following

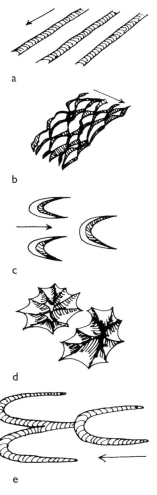

The various types of sand dune pattern: a) Parallel linear (seif); b) Parallel wavy/crescentic; c) Isolated crescentic (barchan); d) Star or radial; e) Parabolic or U shaped.

process (i.e. the wind), but also the process being affected by the form of the ground surface and the supply of sand. The forms also influence the process of plant colonization and succession.

Water

Rivers erode material in their upper stretches and deposit some of it in their lower reaches. Some may be left behind, as meanders gradually move downstream. Additional material builds up on the outside of meanders, as gravel or shingle banks. Levees, natural embankments, may raise the river above the general flood plain; at the river mouth new land can be created from material deposited, where it flows into the sea or a lake. The river may also separate into many channels or braids in areas where its slower speed is inadequate to keep the large quantities of coarse grained eroded material moving. These braided streams vary in size and exhibit classical fractal form.

One of the main depositional landforms to develop in relation to some rivers is the delta. Most deltas form where sediment discharges into the sea or lakes, in places where the currents are weak and where wave energy is low. This means that the sediments are not dispersed but are able to accumulate in one place, building up in layers until they break the surface of the water.

An example of a delta where two rivers empty into an inlet on the west coast of Vancouver Island in British Columbia, Canada. The river flow breaks up into a number of branches and creates a complex pattern of mudbanks both above and below the water surface.

In lakes the structure of deltas or deltaic forms may be simple. Fresh water meets fresh water and mixes easily. The sediments gradually build up and the stream flows over earlier deposits to discharge into the lake. Such deltas are often found at the head or along the sides of ribbon lakes found in glaciated valleys. At the head of the lake a braided stream may discharge, giving a more complex pattern. Along the sides, the fast streams from hanging valleys may be loaded with coarse sediment, gravel or shingle and create substantial deposits, as such material cannot be moved far once it reaches the stiller waters of the lake.

Ocean deltas are more complex. Normally, the sediment is much finer, being silty in character. Fresh water laden with sediment is lighter than salt water and this also affects the way in which these deltas form. Hence, the lighter discharging sediment may flow over the salt water surface for some way before gradually sinking; it may disperse through the heavier salt water at gradually reducing velocities, or it may slide down the face of the delta. As the sediment increases, the river is forced to flow across it at a very low gradient causing much of the fresh sediment to build up as natural embankments or levees leaving swampy ground between them. The river may also start to branch into distributary channels each bordered by levees, possibly caused by gravel bars building up across a channel forcing floodwater to divert and to cut a new channel. Such 'bird's foot' deltas show all the characteristics of branching patterns described in Chapter One. They also have a fractal structure and this gives them the massiveness which, when combined with vegetation, produces landscapes full of coherence, complexity and mystery.

Glacial Depositional Landforms

The erosional processes described for glaciation also produce enormous quantities of sediments of a wide range of particle size, ranging from huge boulders to very fine powder. These become deposited during and after glaciation by the ice sheets or glaciers and by the melting waters flowing from them.

Deposited material left by retreating ice sheets or valley glaciers tends to have a randomly mixed internal structure, but occurs in predictable places due to the glacier's structure and its movement cycles. Such material is usually described as morainic. For example, terminal moraines are made from material pushed along in front of the glacier and dumped when it retreats, whilst lateral moraines collect along the sides of the glacier where it abuts the valley side. They are often perched high up on the steep valley slopes and can be unstable when the glacier vacates the valley. Median moraines occur when two glaciers join up and the two adjacent lateral moraines from each converge and are carried on the ice in the middle of the combined glacier. Moraines have smaller scale rounded and smooth landforms unlike the angular erosional forms, and can impound water to form lakes.

Sheets of ice or large glaciers also have material within or under them. Large deposits of moraines may be left as an ice sheet melts in situ. Drumlins are rounded hills of this material, often left in clusters or groups, sometimes known as 'basket of eggs' topography. The shape of each drumlin may be elongated in the direction of the ice movement. Large areas of the landscape can be covered in drumlin fields. Parts of Ireland have extensive drumlin landscapes where the characteristic repeated, rounded knolls display distinct drainage and soil patterns, creating a very intimate, small scale landscape that combines coherence, complexity and mystery. The pattern of a drumlin landscape is an example of the close packing pattern type described in Chapter One.

Water borne deposits from glaciers are internally sorted into layers of sand and gravel. This is because the seasonal cycle of freezing and melting controls the flow of water from under a glacier and thus its capacity to move heavy stones. Layered material can also build up inside tunnels within the base of the glacier or ice sheet. When the ice melts these are exposed as linear mounds called eskers. They also follow the direction of ice movement.

Sediment washed off the ice surface can form low, irregular ridges like a cock's comb. These are called kames, and may occur in large areas. Although eskers and kames may resemble moraines, they are different, because of their layered structure.

As the glaciation period ended, sometimes sheet ice broke up into large blocks that melted slowly and became surrounded by sands or gravels washed over and around them. Once the blocks of ice finally melted they left holes, called kettle holes. These usually fill with water to form small ponds or lakes, many of which eventually fill with aquatic vegetation to become bogs and marshes.

Depositional landforms also differ in their hydrological characteristics. The finest powdery or clay like particles in the moraines can develop very impeded drainage whilst the layered, coarser textured fluvioglacial structures (eskers, kames) can be very well drained. Some larger areas of sandy material washed from the snout of large glaciers,

Drumlins provide the pattern of landform in this part of Ireland. The repeated, close packed pattern of rounded forms create a small scale enclosed landscape.

called outwash plains, can dry out sufficiently for wind action to form dune structures. Some of the finest grained material may also blow away to build up elsewhere.

Thus, in mountainous terrain, a complete depositional landscape develops in the lower parts whereas erosional structures tend to predominate in the higher elevations. This leads to a distinct contrast in patterns between the angular concave structures high up and the smoother, rounded forms lower down. This contrast in two patterns exhibiting massiveness, in Whiteheadian terms, combines with the intensity proper to give strength and thus the major form of beauty. This can act together with the sense of the sublime to give powerful aesthetic qualities.

A final example of landform resulting from glaciation is the effect of the release of the weight of ice that pressed down on the land. This weight was sufficient to depress the earth's crust and even now, some 10,000 years after the ice sheets melted, the land is still rising in these places. In Sweden, some interesting and characteristic landforms can be seen in two places. The area of the 'High Coast', north of Sundsvall on the east coast is rising at a rate of a few centimetres a year. Thus, rocks that were at one time submerged under the sea are now high above sea level. The wave action and washing by water has left the bedrock completely bare with only a few large boulders remaining on the surface.

On the west coast around Kongshavn, north of Goteborg, the land is also rising but at a slower rate than the High Coast. However, the coastal scenery is quite distinctive. Clean rocky ridges run inland from the sea, bare and smooth, except for a few scrubby trees growing in cracks. Between these ridges, flat areas of silty soil have developed, where crops are now grown. The edges of the fields carry woodland. There is a definite east-west grain to this pattern due to the rock structure and the direction of the ice movement that eroded the ridges and valleys. The lack of glacial deposits covering the rocks is due to their erosion by the sea, so revealing the 'skeleton' of the landscape.

The broad expanse of sand forms this outwash plain at the foot of the large glacier complex to the south of the Vatnajokull Ice Cap in Iceland. The sand can blow into dune formations.

The coastline of southwest Sweden where the land is rising out of the sea. The rock ridges are bare of soil whilst mudflats gradually emerge between them to provide agricultural land. Settlement occupies the narrow zone between sea and rock.

Relevance of Landform Patterns

From this brief excursion into the study of geology and geomorphology, we have identified the essential relationships between landform patterns and processes which produce the underlying structure of the landscape. The plate structure of the earth's crust and the existence of patterns of volcanoes and mountain ranges give the macroscale landform. Interactions with the climate and the agents of weathering, erosion and deposition over the eons provide the landform and rock types suitable for colonization by plants and animals. As a result of the slow pace of landform creation by these processes we can, for practical purposes, treat the landform as a static, stable base.

Many of the more dramatic landforms invoke significant aesthetic responses within us. Massive mountains, canyons, cliffs, waterfalls, meandering rivers and rugged coasts all tend to display strongly fractal structure that fits well with the aesthetic theories of Alfred North Whitehead and lead to the qualities of coherence, complexity and mystery. Landforms and the powers at work to create them can also produce feelings of awe or the sublime. Partly because of this, such landforms have often been chosen for preservation as parts of national parks. Some landforms such as mountains and rivers have been identified by Simon Schama, a British historian, as 'archetypal landscapes' of deep cultural significance. Hence an understanding of their character is of direct relevance to the perception of the landscape that we explored in Chapters Two and Three.

Many landforms also affect the way we have tried to manage or utilize nature. We have tried to predict volcanic eruptions, control the movement of great rivers, dam deep valleys or quarry away mountainsides. Nowhere are people more vulnerable than when living next to active volcanoes or along the flood plains of rivers, yet the attraction of fertile soils has meant that people have been willing to take such risks since time immemorial. Later in the chapter we will explore ways of working within the limits imposed by some of the forces unleashed by landform and climate. We will consider how the urge to control rivers or coastal erosion can be replaced by more harmonious and efficient approaches using a deeper understanding of landform patterns and processes.

In the following chapter we will explore in some depth, the ways in which landform structure affects ecological processes, while in Chapter Seven we will discover how landform has affected the human use of the landscape. The next task is to consider means of analysing landform patterns and processes as a precursor to design.

Analysing Landform Patterns

As the landform is the substrate for all other natural processes and human activities, it is logical to begin with its analysis. The term landform means, literally, the 'form of the land', as we observe its three dimensional shape. Our analysis of landform can be divided into structure and composition. Structure refers to the way its component parts are put together and the results of erosion, whilst composition refers to the types of rocks, their chemical makeup, relative hardness or resistance, origin and duration.

Geology and Landform

Geological maps and descriptions provide the basis for any analysis, but they must be used with care. Maps produced by various national geological surveys use a range of set map scales or dimensions to represent actual measurements of varying degrees of accuracy on the ground. What is shown may be too superficial or coarse for some levels of analysis or too detailed or fine for others. For analysis of smaller areas of land (below 1000 ha) the solid rocks may not vary. Surface deposits may be more variable and soil even more so. At scales of 1000 to tens of thousands of hectares, the scale of geological information provided by existing maps may be adequate or can be simplified into broader categories for the purposes of landscape categorization.

One valuable result of analysis at a regional scale is to produce a map of physiographic units which can be used as a basis for the interpretation of many other patterns (see Landscape Assessment in Chapter Seven).

The main questions for any analysis should relate to its purpose. In the context of this book, we wish to deduce the underlying interactions between pattern and process. In terms of the geology these are:

- The relative importance of the solid rocks to the surface deposits. In many areas the superficial deposits of fluvial, aeolian or glacial origin are deep enough and exert sufficient influence to render the nature of the underlying rocks irrelevant.
- The places where significant changes, especially abrupt ones occur in the solid geology. These include major discontinuities, such as where limestone suddenly changes to sandstone or metamorphic

rock causing major effects on chemical composition, soil creation, erosion and the resulting topography. Fault lines are also important for the same reason.

- The places where the rock is prone to weathering over the time scale of the processes being considered. Soft rocks may be eroded quickly by water as in the Badlands of the USA or along river valleys.
- The examples of unique geological formations that have exerted a major influence on the geomorphology. Igneous intrusions, volcanic plugs and lava flows can determine the structure and the character of a landscape. The city of Edinburgh in Scotland is a prime example of this (see Chapter Seven).
- The examples of geological formation, often deep down in the earth such as oil, coal or minerals of economic value which have led to certain settlement or industrial patterns.

Maps of superficial deposits may already include references to the types and origins of landforms that comprise them, such as moraines, eskers, lacustrine or lake sediments and so on. If the depositional landforms are sufficiently large in size, they will register on the topographic map as contours, depending on the map scale. The correlation between landform and depositional origin is important for later analysis of ecological and cultural patterns. Depending on the scale of analysis, it may be useful to delineate the main groupings of landform types, such as kame-and-kettle, basket-of-eggs, estuarine structures or flood plain morphology, as these groupings may define later subdivisions of landscape character and ecological types.

Erosive structures carved out of the solid geology will display a number of forms, partly dependent on the characteristics of the parent rock. There will also be numerous places where the topographic map correlates with the map of geological structures when overlaid, because the weaknesses provided by jointing, faults or discontinuities are exploited by the erosive agent and show up as variations in topography. There will also be places where rock changes produce no noticeable alteration in the topography, soil or vegetation and therefore these can be ignored.

Landform Shape and Structure

The shape of the landform needs to be described. Landform shape is important because of the wider correlation with hydrology, vegetation patterns and aesthetics. The landform can be viewed as a series of solids or voids, such as a conical volcano, a pyramidal peak, a deep canyon or intersecting V shaped valley system. However, it is more practical to consider them as surfaces, because that is how they act and that is what we tend to perceive (see Chapter Two). The discussion on geometry in Chapter One noted that a landform exhibits aspects of fractal geometry. Hence, surfaces vary from the planar dimension (2D) into the almost three dimensional (3D). It is the degree of variation that needs to be described and, if possible, measured at a range of scales.

Landform surfaces can be analysed using a perspective view, a photograph or a topographic map of contours. A topographic model can also be used, but usually the scale is too coarse to show the fine detail of surface modelling. Topographic maps are also limited by the map scale. However, the topographic map will provide a broad division into areas with similar landform character. This can be done by eye. For example, the contrast between steep, fretted, eroded slopes and undulating valley bottoms and rounded, convex shapes can be identified and mapped. This segments the area for more refined analysis as follows.

Analyse the fractal dimensions of contour lines selected from various places on the sampled area, by measuring the degree to which the length measured in detail is greater than the most direct line between two points along a sample segment. A sketch showing a typical contour line will give its 'fractal signature'. A jagged line could have the same fractal dimensions as a curving one and so the quality of the shape can also be indicated by a diagram. This gives a measure of the convolution of the line and thus of the slope as a whole. If the dimension is similar for analyses of long, coarse grained segments as for shorter, finer grained ones then the landform is truly fractal.

Some landforms will display an obvious fractal dimension at one or two scales, but not at more. This is more likely to be the case with some depositional structures than with erosional ones, due to the operation of the processes that formed them. For example, a moraine may show some fractal aspects of the main shape and one level of detail of topographic subtlety whereas a valley eroded by water will tend to have many more layers of detail, each repeating the pattern of branches.

Analyse the degree of convexity or concavity of landform based on its degree of positive (convex) or negative (concave) curvature. This can

Two sets of contour lines with the same fractal dimension (degree of variation from straight) but very different character or 'signature'.

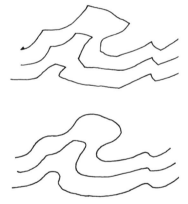

Valhalla Provincial Park in British Columbia, Canada has distinct landform character. The upper portions are highly eroded and jagged in shape as the result of weathering and erosion taking place, including corrie glaciers, while the lower slopes are smoother and more rounded from the erosion by a valley glacier and the moraine deposits left behind.

be performed using a special software programme called 'Convex'. This bases the analysis on a digital elevation or terrain model (DEM or DTM). The scale of resolution is dependent on the DTM, say a 20 m, 50 m or 100 m grid (or wider range). The shape is depicted best by a secondary series of contours, red for convexities and green for concavities (using complementary advancing/receding colours to emphasize the two variables). The greater the degree of curvature the greater the number of contours is produced (p. 236, Fig. 8).

A landform analysis based on the visual design principle of 'visual forces in landform' provides a very useful depiction of the underlying character as well as the hierarchy of the structure. It relates also to the way we tend to perceive landforms (the eye being drawn down ridges and up into valleys) and thus suggests a link to patterns that could be used in a design. Using a topographic map, the idea is to depict ridges as red arrows which follow them downward and to show valleys as green arrows running up them. The main way of doing this is by eye, looking for the stopping and starting points of these structures and the places where ridges or valleys branch off. The hierarchy of major and minor structures is depicted by drawing arrows thicker or finer relative to each other.

It is very useful to project these arrows into perspective so as to relate them to the way we view landform surfaces. This can be achieved using the same methods on a photograph with an acetate overlay or by digitizing the arrows on the topographic map, so that they can be draped over a DTM and viewed from any angle. The resolution once more depends on the degree of refinement of the contours. Some landforms are very dissected with many arrows, others are simpler, reflecting their degree of fractality. It is possible for a computer programme to define the 'lines of force', but in many ways the manual method works best, because an element of learning about the landform is involved, and of judgement in deciding what to include and what to leave out. This partly depends on the ultimate purpose of the analysis and the detail required in any ensuing design (p. 236, Fig. 9).

Examples of landform analysis:

Hazelton Mountain, British Columbia, Canada

The area lies in north-central British Columbia and contains the catchments of two major creek systems, McCully Creek and Date Creek, which flow into the Kispiox River, a tributary of the Skeena. The landform ranges from the wide valley floor of Kispiox River up to high (3000 m) mountains that retain isolated remnants of corrie glaciers and perennial snow patches. A study of the broad structure shows three distinctive macro-units: the once heavily glaciated valley floor, comprising flood plain characteristics of an undulating terrain of old channels and fluvio-glacial remnants; lower slopes of the mountain, generally rounded or bench like, following the effects of valley

glaciation with morainic and other deposits; the upper mountain, deeply sculpted by a series of valley and corrie glaciers with pyramidal peaks and perched glacial deposits on steep slopes. The underlying geology is of folded Triassic sedimentary and igneous rocks. The main peak, Hazelton Mountain, being formed from a granitic intrusion, has a more dominant height and angular, sculpted profile.

A sample of contour lines shows the difference between the landform zones, which are further subdivided. The simpler, less fractal lower slopes contrast with the strongly fractal upper slopes, as do their fractal signatures.

The contours of concavity and convexity show the pronounced angular form of the mountain and the deeply incised side creeks, whereas the lower portions show series of convexities of low emphasis.

The landform analysis emphasizes the intersecting valley/peak formations, with multiple branching and interdigitations (like intersecting fingers) to several hierarchical scales. The lower areas are less complex and are dominated by convex forms with undefined ridges and a few incised valleys. Thus the three dimensional pattern directly reflects the processes that originated the landforms. We will return to this example in order to analyse the relationships between ecological patterns and processes and landform. The landform analysis also relates to the landscape character analysis discussed in Chapter Four.

A view of part of Hazelton Mountain in British Columbia, Canada, used in a major landscape analysis project.

Examples of different contours and fractal signatures from Hazelton Mountain.

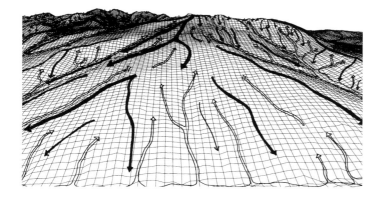

The visual force analysis from part of Hazelton Mountain. This was prepared from analysis of contours and draped over the digital terrain model to show it in perspective. (Reproduced by permission of the British Columbia Ministry of Forests)

A view towards the ridge landform at Vuokatti in central Finland used in landform analysis.

Vuokattinvaara, Finland

This is a pronounced ridge feature in central Finland analysed using the same techniques. The first layer to study is the solid geology that lies beneath the landscape. The rocks are pre-Quaternary in age, composed of distinct areas of basement gneiss, granite, quartzite, schists and various other minor components. All are hard, resistant rocks. When overlaid by a topographic map, a clear relationship stands out between the highest ridge line running north to south and the area of quartzite, one of the most resilient rocks.

The next thing to consider is the superficial geology. This comprises various depositional features of glacial origin as well as the shoreline structures of former glacial lakes and the Baltic Sea in prehistoric times.

The geology of the Vuokatti area in Finland. a) Solid geology, showing the hard quartzite ridge. b) Contours, showing the major ridge line. c) Glacial remains correlated to the movement of ice and the geology.

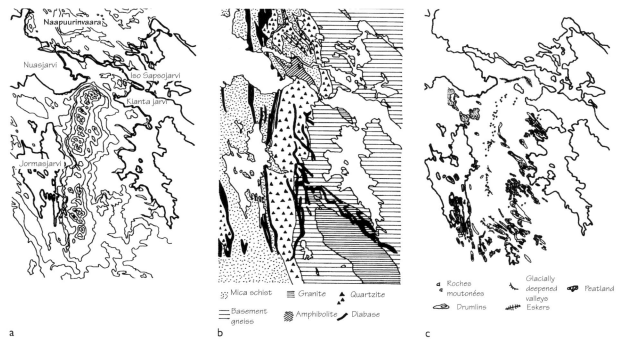

a

b

c

When analysed in conjunction with knowledge of the direction of ice movement, a distinct pattern of depositional and eroded structures emerges. The irresistible force of this northwest to southeast ice movement met the immovable object of the quartzite ridge. Some crevices or valleys through the ridge were gouged and a number of *roches moutonées* or elongated rock knolls were formed by the ice along the summit. The west facing slopes received occasional drumlins, but these mostly lie to the east and are distinctly elongated in form, reflecting the direction of ice movement.

The ice retreat left the area covered in patches of moraine over the main rock ridge. The saddle between Vuokattinvaara and the northern hill of Naapurinvaara, through which most water flowed beneath the ice sheet, has several eskers. The flanks of this ridge also possess various lake or sea coastal deposits such as sand dunes and prominent shorelines. The main hollows have remained lakes on either side of the ridge, whilst a number of other hollows are smaller lakes. Some of the shallow depressions have filled with vegetation, forming peat, since the ice retreated.

The landform shape and composition has affected the drainage characteristics. Gravel deposits are coarse textured and free draining, whilst drumlins often show impeded drainage due to fine textured clay size materials. The superficial moraine offers potential to make better soil than the drumlins.

The visual force analysis shows up the definition of convexities that dominate the form and the strong directional grain reflecting the ice movement. A notable feature is the hierarchy of landforms, especially the small scale modelling along the ridge top which echoes the large scale structure. Hence the landform pattern we see today is a result of the combination of the geological pattern and the erosional and depositional processes of the ice age.

The link between the development of the primal sketch, the movement of the eye, optic flow and Gibsonian affordance with fractal dimension, landform diversity, massiveness and constrasting landform types can all be used to postulate direct links between the landform structure, our perception and aesthetic response.

Analysing Hydrological Patterns

One of the most important relationships between landform pattern and process is the way the hydrological system operates. The landform, especially mountains, influences the type of precipitation (snow, rain, fog) and its distribution. It also directs the movement of ground water and affects rates of flow, storage, release and sediment yield.

In landforms with high elevation, the snowpack collects and is retained longest. Snow on shady slopes melts later and releases water throughout the summer season. Steep slopes lead to high speeds of flow and movement of erodable material, whilst highly fractal landforms produce numerous first order streams. Gentle gradients cause sediment to be deposited and meanders to form, whilst flood plain structures control and are controlled by rates of flow. All of these can be analysed by hand or by computer techniques.

A map of topography and aspect can be annotated with the stream system and areas where snow accumulates, water storage occurs in lake or bog systems, sediment collects or flooding is commonplace. A distinct pattern will emerge, clearly related to the analysis of landform shape and composition. Computer models can indicate factors of rates of precipitation, snow melt, erodability, flow rate and water input/output calculations. These may be more useful for the needs of water managers whilst the mapped pattern may well suffice as an aid to the planning and design of landscapes.

The hydrological pattern is not only related to landform, but it also interacts with the vegetation in the form of a feedback system. Evapotranspiration, snowpack retention and water flow control are all related to the type of vegetation structure and composition that grows on the land.

The analysis of Hazelton Mountain showed pronounced zones where different hydrological processes are at work. The relationship to the landform includes some watersheds, which produce large amounts of sediment and significant deposits due to the composition of the rocks, whilst other watersheds produce almost none (p. 237, Fig. 10).

Design of Landforms to Reflect Natural Patterns

Road construction, extractive industries and quarrying all alter landforms. Some create new ones, but rarely are the final results properly fitted into the landscape and rarer still is any connection made between the resultant landforms and the initiation of ecosystem processes.

The restoration of land that has been used for dumping of mineral spoil, from deep mining of coal or the modelled surface of infilled material following open cast or strip mining, illustrates how current practice misses many opportunities. The disturbed material is treated initially as an engineering and safety issue, so that angles of slopes and drainage are designed to conform to various rules. The landform so created is typically crude, often being of simple Euclidian geometry with no subtlety.

A study of nearby landforms can be used to determine how varied the topography is and to deduce the degree of fractal geometry it exhibits. The fractal signature can then be used to ensure that the modelling of the new landform produces as similar a pattern as possible. Complications can arise where the landforms are necessarily higher than the natural topography, because of the disposal of extra amounts of material. Likewise, the physical structures may not reflect

A coal spoil heap near Bolton, England, in need of restoration. The redesign of the landform is an important task involving much more than engineering and basic drainage.

those of the natural topography, perhaps being more easily eroded. In these circumstances the challenge for the designer is to be more creative, perhaps using the fractal signature of contours to graduate the topographic variation from edge to middle and to incorporate some sculptural shapes, depending on the design objectives.

The simple geometric forms described above often include inadequate drainage patterns that are likely to erode friable surface materials. This is because there are no drainage channels of various sizes to contain and control the flow. By contrast, there is much to emulate from naturally structured landform, which possesses surface modelling that collects rainfall and distributes it at rates of flow and quantities that are less likely to cause serious erosion. Meandering channels also control the flow, permitting the landform to absorb and hold larger quantities of water that gradually flow out of the system. Reinforcement of friable drainage channels can be undertaken to lessen serious erosion, whilst ponds of a natural shape can be used to filter the larger quantities of sediments likely to be produced for the first few years, until revegetation is established.

A varied landform also provides greater diversity of microsite and microclimate, which encourages a wider range of plant species or habitats to develop. However, site conditions are usually difficult, so that vegetation succession and the development of soil forming processes at natural rates often succeed better than too much reliance on technological assistance, such as fertilizers, which tend to suppress natural processes. Thus, naturalistic landform shapes and drainage characteristics can also help the restored site to follow the processes of ecological succession, as long as seed sources are present. In addition,

Examples to demonstrate poor and improved landform design. a) Shows a simple, geometric approach whilst b) shows a more natural approach where the contours reflect those nearby and have a fractal quality more likely to promote natural drainage control and the development of ecosystem processes.

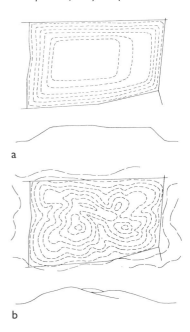

a

b

A limestone quarry within the boundary of Samarskaya Luka National Park on the River Volga in Russia. The terraced profile and vertical cliffs need radical treatment if the landscape is to be successfully restored.

wind movement is modified and the new landscape is likely to be more amenable to human use, especially since many of these are close to settlements and often have potential for use as recreation parks.

Hard rock quarries, once exhausted, often appear as highly unnatural sequences of horizontal benches separated by tall, vertical cliffs. These are not only unsympathetic to the surrounding landform, but can also be extremely dangerous to people and some animals. Some solutions concentrate on technologies of plant cultivation on the benches in order to 'green up' the face as soon as possible. However, some innovative work at Tunstall and Hope quarries in Derbyshire, England, has involved 'creative blasting' to produce more irregular quarry faces with a much greater fractal structure, as well as associated talus slopes and debris fans in a natural idiom, not unlike those seen in the Grand Canyon. Once again, creative solutions have made the faces

A conceptual sketch showing how the use of blasting can convert the regular shape of a quarry face into a more natural, fractally geometric one. The talus fans left by blasting emulate natural erosion structures and allow natural ecosystem processes to start.

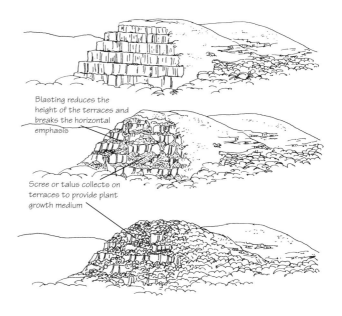

Blasting reduces the height of the terraces and breaks the horizontal emphasis

Scree or talus collects on terraces to provide plant growth medium

A worked out gravel pit near Cambridge, England 'restored' to a water body. The plan shape is too simple, the edges are unnatural and the vegetation is over-managed to say nothing of the transmission poles on their islands.

safer by reducing cliff heights, converted the faces from Euclidian to fractal geometry and, in the talus, provided material upon which natural colonization processes can proceed more easily.

Finally, an understanding of natural patterns can help to improve the design of the landform beneath artificially created water areas. Water areas created by damming or from mineral extraction (gravel, clay etc) can be unsightly and ill-equipped to provide habitats or water recreation, because of their uniform, simple underwater shape. The design in plan and section should provide the correct conditions for plant colonization if the land/water interface possesses a naturalistic fractal structure.

All of these examples can provide ecologically richer and more aesthetically pleasing results, as well as assisting the integration of the new element into the surrounding landform and vegetation. Some can become outstanding landscapes in their own right.

A concept sketch showing how a worked out gravel pit (a) can be made to resemble a natural water body in plan shape and underwater form (b). The pattern of bays, promontories, and different shoreline gradients presents a wide range of habitats for aquatic plants and animals and this helps to determine the ecological sequences of colonization and succession.

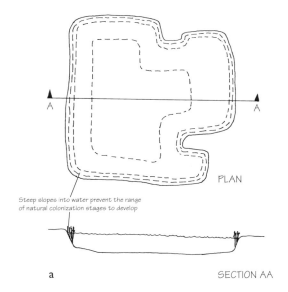

Steep slopes into water prevent the range of natural colonization stages to develop

PLAN

SECTION AA

a

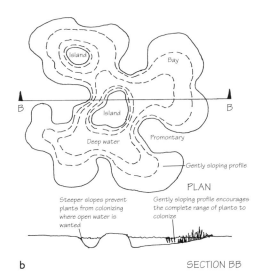

Steeper slopes prevent plants from colonizing where open water is wanted

Gently sloping profile encourages the complete range of plants to colonize

Gently sloping profile

Island

Bay

Island

Deep water

Promontary

PLAN

SECTION BB

b

Rivers and Hydrological Systems

In our study of natural patterns and some of the earlier methods of pattern analysis (see Chapter One) and our analysis of complete drainage systems earlier in this chapter, we were impressed by the intricate, highly fractal and remarkably self-organized structures of river basins. Branching and meandering patterns combine with the underlying landform to produce very efficient water flow control systems. However, the history of human interference with rivers has not been a successful one. From the earliest times, river valleys, flood plains and deltas have been popular settlement and communication locations. The desire for flood control and navigational improvements has meant that rivers have been continuously altered, straightened and forced to adopt simple, Euclidian geometric forms. The uncertain, but periodic flood events are hard to predict and after each bad one there seems to be a propensity to increase the defences further, thus causing a positive feedback loop that constantly makes matters worse.

An additional, often localized, problem is the effect of drainage systems laid beneath the surfaced areas of settlement and roads and agricultural land that speed newly fallen rain through the hydrological system. This prevents much of the natural storage and absorption of water by the ground and exacerbates the local effects of flooding. The cumulative effects of all these alterations to river systems, large and small, is to discharge water out of the system far more quickly than would occur naturally. Thus, serious floods are symptoms of hydrological systems out of balance in terms of the alteration of their natural pattern of flow, sediment collection and delivery and aquifer replenishment.

A river, once natural in its pattern, now canalized by river engineers in an attempt to control it. It presents a sterile, bland picture.

Usually the whole ecosystem structure that interacts with the river processes can be disrupted or lost as rivers are altered. In addition, most of the riparian forest which is important for filtration and collection of sediment, temperature control and bank stabilization has been lost in agricultural drainage schemes that exploit the rich silty soil which grows excellent crops, but erodes quickly during floods.

In developed river basins some fresh ideas are needed to restore or rehabilitate some degree of their natural structure and functioning. Instead of the usual straitjacket of canalized sections between engineered flood dykes, rivers need to be given some room to vary their channels and, most importantly, be allowed to flood in places so as to accommodate fluctuations in water levels without catastrophic damage to settlement and crops.

Jeremy Purseglove in Great Britain pioneered some of this work in the 1980s, encouraging river engineers to restore meanders and to preserve or restore valuable vegetation, including trees, along the banks. Some more adventurous schemes are planned in the USA, where the disastrous results of the 1996 Oregon floods has prompted a new approach. The Willamette River which flows north into the Columbia, has been gradually altered over the years since 1854. The original system of channels, flood plain forest and wetland which once covered an area some six miles or ten kilometres wide has been simplified, into one main channel with a few backwaters, wetlands and isolated ponds. The aim now is to restore a number of the wetland areas in key places, so that the swelling river at flood can spread into areas set aside for it.

The key aspect in such schemes is to change the perception of people likely to be affected by floods, away from the idea of total prevention, towards a model based on uncertainty and probabilities, where the flood is seen as a natural event that can be managed within certain limits, but not entirely controlled. As earthworks are expensive to erect they should only be used to steer the flow and to protect key places, such as settlements.

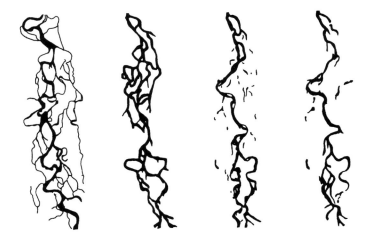

The sequence of gradual loss of the diverse patterns of structure and process along a stretch of the Willamette River in Oregon, USA. The complex natural pattern has become simpler since the 1850s (left) to the present day (right) and the capacities for storage, nutrient cycling and natural riparian processes have become impoverished.

The idea of ring dykes around settlements was pioneered by people in Holland in the early mediaeval period and has been also used to good effect in the Red River basin in Canada, where floods were serious in 1997. By restoring the structure and functioning of the natural flood system the trapping of water will be prevented aiding the effectiveness of defences because less pressure will be placed on them as the flood load is allowed to spread out.

A second aspect is the restoration of the vegetation structure of flood plain forests and wetlands which are key to the success of the river system (see Chapter Six for a discussion of vegetation patterns in river systems). Forests hold natural bank systems together, while wetlands retain some of the flood water as temporary lakes that evaporate or soak away rather than flow to the sea. Thus, these diverse and valuable habitats are also fulfilling an important hydrological function. The revived landscape of such rivers will also increase their aesthetic value as not much beauty or mystery can be attached to a canalized river. Those yet unaffected such as the Skeena River in British Columbia or parts of the Volga in Russia, not dammed for hydroelectric power, retain the distinct multi-channel pattern. Their intact flood plain forests are attractive and retain a strong sense of mystery, because of the inability to see all of their channels and islands at once. The flow of the water gives the river its coherence or unity as a complete system. Thus, any action to restore river systems and associated forests towards their natural condition could be a stimulus for ensuring that the beauty of natural channel patterns, meanders and vegetation patterns is used as a template for such work everywhere.

Natural floodplain forest on the River Volga in Russia. The natural bars and islands and the shore of the river offer a diverse pattern of habitats that help stabilize the shifting materials and is a major corridor for wildlife and human movement. The pattern exhibits fractal structure in the similarity of scale of mud-banks and channels. This is an indicator of correct structure for the restoration of natural processes in a previously simplified system.

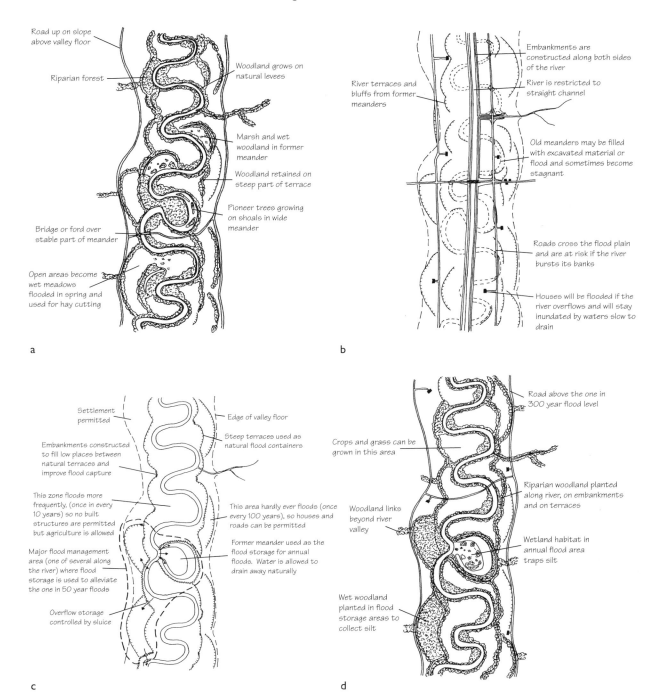

a)

Road up on slope above valley floor

Riparian forest

Woodland grows on natural levees

Marsh and wet woodland in former meander

Woodland retained on steep part of terrace

Pioneer trees growing on shoals in wide meander

Bridge or ford over stable part of meander

Open areas become wet meadows flooded in spring and used for hay cutting

b)

River terraces and bluffs from former meanders

Embankments are constructed along both sides of the river

River is restricted to straight channel

Old meanders may be filled with excavated material or flood and sometimes become stagnant

Roads cross the flood plain and are at risk if the river bursts its banks

Houses will be flooded if the river overflows and will stay inundated by waters slow to drain

c)

Settlement permitted

Edge of valley floor

Embankments constructed to fill low places between natural terraces and improve flood capture

Steep terraces used as natural flood containers

This zone floods more frequently, (once in every 10 years) so no built structures are permitted but agriculture is allowed

This area hardly ever floods (once every 100 years), so houses and roads can be permitted

Major flood management area (one of several along the river) where flood storage is used to alleviate the one in 50 year floods

Former meander used as the flood storage for annual floods. Water is allowed to drain away naturally

Overflow storage controlled by sluice

d)

Road above the one in 300 year flood level

Crops and grass can be grown in this area

Riparian woodland planted along river, on embankments and on terraces

Woodland links beyond river valley

Wetland habitat in annual flood area traps silt

Wet woodland planted in flood storage areas to collect silt

A concept sketch showing how a pattern of natural structures can be restored in a river, starting with reinstatement of meanders and places that flood at varying frequencies: a) shows the original river pattern with associated vegetation; b) the engineered, canalized system; c) restoration of the meanders with some flood control measures fitting the natural pattern; d) the vegetation restored to the reinstated meander pattern.

Summary and Conclusions

In this chapter the patterns and processes of landform have been explored. We have seen how the creation of new land, its weathering, erosion and deposition, forms the substrate for all life and for all human activity. We have noted that some very complex, self-organized patterns emerge from the interaction of landform and geomorphological processes; patterns which are frequently extremely similar at various scales also exhibit fractal geometry.

The perception of the landscape partly depends on our ability to detect patterns in the landform. We see edges, lines, textures and repeated similar shapes. The coherence of many of them, their inherent complexity and sense of mystery contribute to our sense of beauty, while the sheer scale of some landforms overwhelms us and creates a feeling of the sublime.

By analysing the physical and aesthetic components of landforms, and linking the patterns to their originating processes, we can discover how, in activities that alter existing landforms or create new ones, we should respect their natural characteristics. We can be creative and fulfill the urge to leave our mark on the landscape without insensitively interrupting the continuing natural processes that are so important for our well being.

The next chapter will relate the landform to its effect on ecosystem processes, demonstrating a fundamental link between all processes and all patterns in nature.

CHAPTER SIX

ECOSYSTEM PATTERNS

Introduction

All the landform patterns described in Chapter Five form the basic structures upon which vegetation, ecological and human activity has developed. The next stage in our quest for pattern/process relationships and their application to design turns to vegetation, its distribution and dynamics. Vegetation is one of the major components of the terrestrial ecosystem, so the interactions that occur between vegetation, landforms and climate are of fundamental importance.

The development of vegetation follows three stages, each of which may exist simultaneously in any landscape: colonization, succession and disturbance. Colonization is the act of plant species or communities moving into areas that they do not already occupy. Succession is the process of vegetation growth, competition among plants, compositional and structural development towards a mature stage. Disturbance occurs when the vegetation is changed or destroyed in some way, allowing re-colonization, setting the successional clock back to zero or altering the successional path in some way.

All new land emerging from volcanic eruptions, sedimentary deposits or glaciation is available for colonization. The type of vegetation that colonizes, and the way this occurs, depends on several factors such as the availability of seed or propagation material, the climatic conditions of warmth, moisture and a length of growing season, and the structure, as well as the nutrient status of the substrate.

At a site level new substrate may be patches of solid rock or shifting sand, with little or no available moisture, where individual seeds cannot germinate or survive. However, at the larger landscape scale, such small incidents are subsumed into a wider pattern, where even desert vegetation occurs repeatedly enough to exhibit a distinct pattern of distribution and structure.

Landform Effects on Ecosystem Patterns and Processes

Before exploring the dynamics of the plant communities, it is important to understand the interactions between landforms and ecosystem processes and patterns. Vegetation colonization may develop after the geomorphology is in place or can occur concurrently with landform development and express, directly, the pattern of those processes. Geomorphological processes may also occur after vegetation is present, thereby heavily influencing the vegetation. The interactions between landform and ecological processes may occur at a range of scales, from individual plants, binding soil particles together, to the influence of large mountains on temperature and moisture gradients.

Swanson, Kratz, Caine and Woodmansee, an American group of ecological researchers, examined landforms and found them to be significant regulators of the distribution of organisms, especially plants, and ecosystem processes. They classified four main types of landform effects on ecosystems, none of which is found exclusively, and all occurring to greater or lesser extents in most places:

- Landforms cause environmental gradients

- Landforms affect the movement of materials and energy

- Landforms affect ecosystem disturbances

- Landforms affect local geomorphological processes

Landforms Cause Environmental Gradients

The first effect is where landforms cause variations in environmental conditions known as gradients. Elevation and aspect are major gradients and can easily be seen. Higher elevation causes a decrease in temperature, affects solar radiation and increases rainfall, whilst aspect affects solar radiation (gained more on slopes facing the sun, which are warmer), snow melt (slower on shady slopes, which are cooler) and rain shadow effects (aspects to the leeward of rain storms can be considerably drier). Fog may also cling to one side of a hill or mountain. Other gradients can include soil moisture and nutrients (linked to the second class of effects.)

This scene in the Mount Hood National Forest in Oregon, USA, shows the abrupt changes to vegetation between damper, cooler, shady north facing slopes (to the left of the picture) and drier, warmer, sunnier south facing slopes (to the right). The change from dense fir on north facing slopes to open oak on south facing slopes is distinctive and is sensitive to small changes in aspect.

The Cascade Mountains in the USA show the effects of many of these gradients. The Columbia River Gorge, which cuts east-west through the Cascades, provides an almost sea level transect across the breadth of the mountain range, where the rain shadow effect is dramatic. The western slopes have much higher rainfall and are dominated by Douglas fir forests that differ from those on the drier eastern slopes, characterized by pine or oak. On the east side of the mountains local aspect effects can also be observed; north and east facing areas tend to be occupied by fir and pine, whilst open oak groves and grassy areas grow on south and west facing slopes. Depending on the complexity of the landform, the vegetation also exhibits a fractal pattern; the mosaic created by the gradient is dependent on the scale of aspect change.

The elevational gradients are shown by the changes in forest structure and composition with increasing elevation until the irregular tree line is reached. This variation is dependent on the scale of the landscape. In some places, like the conical volcano of Mount Hood, changes occur gradually with both elevation and aspect, but in more complex eroded areas the slightest change in aspect of a slope can result in rapid alterations to the dominant vegetation community. Once again, the pattern has a fractal character

Elevational gradients can also be seen in a different way in the Colorado Rockies in the USA, where at lower elevations the rainfall is the limiting factor, causing grassy prairies to be the dominant vegetation. Higher up, the rainfall amount increases, allowing forest to develop gradually and become dominant. At highest elevations, the temperature gradient becomes the limiting factor and the forest is replaced by alpine tundra. Thus the mosaic pattern can be defined at a large scale by such gradients.

An area of the Rocky Mountains in Colorado, USA, where rising elevation causes prairie to transform into forest as rainfall increases whilst forest gives way to alpine tundra as temperature decreases with further increases in elevation.

Moisture gradients in the soil, determined by landform and drainage characteristics, can also affect vegetation patterns. On Nootka Island in British Columbia, Canada, the west coast slopes receive as much as 4 metres annual rainfall. The soil is frequently saturated and the distribution of forest communities depends on the degree of drainage afforded, in relation to the degree of slope. A slight reduction in the gradient, producing wetter conditions, causes the hemlock/balsam forest to switch to cedar/hemlock, whilst the flatter parts may be so waterlogged that sphagnum bogs develop and few trees, other than Shore pine, can survive. In the valley bottoms and along the shoreline, the nutrient and salt gradients (from riverine silts and seaspray respectively) result in local dominance by Sitka spruce. All these patterns are determined more by landform and moisture interactions, than by rock, soil types or elevation.

Different forest types on Nootka Island, British Columbia, Canada. Their distribution is mainly correlated to drainage. Thus pine dominates on the flattest, most poorly drained coastal shelves with cedar in the valleys whilst hemlock is dominant on the steeper, convex ridges.

Gradients on a very small scale can also be seen in bog/forest complexes and in coastal mudflats. The slightest increase in dryness causes changes to the vegetation that stand out as distinct patterns characterized by fractal geometry. The distribution pattern is also related to the varying probabilities of successful colonization, where vegetation is most likely to develop best on the drier places and fare less well on the wetter ones.

Landforms Affect the Movement of Materials and Energy

The second landform effect concerns the movement of materials, organisms, propagules (seeds, fungal spores or rootable pieces of plant material) and energy. The hydrological gradients, described previously, interact with this effect in terms of the flow of water in and over the ground. Flow is determined, both in direction and velocity, by the shape and steepness of landform.

The movement of animals may be directed by the landform. Some live in particular zones of elevation and move across slopes. Their range may be limited by deep ravines or knife-edge ridges. Others may move up and down slopes using valleys or ridges. Many may be also constrained by the existence of the vegetation types they need for food or cover; for example, alpine tundra only occurs at high elevation, forest lower down. Boggy areas might favour some species or may limit others. As animals often aid the distribution of plants by carrying seeds, their movement in turn affects vegetation patterns. Methods of analysis of the movement patterns of such flows will be examined later in this chapter.

Propagule dispersal, particularly by seed or spores may be directly or indirectly affected by landforms, depending on their dispersal mechanisms. Heavy seeds may be moved by gravity, water or snow flow, whilst wind, consistently funnelling through valleys, may tend to blow light seeds in one direction. Animals and birds, moving around, may spread seed more densely in some places than others. This can have a pronounced effect on the composition of vegetation, depending on the competitive strengths of different species under different climatic circumstances.

The patterns of movement are likely to reflect the character of the landform, where more defined patterns result from strongly structured, highly fractal topography. Where branching and meandering patterns are also present, the movements are likely to follow them.

Landforms Affect Ecosystem Disturbances

The third effect is the interaction between landform and natural disturbances, other than those caused by geomorphological processes. Landform affects wind movement and this can disturb forests. The venturi effect of wind, gaining velocity as it funnels into narrow

This diagram shows how wind flows around a mountain. In some places the landform channels the wind whilst other places are almost continually sheltered. The pattern is a turbulent one within the context of chaos theory although it is more predictable because of the influence of the fixed landform structure. (After Arno and Hammerly, 1984)

confines of valleys or blows over ridges, increases its energy and ability to blow trees over. Conversely, landform also provides shelter against wind damage from certain directions. For example, the eddying effect of wind blowing over ridges may confine damage to localized places. Wind speeds also increase with elevation, which increases the dessication of vegetation and this encourages species that are more resistant to this effect. Wind disturbance patterns will be considered in more detail later in the chapter.

Fires are another major disturbance factor of many vegetation types whose pattern of movement can be heavily influenced by landform. The wind may affect the direction and speed of a fire, but ridges and valleys frequently break the spread of fire if it runs across slopes. Also, fires tend to run up ridges if started by lightning strike lower down, because of the rising convection currents of hot air. Moisture gradients induced by landform may also restrict the spread of fire. Forest fire patterns will be explored in more detail later in the chapter.

As in previous examples, the pattern of disturbances tends to conform to fractal characteristics, especially where the landform is more fractally complex. Mosaic patterns, composed of patches of strongly defined, contrasting edges, develop at a scale that reflect the underlying landform.

Landforms Affect Local Geomorphological Processes

Since landforms control the distribution of water across a landscape, they also affect the disturbance caused by heavy rainstorms, by limiting or concentrating the pattern of disturbance in relation to the shape of valleys and by the indirect effect of rain shadow. The storm water interacts with soil, moraine deposits or other superficial material to cause landslides. This is an example of the fourth effect, of local geomorphological processes that occur within the timescale of ecological processes.

Landslides are one of the most dramatic of these geomorphological processes. Soil can collect slowly in hollows in steep topography. The soil may be loosened by surface erosion, thrown up by trees blown or fallen over or shifted by gravitational effects, such as surface creep. Animals and people may also cause erosion. The soil accumulates in a loose structure, too deep to be consolidated or anchored by plant and tree roots. Heavy rainfall may saturate the soil and act as a lubrication at the base of the accumulation, causing it to flow down hill, often at great speed. Trees and structures in the path of the landslide may be demolished, buried or pushed out of the way. The soil accumulates again, as fans or cones at the base of the slope. Landslides can be repeated at intervals, depending on the time taken for debris to build up and the frequency of heavy rain events, particularly following snow.

The size and frequency of landslides depends on the structure of the landform, so that there is likely to be a fractal pattern to their occurrence correllated to that of the topography. This was observed in the character of the pattern of debris fans noted at the Grand Canyon, in Chapter Five.

In some circumstances, where landslides are very frequent, vegetation colonization and succession may be restricted. This is found in snow avalanche tracks that act in the same way, but more frequently, occurring every year and sometimes several times during a year.

Another landform influence on geomorphological processes, affecting patterns of vegetation, involves river meanders within valleys.

The result of the 1996 mud slides in Oregon, USA. Here a massive flow including large boulders released material that had accumulated for hundreds of years. The slide spread down the valley and across the open land at the foot of the slope, submerging buildings and filling in streams. This example is from the Columbia River Gorge.

The valley structure controls the size and number of meanders, particularly in flat bottomed glaciated valleys, where the river has minimal erosive power compared with the original glacier. The effect of this constricted erosion and deposition can result in constant disturbance to river bed characteristics, banks and vegetation. New material of low nutrient status is constantly exposed, thus restricting vegetation to pioneer species (including trees) able to cope with these exacting conditions. The new material always conforms to the characteristic pattern of the river system, fitting into the meander structure, braided or branching streams.

The four classifications described above can occur simultaneously in many places and interact in complex ways. It is important to evaluate these landform influenced events as they provide indicators for understanding the dynamic patterns of nature. Generally, pronounced landforms have more influence, but this is not always the case. In some circumstances, one type of influence may be overridden by others of greater magnitude. The short term effect of a catastrophic disturbance may temporarily mask or reset the longer term, smaller scale effects of aspect and exposure. Conversely, the longer term, subtle pattern effects may survive or limit the pattern of the short term dramatic event.

As we noted in Chapter Five, our aesthetic response to landforms is related to their coherence, complexity and mystery. Because ecosystem patterns and processes are themselves influenced or defined by landforms, it stands to reason that we see them as coherent, complex and mysterious in turn. The Whiteheadian quality of massiveness is also likely to be evident, though dependent on the scale at which ecosystem patterns occur.

Vegetation Patterns: Structure and Dynamics

In a wide range of landscapes, the patterns of vegetation are consistent with landform, drainage and soil patterns derived from the influences described above. Some are easy to interpret, others are more difficult. For example, the tropical rainforest looks very monotonous from exterior views, as the only visible part is the canopy of dominant trees. Beneath the canopy the structure is so complex that distinct patterns are difficult to detect and it is easy to become disorientated. This is because the small scale changes to the forest structure depend on the death of individual trees and the rapid regrowth in the gap created. The greater the available light and nutrients released by decay, the faster is the rate of growth. The landform and soil are less relevant. By contrast, the patterns of vegetation in places where strong environmental gradients occur are usually prominent. Edges, margins and transition zones between vegetation types are particularly interesting, not only because of the obvious patterns, but also due to the dynamics at these interfaces. This fits well with Richard Forman's observations of gradient versus mosaic characteristics in heterogeneous landscapes as described in Chapter One. The strength of definition of edges, margins and transition zones helps us to understand and make sense of mosaic landscapes; they become coherent. There are also likely to be links with the aesthetic theories of Aldo Leopold as outlined in Chapter Three.

Plant Colonization and Succession Patterns

The ultimate edges of forest areas, where they succumb to the extremes of temperature, windchill and dessication at high altitude and latitude represent the current frontiers of colonization that started when the land emerged, perhaps from the grip of the ice age. We can imagine, for example, the gradual retreat of glaciers up valleys exposing fresh moraine, eskers, river beds and bare rock. These areas are now available for propagules of plants to land on. Whether the growth of the plant will be successful, depends on whether the site it lands on is available and suitable.

Newly exposed areas tend to be difficult for the survival and growth of some plants, because of the absence of nutrients (especially nitrogen), unstructured soil with problems of water retention (free draining sands dry out very quickly, whilst heavy clays hold too much water), or absence of soil forming materials in substrates such as bare rock, talus or boulder fields. Species able to colonize such areas are commonly called pioneer species. They usually have light, windborne seed that spreads easily onto newly available sites, low nutrient requirements, tolerance of water fluctuations and can complete their growth cycle within short growing seasons. Certain species manufacture their own nitrogen to overcome nutrient deficiencies. Some of the seed or other propagules, such as spores of lower plants like mosses, will germinate, grow and reproduce, where others will fail.

The resulting pattern usually has a distinctive character and fits the landform very closely, showing clear signs of organization. These patterns are not designed, but are self-organized. They are not completely random, nor are they entirely predictable. According to the principles of chaos theory, there is a high degree of order to the plant distribution; this is dependent on the influence of the underlying substrate and microclimate, which affects the probabilities of survival and growth of each seed or spore as it lands on a particular microsite. Better sites indicate a greater probability of more seeds surviving to germinate, grow and reproduce themselves. Other sites may result in total failure of seed development; for example, open water, bare rock or residual ice. The more variable the site, the stronger the mosaic pattern that will develop and the more fractal it is likely to be.

Sites with variability at a small scale (for example hummocky terrain) will give, locally, more variable patterns. These patterns can be observed to display fractal geometry by being repeated at a range of scales, from the major distribution patterns determined by the main ridges and valleys to the minor variations induced by the effects of local landform. Conversely, homogeneous areas will result in more even growth, as on mountain slopes that are less complex where the general limit of the treeline often follows the contour to give a horizontal edge.

The earliest colonizing by pioneer species begins the process of soil formation. Plant remains build up and decay, weathering of minerals, exposed to the air and water, releases nutrients and activity by roots and soil fauna develop structure. Eventually conditions become suitable for other, more demanding, species of plants to establish themselves. Some need better soil, the microclimate of shelter and shade, provided by pioneer woodland, or they rely on their seeds being brought into new areas by birds or animals, who need woodland conditions. Some colonization takes decades or centuries to be completed until the typical 'mature' phase of the vegetation develops. This process is called succession. The leading edge of the forest at the treeline represents the furthest possible line of advance, given the existing climatic conditions.

Classic succession sequences, in places like Iceland, start with bare, newly exposed rock, where the growth of lichens and mosses, and their contribution to weathering and capture of nutrients, gradually forms enough substrate on bare rock to allow herbaceous species to grow. The gradual accumulation of litter, continuing weathering of the parent material and capture of water or airborne particles slowly builds up a soil that permits the growth of woody vegetation and, eventually, long lived tree species. Distinct mosaic patterns of vegetation appear that depend on the rate at which soil can be formed, at a scale determined by the variability of the substrate and its weathering characteristics.

In places in the northern hemisphere, where pioneer tree species are able to colonize at an early stage along with lower order plants, the

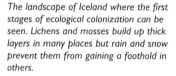

The landscape of Iceland where the first stages of ecological colonization can be seen. Lichens and mosses build up thick layers in many places but rain and snow prevent them from gaining a foothold in others.

succession can develop from pioneer forest of birch, alder or willow, to oak, pine or spruce. The pioneer tree species are able to survive in low nutrient environments, are light demanding and relatively short lived, by comparison with most trees. Later successional species require more nutrients, are increasingly tolerant of shade and are long lived. They used to be described as 'climax' species, because it was considered that once a vegetation type reached a late stage of development, it was very stable and would continue, almost unchanged, in that state indefinitely. Recently the concept of climax ecosystems has been revised as more understanding is gained of the dynamics of all ecosystems and the importance of disturbance as a process.

At present, the climax stage of vegetation refers to late successional species that persist until disturbance takes place, causing succession to recommence. Sometimes the theoretical 'climax' or late successional state is never or rarely achieved, because disturbance usually intervenes or local site conditions prevent it. Such arrested succession may occur where heathy vegetation, such as heather may dominate and prevent succession to woodland, because of either its competitive advantage or its artificial maintenance by human or animal intervention (burning or grazing). Another example is Lodgepole pine which is sometimes called a seratinous or 'fire climax' species, because it is a pioneer that is usually burnt before later successional stages can develop.

Succession can also lead to the formation of completely new habitat types; the open water of a pond or lake may eventually fill with silt and fen moss, become a bog and then dry sufficiently for pioneer forest to colonize and develop into late successional woodland. All these stages can be seen in places where glaciation left ponds or lakes of varying depths, nutrient status and water flow, where the shallowest have already dried out and converted to woodland, whilst the deepest remain as open water.

Landscapes at a late successional stage tend to show a characteristic pattern of species composition and structure. In much of the temperate (warm to cool) zone, mixed woodlands are normally regarded as late successional ecosystems. Species composition tends to vary spatially across the landscape. For example, in parts of the Acadian Forest of New Brunswick and Nova Scotia in Canada and Maine in the USA, it is typical for shade tolerant broadleaves such as Yellow birch and maples to be located on ridge tops, whilst conifers such as Black spruce, White spruce or White pine are found on slopes and in draws or gullies. Aspect can affect this distribution. In landscapes with higher hills, such as in Vermont or New Hampshire in New England, the pattern can be reversed, with higher ridges and cooler aspects being dominated by conifers such as Black spruce, whilst broadleaves of different species are found on lower ridges, in valleys or on side slopes of warm aspect. The contrast of these species, their textures and colours, contributes to their aesthetic value because they are coherent and complex. Seasonal changes and the dramatic autumn colours

This hillside in Vermont, USA, shows a pattern of vegetation distribution related to topography. The upper slopes tend to be dominated by conifers or conifer/deciduous mixtures. Lower down the deciduous species dominate and are divided into different types.

enhance their diversity and the sense of beauty they provide; the colour patterns relate to the species (orange-red maples, golden birch) that grow on different sites according to landform.

Distribution patterns can also arise due to the chemical composition of the soil. In parts of Idaho in the USA, Jeffrey pine will only grow on mineral deficient, volcanic soils, because these are not occupied by sagebrush that competes with the pine and prevents its establishment.

In many places, it is difficult to see late successional patterns in their natural state, because so much interference or disturbance, principally

The distribution of forest on this volcanic landscape is determined by the chemical composition of the rock and the available moisture. Here Jeffrey pine can survive because sagebrush does not grow but it is most successful in the valley bottoms where moisture accumulates. Craters of the Moon National Monument, Idaho, USA.

by human activities, has taken place. However, it is possible to reconstruct the pattern of late successional plant communities by analysing soil and site types in terms of existing plants and their usual associates that should also be present. This approach can be useful for restoring damaged landscapes and will be described later in the chapter.

Stand structures are less easy to perceive as identifiable patterns, partly because they are more complex, and often occur at a very small scale. However, some of the vertical structure is normally dependent on local microsite variations, so that shrubs, herbaceous and other vegetation can show sensitivity to variations in moisture. This is very noticeable in the vicinity of rivers or lake edges, where the wetter soil, shelter and moist atmosphere create a pattern to the vegetation structure that is normally developed in conditions of deep shade. Elsewhere, the structural pattern can be influenced by variations in light intensity as much as by microsite. This is caused by the death or collapse of canopy trees, whose distribution may not be according to a defined or predictable pattern. Hence, someone walking amongst a forest may find it difficult to perceive a coherent pattern except where the edge structure is more clearly defined. The aesthetic value of edge landscapes may partly depend on our ability to comprehend them.

Some structures arising from succession take many centuries to develop and this is dependent on small scale disturbance in the early stages. Coastal old growth forest in the Pacific Northwest of the USA and Canada is an example of late successional forest that relies on the death of long lived canopy species to develop and continue. As the successional stages of a forest develop, each persists for a variable length of time and shows a change in the height of the trees, the species composition and the stand structure. The forest ecologists Oliver and Larsen in the USA have presented successional models which link to different disturbance agencies. The typical stages are as follows, although stage 6 is not always present.

1. **Stand initiation,** where the bare or disturbed ground re-colonizes with vegetation.
2. **Stem exclusion,** where competition for light and space amongst the colonizing plants causes high mortality. This process starts with an open canopy, so that competition includes all vegetation, and continues into closed canopy.
3. **Understorey reinitiation,** where light is able to penetrate below the canopy and permit vegetation to grow once more.
4. **Young forest, multi-strata,** where the stand develops many vegetation layers.
5. **Old forest, multi-strata,** where the trees become mature and some dead and decaying trees and fallen wood add to the structure.
6. **Old forest, single stratum,** where one species, usually a shade tolerant one eventually dominates and shades out the rest of the vegetation.

This diagram shows the typical stages of forest succession for an interior cedar/hemlock type from British Columbia, Canada. The succession paths are prone to variation as a result of disturbances which can advance or retard succession or revert to stand initiation stage.

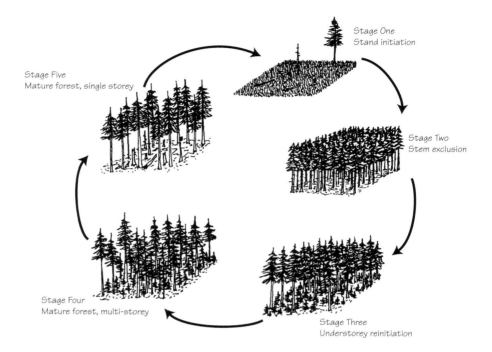

Stage One
Stand initiation

Stage Two
Stem exclusion

Stage Three
Understorey reinitiation

Stage Four
Mature forest, multi-storey

Stage Five
Mature forest, single storey

Whilst the patterns of vegetation within a temperate forest are described above, it is at the edges that the greatest contrast and definition of patterns is to be found. Examples of this are treelines, where the forest patterns are due to the effects of elevation or latitude, forest/bog interfaces, coastal sand dunes and areas of mudflats, deltas and riverbanks.

Treelines

Steven Arno has explored the character and processes giving rise to treelines, and some of his findings are summarized here. Tree height declines with increasing altitude and latitude, because growth rates are much slower and species composition changes as the climate conditions become more severe. However, at a particular elevation (the precise point varies depending on aspect and latitude), the structure of the forest changes. The continuous canopy starts to become patchy and gaps appear. The trees then become clumped, occur in isolated patches or appear as individual trees (alpine parkland). Most of the trees also become stunted, assume bushy structures or spread out horizontally. These patches are scattered across a zone where the horizontal, bushy form eventually becomes the only type to withstand the climate (a distinctive type known as 'krummholz'). Finally, even these peter out and disappear. The pattern created by these changes is known as the treeline.

There are three basic varieties of treelines:

- Upper elevation or alpine treelines, defined as the limit of adequate summer warmth.
- Lower elevation treelines, where summer drought limits tree growth.
- Latitudinal or arctic treelines, also resulting from inadequate summer warmth.

The different characteristics of a treeline pattern as the forest gradually gives way to open alpine tundra.

Tree species line

Timberline   Treeline

Although upper elevational and latitudinal types arise from similar factors, the former occurs over a few hundred metres/yards, whilst the latter takes some dozens of kilometres/miles to develop.

There is a terminology to distinguish between different parts of a treeline. The 'timberline' refers to the upper limit of continuous canopy forest. The 'treeline' is the limit for individuals to grow erectly up to two metres tall and be recognizable as trees. The 'tree species line' defines the limit where trees will grow, although by this time they are stunted and deformed. The area between the timberline and the tree species line is called the 'kampfzone' (zone of struggle), where the decrease in height, density, canopy continuity and increase in shrubbiness and presence of dwarf trees occur.

Under current climatic conditions, the absolute limit to the survival of tree species is reached when individual plants cannot maintain a positive carbon balance. This means they cannot grow enough woody material during the growing season to offset the losses from damage or decay. The tree form, being vertical and usually single stemmed, is best suited to maintaining a positive carbon balance in circumstances of extreme competition for solar energy, such as those found in the closed canopy of the forest. At high elevations or latitudes other factors become more important, accounting for the changes to plant form, such as the small shrubby structure of multiple stems; this needs less carbon for wood production, so making it easier to maintain the positive carbon balance.

As noted, the main factors that contribute to the pattern and character of treelines of all types are climatically related and interact with topographic variables.

Characteristics of Treeline Patterns

1. **South versus north facing slopes:** The effect of greater exposure to the sun (insolation) on south facing slopes in the northern hemisphere is very marked, especially at latitudes greater than 40 degrees, because of the lower sun angle. The greatest insolation occurs during the afternoon so that southwest slopes are the warmest and northeast the coolest.

   Furthermore, in many places in the northern hemisphere, the prevailing wind blows from the southwest. This can blow some of the snow from southwest facing slopes onto the northeast aspects. This intensifies the moisture differences and heating, the length of time the snowpack lies, and access to water during dry summers in continental mountains. Hence, sites with the same air temperature can occur several hundred feet/tens of metres higher on south facing than north facing slopes, as does the alpine upper treeline. The plant species tend to differ between south and north facing slopes.

2. **Ridgetops and basins in strong relief:** Convex slopes are often warmer than concave ones. This is because cold air, descending at night, collects in valley heads and can produce air frosts even during the summer. Certain landforms, such as corries or cirques, may contain moraine dams at their mouths which prevent this cold air from draining. In maritime climates, heavy winter snows often persist in hollows and cold air can drain from glaciers. This results in the treeline ascending on ridges, whilst the valley heads remain treeless. This pattern is also seen in the tropics, where broadleaved species are less cold tolerant than conifers. It is an inverted treeline, because it is the opposite of that formed by the more common distribution of plants, where better growth is concentrated in hollows and sparser growth on ridges.

   Where there is severe summer drought, such as in continental climates, the most prominent ridges tend to remain bare because they are too hot, dry and windy. The deeper valley heads or corries also remain treeless, but the intermediate concave slopes carry trees that often rise higher on one side of a valley head, because of greater warmth, moisture or shelter depending on the local limiting factors.

3. **Gentle topography:** on plateaux, mesas and broader ridgetops the more gradual altitudinal increase does not cause abrupt transitions in the upper treeline. Instead, other patterns are able to develop,

This view shows the distinct pattern at the upper forest treeline on Hudson's Bay Mountain, British Columbia, Canada. Much of the most stunted krummholz remains buried by the snow. The repeated linear pattern relates to microclimate variations in the local landform and to the way snow accumulates, thus providing protection to the trees during winter conditions.

This treeline in Newfoundland shows a distinct shape where it rises into better, more sheltered hollows and is lowered on the exposed ridges.

such as ribbon forest, snow glades and rings of trees known as 'timber atolls'.

In the Colorado Rockies there are high altitude basins or plateaux of prairie that rise abruptly into the final peaks. The upper treeline is irregular, reflecting changes in topography and microsite conditions. The lower treeline occurs at the foot of steeper slopes, where these grade out into flatter landforms and treeless prairies. In many natural forest areas there is no lower treeline, but where moisture decreases, desert or grassland becomes dominant, such as in Colorado. The arctic treeline develops on the gentle topography of the Canadian Shield or similar landforms in Siberia, undulating in nature as a result of the ice sheets. This yields various patterns depending on the degree of wetness and the soil forming or rooting capacity of the base material.

4. **Size of the mountain mass:** Large mountainous masses slow the rate at which temperature decreases with elevation. This

'massenherbung' effect leads to higher treelines in ranges, such as the central Colorado Rockies, the Himalayas or the Andean altiplano, than on isolated peaks at the same latitude. This occurs because the larger land masses cause the bulk of an approaching warm air mass to rise and lift over the top, whereas such air is more easily able to slide around and past an isolated peak, such as one of the Cascade volcanoes, leaving it much cooler. Winds are also less severe and larger mountain ranges tend also to occur in areas of continental climate.

Within the context of the prevailing climate and landform, the success of treeline formation and development rely on a number of specific environmental factors either singly or when combined.

1. **Temperature:** The critical factor is whether there is a minimum season, of around two months, during which trees can complete their annual growth without the risk of frost damage. This factor not only determines the elevation of the treeline (which varies locally according to aspect), but also the species within it. Some species cannot compete because they are not frost hardy.

2. **Wind:** Violent winds can occur all year round on exposed peaks and ridges causing trees to become misshapen, or wind trained. Such shapes arise due to physical damage inflicted by the sheer force of the wind, and by lashing branches and ice pellets. Tree growth is then greatest in sheltered places and on those parts of the tree facing away from the wind direction.

   Warm winter winds (chinooks or foehns) can melt ice and evaporate moisture in leaves causing dessication. If the soil around the tree roots remains frozen these water losses cannot be made good and trees or affected parts of trees can die.

3. **Snow:** Snow can protect trees by collecting in hollows or completely enclosing or jacketing individual trees. Krummholz may depend on the pattern of snow accumulation to develop and survive. Snow jackets may allow otherwise cold intolerant trees to survive. Snow prevents dessication and wind damage. It can also be too heavy, causing trees or branches to break.

   Snow avalanches break, flatten or scar trees and can lower the treeline in larger basins. Lingering snow can also prevent forest establishment on shady slopes (northeast facing). Conversely, trees can grow better on ridges than in basins or valleys because snow pack is thinner and melts sooner. The treeline may advance during periods of lighter than average snowfall that allow sufficient time for seed to germinate and establish.

4. **Precipitation and moisture:** Moisture affects species composition within the treeline zone. Moisture availability is coupled with the distribution of precipitation, temperature, evapotranspiration rates and soil/substrate drainage/moisture retentiveness. In Alaska in the USA, very low precipitation is not a problem, because the evapotranspiration rate is low and soil drainage is poor.

A dearth of moisture causes a lower treeline to develop in semi-desert or continental interior forests. The typical character is of dense forest gradually thinning out as elevation descends, becoming park or savannah like with scattered trees and denser patches in moister places such as draws or gullies.

5. **Soil and geology:** In glaciated topography, where altitudinal and latitudinal treelines typically occur, the undeveloped soils are frequently of poor structure and markedly affect the treeline pattern. Glacial deposits are commonly either free draining gravels or poorly draining morainic tills and clays.

Some trees are able to thrive on coarse textured soil where more moisture is available and competition with grass and herbs is less than with fine textured, clayey or silty soils. In the palouse areas of eastern Oregon in the USA, pine is restricted to coarser soils because it will not grow on the silty ones. Where patterned ground is present, such as described in Chapter Five, the coarser stony parts of polygonal and striped areas provide the sites for pine.

6. **Frozen ground:** The polar/arctic treeline is found in areas where the soil is permanently frozen. Summer thawing only penetrates a short way into this deep permafrost, except where deeper gravelly deposits occur. In Canada, the northern limit of the forest/tundra

The treeline in Finnish Lapland. The pine and spruce gradually peter out whilst birch, willow and juniper, especially prostate varieties, become the main species at the treeline. The simple, domed landform produces fewer areas of shelter so that the trees are more evenly distributed across the slopes.

zone coincides with the southern limit of continuous permafrost. From there southwards the permafrost is patchy (related to solid and superficial geology) and the seasonally active surface of the soil is thicker. Permafrost restricts the growth of all trees, but to varying extents. Black spruce in Canada will grow on very shallow thawed places whilst in Siberia, *Larix dahurica* can grow on top of permafrost. White spruce, Balsam poplar and Alaskan paper birch find 3-4 feet/one metre of thawed soil adequate but prefer deeper sites that drain better such as gravelly areas and river terraces. Hence, much of the forest patterning relates to the microrelief of the surface topography and the thickness of the active soil layer.

7. **Light intensity:** Too much light and ultraviolet radiation can cause a loss of chlorophyll and a reduction in photosynthesis which reduces the chance of trees maintaining their positive carbon balance. This can make seedling survival difficult. Some species are limited to shadier slopes or the shade of other trees.

8. **Tree species:** The actual position of the treeline depends on the availability of species able to use diverse sites to the limit of their growth capacity. In parts of the tropics the treeline is lower, because the cold hardy conifers are not present in the ecosystem. Some species are especially adapted, such as Mountain pine, which grows in a prostrate form, or some forms of trees may have narrow crowns that can shed the snow more effectively.

When all these factors are understood the patterns of the treeline are a dramatic manifestation of the struggles of vegetation to exist. Chaos theory is at work in these places, leading to a self-organized fractal pattern. The pattern seen in patches of krummholz contributes to the greater one that reflects the gradual advance or sudden retreat of the forest front.

Treelines are thus zones where the vegetation presents highly defined patterns that are both coherent and complex. They relate directly to the interaction of landform and climate. Such places also demonstrate massiveness, with a diversity of structure at a range of scales. Hence they should be aesthetically pleasing, which they tend to be, judging by their attractiveness to people as places to hike or as components of highly valued scenery. Some of the qualities of a sublime landscape can be found where the treeline demonstrates the power of the forces of nature.

Forest/Bog Edges

Bogs, waterlogged peaty deposits formed by the accumulation of mosses, mainly sphagnum, provide an example of moisture gradients, that interact with the distribution pattern and structure of vegetation.

Many bog systems are active, growing and spreading during periodic wet phases of the climate or drying and shrinking during drier phases. In a number of areas, like the north of Scotland, climatic variations such as the post glacial change from warmer to cooler conditions some 8000 years ago, caused expansive blanket and raised bogs and mires to form. The cooler temperatures reduced the amount of evapotranspiration and allowed soils to become wetter, leading to the build up of sphagnum moss, which does not decay in the acidic, waterlogged conditions and accumulates as peat. These bogs expanded and engulfed adjoining forests, whose stumps can be exposed when peat is removed or excavated. During warmer, drier periods, the surface of the bog starts to dry out at its margins, enabling it to be colonized by trees and shrubs. Trees already present during drier periods may survive for a while into the next wetter cycle, explaining the partly dead and dying pattern of trees on some bogs.

At ground level, the gradual decrease in number and size of trees from solid canopied forest, some distance from the bog, to scattered, stunted, half dead trees on the sphagnum surface, shows distinct and structured patterns. Bogs are frequently hummocky, with locally drier patches and open pools of water. Trees or shrubs can colonize the drier hummocks and contribute to more drying by their transpirational power.

From the air the patterning of many of the bogs is clearly evident. In Finland or Newfoundland, bogs often display a distinctly striped appearance of low linear, drier ridges colonized by ericacious vegetation such as cloudberries, interspersed with the wetter zones, where standing water lies on the surface for much of the time. The ribbons and pools both seem to persist once formed, but the reasons for their formation are uncertain. One theory is that surfaces of the

The pattern of forest and bog on Vancouver Island, British Columbia, Canada. Trees which colonized and grew on the bog are now dying whilst the bog spreads into the forest edge to smother some of the trees. During drier phases the forest will be able to advance once more on to locally raised patches of the bog surface. The character of the edge relates to the classification made by Richard Forman.

A diagram showing some of the forest/ bog edge dynamics. The resulting edge can be described as a meandering pattern.

Forest advances onto bog where it is driest

Bog advances into forest where it is wettest

Bog

Forest

ribbon bogs erode when they thaw and melted snow flows over the frost-loosened surface. The ridges between the eroded channels dry out and are colonized by vegetation. The tree/bog interface has a similar structure to the elevational treeline; the closed canopy forest is punctured by small gaps, becomes fragmented and eventually breaks into small patches and individual trees. Size and health decreases with the distance out into the bog. Unlike the relative stability of elevational treelines, the forest/bog edge is more dynamic.

However, the general fluctuation of the bog edge over time does not explain how the structures of the patterns originated. A tree seed may fall on the bog. Its chances of survival increase or decrease, depending on the local moisture gradient; the bog grows into the forest - its chances of takeover depend on the transpirational power of the trees being less than the supply of moisture required to sustain the sphagnum. Thus, the edge structure describes a front of complex irregularity between winners and losers resulting from chance such as that randomly occurring on the throw of dice. In this case the front is

An aerial view of a Finnish pattern or ribbon bog. There is the typical, irregular edge structure and within the bog, perhaps on a slightly sloping section, the ribbon pattern has developed. This could be caused by some channel erosion of the peat during snow melt and colonization of the intervening, drier ridges. Such patterns, once formed, are quite persistent.

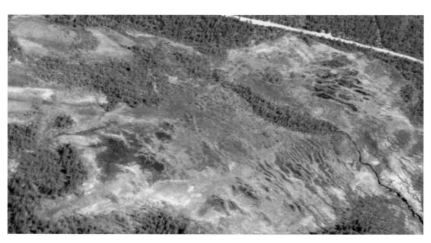

not completely random, being more predictable on the basis of probabilities, but is one more example of self-organization and fractal geometry. The edge line often describes a meandering pattern and the structure neatly fits Richard Forman's edge classification.

The presence of bogs in a forested landscape contributes to its mosaic character. The fractal edge, reflecting both moisture and competition, presents coherent, complex and mysterious qualities that enhance the aesthetic value of these patterns.

Coastal sand Dune Colonization

The new substrate produced in coastal areas where sand is deposited by the sea, provides another fascinating example of self-organized patterns. The structure of the dunes, formed by the wind, creates a pattern of landform with various gradients of moisture and stability. Depending on the size of the area, a series of dunes is commonly found, decreasing in mobility from the developing dune near the sea to those inland, colonized by vegetation whose roots stabilize them completely. The dune falls into the meander pattern type described in Chapter One, with a distinctly repeated ridge and valley structure.

The hollows in between dune ridges tend to be moister and may flood at high tides or during storms. Gradients of moisture vary with the depth of these hollows or 'slacks', the distance from the sea and the degree of flooding. As well as the macroscale variation between each dune, there is a microscale variation of small hillocks or convexities and minor hollows or wet spots (showing a fractal structure). Some of this microscale variation comes from the local success of vegetation in stabilizing sand, so that the wind removes more in the less stabilized areas. This is as much an example of vegetation determining the local landform as of landform determining vegetation; there is a continuous feedback loop between pattern and process, leading to subtleties and refinements that change frequently, particularly near the sea.

A view of active coastal sand dunes in Oregon, USA. Open moving dune areas can be seen together with grassy areas, shrubby cover and forest. This vegetation anchors the dunes. The forest offers greatest protection, but storms can breach the most weakly anchored sections.

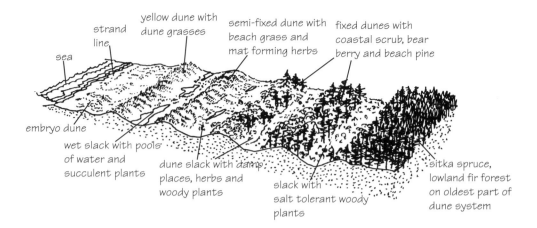

A typical section through a coastal sand dune system in Oregon shows how vegetation colonization progresses once the sand is stabilized and the salt is flushed out by rainwater. The dune structure consists of meandering waves that provide different degrees of moisture or dryness.

Occasionally major storms may have sufficient force to break the seaward dunes or remove the stabilizing vegetation and cause the whole dune system to become mobile. In some instances, this movement has buried villages built behind the formerly stable system. Erosion by human activity may also disturb the fragile stability and cause sand to blow again.

The plants follow a succession from pioneer stabilizers on the dunes such as marram grass, to shrubs and eventually to trees. The dune hollows or slacks have their own vegetation of plants tolerant of frequent flooding and salt, as well as drying. Distinctive patterns of a very fine scale can be observed amongst these small, specialized plants, which also partly stabilize areas of the sand in the bottom of the slacks.

When exploring coastal sand dune systems, we can perceive the repeated ridge and valley pattern that provides coherence for us. The complexity arises from the variability of dune structures and the changes to vegetation across them. As we can only see part of the pattern at any one time, there is a sense of mystery. Thus, coastal sand dune landscapes are aestheticaly valuable. We may find beauty in them and also a degree of the sublime, when the power of storms to breach and change them is displayed.

Mudflats, Deltas, Lakes and Flood Plains

A final example of the outstanding beauty of self-organized patterns, as plants colonize newly emerging land, is related to the extensive fractal patterns of mudflats and deltas described in Chapter Five. The movement of the water and the distribution of the substrate provides gradients of moisture, nutrients and degrees of stability, exploited by plants in different ways.

On estuarine mudflats, the pattern varies from the older, drier parts with established plant growth to the newly accumulating edge. Tidal water, mixed with the river water, floods these areas twice daily, leaving more mud or washing some away. As the waters recede and flow out to sea, a network of channels of intricate tracery is created. Plants tolerant of salt water and flooding colonize from the drier edges and trap mud against their leaves. This allows the mud to accumulate to levels where it is only rarely inundated. Fresh water from the river or rain may then flush the salt and create conditions suitable for other plants to take over.

At deltas, the multi-branched network pattern of channel structure is accompanied by variations in level produced by deposition along stream banks during floods. These natural levees are often above the water level. They are frequently the first areas to become colonized by woody plants, such as alders, poplars or willows, that are adapted to wetter conditions and succeed best there. The banks of the streams are characterized by this pattern, whilst the intervening spaces accommodate swamps or wetter soils that support woodland of the most water tolerant species such as alders, willows or mangroves.

As flooding leaves plenty of silt and nutrients in these places, they are very diverse in vegetation. Occasionally, where the delta has a simple structure with only one stream running into a lake, it may be entirely wooded, with older stands located nearest to the original lake shore whilst the freshly deposited material is colonized from the younger, leading edge of vegetation. Where the accumulating material slopes down, gradually into the water of a shallower lake, a gradient of water depth and moisture produces a pronounced progression from submerged plants to wet woodland. The undulation of the surface also gives rise to local variations. Eventually vegetation fills shallow lakes completely, to become dry land. The vegetation reinforces the underlying landform pattern and gives it more vertical structure. Complexity is added by the different textures and colours of the vegetation that reflect the landform structure.

An aerial view of a river delta in British Columbia, Canada where the fractal pattern of distribution channels is well developed. The mudflats are currently colonized with grasses whilst the forest is moving on to the margins (right hand side of picture). Deciduous pioneer species such as cottonwoods are the first to thrive on such sites.

On landform derived from glacial deposition, such as kame-and-kettle topography, where numerous kettle hole lakes were left by melting blocks of ice separated by gravel deposits, there may be a distribution of stages of colonization and infilling. Some larger, deeper lakes linked by streams might be flushing, open water with few deposits at the entrance. Others, fed by springs or ground water rather than streams, may still to be too deep for infilling to have commenced. Shallower pools may be ringed by fens and wet woodland. Others may have filled with mosses and fen vegetation, whilst the shallowest may have been colonized by trees or be completely wooded. In this case, the pattern of vegetation colonization has been determined by the underlying landform and associated water movement. This pattern can become a very complex mosaic. Coherence comes from the repeated patterns of kettle holes.

Flood plains of rivers exhibit similar vegetation patterns to deltas. The flooding river and the movement of meanders down stream produce a variety of microtopography, ranging from levees and terraces to ox bow lakes and vacant meanders. The ridges or terraces are mostly dry, whilst the lowest lying places are mostly wet. The frequency of different intensities of flood will affect lower places more often than higher ones, depositing nutrient rich silt over a gradient and also waterlogging or inundating some areas more often than others. As with deltas, trees and shrubs growing on levees will stabilize the banks and collect debris during floods. A varied, but highly structured vegetation

A rich mosaic of vegetation has developed on the flood plain of this meandering river. Mature mixed forest has been able to develop on the larger, more prominent gravel bars whilst others are disturbed by floods and shifting channels. Driftwood helps to trap sediment and start the construction of shingle bars. Some backwaters, from former channels, now out of the regular water flow, are filling with fen species. Slocan River, British Columbia, Canada.

pattern results that interacts with the processes of flooding, erosion and deposition in an intimate fashion. The meandering patterns found in the river valley landforms are reflected in the vegetation. The dense tree growth on levees along old meanders adds to the coherence of the whole pattern.

In our exploration of visual perception and aesthetics, we acknowledged the importance of pattern recognition in making our environment coherent. Vegetation patterns can be easy to perceive, if they contain contrasts of texture and colour and have defined edges. They are most unified, where the shapes relate strongly to those of the underlying landform. The most attractive scenes contain the qualities of coherence, found in the strength of the patterns, especially repeated basic ones such as meanders; complexity, found in the mosaics of vegetation; and mystery, where we cannot perceive all of the pattern at once. This is a common characteristic of diverse natural vegetation patterns, especially forests, which are three dimensional; much of their pattern is not discernible from within.

Natural Disturbance in the Landscape

Earlier in this chapter the concept of the stable, climax ecosystem was challenged. However, most climax ecosystems fail to arise because the developing vegetation is disturbed in some way, causing it to revert to an earlier successional stage, possibly the earliest one. Far from being aberrations that prevent the attainment of perfection, disturbance is an inherent part of all ecosystems, whose functioning and resilience depend on it. Disturbance is also one of the main mechanisms driving the maintenance of landscape diversity. It can also cleanse the landscape of pathogens, such as a fire consuming fungal spores or insect pupae.

The definition of disturbance depends on the scale of space and time under consideration. Some ecosystems are stable at a large scale and over long periods, whilst being unstable at a smaller scale and over short periods. Others suffer large scale catastrophic disturbance frequently, but exhibit little at the small scale or short term. Usually different types of disturbance interact in quite complex ways at various spatial scales and time periods. There are six types of natural disturbance:

- Soil and earth movement
- Water - as liquid, snow and ice
- Wind
- Fire
- Pathogens, including fungi and bacteria
- Animals, including insects

When assessing the impact of disturbances on vegetation patterns, there are four factors to consider: the frequency of the event, its intensity, the severity of the disturbance and its duration. Many events

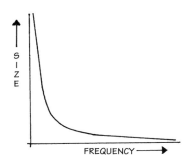

A diagram to show a 'log normal distribution' of the frequency/size relationship of natural disturbance events. Such a distribution helps to ensure the fractal quality of many natural patterns.

demonstrate a relationship between frequency and severity. For example, some forest types may experience frequent fires of low intensity, whilst others may be unaffected for long periods only to succumb to a rare fire of great intensity. Wind of moderate intensity is very frequent, whereas hurricane force events are relatively rare. Such distribution patterns over time are common to most disturbances and are known to statisticians as 'log normal distributions'.

Intensity may also be correlated with duration: ice storms last only a few hours, as do tornadoes or locust swarms, yet they do immense damage compared with less intense events of longer duration, such as some fungal attacks.

All disturbances contribute to the development of heterogeneous, mosaic landscapes as defined by Richard Forman. The effects of many can be widespread, intense and, because they may occur over short duration, dramatic. The aesthetic effects may initially be negative, as landscapes we have become used to suddenly change. The aesthetic response to disturbance will be considered more fully after their patterns and processes have been described.

Soil and earth movements are one of the interactions of landform and ecosystem processes. Landslides remove the vegetation, causing succession to revert back to new colonization by pioneer species. The new material may be fresh subsoil, containing little or no humus or seeds, or it may be the movement of soil and debris rich in organic material, seeds and other propagules. The pattern of slides depends on the stability of the substrate and the frequency of events which trigger them, such as very heavy rainfall. Sometimes this movement may be frequent enough to maintain bare ground conditions permanently. Frosts can aid this, continuously loosening roots developed over the previous growing season.

An example of this kind of constant disturbance can be found along the banks of the Fraser River in British Columbia. The undercutting of loose, finely textured soil by the river, together with occasional heavy rain in a fairly dry climate, has eroded this material in a fractal pattern. Forest grows on the less eroding areas to give some stability, grasses and herbs colonize bare areas but are unable to gain a foothold on the most disturbed places. Thus, there is a distinctive pattern to this kind of disturbance, which relates to the original landform and vegetation history.

A slower and less catastrophic variety of disturbance is the more gradual movement of soil under gravity. Smaller scale occurrences are known as soil creep, whilst the larger scale involves the slow, downward flow of the whole hillside. This earth flow inhibits the establishment of deep rooting plants, such as trees with tap roots, and also disturbs the growth of trees that do become established. This process may not cause succession to revert to the starting point, but it prevents late successional stages from developing. This occurs on slopes

This pattern of constant erosion along the valley side of the Fraser River in British Columbia, Canada, shows how constant disturbance maintains the site at an early successional stage. Grasses manage to colonize some slopes and trees can find a foothold in other places less prone to disturbance.

overlaid by deposits, which do not become fluid when wet or where the slope is not steep enough to render catastrophic failure likely. As earth flow progresses, the upper portion may tend to be less vegetated than lower portions, where considerable depths of material accumulate. Other disturbance agents such as fire or wind may change the character of the flow if the limited stabilizing effect of roots is reduced or the ground becomes more open to rain percolation. Earth flow helps to maintain a heterogeneous vegetation mosaic.

Water disturbs landscapes and ecosystems as a liquid and as snow and ice. These act in different ways. Running water is an integral part of the landscape and is an important pattern creator. It acts as a disturbance agent when it occurs in quantities and at times or over durations that are outside the 'normal' ranges in which it functions. Disturbance by running water can be direct or indirect. Direct effects include floods washing away plants, soil, rocks and altering long established patterns of river flow. Heavy rain can effect similar changes, especially in dry or semi-arid climates, where it is an extremely rare event, but one of great intensity and short duration, such as in the badlands example described in Chapter Five. Secondary effects include landslides induced by heavy rain soaking into potentially unstable soils or other deposited materials or where debris carried in flood waters bury an existing ecosystem.

The disturbance effects of flood waters were seen in early 1996 in Oregon in the USA. In one river, the complex pattern of pools and riffles (gravel bars) built up over decades was completely altered, so that the channels moved, pools filled and riffles were scooped out to become pools.

This west facing mountainside shows the evidence of frequent avalanches. The parallel straight tracks occur in slight hollows. Snow collects along the ridge top until an avalanche is triggered by warmer weather.

Snow causes disturbance at large and small scales. Avalanches occur mainly on south or west facing slopes (in the northern hemisphere), where greater temperature fluctuations cause snow accumulations to become unstable. The power of an avalanche is very great, so that trees and shrubby plants are flattened and ground vegetation can be eroded. In many mountain ranges, there are distinct and regular avalanche tracks down forested slopes with a broad expanded area at their foot. There may be avalanches at least once a year so that vegetation has little chance of establishment.

Snow can also bend, break or de-branch trees, if it is particularly heavy and wet. Such snow may be common in some places, such as coastal mountain systems, where many tree species and growth forms have evolved to withstand it. In other places, such snowfall is rare and can cause widespread damage. This can range from whole stands of trees being broken and flattened, to considerable thinning of the forest canopy, letting light enter, as well as resulting in large quantities of dead wood. The pattern of damage may be determined by the prevailing wind direction during such events, the topography (causing a greater likelihood of snow accumulating on sheltered trees, where it cannot blow off to reduce the load), together with the forest type, species composition and successional stage.

Ice can also build up on the top of trees and cause the whole tree to collapse. The tops of some may snap under the weight of ice. Others, more flexible, may bend double. In the winter of 1995 an ice storm blew across the Christmas Mountains in New Brunswick, Canada. The trees might have withstood the strength of the wind but could not stand the combination of wind and accumulated ice. Very large areas were flattened during a single night. Thus the disturbance contributed to the development of the landscape mosaic at varying scales, from lots of small patches to a few large ones.

Wind affects many landscapes and sometimes it may be difficult to distinguish between wind as a normal part of landscape processes and as a disturbance agent. Trees and forests are particularly prone to alteration and development by wind. Individual trees or forest edges can be sculpted by persistent wind blowing in a consistent direction. Wind can also disturb much broader patterns of the landscape.

Wind moves like a fluid and is subject to turbulence and internal instabilities that show patterns related to chaos theory. Intense wind storms contain a pronounced structure, from which vortices or eddies (tornadoes) may spring. The patterns perceived in this process are repeated, but are extremely difficult to predict or to measure.

The flow of wind over a landscape will show patterns of flow and speed that result from these interactions. Wind speed increases over ridges and through narrowing valleys, due to the venturi effect. If strong winds flow from a particular direction, a map of windiness can be assembled. This windiness pattern can be reflected in the structure of a forest canopy; a smooth, tightly packed structure results from persistently strong winds, whilst coarser textured, more open canopies develop in regions with lower wind velocities. Seasonal effects can be observed between deciduous and evergreen trees. The former, being leafless in winter, are less affected by strong winter winds than by prevailing winds in summer, when their canopies are densest. Thus the mosaic pattern is likely to show scale characteristics depending on the pattern of windiness as defined by the landform.

Wind shaped, wave forests are a prime example of dynamic systems with internal patterns created by instabilities. They can be found in a number of places such as Japan, the Adirondack Mountains of the USA and Newfoundland in Canada, as well as other places where they have recently being identified. Sandy Robertson, a forest researcher in Canada, has produced a fascinating study of wave forests and their inherently fractal geometry.

Wave forests are thought to originate from weather systems that can show a wave like pattern at mid latitudes. This pattern travels eastwards and exhibits a degree of coherence, contrasting with more chaotic systems of regions noted for the passage of storm tracks. Newfoundland lies in one of these routes. The weather systems over continental land masses tend to be more predictable than those over the ocean and in Newfoundland, as in Japan, the two types converge so that stable patterns occur within the more turbulent areas. The wave forests are the reflection of the rolling vortices that flow off the turbulent weather systems across the land, once they reach chaos. These vortices flow in waves and their strength causes the forest to develop a repeated pattern of disturbance: wind shaping and blow-down, also in a wave pattern; the exposed edge is affected by successive events, to be followed by recovery and regrowth. Thus in section they present a series of wave like forms that progress across the landscape in the direction of the wind.

An example of a wave forest pattern under formation in Newfoundland, Canada. Each blown strip is evenly spaced across the slope. The pattern will gradually move across the landscape.

More conventional wind disturbance is caused by hurricanes or other extreme climatic phenomena. Studies of hurricane passages across forests have uncovered some interesting patterns, dependent on the structure and interaction of the storm system and the terrain. The effects of a hurricane upon a forest are not solely due to the forces of wind and rain. Their strength of impact is regulated by the landform, the successional stage and structure of the forest.

The influence of landform can range from maximum exposure on ridge slopes, facing the direction of the storm, to maximum shelter low down on lee slopes. Hence, this should give a pattern to the degrees of exposure based on a given wind direction, and the likelihood of eddies that cause locally severe damage, where there is greater variation in the direction of tree fall.

Early successional stages of the forest tend to be damaged less than later ones. Younger forests may already be present, due to previous

This view shows the pattern of wind damage in English woodland after the Great Storm of 1987. Trees are uprooted and snapped. The trees were later removed but left to itself new woodland would have developed through the tangle of debris. The upturned root plates provide fresh soil conditions, ideal for colonization by early successional plant species.

hurricane damage, resulting in a different pattern from a forest of less varied ages. If the forest is more fragmented, there will be more edges where older trees abut younger ones. These more exposed edges will be prone to greater damage where they face the wind. Tall trees, with crowns concentrated near the top, are more likely to be blown over than trees whose crown is deeper. Some shallow rooted species are more prone to uprooting than snapping and this may result in different damage patterns. Thus the mosaic pattern existing at the time of a hurricane will affect the subsequent mosaic and the future development of a landscape.

The intensity of the damage is related to the scale: the most intense action and the greatest damage is very localized, whilst lesser damage is generally more widespread. The competitive advantages of species may alter in the short term, because of the damage to foliage and root systems and the new levels of light penetrating the canopy. Some trees recover more quickly from damage than others. Hence, recovery from the damage, or rates of secondary succession are both short and long term in character.

It is now increasingly apparent that tropical forests, once believed to be fragile, unchanging ecosystems, have experienced large scale changes over, at least, the last 14,000 years, due to hurricanes. These periodic changes produce variations in species composition, biomass quantities and rates of forest cycling. Tropical forests may be adapted to or require periodic disturbance. Data on the characteristics of disturbances are very rare in terms of their scale, frequency, duration or intensity. From events such as Hurricane Hugo, which passed over forests in Puerto Rico in 1989, some inferences can be drawn. This storm moved across the landscape at a slow rate of 10 knots. When compared with a faster moving storm, the rate of energy dissipation per hectare was much higher, giving rise to greater damage. Within the hurricane, there is a complex system of wind gusts, sustained winds, violent changes in direction and tornadoes, all of which are impossible to predict or reconstruct and which have very localized effects.

The damage caused by Hurricane Hugo reflected the combined influence of storm dynamics, landform and forest structure described above. As tropical landforms tend to be formed by water erosion, they are usually strongly fractal and full of dendritic branching patterns. Thus, the damage also tends to show a basic fractal pattern overlaid by that of storm turbulence. The result adds to the heterogeneity of the vegetation mosaic.

Hurricanes have also been studied by Foster and Boose in New England in the USA, where there is some record of past events across the same area. Hurricanes can travel along a relatively small number of paths, one of which is most likely to generate catastrophic wind. Storms travelling, mainly, across land quickly dissipate, because of the greater surface friction, compared with the sea and because they are cut off from their energy source, which is the ocean. Storms travelling over

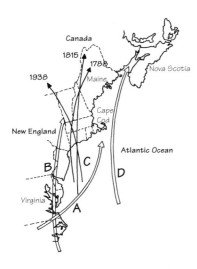

A map showing the pattern of hurricane movements over New England in the USA. Track C is the one that produces the most damaging effects.
(After Foster and Boose, 1992)

the ocean maintain their full strength longer. They rotate anti-clockwise in the northern hemisphere and the highest winds are normally found on the east side if they travel north, where the general forward motion of the storm coincides with the direction of rotational winds around the storm centre.

Storms passing northward over the Atlantic along the eastern seaboard of New England into Maine are the most damaging, where winds blow from the south and east. Hurricanes in 1635, 1788, 1815 and 1936 followed this route and so repeatedly affected the same area. The eastern mixed broadleaved forests take around 100 years to achieve late successional conditions. Assuming the absence of human intervention over the period, the 1815 event would have caused less damage to areas affected in 1788, because the regenerated area following complete blowdown would not have fully recovered. Between 1815 and 1936, stands would have approached a late successional stage and so be ready for another catastrophe. Thus the landscape structure (in the absence of human clearances) would theoretically contain a diversity of stands, in terms of size, shape and successional structure, from repeated hurricane episodes. Within this landscape variations in storm intensity may also have contributed to diversity of structure. Damage would range from slight snapping of branches and stems, partial blowdown of certain species leading to a more open canopy, to places of complete blowdown, as well as a concentration of scattered smaller areas where extremely intense damage would have taken place.

Thus, the picture straight after a storm or hurricane event is likely to show a pattern of forest patches of different structure and composition. This will affect the future succession and changes to the landscape, due to environmental conditions such as light, shelter, evapotranspiration rates, surviving vegetation and the availability of propagules. These lead to differences in the rate of forest regeneration which affect the likelihood of damage from the next event.

In Great Britain, a particularly windy country, the forests planted since 1919 on poorly drained and exposed upland sites are prone to wind damage. Studies of the patterns of wind speeds over several decades show the typical distribution of a few large events embedded within numerous smaller ones. What is significant is that every winter there are storms of sufficient strength to blow mature forests, or parts of them, down. Thus wind disturbance is endemic to such forests, a fact only recently realized (p. 237, Fig. 11).

Fire: Natural fire has been and continues to be a major cause of disturbance in the landscape. Forests, grasslands and tundra are all affected. The occurrence, frequency and patterns it creates are varied, depending on a large number of factors.

Natural fires are virtually all caused by lightning (exceptions include volcanic eruptions). Excepting ice covered areas, lightning fire occurs in all terrestrial landscapes, even moist tropical rainforests (rarely) and contributes to the great mosaic of vegetation types. In tropical landscapes, the lightning may be frequent and concentrated enough to kill and break up patches of vegetation, even if it is too wet to catch fire. Temperate forests, savannah, prairie, tundra, chaparral, desert and marshes all burn from lightning fires.

Like the log normal distribution patterns over space and time, described for floods and winds, lightning shows a large number of discharges, but a small number of fire starts. Lightning is unable to ignite fires if there is insufficient material in a combustible state. In the tropics, there is the greatest amount of lightning activity, but natural fire is rare. In higher latitudes of boreal forests, lightning is much rarer, but fires are started more easily and can become very large conflagrations. 'Dry' lightning storms are most effective at starting fires, as they produce very little precipitation and do not douse any fires that start. They occur with varying frequency; for example, several times a decade in the northern Rocky Mountains or almost annually in California and Arizona in the USA.

Fire behaviour is very complicated and difficult to forecast, but its patterns are more predictable. The sequence of events and the progress of particular fires may be chaotic, but the character of the pattern is influenced by the structure of the landscape, as has been observed for other disturbances and explained by Stephen Pyne as summarized below.

Whereas wind storms destroy vegetation, but leave the pieces behind, combustion processes consume much of the vegetation. There are three stages to the process of combustion :

1. **Preheating**, where the vegetation and other fuel, such as dead wood, is brought to the temperature at which it will ignite. The initial lightning strike can reach extremely high temperatures at one spot, so that on tinder dry vegetation the ignition point is reached immediately. Once a fire is established, it can spread heat to nearby areas by convection, such as heat rising up slopes from the fire, by radiation from the front of the fire to vegetation close by or by conduction. The preheating induces pyrolysis, where hydrocarbons such as resin are vaporized, water evaporates and solid material becomes gaseous.

2. **Flaming combustion** commences when the gases ignite. This is an ephemeral state where a wave of flame advances, releasing huge amounts of energy as it does so. By the time the deeper layers of wood in a log or tree are exposed, the flaming front has passed by, blown by the wind and attracted by freshly pyrolysed gases. This results in the fire site being covered in charcoal debris.

3. **Glowing combustion** continues after the flaming front has passed over. The charcoal from the flaming stage oxidizes and the carbon burns. This phase may last a long time or may be doused by rain.

A diagrammatic section across a fire, showing the different phases.

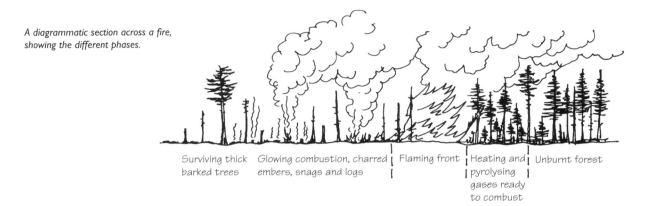

Surviving thick barked trees | Glowing combustion, charred embers, snags and logs | Flaming front | Heating and pyrolysing gases ready to combust | Unburnt forest

Rarely does the entire vegetation burn or the soil become so heated that all organisms are killed. However, the fire does 'purify' the site and reduce the amount of pathogens that might be present. Dead vegetation may be almost entirely consumed whilst green trees may be killed or part burnt and become the substrate for specialized organisms or fuel for future fires.

The pattern of a fire usually starts as a compact shape, spreading out from the point of ignition. If lightning hits a fairly uniform patch of vegetation and the weather is calm, the fire will expand fairly evenly. However, the wind will usually drive it in a particular direction and as it veers or backs, the fire will spread in different directions. Local topography, wetter places or different amounts of fuel will also affect how intensely the fire burns or where it may peter out completely. Thus the fire develops peninsulars and branches, fingers and palmate patches. These are the kind of pattern shapes noted by Richard Forman and discussed in Chapter One. The wind may blow burning brands ahead of the flaming front and start new fires, which extend and subsequently affect the continued spread of the main fire.

The pattern of burnt and unburnt forest on a landscape in Labrador, Canada. The fire has left substantial unburnt patches in deeper valleys, hollows and on rocky bluffs.

A ground fire burning in a Scottish pine forest. The fire will kill much surface vegetation but leave the roots of many plants alive. This fire will also scorch the bark of the large, old trees but it is not likely to kill them. There is insufficient structure to allow a crown fire to develop.

In a forest, the principal fire may be a ground fire, mainly of the glowing combustion variety; it may develop into a surface fire, which has a flaming front and burns fuels such as dead wood, and shrubs; a crown fire occurs when the tree crowns, heated by convection, erupt into flames in spectacular fashion. A crown fire needs a 'fire ladder', such as a dead and dry tree, to climb into the canopy, and a surface fire to sustain it. The transition from surface to crown fire, from steady state to acceleration, needs a huge accumulation of heat from combustion of large amounts of fuel on the ground; it also requires a deep flaming front of sufficient size to provide an area of heat, rather than a point or line. The rate of energy release has to be great enough to interact with the surrounding air, especially the wind, so that it can generate its own convective wind with a positive feedback (where the greater heat sucks in more oxygen and generates even fiercer heat).

A diagram showing the pattern and structure of a forest landscape burnt by a crown fire. Patches of unburnt trees, both living and dead, a fringe of dead trees and isolated living trees whose thick bark has protected them are distributed over the site.

The structure of a forest, after a severe fire has passed by, will consist of a significant area of almost completely burnt material, with the skeletal remains of larger trees scattered about. Islands and promontories of unburnt forest will persist. Some will be dead from the scorching of the surface fire, others will be still alive, being bypassed, due to chance wind changes or because they were sheltered or in damper patches. A fringe of dead trees will mark the margins of the fire, whilst some thicker barked, older and taller trees will have survived in places: these may have withstood 3 or 4 fires in their lives.

Where the landform is regular, with few breaks in slopes, ridges, valleys or other natural obstacles and the forest is uniform in species and structure, a large spreading fire will have nothing to stop its progress. On broken sites, microsite differences will contribute to a more diverse pattern, less continuous and with more untouched patches left behind. At the larger landscape scale, there will be major differences in the frequency and intensity of fires, depending on the aspect and elevation of the area. In the northern hemisphere, south and southwest facing slopes are likely to burn more frequently than north and east facing slopes, because they are warmer and drier. The north and east slopes lose snow later and more slowly making it difficult for fires to start. It takes the periodic drier intervals that occur every few hundred years for north and east slopes to reach a level of dryness that will burn and do so more intensely, because much fuel has been accumulated. More frequent fires reduce the amount of fuel to a degree, although by killing trees they also create it.

Fires as they move, can also jump across deeper gullies or hollows and leave the vegetation in them untouched. Such areas act as refuges for seed, propagules and wildlife to re-colonize the burnt area. Ridge lines may be the point at which a fire peters out because the rising heat prevents vegetation on the other side of the ridge to heat up for ignition, or the change of aspect may mean that the fuel is not dry enough to burn.

Vegetation varies in its flammability and response to the effects of fire. Different forest species may be more flammable, such as resinous pines, firs and spruces. Broadleaved trees will be killed by a hot surface fire, but are unlikely to burn. Larches also tend to be less flammable. A number of species are fire dependent to some degree, and are genetically adapted to respond to fire. Lodgepole pine is one of these. It bears seratinous cones (meaning delayed opening) that are opened by the heat of the fire to release seeds, which then colonize the burnt landscape and produce a secondary succession of pine. Parts of the North American forest are 'fire climax' of Lodgepole pine which burns every 70-80 years or so and re-colonizes the burnt landscape. Some eucalyptus species in Australia act in the same way; bush fires are needed to reduce the litter layer, consume oils that accumulate at the surface following leaf decomposition and open the seed cases. These seeds can accumulate for decades before release.

Whilst trees with seratinous cones are well adapted for re-colonizing after a fire, some individuals of the same species will not have them; this seems to ensure that in rare periods, when the fire return interval is long, the trees are able to reproduce in its absence.

Some forest types are not destroyed, but are sustained by fire. Ponderosa pine develops a multi-layered forest structure in a semi-arid climate. It develops thick, heat resistant bark quite early in its growth and requires frequent surface fires to keep other trees from colonizing, such as firs (*Abies spp*) that are shade tolerant and would eventually shade out the pine. Fir is thin barked and extremely resinous and so it burns extremely easily.

Following a fire the ash gives a boost to nutrients such as potassium, but nitrogen will have been lost. Thus, plants recolonizing can take advantage of the nutrient flush, but those capable of capturing or coping with low levels of nitrogen, or having stores of nutrients in their roots, may take better advantage of the site. Other plants can adapt to the regular presence of fire by developing thick bark or outer skins resistant to heat, tuberous roots deep in the soil or by resprouting from underground parts soon after the fire passes. Leguminous plants are often early colonizers, because they can fix nitrogen.

When fire occurs in a cluster over a relatively short time, such as a decade or two, the repeated events may leave the vegetation little or no time to recover fully and rebuild the nutrient regime. Soils may become progressively exhausted and convert from the original vegetation to another type. Forest in the taiga may become muskeg, because, without evapotranspiration, the soil becomes wetter and boggy. The same may happen at the elevational treeline, because of the very slow growth rate of trees. In the Mediterranean region, fires (not all natural) prevent the oak/pine forests from returning and maintain a scrubby vegetation. In extreme circumstances, repeated fires in drier climates may contribute to desertification.

Human use of forests and fire have gone hand in hand since the earliest times. Whilst floods and wind storms are events that cannot be controlled, fire can be started and to some degree controlled. Early humans are likely to have seen the effects of fire producing fresh vegetation growth, which attracted animals and made hunting easier. Thus wild fires cannot easily be separated from human induced ones, as described in Chapter Seven.

Fungi and Pathogens: Whilst floods, winds and fires are exogenous, originating from outside the ecosystem, fungi and natural pathogens (bacteria and viruses) are endogenous, originating from within it. These may remain endemic components of a system, persisting at low levels in the ecosystem and affecting small proportions of trees or other plants, but periodically may flare up into an epidemic, killing large numbers of the host plants. This can cause stand replacement or even substitution of one species by another.

There are many fungi and pathogens that create or contribute to the development of landscape pattern. Fungal root rot in conifers may start a centre of infection and spread slowly through root grafts to neighbouring trees. As the trees die, light reaches the forest floor and secondary succession proceeds in small patches. This results in a very complex vegetation structure. Such patch-based forest dynamics may be an important process, leading to mosaic development in vegetation types not prone to other kinds of more catastrophic disturbance. In conifer forests, there may be succession by broadleaved trees in the gaps created by the root rot. These eventually revert to conifer, but the interval may help reduce the occurrence of root rot if the broadleaves are not also susceptible.

Epidemics may arise from a number of factors, such as drought that causes stress in trees, making them less able to withstand an attack. Moist conditions may be favourable for the production of fungal spores, or the fungus may be a secondary infection following a fire or windstorm.

Some major epidemics have affected the appearance of whole landscapes. Chestnut blight in the Appalachian Mountains in the USA virtually wiped out the American chestnut, a major species, in the early years of the 20th century. In Great Britain, Dutch elm disease severely diminished most species of elms, which were an important component of the lowland landscape. The elms grew from suckers, so that when one tree was attacked, the fungus could spread along a hedge, killing all the trees. This disease needs a beetle to transmit it, which can only burrow into branches of a certain thickness. The elm resuckers after the disease has passed through but when new growths reach the size suitable for colonization by the beetle carrier they succumb once more.

Other extreme examples are rust fungi that will kill part or all of the foliage of plants, especially trees. This may be restricted to certain species, reducing their competitiveness or the degree of shade they cast. Frequently such trees take several years to succumb to an attack. Rusts may also only attack certain species such as White pine blister rust. Other species of plants may also have their own rusts.

It is often believed that the effects of pathogens are more catastrophic where crops are grown: monocultures of food plants provide a large host population in one place, so that spread of the pathogen can be very swift. In natural environments, the plant communities are usually more mixed, so that monospecific pathogens may only affect one component. However, locally, there may be quite extensive patches or stands of the same species, whose death or debilitation by a pathogen will affect the landscape structure, alter competitive advantage and may permit other species complexes to assert domination. The chestnut blight mentioned previously did not kill the whole forest, but changed the competitive relationship amongst the remainder. The pattern of pathogen attack relates to the pattern of vegetation distribution, itself related to landform. Thus, the contribution of pathogens to the landscape mosaic is to reinforce many of the patterns already present.

Insects: Insects are major disturbers of all ecosystems. There are huge numbers of species, so it is possible for all plants to play host to one or more specific insects. Some use plants in a non-lethal fashion, such as aphids sucking sap which reduces growth, but does not kill the plant. Others defoliate whole areas of forests, prairies or farmlands. As with pathogens, they are prone to extreme fluctuations in numbers, rising quickly to epidemic proportions and then collapsing to endemic levels. The main ways insects disturb landscapes are defoliation, where they eat the green parts of plants, and shoot or bark invasion, where the cambium is killed by boring insect larvae. Nearly all forms of infestation are by larval stages, the main part of the insect life cycle, which need large quantities of food.

An exception are locusts, where the voracious winged adults fly in vast swarms and eat all vegetation in their path. This is an extremely intense, shortlived event on a par with a hurricane or a fire. The movement of the insects depends on their detection of further supplies of food and they need to move continuously as food runs out. There may be some links between these outbreaks and climatic factors.

The population of many defoliators can increase dramatically in a few years, if each adult pair is able to lay large quantities of eggs. The timing of each outbreak may be related to the age of the host plant and the climatic conditions. If the winters have been milder or sunnier than usual, a larger proportion of overwintering pupae survive severe frosts enabling further substantial increases in population levels. When Eastern spruce budworm attacks Balsam fir in the northeast USA and eastern Canada, the forest can be almost entirely killed; it regenerates as a completely even aged stand of Balsam fir and grows to around 70 years before becoming prone to another attack. It is possible that the trees' defences are weakened, when they start to suffer the stress of old age or competition. These epidemic outbreaks tend to be most severe in forests in higher latitudes.

An aerial view of a Balsam fir forested landscape in New Brunswick, Canada, which has been attacked by spruce budworm (pale grey area in centre of photo). The attack partly depends on the presence of the correct species of tree at a susceptible age as well as factors of insect population patterns.

The Western spruce budworm, the Mountain pine beetle, Larch sawfly, Hemlock looper, Pine beauty moth, Gypsy moth and Douglas fir tussock moth also affect large areas at a time. In some outbreaks the pre-epidemic levels of populations may increase between 150 and 450 fold over two to three years, at the low end (tussock moths) to 18,000 fold at the high end (the Larch budmoth population in Europe).

The development of an epidemic has several phases. Firstly, the release phase is characterized by insect numbers increasing past the level at which natural control can cope. The peak phase sees populations increase exponentially (the population doubles in size during each period of measurement) to the maximum. This is followed by a decline phase, where the decrease may be swifter than the increase during the peak phase. This happens because the food runs out or the predator population catches up or both. The rate of decrease reduces during the post decline phase.

Some epidemics are cyclical, occurring on reasonably predictable cycles such as around eight and a half years in the case of Swiss Larch budmoth outbreaks. Others are eruptive: they occur at irregular intervals and fluctuate erratically. Some populations may be stable in some places and eruptive in others.

When insects are restricted to certain hosts, the pattern of their activity is clearly related to that of the vegetation and its age structure. Thus, there may be complete killing of large areas of single species or changes to the texture and diversity of areas of mixed species, where one species is selectively killed. Once again, this type of disturbance helps to create and maintain a landscape mosaic of different vegetation types and successional stages.

Animals: Very high levels of browsing herbivores, such as rabbits, can reduce plant populations and cause reversion to early successional stages. The plant composition may change, due to grazing or browsing, so that only species tolerant of this can survive. Hard winters or food shortage may cause animals, like deer or porcupines, to eat plants or parts of plants that they would normally avoid, such as bark, thereby killing trees. Natural disturbance of this sort may be quite rare compared with human induced examples, such as pastoral animals, introduced species or predator removal, causing unnaturally high numbers in some populations that can damage or severely inhibit the growth and regeneration of a wide range of plant species.

Interaction Amongst Disturbance Types

Most landscapes are affected in very complex ways by the interaction of the various disturbances described above.

Various cycles of disturbances may occur. In some forests where large fires or windstorms may be anticipated at long intervals, there may be other, smaller disturbances at more frequent intervals, such as lesser fires, root rot pockets, insect attacks or landslides, avalanches and snow breaks. If a stand of approximately uniform species and age was regenerated after a large fire, it would follow through the various phases of secondary succession. If it reached late successional or a mature phase before being replaced, it is likely that a patchy structure would start to develop. Root rot might open the canopy, allowing other species to develop; wind snap, avalanche, landslide or snow break would also open various sized patches in different places, leading to other structural variations and changes to the plant communities. Many of these agents would also be adding to the fuel and increasing the overall risk of catastrophic fire.

Trees blown over by hurricanes, but not killed, become stressed, because their root systems are damaged. This may increase the chances of pathogen or insect infestation in those areas, hastening their deaths. If the forest is prone to lightning strike, the large quantities of fuel from dead fallen trees and dead trees leaning into intact forest canopy, will increase the chances of intense crown fires.

The Lodgepole pine forests of North America are prone to large scale stand replacing fires. It is not a long lived species so that, in the absence of another disturbance, the forest will eventually be succeeded by shade tolerant trees such as fir. However, Lodgeploe pine is also prone to attack by Mountain pine beetle, which follows the epidemic pattern described above. Thus large areas of trees die as the bark burrowing beetles kill the cambium layer. The large patches of dead trees add to the fuel levels in the forest, so that intense fires are more likely. These fires consume the dead trees and kill any remaining beetles, so sanitizing the forest. Severe fires are needed to release seed from the cones and the forest regenerates. The pattern this sequence creates varies, depending on whether the Lodgepole pine comprises pure or mixed stands. Mixed stands are less likely to burn so severely, leading to a patchier pattern.

Balsam fir in eastern North America can be almost entirely killed by the budworm. The timber soon starts to rot and the dead trees start to break up. If there is no fire the Balsam can regenerate, partly shaded by the skeleton of the previous forest. This shade prevents colonization by light demanding pine or broadleaved species. If a fire does occur, the dead material is excellent fuel and the resulting ashes and available light make an ideal site for light demanding pioneer broadleaves such as poplar or White birch. Pine may also colonize (Red pine or Jack pine). The seed of the Balsam fir may have been incinerated so that the pioneers may then be succeeded by spruce. If Black spruce succeeds, this is a very long lived stable forest type compared with the Balsam fir so it might be a long time (200 years or more) before a severe fire occurs. This might cause succession to spruce, to broadleaves, or to Balsam fir.

In the dry savannah or sahel regions near the Sahara desert, the process of desertification may advance when swarms of locusts eat all the vegetation that has been stabilizing the dry, friable soil. If this happens during a drought period the soil may blow away and it may be difficult for new vegetation to establish.

Human Influence on Disturbance

It was suggested previously that humans probably started to use fire as a tool to aid hunting from a very early period. In the USA, it is possible that some of the largely treeless, prairie landscapes developed from hunting clearances, which in turn supported large numbers of herbivores such as bison. These kept the prairies open by grazing, whilst the nomadic people burnt areas to promote fresh grass growth.

If people also observed certain tubers and grasses regrowing quickly on patches burnt by a lightning strike fire, they could have developed primitive forms of cultivation, emulating this effect, such as slashing and burning existing vegetation. This disturbance, controlled by people, would tend to reduce the risk of large scale natural fires, lead to a patchier landscape and affect the populations of animals and birds. Species requiring edge or more open habitats would be favoured, whilst the presence of early successional 'weed' species of plants would increase. These changes to the pattern of the landscape could have been sustainable, whilst human populations remained at relatively low levels.

Natural fire keep the landscape in a particular mosaic of vegetation patches which then all succeed to a late successional type in its absence. However, people have also deliberately suppressed forest fires. This may reduce the degree of patchiness in the vegetation pattern, causing a monotonous late successional stage to persist and depriving wildlife of certain habitat types such as open, early pioneer stages. Moreover, the suppression of fire in certain forests such as Ponderosa pine in the USA, can have calamitous effects for its survival (see Chapter Seven).

Human disturbances of an artificial nature are also introduced into the landscape. Forests that are harvested or logged, present disturbance patterns very different from natural ones. The size, shape and distribution of clear cut areas may lead to fragmentation of the forest, oversimplified stand structure, loss of legacies to the next generation of forest and a huge increase in the amount of edge. Road construction may place large quantities of earth in places where landslides may occur (if the excavations are badly constructed). These slides may deposit larger amounts of material into a hydrological system than can be coped with by the natural levels of control within the system.

Farming constantly reverts the ecosystem to early successional conditions by ploughing and harvesting. Quarrying, mining activities such as spoil heap placement and landfill of refuse, all add disturbances to the landscape out of step with natural processes. It is difficult to see the influence of natural disturbance in many landscapes nowadays because they are so altered by human practices.

One of the ideas, to be presented later in the chapter, is to use an understanding of natural disturbance in the landscape as a means for maintaining its health by designing and managing the landscape in ways that are compatible with its various forms.

A mosaic landscape of evergreen conifers and deciduous aspen. The aspen is a pioneer species and owes its distribution pattern to human disturbance, in this case probably traditional practices of burning to create better browse for animals hunted by native people. Fort St James, British Columbia, Canada.

Aesthetics and Natural Disturbance

In Chapter Three we explored the aesthetics of the landscape. One of the issues concerning the perception of beauty in natural landscapes is whether a disturbed scene, such as a forest that has been burnt, blown down or killed by insects can also be beautiful.

The appearance of newly disturbed landscapes can be shocking to us. If we are familiar with a particular scene, perhaps having grown up with it, the impact of change is likely to be greater. We may become more easily adjusted to frequent, smaller scale disturbances, such as minor changes to the pool and riffle structure of a river, small continous landslides, or small areas of forest blowing down every winter. However, the experience of a catastrophic disturbance may be so rare, perhaps only occurring once every few generations, that it upsets our sense of the world and our place in it. The experience of a catastrophic event like a fire or hurricane may be a sublime one, yet not very positive.

Such disturbances are necessary for a diverse landscape to exist in a healthy state, which suggests that while we may not like the initial effects, the new growth and the healing scars, lead to a restored beauty. Moreover, the mosaic patterns produced by disturbance contain the necessary edges, textures, colours and shapes to help in our perception and understanding of scenes, which also contain many more affordances.

Given that we have lived in and utilized the natural world for millennia, it seems nonsensical to regard nature and natural disturbances as completely inviolate and segregated from ourselves. The engagement with our environment, as proposed by Arnold Berleant, becomes more compelling and fruitful when we understand more about natural patterns and processes. Perhaps the main distinction to be drawn is not between purely 'natural', wilderness environments and completely 'cultural' ones, but between those landscapes where natural processes (and therefore patterns) dominate and those where cultural forces and patterns dominate. Along this continuum are also a large number of landscapes where humans and changing nature can live in harmony.

We prize the most natural landscapes for their rarity and aesthetic qualities. Ironically, we have also tried to prevent many of the natural disturbance processes that have produced the predominantly natural and healthy ecosystems from occurring. At Yellowstone National Park in the USA during the late 1980s, the long practice of suppressing fire eventually led to catastrophic conflagrations, because the ecosystem became stressed. Such eventualities are not yet accepted by many people, especially non-ecologists, as an inevitable consequence of misunderstanding natural forces.

With the current emphasis on sustainable management of natural resources, it is necessary to know the potential range of patterns in a landscape and their ability to change. This enables the management of the landscape structure and composition to maintain the appropriate populations of flora and fauna, or to extract natural resources, such as timber, within the ecological carrying capacity of a forest. Restoration of damaged landscapes and substitution of natural processes, including disturbance, by human ones, also require this awareness and appreciation. Using or changing landscapes, without a prior understanding of the processes that create and change its natural patterns is flawed and could lead to suboptimal solutions or serious damage to natural systems.

Analysing Ecological Patterns

Following the discussion so far on the patterns formed by vegetation and the interaction between landforms and ecological processes, we need the ability to analyse ecological patterns. A good starting point is to classify vegetation and then seek the underlying relationship between landform, site, climate and our perception and aesthetics. There are a number of ways of classifying vegetation into types with a homogeneous character. Some rely on data collected from remote sensing by satellite or aerial photographs, which are then interpreted by a trained person into predetermined categories. These methods have to be verified on the ground, using sample sites that are visited by surveyors. Other methods use a large number of samples from a range of sites, which are interpolated to produce a larger pattern. Two approaches that have produced very useful results will be examined.

Biogeoclimatic Ecosystem Classification

The Biogeoclimatic Ecosystem Classification (BEC), developed in British Columbia, Canada, over the last twenty years, uses a synthesis of vegetation, climate and soil data. At the province level, the classification map depicts a very distinctive pattern. Regionally, locally (landscape) and at the site level, the classification is integrated in an hierarchical fashion (p. 238, Fig. 12).

One of the practical problems that has to be overcome with any classification system is that similar sites can carry different plant communities. Hence the originators, the forest ecologists Klinka and Krajina and their colleagues, decided to use the concept of biological or ecological equivalence, meaning that sites with the same physical properties have the same potential and could develop to the same 'climax' or late successional vegetation type. Thus within one of the BEC zones, vegetation may differ, depending on the current successional stage or due to disturbance.

Instead of trying to classify each type separately, the system recognizes zones based on the climax vegetation. The climax type is complicated, because in British Columbia the vegetation (mainly forest but also alpine tundra, grasslands and parkland) may exhibit fire climax or edaphic (soil limited) climax as well as that controlled by climate, so that in many areas the theoretical climatic climax rarely occurs. The zones reflect this using maturing successional stages as the diagnostic types. Where vegetation is in an early successional phase, the usefulness of the concept of potential vegetation is demonstrated. Combining the understanding of successional stages with the use of understorey vegetation to indicate site quality, enables an accurate prediction of the potential vegetation and hence, the appropriate zone.

The basic vegetation descriptions are set in the context of regional climate. This is interpreted from climatic factors such as accumulated warmth, the average number of frost free days, length of growing season and average annual precipitation. These factors vary from north to south (latitude), west to east (oceanic versus continental influences), with altitude (there being substantial mountain ranges in the province) and the rainshadow effect of the coastal mountains; all these exert significant effects on the broad vegetation patterns.

Sites within each climatic zone may possess a variety of soils derived from different parent materials. The soil characteristics, which exert most influence on vegetation are soil moisture and soil nutrients.

Soil moisture regimes are based on the average amount of soil water available to vascular plants. These also vary regionally, locally and at the site level. Instead of a continous scale running from the wettest to the driest sites province-wide, a nine class system was developed to be applied to each climatic zone. For example, the wettest zone on the west coast of Nootka Island ranges from *hydric* (the wettest) to *xeric* (the driest), as does the driest semi-desert interior climatic zone at Osoyoos.

Soil nutrient regimes reflect the average amounts of essential nutrients found in the soil and available to vascular plants. The quantitative assessment of this is difficult, due to complexities amongst the soil, climate, soil microorganisms, topography and nutrients received by a site from outside. However, some key properties, such as the availability of chemicals and the use of indicator species of plants, were used to develop a six class system, ranging from very poor to very rich and applied to each climatic zone.

Soil moisture and soil nutrients can be arranged to make a grid. The combination of each axis creates fifty four boxes. Each plant community within a climatic zone, lies within one or more of these boxes. Hence, this analysis produces a multi-dimensional framework of climatic zone and site, which has to be synthesized with the 'climax' vegetation potential to give the major BEC zones. Each zone represents the average or *zonal* condition for the vegetation type (located on sites with loamy soils and no major microsite or microclimate extremes). Subzones occur around these zones, based on the range of soil moisture, soil nutrients and microclimatic variations.

As already noted, much of the province is not currently in climax condition as the vegetation either relates to a successional stage or may be in another land use such as agriculture. Thus, knowledge of the successional paths for each BEC zone is needed to ascribe the sampled site to the correct category. This ensures that the system is robust, as the classification is never solely a snapshot of the time it was carried out. This successional information is also useful when applying the classification system and incorporating the dynamics of the landscape.

The most recent development of the system is to ascribe natural disturbance regimes to each zone or subzone. Currently they are divided into four general types: three stand replacement types, of rare, infrequent and frequent (depending on the fire return period), and one stand sustaining type. Thus, the system can be used in a number of ways as an objective and robust basis for further ecological analysis at the landscape and site level.

The system is structured as an hierarchy, but it is compiled from sampling at site level. Various analysis tools are used to complete the maps from the samples; with a well defined framework it is straightforward to categorize a single site into the appropriate subzone, on the basis of the diagnostic site and floristic composition. The main scales for mapping are 1:2,000,000 and 1:250,000. This presents a clear pattern at the provincial and regional scale, with a useful amount of detail. However, when used at the main planning scales of 1:50,000 or 1:20,000, the precision of boundaries is lost. The lines separating zones or subzones tend to follow contours at the 1:250,000 or greater scale, yet earlier in this chapter, we saw that vegetation patterns tend to follow landform, due to its effect on soil conditions. Thus, a more detailed scale of interpretation is needed to produce a more useful pattern, when working at smaller scales. In mature or late successional forests this is relatively easy, because the zones are based on the potential 'climax' and the forest cover maps show the tree species composition from aerial interpretation. The actual boundary line (not a completely distinct one, but more of a gradual change or 'ecotone') can then be plotted.

The British National Vegetation Classification

The BEC system is relatively straightforward to compile, because much of the landscape still has its natural vegetation. In Europe, with its long history of clearance and management, ecological classification is more challenging. There is a temptation to ignore the cultivated land and to concentrate on the protection of rare, semi-natural habitats of high ecological value, even though many of these are fragmented or are artificially maintained at various early successional stages. To recreate a picture of the landscape possibilities, in order to extend or restore natural vegetation types, a similar approach to the BEC is needed, one that identifies potential vegetation as well as classifying what is present. The British National Vegetation Classification (NVC) is designed primarily to classify existing plant communities, but can be extended to describe potential vegetation types. Given that the majority of vegetation in Great Britain is not in a natural late successional stage, undertaking the latter exercise is no mean feat.

The approach adopted in extending the NVC was based on phytosociological or plant community principles in the data collection and classification system, assisted by multivariate analysis by computer. Beginning in the mid 1970s, under the direction of the plant ecologist John Rodwell and a small team from Lancaster University, for the Nature Conservancy Council of Great Britain, samples of almost all natural, semi-natural and many managed vegetation communities were examined using the tested methods of quadrats of various sizes (smaller for fine complexes, larger for scattered trees and woodland, linear for hedges). The plants in each quadrat were identified and measured for abundance according to the *Domin* scoring system (where 91-100% cover scores 10, 70-96% = 9, 51-75% = 8 and so on down to less than 4% scoring 1, 2 or 3 depending on the number of individuals).

Environmental data such as soil, landform and climate were also collected, although they were not used for the initial analysis and classification, which was solely based on the phytosociology. The types that emerged from this are not hierarchical like the BEC system, nor are they of potential vegetation. Instead, they represent a range of communities, which may be partly climax or late successional, with some seral and others persistent; all are dependent on continued management. Some communities can be split into sub-communities or variants. The environmental data was used to explain the distribution of the communities, since the samples showed distinct geographical ranges for each type. This enabled a landscape scale pattern to be established for the plant communities in relation to climate, geology, soil and microsite variations.

The data and the plant communities that emerged from the analysis were grouped under main headings such as woodlands, grasslands, mires and so on and were named simply on the basis of the 2 or 3 most common plants found in them. This became the NVC.

The NVC meshes with site classification, so that certain vegetation types occur on particular sites. Thus, a map of potential vegetation can be devised, despite the absence of the semi-natural vegetation. This also works with potential climax or late successional vegetation, usually woodland. Sites within an area may possess variants of semi-natural vegetation that provide indicators of the woodland type most likely to have existed. Certain of these indicators, known as optimal precursors, can be mapped at the scale of microsite variation and from this a likely natural woodland mosaic can be reconstructed. This technique has gained wide acceptance as a means of recreating native woodlands in Great Britain.

A British version of ecological site classification, similar to that of British Columbia, has been developed by the British soil scientist Graham Pyatt and meshed with the NVC. It has recently been completed for a substantial area of Glen Affric in Scotland. Here, a number of sample transects were laid out and the vegetation and site conditions were sampled at 100 metre intervals. Plant composition, soil type, soil moisture and nutrient regimes, slope form (concave to convex), steepness, aspect and elevation were recorded or obtained later from computer based terrain information. A database of these samples was assembled and multivariate analysis was performed on the data.

A view of Glen Affric in Scotland showing some remnant pine forest. There is a pattern of site types and potential forest vegetation which can be used to reconstruct the way native vegetation would be distributed across the landscape.

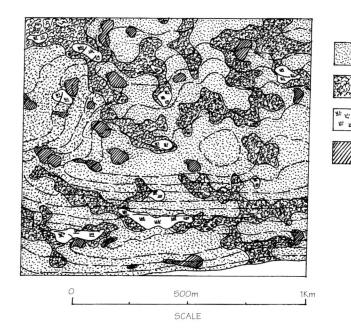

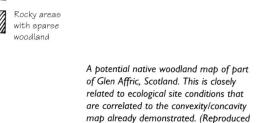

Mainly pine

Mainly birch

Open boggy areas

Rocky areas with sparse woodland

A potential native woodland map of part of Glen Affric, Scotland. This is closely related to ecological site conditions that are correlated to the convexity/concavity map already demonstrated. (Reproduced by permission of the Forestry Commission). See also p. 236, Fig. 8).

0   500m   1Km

SCALE

From this analysis, a range of ecological site types and potential woodland NVC types was identified, which could be extrapolated to produce a map of potential woodland types; this showed, in some detail, how the structure of the landscape might look over a substantial area. Some aspects of the model were not successful; for example, the position of the upper treeline related to aspect could not be determined, because of a lack of adequate microclimatic data across the samples.

This type of landscape analysis leads into the examination of the dynamics of the landscape, where the pattern, the processes at work and the overall ecological functioning are analysed. This is the realm of landscape ecology.

Landscape Ecological Analysis

Landscape ecology is the study and use of information about the patterns and processes of ecology and their interaction with landform at a scale ranging from parts of hectares/acres to many square kilometres/miles. The key requirements for successful analysis are the choice of the size of area to be analysed, the coarseness of resolution of components to be described and measured and the rates of change considered relevant. Each of these depends on the purpose of analysis and the inherent structure of the landscape. For example, a drainage system may be a suitable unit, because the landform structure and hydrological system can be linked to the processes operating in a series of sites that are separated from adjacent drainage systems. However, as each study area is not usually an island, any analysis must not overlook the connection both upwards and downwards to larger or smaller scale patterns emanating from the study area (see the discussion of pattern hierarchies in Chapter One.)

The main objective of analysis is to understand the way the ecosystem functions at present and how the dynamics of change affect it now and into the future. Thus, the components to be included need to be chosen with care. Indices used to quantify aspects of the landscape are also required. Landscape ecological analysis can be undertaken by descriptive methods or by sophisticated computer based modelling. The latter usually needs information from the former in order to set the starting conditions and rules of operation.

Analysis of Landscape Structure

The analysis of a landscape usually starts with a description of its constituent parts or elements. The basic types of element are often described as follows:

- A mosaic landscape usually consists of a number of different patches of vegetated and non-vegetated areas.
- Corridors are linear patches that are used for movement by water, wildlife or people within the landscape. The structure of the element enables movement to take place and is important.
- Pathways are linear routes also used for wildlife movement, but are not associated with a distinct vegetation or other structure.
- These patches, corridors and pathways may be set within a matrix, that is the landscape element most strongly connected across the landscape, which exerts a major influence over the functions within it.

The first task is to map and describe these elements. Key descriptors are size, shape, structure, composition and origin. Size is the absolute area in the units being used. Perimeter might also be important, because some indices use perimeter/area ratios. Shape can be described as angular, curvilinear, interlocked, geometric and so on; to some extent the irregularity can be measured using a fractal dimension index. The character of the shape can also be depicted using a sketch of its 'fractal signature'. The fractal dimension (see Chapter One) is the degree of curvilinearity of the boundary of a patch and is susceptible to measurement at varying scales of resolution. Some patch boundaries are self-similar and others indicate the character, origin and function of the patch. One key relationship is that a high fractal dimension denotes that a natural process has been the origin of the patch, whilst a low fractal dimension tends to suggest it has occurred as a result of human influenced processes (see the discussion of Richard Forman's work in Chapter One).

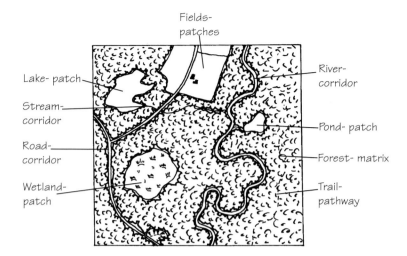

Fields-patches

Lake- patch

Stream-corridor

Road-corridor

Wetland-patch

River-corridor

Pond- patch

Forest- matrix

Trail-pathway

The definition in landscape ecological terms of patch, matrix, corridor and pathway.

For example, patch structure refers to the various layers of vegetation it comprises. A forest patch can be simple in structure, if composed of one age of tree with no ground or shrub layers. It can be complex, if it has several overlapping layers of tall trees, shorter trees, shrubs, herbaceous plants, epiphytes, dead wood and so on. Patch composition refers to the range of species of plants or the types of material it is made from, such as rock, sand or water. Some distinct patch types may be associated with particular vegetation zones and stages in the natural succession process.

The structure and composition of patch edges is of particular interest. As well as the fractal dimension, there is the degree of contrast between the structures at the edge of the transitional zone. Earlier, the importance of edge structure and environmental gradients was noted. The description of the edge character can be correlated to gradients of temperature, light, air humidity, soil moisture, changing plant composition, water flow and the degree of browsing or predators. Forman observes that soft boundaries (with a high fractal dimension, a strong degree of inter-digitation and definite gradient across the edge) are more absorbent and may exert a dampening effect in the adjacent system. Floods, fires, winds and pest movement may all be reduced in severity when they meet such boundaries, as opposed to hard, geometric, simply structured ones.

A further aspect to explore is the relationship between size and shape. Forman has demonstrated that there is a positive correlation between increasing size and increasing irregularity. This makes sense, because small disturbances start with a fairly regular shape; often the size is also related to the number of plants removed by the disturbance. For example, the hole created in a forest canopy by a small fire, consuming a few trees, can only be relatively regular, but as it spreads and more trees are burned the pattern can become more irregular.

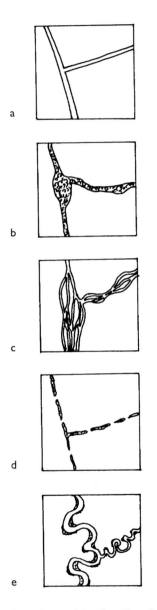

Some characteristics of corridors: a) straight, parallel; b) variable width; c) braided; d) discontinuous; e) meandering.

As patch size increases, so does the effect of microsite as more topographic, moisture and soil variations are enveloped; there is a greater tendency for lobes, bays and promontories to appear. This seems to indicate a relationship to more generic form-generators in nature (see complexity and chaos in Chapter One) due to initial fluctuations in composition which, through positive feedback, become exaggerated. This may be the case with expanding edges, where a patch expands by colonization or due to wind eddies, wind funnelling and fire spread. Where lobes, bays and promontories develop, there may be a harmonic to be measured, that is the frequency and amplitude of the shape. Multiple harmonics indicate a fractal structure. The number of lobes, bays and promontories per unit area, their length to width ratio and the degree of similarity of shape between patches of similar structure and composition can also be measured to assist characterization.

The origin of patches is the final requirement. If they are natural, they may originate from erosion, deposition, hydrological processes, vegetation colonization, succession or disturbance. Human caused patches can arise from a wide number of activities that may have similar effects to natural ones, such as excavation, dumping of minerals, artificial water storage, planting, management of vegetation, cutting etc. The origin of patches is highly correlated to their shape and size (see discussion of disturbances earlier in the chapter).

Corridors can be described in exactly the same way as patches. Their size is measured in terms of length and width. There may be variations to the width that might be significant. Shape can be very important, varying between completely straight to various degrees of curvilinear, culminating in meandering patterns, branching structures or braids. The degree of meander can be measured by fractal dimension and harmonic, much like the edges of patches.

Corridors can also show different degrees of continuity from complete continuity to gappy or discontinuous. Their structure is important, as they have a high edge to area ratio, so that edge effects may be dominant in some circumstances. Because corridors are used for movement across the landscape their structure and composition are especially significant in understanding their function.

Pathways are considered in terms of location, direction and route. These factors may change, depending on what moves along the pathway. Their relationships to patches (as destinations for the pathway) and to the underlying landform are important aspects to disentangle.

The matrix is defined partly as the most connected part of the landscape. In some places, a number of patches linked by corridors of the same structure and composition, may be the most connected part and so constitute the matrix. An example is the hedgerow landscapes of some countryside in Great Britain. The fields in between the hedges are the patches. The hedges link with small ancient woods and form a vital network of habitat that has provided for a range of plants and animals for thousands of years.

There are examples where a matrix does not exist and where the landscape consists entirely of patches, corridors and pathways. In many natural landscapes the matrix has no boundary at the scale being analysed, because it is continous and extends beyond the limits of the study area. Its structure and composition should be described, especially where the matrix represents the late successional stage of the main vegetation type for the area. It may be necessary to subdivide the matrix into several components such as different vegetation classes, although the change between them is gradual and is of composition rather than structure.

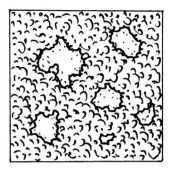

a

The matrix changes as patches develop and change. A disturbance to a matrix, such as an area of late successional forest, creates a patch. At a certain stage of succession the structure and composition of that patch will become the same as the matrix again. Hence, it is important to define the stage at which matrix conditions are reestablished.

A matrix can have an edge, if it bounds another area of a different character. An area of late successional forest can abut a prairie, alpine tundra, cultivated fields or blanket bog, where each is extensive enough to act as matrix. The edge character and structure is likely to be important, because each matrix can act as separate components for the habitat of animals with large territories.

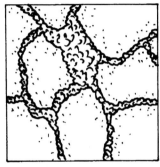

b

Characteristics of matrix patterns.
a) The woodland is the most connected and the most extensive in area.
b) The woodland is the msot connected but not the most extensive. However, both can be defined as matrix.

While it is easier to categorize the components separately, it is the overall pattern that is also important for ecosystem functioning. Fragmentation of the matrix by many patches can be measured by the relationship of number and size of patches in proportion to the area of matrix, edge to area ratios and the degree of connectivity, relative to the number of breaks in the matrix. The degree of patchiness, the numbers of different patches per unit area and the amount of contrast across the landscape, help to measure how diverse a pattern is at a particular scale of resolution. These measures have to be set against a baseline of 'natural' patchiness or connectivity; for this some knowledge of the natural range of variability is necessary.

The final part of the analysis of landscape structure is to determine how much is related to the physical structure underlying the ecosystem: the landform, soils, climatic influences and hydrology. The ecological classification and landscape structure maps should be compared with the landform and hydrological analyses to see how well they correlate. This can be done visually or by sampling aspects of each layer and performing a multivariate statistical analysis. In most landscapes, there will be complications with the patterns of disturbance, which may not be landform or climate correlated, especially if they are of human origin. Failure to probe beneath the existing patchiness for the 'natural' pattern and resolution of the mosaic can lead to misunderstandings and incorrect planning, so that disentangling the layers is vital.

An interesting aspect of pattern analysis is the use of spatial cues, networks and graph theory which are explained in ensuing paragraphs. The use of spatial cues such as the degree of similarity of shape,

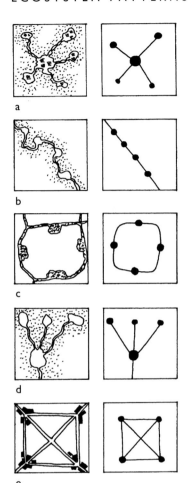

Graph theory examples: a) a spider pattern of small wetlands linked by streams; b) a necklace of small open areas linked by corridors; c) a graph cell of small woods linked by hedges; d) a candelabra of small openings linked by corridors; e) a rigid cell of settlements linked by roads.

structure, composition or internal rhythm, gives a measure of regularity or irregularity of a pattern.

They may also determine if there is a natural repeatability across an area and at varying scales (an apparently random pattern of sizes of patch may be the effect of scale changes, associated with 'log normal' frequency/size distribution, as described earlier in the chapter). Aggregated patterns may be discerned from density or proximity relationships. Linear, parallel or braided patterns may also be present.

Networks can be identified on the basis of degrees of similarity and proximity amongst structures, within statistical limits of scale. Hence corridors and patches of similar structure and composition either joined or near each other (based on a threshold value) can be linked as a network that may be of significance later on.

Graph theory is a technique for depicting patterns in a shorthand way (see Chapter One). For example, circles represent nodes connected with lines. This simplifies and makes the actual pattern of variably shaped and sized patches and corridors easier to visualize. It is believed that only a limited number of these patterns can occur such as 'spiders', 'necklaces', 'graph cells', 'candelabra' and 'rigid cells'. Care is needed to avoid the error of trying to fit all patterns into the general classification of the theory, despite significant discrepancies.

Analysis of Landscape Flows

So far we have concentrated on landscape structure for information about aspects of the ecosystem. The patterns that occur in landscape also have to be considered because of their intimate relationships with processes at work. This entails examining the inputs, outputs, capture, storage and cycling of the ecosystem. These processes occur in plants and animals as a result of the effects of water, heat from the sun, wind, weathering of soil, death and decay of organisms and so on. Landscape ecology is concerned with particular scales of processes, such as those acting throughout a landscape and between a particular landscape and its surroundings (inflows and outflows.)

Flows are things like animals, water, people, plants, propagules, nutrients and energy that move around the landscape (in the air, on the ground, through the vegetation and in the soil). The first task is to exclude disturbance agents, because at this stage we are interested in interactions with the existing structure not its destruction. The boundary of the analysis area and its size should be used to determine which flows are significant. For example, some animals migrate in and out and across the landscape, whereas others complete their life cycle within logs, beneath stones or within small patches. Those that use the whole landscape are most relevant for analysis.

Another criterion for the selection of flows for analysis, is to concentrate on species high in the food chain or especially significant, as indicators of the health of the ecosystem. An example of this is a

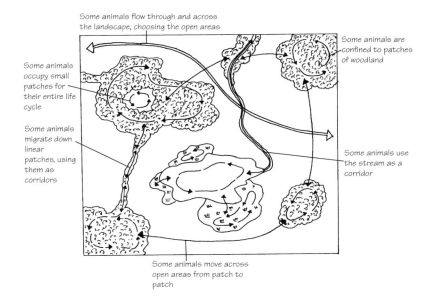

Some animals flow through and across the landscape, choosing the open areas

Some animals are confined to patches of woodland

Some animals occupy small patches for their entire life cycle

Some animals migrate down linear patches, using them as corridors

Some animals use the stream as a corridor

Some animals move across open areas from patch to patch

The relationship of flow patterns of different animals at different scales in a mosaic landscape.

large predator that depends on a range of prey species. If viable breeding populations of this predator survive, the prey species and their habitats must also be viable. Hence, the success or otherwise of the predator can indicate the status of all the other flows upon which it depends. Thus, there is no need to analyse all of the potential flows.

Water is always a key flow, although that part of the analysis should have been completed when considering the hydrological system in relation to landform. Water also interacts with the vegetation patterns for all the processes of capture, storage, cycling and loss of water within the ecosystem. Water flow patterns are also some of the easiest to determine, compared with those of many animals or birds.

Since this analysis is not restricted to natural or wild areas and can be applied equally to cultural landscapes (frequently the main areas of landscape ecological study), the inclusion of people is relevant. In addition, there are psychological and aesthetic issues of human/environment relationships to consider, as discussed in Chapter Three. A useful way of examining the flow of people is to split the effects of living and working in the landscape from recreation.

Amongst the interactions between landscape structure and human use are the perceptions, aesthetic and emotional issues as well as practical and physical ones. In places where a colonizing human population co-exists with an indigenous one (as in parts of Canada), a further distinction may be made, as native people often have completely different patterns of use, based on a long cultural tradition.

Plants also flow around the landscape colonizing areas, spreading out gradually or moving readily to utilize freshly exposed sites. Some are slow to move, exhibiting sensitivity to particular site conditions.

They can be used as indicators of late successional forest or ancient woodland, a relatively stable and long lasting element in a landscape.

Propagules such as pollen, fungal spores or seeds can be spread across a landscape by wind, water or animals. Such spread may be important for genetic variability, for infection of plants or for colonizing disturbed areas. There may be instances when native plant pollen may mix with non-native varieties to the detriment of the gene pool; the spread of fungal infection may be more likely along the direction of the prevailing wind from an already infected site.

Nutrient flow may be associated with water movement from sources such as weathering rocks, places with accumulated organic materials or leaching of excess nitrate into the water table from intensive farming. In chains of lakes, those lower down the hydrological system tend to be richer in nutrients than those above.

Energy flows can include warm or cold air movement across a landscape, heat currents in lakes or rivers that affect ecosystem function, such as growth rates of local plants or use by certain wildlife. Hot springs flowing into a stream, warm ocean currents flowing along a coastline, the energy accumulation in cities due to traffic and buildings expelling heat, may affect a number of ecological functions at a regional or local level.

Following identification and description of the relevant flows, their movement patterns should, as far as possible, be mapped so that the spatial relationships with landscape structure can be understood. Some of them can be plotted quite accurately; for others, a more general picture of their scale and direction of movement will suffice.

Interaction of Structures and Flows

The next step in this analysis is to interpret the interaction between each flow and each structure. A simple and very effective means of doing this is to fill out a spreadsheet, where the columns are the flows and the rows the structures. This builds up a comprehensive picture of the existing pattern/process interaction. For example, the interaction of water and alpine tundra involves water being collected (captured), stored (as snow, ice and in peat) and released during the summer as the ice and snow melts. Water interacts with tropical rainforest by being partly intercepted by the canopy and evaporated, some reaches the ground and is taken up by plant roots (captured), some soaks in and reaches an aquifer (storage), whilst a proportion is transpired by the plants back to the atmosphere, where it condenses again to fall as rain (cycling).

An animal like a Grizzly bear may use a range of habitats for feeding, hibernation, breeding, travelling and so on. Alpine tundra may provide berries, small animals and rocky areas for denning. Old forest provides rotten logs for insects to be found, piles of logs and upturned roots for dens. Rivers provide fish for food to fatten the bears in preparation for winter. If any of these structures are absent the habitat and range of the bear might be curtailed to a critical degree for its survival.

On completion of the spreadsheet a pattern will emerge. Some structures will be highly significant for a wide variety of the flows. Some flows will be confined to a narrow range of structures, whilst some structures may be neutral to most flows or may invoke negative interactions. The analysis may also show that some important structural elements are absent from the landscape (perhaps due to past management). Conversely, the range of structures may be ideal, but there is no population present, perhaps due to local extinction.

Disturbance and Succession

Earlier in the chapter many different disturbance regimes and their patterns were discussed. These form the basis for introducing the dynamics of the landscape. For the landscape under consideration, each relevant disturbance type should be listed and a table constructed to record its frequency or return period, scale, duration, intensity and the resulting vegetation structure. Both natural and human disturbances should be included. Where these can be related to particular parts of the landscape, they should be mapped. For example, fire may differ in its likely character, depending on exposure, aspect and microclimate. Human disturbance may be highly localized, such as quarrying.

Each disturbance initiates succession. Sometimes the successional path is straightforward. At other times several routes are possible. In a few instances succession is constantly arrested by more disturbance. Where several different disturbances operate on the same area, succession may advance or retreat. For example, a fire occurring at any successional stage of a susceptible forest will revert it to the stand initiation stage whereas a fungal infection, by killing trees, may advance the time of development of the understorey reinvasion or multi-storied forest stages earlier than in the absence of the disturbance. Burning heather moor constantly maintains a shrub stage, so that natural forest never returns; annual ploughing of a field reverts the weed invasion stage to bare ground; coppicing, where trees are cut every few years and resprout, constantly keeps a broadleaved woodland between a type of stand initiation and stem exclusion stages.

For each vegetation zone and local microsite variation, a chart or flow diagram should be developed, showing successional stages with descriptions of structure, composition and duration, interwoven with the effects of different disturbances on these stages. This will be used to help define the rate of natural ecosystem processes and to aid any design project that is proposed.

As part of the culmination of the landscape ecological analysis, it can be very useful to categorize the landscape elements in one of three ways: as *critical natural capital*, *constant natural assets* or *liabilities*. If the area under analysis is mainly a cultural landscape, then cultural capital and assets can be incorporated.

Critical natural or cultural capital comprises those features of the landscape, which are so significant for ecological functioning and for the well being of society, that they must be maintained and protected as they are. Some may be permanent, while others may persist for a sufficiently long duration to be treated as such. In a number of cases, their location is also preordained so that they cannot exist elsewhere in the landscape. Examples include lakes, streams, wetlands, ancient forest or woodland, ancient hedgerow patterns, archaeological sites and features, locations of important historic events, places with a strong spirit of place or *Genius loci*, traditional buildings, alpine tundra and rock formations, to name only a few.

Constant natural assets include all features that are necessary in the landscape for ecological functions to operate effectively, but are not fixed in location or time. These are the elements most affected by disturbance, succession and human management activity. Successional stages of the main vegetation types such as forest zones, or of certain managed vegetation types such as heather moorland or unimproved pasture, might be typical examples.

Liabilities are those elements present in the landscape, which interfere with or prevent ecological processes from operating. Frequent examples are human created features, such as mine spoil or tailings, sources of pollution, eyesores, noisy highways, over-intensively managed farmland or inappropriate engineering structures.

Landscape Ecology and Analysis at Hazelton Mountain, British Columbia

The Hazelton Mountain case study, cited earlier under landform analysis, will also be used to demonstrate the application of landscape ecology. The purpose of the analysis is to develop:

- a set of landscape objectives related to the resource values identified as important to the community
- the pattern and structure of the landscape required to meet those values in a sustainable manner.

The process of analysis uses the descriptions of the structure, flows, their interactions, the effects of disturbance and succession; this leads to combinations of these factors related to landscape zones. Finally, these are synthesized into desired future ecological conditions and their ability to sustain management for different resource values in each zone.

Landscape structure description for the 40,000 ha area identified the following three types of matrix:

- Alpine areas with slopes greater than 20%, icefields, bare rock, scree and grass, herb and shrub vegetation.

- Mature (late successional) conifer forest on the upper slopes above the main Kispiox River valley. This is very continuous and similar in character, representing two biogeoclimatic (BEC) zones (Interior Cedar/ Hemlock and Engelmann spruce/Subalpine fir), also lying on slopes greater than 20%.
- Disturbed coniferous forest in the lower valley, where many patches have broken up the continuous nature of the forest. This contains the Interior Cedar/Hemlock BEC zone, has less than 20% slope and mesic site conditions (average for the zone).

The strength and extent of these matrices was a significant aspect of this landscape.

Patches were present, some almost permanent in the time scale under consideration, others ephemeral:

- Krummholz patches in the treeline transition.
- Wet meadows on a plateau forming a complex of forest edges, lakes and boggy places.
- Lakes in hollows such as kettle holes, all being the sources of streams and roughly ovoid in shape.
- Rock faces or slopes amongst the forest matrix where bedrock is exposed.
- Cultivated fields in the valley bottom, where fertile ground had been cleared, often showing geometric shapes.
- Cedar dominated stands of old forest on wetter, less disturbed areas that permitted their slow emergence through the canopy.
- Logged areas with various amounts of woody residues and geometric shapes with abrupt edges. Some were regenerating, others had been recently cut.
- Mosaics of patches interwoven with each other, set amongst the disturbed forest matrix, including broadleaved trees, shrub areas and Black spruce in wet places.

Each of these was described in terms of structure, composition, origin and character.

Corridors and pathways were present. They included:

- Streams of varying size and flow rate in valleys, ranging from shallow descending depressions to deep canyons.
- Forested ridgelines and unforested ridges.
- Gravel roads in the lower area, following contours.
- Trails with some surfacing and bare soil.
- Avalanche chutes on steep south and southwest facing slopes below the alpine areas.
- Pathways used by Grizzly bears, but displaying no structure.

Maps were prepared of these structures, so that their spatial characteristics were evident (p. 238, Fig. 13).

The analysis of flows in the landscape concentrated mostly on animals at the top of the food chain and those using seasonal habitats, with the exception of a group of species, known to be dependent on riparian corridors. The flows were as follows:

- Water, collecting in the alpine areas as snow and flowing into the two watersheds showing different characteristics of erosion and deposition (see the hydrological analysis section earlier in the chapter.)
- Black bears preferring the lowland mixed forest mosaic, although they can use any type of forest. They hibernate in big cottonwood or cedar trees.
- Grizzly bears and wolverines, treated together, because their habitat and movement patterns are very similar. They use the high elevation wetlands, den in high elevation areas and make use of avalanche tracks for feeding. In the late summer and autumn, they move to the river to collect salmon and berries to prepare for hibernation. They are attracted to the early seral forest for berries.
- Mountain goats only use the high elevation and canyon side rock walls; they migrate along mountain ridges. They do not breed in the study area, but juvenile animals disperse into it. South facing rock walls are preferred.
- Moose and Mule deer use the lower mixed slopes of the valley floor as their wintering range; in the spring they disperse across the landscape and in summer, up into the alpine areas to feed and escape insects. Moose also favour the wetland complex.
- Fish inhabit the river and creeks. Migrating fish (Steelhead trout, Coho and Chinook salmon, Cutthroat trout and Dolly varden) spawn in the Kispiox, but they also use Date Creek and McCully Creek as far as the falls. Cutthroat trout are resident in the lower elevation lakes and in the creeks.
- Wolves follow their prey species of moose, deer and goats, so that during the winter they inhabit the same ranges, whilst in summer they move to the upland areas for denning, breeding and hunting.
- Eagles (Bald and Golden) fly in from the coast and may follow some of the creeks, where they can hunt and fish. One migratory route for Bald eagles is known to be between the Kitwanga Valley and the Kispiox, over the saddle at the head of the upper McCully Creek. Golden eagles use the upper forest, alpine areas and valleys with rock exposures where they nest.
- The riparian species group includes otter, beaver, amphibians, ducks, osprey and other species. They inhabit and rely on the river and all the major creeks with shallower gradients; also used are valley slopes together with associated forest and wetland complexes.

- People make limited use of the area. There is little recreation, while economic use, such as logging has not been heavy. Traditional uses by native people continue to be widespread and light, so impacts have been low, except for land along the river valley floor, where a long tradition of wood cutting and burning, to increase the area for habitat and settlement, has produced a mosaic structure.

These flows were also mapped. Their pattern was then overlaid on the map of landscape structures in preparation for the next step, an analysis of the interaction. The following table shows a sample of these interactions.

FLOWS

Structure	Water	Grizzly & Wolverine	Moose	Fish	Wolves	Eagles
MATURE FOREST MATRIX	Reduces snow melt & water evaporation, keeps soil moist & cool.	Travel, foraging, hunting, denning & berry foraging.	Movement, forage, mating, breeding, calving, cover & shade.	No interaction.	Travel, denning & hunting moose & deer.	No interaction.
ALPINE MATRIX	Source of melting snow, rain, glacial sediments & erosion.	Summer use for foraging, winter use for denning.	Summer use to rub velvet, escape flies, forage.	No interaction.	Summer use hunting of small mammals.	Hunting and scavenging, especially goat kids by golden eagles.
WET MEADOWS & SWAMPS	Storage, filtration, flow control into creeks, nutrient provision.	High value spring and summer forage.	Very high use to escape predators & flies, forage & cooling in summer.	No interaction.	Difficult territory in summer.	No interaction.
LAKES	Storage, release, sediment capture, nutrient influence (pH).	No interaction.	Escape predators & flies and cooling in summer.	Some fish resident in some lakes.	Travel over frozen surface in winter.	Fishing by bald eagles.
DECIDUOUS STANDS	Snow melts early, higher evaporation, high water table.	Fall feeding, spring foraging & summer berry picking.	Heavy use especially as winter range.	Source of litter, insects & nutrients into streams & lakes.	Hunting of moose & denning.	High use for nesting & hunting.
WET CEDAR	Evapotranspiration & storage.	Forage on skunk cabbage.	Little use.	No interaction.	Low use.	Limited use.
BLACK SPRUCE	Storage, flow control, interception.	No interaction.	Escape predators & flies & cooling in summer. Poor forage.	No interaction.	No interaction.	No interaction.
STREAM CORRIDORS	Main routes of flow out of the area.	Fishing and travel.	Used as routes.	Habitat of a range of species except where barriers prevent further access.	Drinking, travel. Winter use, scavenging & fishing.	Hunting & fishing.

As a result of this analysis, it became clear that some of the structures were more significant than others:

- Streams and riparian areas are consistently important for many flows.
- The settled and cultivated areas, although man-made, provide a range of habitat needs.
- Roads and trails will often be used by wildlife for travel, although there are dangers of collision with vehicles and increased hunting, due to the access provided.
- The valley bottom broadleaved areas are another example of a human-altered landscape providing a valuable habitat for a whole range of species, especially over the winter.
- The forest matrix performs major functions and gives cover and forage to almost all the wildlife.
- Logged areas, despite being artificial, supply an early successional habitat of importance to many species.
- Alpine areas are a stable landscape type, much valued by a range of major species during summer and winter.

Younger forest habitats were in short supply and more could be useful as long as these are of natural character, containing legacies of wildlife tree patches, large woody material, snags and other remains of natural disturbance.

The next step was to consider the dynamics of disturbance and succession. A range of disturbance types was considered:

- Fire
- Various insects, some restricted to certain tree species
- Wind
- Fungal diseases
- Flooding
- Slumping of soil and landslides
- Avalanches
- Ice and snow
- Browsing by deer, moose and goats
- Logging (as a contrast to the natural disturbances)

A comprehensive table showing the frequency, intensity, scale, duration and stand characteristics associated with each agent, was then assembled. This showed that there are different cycles and scales between and within different areas.

Successional paths for the main biogeoclimatic zones were then considered. Complications arose where several paths could develop after disturbance. Seven structural stages were identified (see Chapter Five) and diagrams of their paths compiled. The disturbances were also

	FREQUENCY	INTENSITY	SCALE	DURATION	RESULTING STAND CHARACTERISTICS
FIRE	200-350 years for stand replacing fires, more frequently for smaller patches. Some aspects are more likely to burn, e.g.those facing south.	Fires tend to be intense because the moist climate enables fuels to build up for long periods.	Larger fires tend to range from 20 to 1000 ha.	The smaller ones last a few hours, the larger several days.	Very irregularly shaped and patchy burns result from the broken, dissected landform and presence of wet areas. Lots of legacies are left, especially lower down the slopes.
INSECTS & DISEASE	Insects are species specific and vary in frequency, e.g. mountain pine beetle attacks 60-80 year old stands.	Depends on the size and purity of the stand. Diseases tend to affect small patches.	Depends on the size of patches of the host stands. Diseases such as root rot tend to be small in scale but widespread.	These tend to be endemic and flare up periodically when larger stands reach a susceptible age.	Patchy stands where even aged areas tend to become more broken and complex in structure. Large amounts of dead wood develop.
WIND	Every 3-5 years	Locally very intense damage, both snapping of stems and throwing of entire trees.	Patches of up to 30-40ha, especially on ridge tops and wet exposed slopes.	A few hours.	Snapped trees, thrown trees, tangled areas, mineral soil exposure and fast regeneration after the event.
FLOODS	Range from 5-10 year to 50/100 year events.	Intense but confined to stream system.	Flood plains determine the size at 10s - 100ha.	1-2 days or 4-5 days.	Changes to the stream character, logs washed into streams and some changes to the riparian area.
SLUMPING & LANDSLIDES	Annual events somewhere in the landscape but individual slides may happen every 100 years or so.	Very intense.	Small and localised.	A few moments for catastrophic landslides, some earth flows take a long time and move continuously but slowly.	Open areas are maintained at early successional stages of vegetation or bare soil.
AVALANCHE	Annually.	Very intense.	Limited to slide tracks but some bigger ones may spread.	Seconds.	Areas are kept at early successional vegetation in annual slide tracks and flatten trees where they spread more widely.
ICE & SNOW	Annually.	Moderate intensity of crushing trees by snow and ice.	Widespread patches of small size.	Weeks or months over the winter.	Areas of snapped, bent and fallen trees, especially deciduous species.
BROWSING	Seasonally.	Locally severe.	Depends on the size of early successional areas.	Several years until trees are too big.	Even aged stands become more varied in character.

integrated showing how some, like major fires, return any successional stage to the stand initiation phase, whilst others, like wind or some insects, advance succession.

At this point, an analysis of landscape character was undertaken, to divide the area into zones, on the basis of landform and vegetation. Each of these was described. Following this, the ecological analysis and landscape character zones were synthesized together. From this point, the analysis related to the scale of each zone as opposed to the whole study area. Ten zones were identified. Here are a couple of examples:

Steeply Incised Headwater Valleys

Structures: Alpine areas, krummholz, some mature forest, upper elevation lakes, rock faces, streams, avalanche chutes, riparian and ridges.

Flows: Water, goats, Grizzly bears, wolves, Golden eagles, people and hunting.
Disturbance: Avalanche, ice and snow, slumping and landslides.
Succession: Not applicable, because of the climatically controlled dynamics and extremely slow growth.
Critical Natural Capital: Alpine areas, headwater streams and rock faces.
Constant Natural Assets: Alpine vegetation.
Liabilities: None.

Steep, Mid-Elevation Slopes

Structures: Mature forest, roads, trails, logged areas, riparian and streams.
Flows: Small streams, riparian species, wildlife generally and people at work and recreation.
Disturbance: Mainly wind, slumping and landslides and logging.
Successional Path: ICH mc (Interior Cedar/Hemlock, moist, cool subzone type).
Critical Natural Capital: Small streams, deep, fertile soils, trails, very old forest.
Constant Natural Assets: Mature interior forest, scenic views from the valley.
Liabilities: Unstable slopes, geometric logging blocks.

At this stage the initial analysis was concluded. Its use in developing design and management strategies will be explored next.

Designing Ecosystems

The idea of ecosystem design and management, using the understanding and characteristics of natural processes and disturbances as guides for forestry or protected area management, has become well established. As the landscape will be changed by any management, it is necessary to know, in advance, the direction and character of such change, to ensure that the desired ecological condition will be maintained or achieved.

For example, the outcome of the landscape ecological analysis, described earlier in this chapter, could provide a good starting point for identifying significant types of disturbance and succession characteristics. Together with the analysis of landscape character, especially landform, the places where these disturbance types are most likely to occur can be designed as future management units. It is in forestry management that ecosystem design is most advanced. An example will show how it can be achieved.

An ecosystem design, integrating ecological, practical and aesthetic requirements, was performed at the West Arm Demonstration Forest

A view of part of the West Arm Demonstration Forest (WADF) near Nelson in British Columbia, Canada.

near Nelson in British Columbia, Canada in 1994. As discussed earlier in the chapter, a set of objectives was assembled, based on the identification by a number of stakeholders of a range of ecological, economic, aesthetic and spiritual values. Following a comprehensive inventory, a number of separate but connected analyses were undertaken.

A landscape ecological analysis identified, for each biogeoclimatic subzone, typical disturbance and succession characteristics. These varied according to elevation, soil moisture and aspect; for example, fire as a significant disturbance would be expected to be rare in valley bottoms, due to the moist forest conditions. Fire is likely to be more frequent and hotter on south and southwest facing slopes, resulting in a mosaic pattern of patches of irregular shaped areas; each of these would contain some unburnt remnants and individual thick barked trees that would survive an intense fire. On cooler north or northeast facing slopes, the probability of large fires would be less; their return period might be some hundreds of years; hence, disturbances like beetles or root rot fungus might be more significant in changing the structure of stands. These structural characteristics were translated into potential silvicultural models and applied to defined units that fitted

A sketch sequence (pp. 227-229) showing the steps of design for the WADF. a) The landscape character analysis (in plan and perspective); b) The constraints and opportunities analysis; c) The landscape ecological analysis; d) The sketch design of management units; e) The forest as it might appear after the first silvicultural operations.

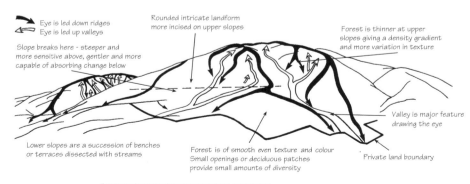

Eye is led down ridges
Eye is led up valleys

Rounded intricate landform more incised on upper slopes

Forest is thinner at upper slopes giving a density gradient and more variation in texture

Slope breaks here - steeper and more sensitive above, gentler and more capable of absorbing change below

Valley is major feature drawing the eye

Lower slopes are a succession of benches or terraces dissected with streams

Forest is of smooth even texture and colour Small openings or deciduous patches provide small amounts of diversity

Private land boundary

a

Foreground is more diverse: private land development

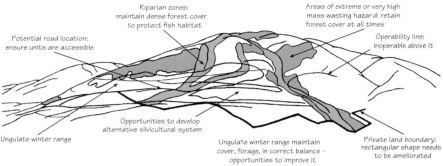

Potential road location:
ensure units are accessible

Riparian zones:
maintain dense forest cover
to protect fish habitat

Areas of extreme or very high
mass wasting hazard: retain
forest cover at all times

Operability line:
inoperable above it

Opportunities to develop
alternative silvicultural system

Ungulate winter range

Ungulate winter range maintain
cover, forage, in correct balance -
opportunities to improve it

Private land boundary:
rectangular shape needs
to be ameliorated

b

On north and east slopes, moister conditions prevent burns except on long cycles. Smaller disturbance from root rot, wind and insect attack create stands of varied ages and sizes. Management to create groups and thus reflect these small disturbances is appropriate.

These areas are prone to fires on 100 year cycle and create patches of between 50 and 100ha. These contain islands which remain unburnt and large old trees with thick bark. Management to mimic such burns is appropriate.

Englemann spruce/sub alpine fir zone. Areas on the top of the mountains typically burn at 300+ year cycles, in areas of 100 - 150ha. They are not accessible for control so non-intervention will be appropriate. Patches will be left unburnt in wet places. Dead trees will remain standing.

Interior cedar/hemlock, dry and warm sub zone. This area, on south and west aspects is the most dynamic, with frequent small fires every 50 years as well as disease and insect attack giving hardwood patches. The fires are not intense so lots of trees remain alive and wet patches emerge. A multi-storied forest results. This provides ideal deer and elk habitat, tall trees for nesting ospreys and lots of timber Management by small units cutting conifer, leaving wet patches, hardwoods and tall trees will give the two storey structure.

Riparian areas are the moistest parts, the most sheltered and the least likely to burn. The forests can develop and survive long periods with only minor disturbances as individual trees fall. Selection of single high value trees is all that can be tolerated, the old-growth character being important for water quality, fish habitat and species continuity.

c

UNIT DESIGN The basic biogeoclimatic zones are broken down into management units related to landform, landscape scale, operability and access, risk of mass wasting (landslide) etc. The management of each unit will be phased time to spread the disturbance and provide a range of structural types at any one time.

d

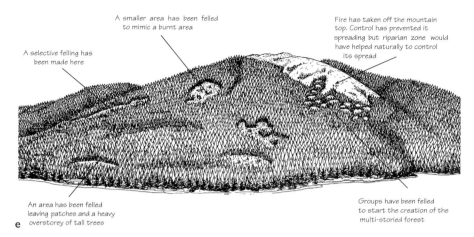

A smaller area has been felled to mimic a burnt area

Fire has taken off the mountain top. Control has prevented it spreading but riparian zone would have helped naturally to control its spread

A selective felling has been made here

An area has been felled leaving patches and a heavy overstorey of tall trees

Groups have been felled to start the creation of the multi-storied forest

e

the landscape character. Management activities would be spread over time periods that reflect the natural rates of change.

The next step was to undertake a landscape character analysis, using the underlying landform shape and the vegetation patterns as the key. The landform was described using the technique of visual force analysis as described in Chapter Five, and the descriptive method explained in Chapter Four. This was presented in plan and perspective for a number of views. The analysis showed how the landscape comprised areas of different character and how it could be subdivided into management zones, on the basis of the relationships of vegetation pattern, disturbance regime and landform. The characteristic shapes of different landforms and vegetation patterns provided the inspiration for the kind of shapes the management units could take, so as to blend into the changing landscape, be unified with it and maintain the appropriate level of diversity.

The landscape character analysis thus underpinned the development of the pattern of management units. Now their shapes, sizes and the way they intermeshed needed to be designed to reflect the landforms and vegetation patterns present. This is the creative part of the design: it is the ability to develop the conceptual solution that best satisfies all the analyses and objectives in an integrated way from the outset. The creative component lies in assessing, amongst all of the possible patterns that could occur, which is the best suited to meet the current objectives. However, in this case creativity is constrained by the intersecting analyses and the underlying structure of the landscape.

The concept for the West Arm Demonstration Forest arose once the relationships between disturbance types, landform and microclimate were converted into the basis for silviculture. The visual understanding of the relationship of vegetation patterns to landform, primarily using the visual force analysis, enabled the concept to be developed into a design. The management units were defined using naturalistic shapes that followed the landform by rising in hollows and falling on ridges;

the detail of their shapes was borrowed from the character of vegetation patches or the expected pattern of disturbances such as fire. The shapes of the management units also had interlocking boundaries with a fractal signature similar to that of the landform. The size of units reflected the topographic diversity, the natural scale of the landscape and the variation in size of the natural disturbance types (where smaller patterns and disturbances tend to occur lower down the slopes and larger ones higher up).

Within each management unit there was a further, detailed level of design. For example, if the unit was to be managed to emulate the effects of a natural fire, the character of the edge, the pattern of patches likely to remain unburnt and the incidence of individual surviving trees was designed to ensure the best natural fit with this disturbance agent.

The emerging concepts required modification, due to the effects of various physical, social, legal or economic constraints or opportunities such as access, riparian management and pest control; all affected the scope of management. Inevitably, there is still much uncertainty in the ecosystem. No one can be sure how it will develop before any long term plan can be implemented in its entirety. Thus, regular reviews and revisions are built into the process, allowing for the design to be flexible, if unforeseen circumstances occur.

Thus, over time, the forest mosaic will take on characteristics of natural patterns, structure and dynamics, although the changes will be by human rather than natural processes. This may not be acceptable to those who hold the integrationist position on landscape aesthetics as discussed in Chapter Three, for whom the purity of appearance and origin in a scene is important. However, such an approach fits well with the idea that pattern and process are indivisible and that the pattern affects functioning in positive or negative ways. Thus we can approach the position taken by Aldo Leopold in his thoughts on ecological aesthetics, particularly his land ethic.

In terms of basic perception, the approach described here contains the factors which are likely to help us perceive a unified pattern, because the gestalt laws such as closure, figure and ground and similarity are fulfilled. Furthermore, in terms of Whitehead's criteria, the natural pattern displays massiveness and intensity proper, thus possessing strength, as described for a forest example in Chapter Three. Finally, the aesthetic qualities of coherence, complexity and mystery are also present. Thus, the majority of people should find the end product of this ecologically based design aesthetically fulfilling.

The approach briefly outlined above is applicable to the restoration of ecosystems of all types. For restoration projects, the potential patterns of vegetation such as woodland, which might be found on a particular landscape, can be established using a technique like the British National Vegetation Classification. This can be used for a range of habitat or ecosystem types and be applied at successively smaller scales, depending on the microsite variation, the resources available

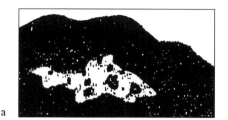

a

b

c

A concept sketch of a fractal design for a management unit or patch within a forest, to be harvested to emulate the natural pattern. Each magnification reveals more detail. a) The main shape related to the structural features of the landform. b) The first layer of detail responding to smaller landform structures. c) The final detail to develop the ecotone structure of the patch edges.

and the need for greater detail. In restoration it is important to remember that the initial pattern, established by seeding or planting, will be affected by the sequence of succession, species competition and some disturbance.

A further example of the use of this approach is where natural processes are reflected more closely by the introduction of prescribed fire into forests in which fire suppression has altered the natural structure. This has been implemented in a number of parks where management is needed, but where maintenance of natural character is paramount (p. 239, Fig. 14).

When we examined the fractal quality of natural vegetation along edges or ecotones, we saw that, often, the major patterns are repeated at smaller scales. This phenomenon can be used as the template for plantings of trees, shrubs or herbaceous species as part of habitat restoration. Thus, an intricate and naturalistic structure can be established for microsites occurring within larger arrangements. The aesthetic result of this is likely to be of a high value, because it would reflect the massiveness in the multi-layered detail giving coherence and complexity at all levels and points of view. The key aesthetic objectives of unity, diversity and reflection of spirit of place (*Genius loci*) can be achieved using the inspiration of natural patterns and processes.

Summary and Conclusions

In this chapter we have seen that a wide range of natural vegetation patterns occur in the landscape. They are defined by the underlying landform and its processes, the process of colonization and succession and the effects of disturbances. This produces a complex and dynamic mosaic, whose patterns show a number of relationships to the basic types discussed in Chapter One.

There are several techniques and methods for analysing the patterns, processes and underlying functioning of ecosytems that can be used as a basis for design, both for managing exisiting ecosystems or for restoring damaged ones. They can also be combined satisfactorily with the aesthetic dimension; without an understanding of landscape character expressed visually, it is impossible to achieve the complete fulfillment of the ecological potential.

1. The advent of space travel and orbiting satellites have enabled us to see the whole earth. The patterns of land and sea, the colours of the terrestrial surface vegetation and the masses of weather systems give us a sense of the interactions of patterns and processes that are continually present.

2. The vegetation zones of the world present a large scale pattern which is the manifestation of interactions between climate and landform. The established patterns of weather systems determine where rain falls as do mountain ranges and the distance of land from oceans. In this satellite picture the vegetation patterns of Europe are quite clear.

3. A landscape in the Rocky Mountains of Montana, USA, shows edges defined by light intensity (light and shade) and different wavelengths (colour) which are sensed by the retinal cells of the eye to build up a retinoptic map as the first step in the visual perception of the scene.

4. Somewhere in this scene there is a bird, a nightjar. It is well camouflaged. This illustrates how the gestalt laws operate. We cannot perceive much of a figure so that the main impression is of ground. Other figures such as light coloured twigs attract our attention first.

5. This scene in the Yukon, Canada, could be described as beautiful in the terms used in Chapter 3. It is a landscape where the parts fit together and there is no element out of place. It happens to be almost completely natural. Our preferences for environments which yield positive feelings are linked by research to qualities like coherence, diversity and mystery, all present in this example.

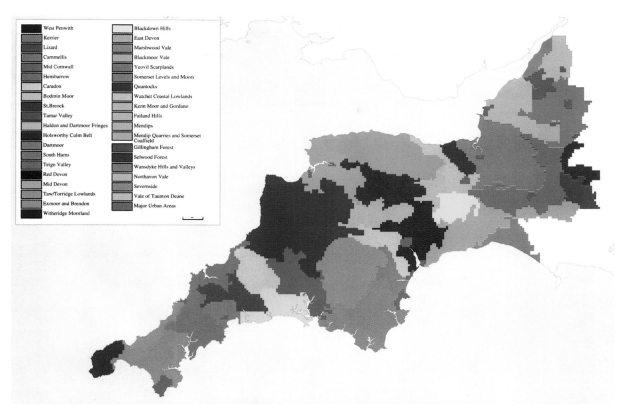

Legend:
West Penwith | Blackdown Hills
Kerrier | East Devon
Lizard | Marshwood Vale
Carnmellis | Blackmoor Vale
Mid Cornwall | Yeovil Scarplands
Hensbarrow | Somerset Levels and Moors
Caradon | Quantocks
Bodmin Moor | Watchet Coastal Lowlands
St.Breock | Kenn Moor and Gordano
Tamar Valley | Failand Hills
Haldon and Dartmoor Fringes | Mendips
Holsworthy Culm Belt | Mendip Quarries and Somerset Coalfield
Dartmoor | Gillingham Forest
South Hams | Selwood Forest
Teign Valley | Wansdyke Hills and Valleys
Red Devon | Northavon Vale
Mid Devon | Severnside
Taw/Torridge Lowlands | Vale of Taunton Deane
Exmoor and Brendon | Major Urban Areas
Witheridge Moorland

6. A map showing regional character zones in the southwest of England based on analysis by the TWINSPAN computer program. The basic information was based on kilometre squares, resulting in the zig-zag stepped boundaries. The map is the result of a synthesis of many layers of information. (Reproduced by permission of the Countryside Commission).

7. A computer generated perspective showing the expected appearance following landscape change, in this case logging. The model is built around the perspective as seen from a viewpoint using a digital terrain model and information about the forest cover, roads, rocks and other features. Such an image enables visual impact and design quality to be established with some confidence before the felling takes place. (Reproduced by permission of Richard Kyle).

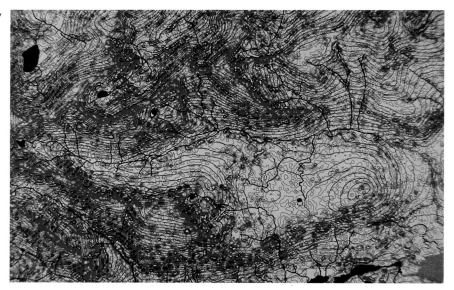

8. A map showing contours of convexity (red) and concavity (green) for part of Glen Affric in Scotland. This analysis emphasizes the landform pattern, allowing it to be related better to patterns of vegetation. (Reproduced by permission of the Forestry Commission)

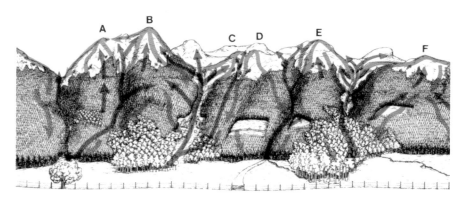

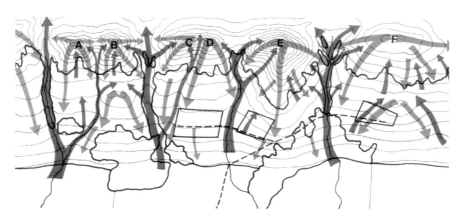

9. A sketch perspective and plan showing a landform analysis using the concept of visual forces in landform. The result is a distinctive pattern, relating to the structure of a landform that we perceive.

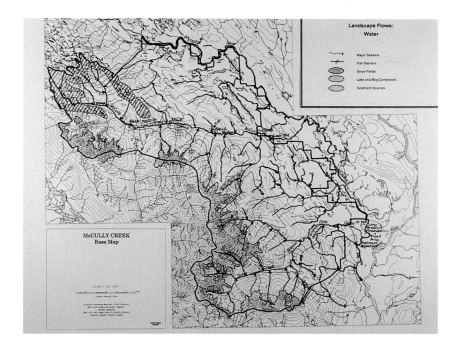

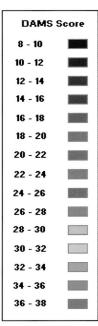

10. The hydrological analysis for Hazelton Mountain, British Columbia, Canada. Three zones are identified, a zone where sediment is produced, a zone mainly of sediment transport and a zone mainly of deposition. (Reproduced by permission of the British Columbia Ministry of Forests).

11. This map shows an analysis of windiness in Glen Affric in Scotland based on relative degrees of topographic shelter in relation to prevailing winds. Any forecast of disturbance to a forest in the area should be strongly correlated to this pattern, both in frequency and extent. DAMS stands for Detailed Aspect Measurement of Scoring, where 8-10 is the most sheltered and 36-38 the most exposed topography. (Reproduced by permission of the Forestry Commission).

DAMS Score

8 - 10	■
10 - 12	■
12 - 14	■
14 - 16	■
16 - 18	■
18 - 20	■
20 - 22	■
22 - 24	■
24 - 26	■
26 - 28	■
28 - 30	■
30 - 32	■
32 - 34	■
34 - 36	■
36 - 38	■

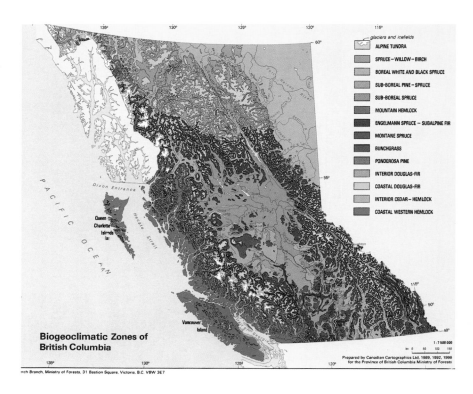

12. The map of the main biogeoclimatic zones of British Columbia, Canada. The pattern is distinctive with north-south and east-west gradients and greater variation where there are mountains. (Reproduced by permission of the British Columbia Ministry of Forests).

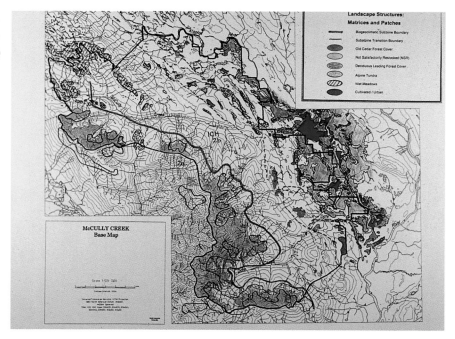

13. The landscape structure map for Hazelton Mountain, British Columbia, Canada. (Reproduced by permission of the British Columbia Ministry of Forests)

14. An area in Banff National Park, Alberta, Canada, where prescribed burning was carried out as a management tool to restore some of the patterns of natural disturbance and succession in the landscape.

15. Some houses at Mora in Sweden, recently constructed using traditional forms, materials, colours and layout whilst providing modern amenities.

16. The old colonial city of Guanajuato in Mexico, a fine example of a self-organized layout reflecting a constraining landform. There are many major public buildings tightly incorporated into the urban fabric. This pattern reflects the site, the human scale, the rich aesthetics of engagement and a concern for the urban functions. Due to the terrain cars are a minor feature of the streets so that there is the capacity to live the indoor-outdoor style that warm climates permit. In addition the fractal layout produces a rich edge structure, blurring or grading some of the distinctions between public and private spaces.

17. In this scene from Losotho in southern Africa, there has been massive overgrazing and deforestation resulting in the bare appearance seen here. This is a common problem in many developing countries and needs extensive ecological restoration using the methods described in this book. (Courtesy James Ogilvie).

CHAPTER SEVEN

HUMAN PATTERNS

Introduction

In the last two chapters, the patterns and processes of nature (landform and ecological patterns) were explored in an effort to explain how the landscape has developed in such an organized way over a wide range of scales. However, it is difficult to find a truly natural landscape, one that is wholly devoid of even the slightest traces of human activity or has not been subject to some influence at some time. After all, human societies survive everywhere from the hottest deserts to the coldest polar regions. Only the highest mountains, ice caps and antarctic regions may have escaped direct influence. Even here indirect human influences have been felt. When we explored the notion of environment in Chapter Three, we acknowledged that we are an integral part of it. Thus, the search for a landscape without human influence is futile.

Nevertheless, the idea of distinguishing between natural and cultural or man-made places is a recent one, stemming from the time of philosophers who sought to separate man from the rest of creation. At first this was seen as a positive aspect, raising humanity above the level of animals and placing people in a position of power and authority over nature. This could mean that people either had responsibility for the well being of the world or the freedom to exploit it as they saw fit. There is a widely held view that exploitation has been the more dominant force and that landscapes which result from this are impure, inferior and in modern terminology, unsustainable.

However, if we review the past, the distinction between natural and cultural landscapes only occurs if two ends of a spectrum are examined separately. As more knowledge is gained about the history of landscape development, it is becoming more evident that many places recently considered 'natural' are actually the result of human intervention of varying degrees of intensity.

An example is the dry Ponderosa pine forests of parts of western North America. These have an open character of large, thick barked trees of various ages, beneath which herbs and grasses dominate. The structure of these stands is maintained in this way by fire, which might arise from natural lightning strikes or be set alight deliberately by native people. It is possible that early inhabitants noticed that some fires, perhaps at certain seasons like early spring, helped to produce a flush of new grass that was especially attractive to game species of importance to these people. Such fires do not damage the forests in the way that hotter fires might do later in the summer; in fact, they reduce the risk of more serious conflagration. So, it is believed that the native peoples started their own, controlled fires to improve the habitat for the game upon which much of their survival and culture was based.

Ironically, later human intervention in the form of fire suppression has caused serious problems in these pine forests. The suppression was either in the form of removing the agencies for starting fires (moving the surviving native peoples out of the forest) or acting quickly to put out the fires that started from natural events. The result of this action allows shade tolerant species such as firs to grow beneath the pines. At

A typical multi-layered stand of Ponderosa pine in Oregon, USA. This forest requires regular ground fire to maintain its stand condition. Native people probably contributed to this early form of management. Recent forestry practices have encouraged a denser structure with fir invasion which creates conditions where catastrophic fires are more likely.

first this seemed to be desirable to foresters, because it increased the timber volume. However, in very dry seasons like the early 1990s, stresses placed on the firs made them susceptible to Spruce budworm, which killed many of them, especially in the Blue Mountains of eastern Oregon. Dead fir trees make excellent fuel, so that when fires start they are very hot and their suppression is difficult. Such fires destroy stands rather than maintain them, especially as they kill even the oldest, thickest barked pines. They also scorch the earth damaging the soils and its microorganisms.

This example illustrates the complexity of human interactions with natural processes. In many places the relationship is almost a symbiotic one. The landscape is more or less dependent on some form of human intervention for its naturalness, whilst to yield the values and products we seek from it, nature must be worked with and not against. Many other examples can be cited and the theme of this chapter is to explore the patterns and processes that lead to cultural landscapes together with some of the tensions that arise.

Early Cultural Landscapes: Hunter-Gatherers

The earliest hunter-gatherer societies tended to leave very little evidence from which we might ascertain the ways in which they may have changed the landscape. In any event, later generations have had far more profound effects by obliterating most of these early traces.

Occasionally there are glimpses, such as the remains of a hunted animal that tell us something about its life and the landscape in which it lived and died. Early hunters, being dependent on game, could improve their prospects in two ways. One was by following the game, which often embark on seasonal migrations, as described in Chapter Five. The other was to try to keep more game in an area by some kind of habitat management. Most tribes may have done some of both. Caribou/reindeer herds migrate very long distances and require certain habitats for their food. The same applies to further types of deer, bison, horses, llamas and other animals, some of which were later domesticated. The Lapp people (or Sami) in northern Scandinavia follow the reindeer, whilst performing some habitat management; Plains Indians used to track the immense herds of buffalo across the Great Plains of North America and probably also burned the prairie grasses from time to time to improve the grazing.

Other types of habitat management were probably also carried out for purposes, such as berry production. Gathering wild food and primitive forms of cultivation or vegetation selection were the other main ways early societies tried to maintain food supplies. Many berry producing plants in cool, temperate climates belong to the *Vaccinium* family and their productivity can be improved by periodic burning. Blueberries, huckleberries and the like were important to native tribes of North America and parts of Europe who maintained open patches in the forest for their growth.

In more favourable climates, such as the tropics, a wide range of plants provide edible fruit, roots and other parts such as tapioca bark. Native people undoubtedly increased the proportion of these plants in areas they inhabited. This in turn may have helped increase the numbers of other animals like monkeys, who eat similar fruit and also provide prey for hunters. Shifting cultivation would have added to this structural diversity.

In more recent times, population reduction by smallpox and tuberculosis, caused this type of forest management to decline and its structure to become denser and less open than was historically the case. Hence, it has been suggested that tropical forests are significantly more affected by native people than previously assumed.

We can envisage a landscape containing low human populations, who were able, using simple tools, to manipulate the vegetation structure to suit particular species of plants and animals that were important for their survival and way of life. This is little different from the current situation in the world; it is the rapid rate of change and degree of manipulation of landscapes that has altered today. However, primitive peoples may have changed the landscape to a greater degree than we formerly believed. Forests may have been patchier and prairies more open. This could have created a pattern of dynamics in the landscape, which altered those provided by natural disturbances as described in Chapter Six. Natural fires are likely to have been less prevalent where native people carried out controlled burning; the small openings caused by blown down trees or fungal attacks could have been supplemented by small tracts of burning. In turn, some wildlife may have adapted to the changing landscape and become dependent on a habitat structure that was more cultural than natural in origin.

As well as the utilitarian manipulation of the landscape for improved survival, there is the possibility that people have always altered landscapes to create places more suitable for habitation in the sense of providing greater safety or some primitive aesthetic quality. Because it is thought that the human species developed in the savannahs of East Africa, it has been suggested that we may prefer and be better adapted to semi-open park-like landscapes containing plenty of hiding places, combined with good visibility. This is partly because our erect stance and stereoscopic vision gave us good sight to see danger or to look for prey, but, relying more on keen intelligence than brute strength, we also need to anticipate problems ahead. This 'habitat theory', advanced by Jay Appleton amongst others, suggests that people subconsciously prefer and therefore create edge habitats with a complex structure. This edge diversity also provides more habitat for game as well as varied food plants. This theory can be neither proved nor disproved, but it does raise questions about the character and structure of landscapes that make us feel more comfortable. What tends to be ignored in this theory is the extent to which cultural preferences might mask the primitive, evolutionary response. Nevertheless, the theory suggests that early landscape manipulation could have had an aesthetic component.

Pastoral Landscapes

The development of human culture coincided with the domestication of animals. The Lapps and other Arctic tribes have semi-domesticated reindeer, elsewhere cattle, sheep, pigs, goats, llamas, horses and yaks are major domestic animals descended from wild predecessors. These grazing animals were probably originally managed much like the following of herds of wild livestock by earlier people.

The tribe would follow the herd or drive it to certain areas for grazing at different times of the year. The pressure of grazing by large flocks or herds could have quickly altered a landscape. Overgrazing can be blamed for the transformation of once wooded areas into grassland or even desert. In many countries around the Mediterranean Sea the open, rocky landscapes of sparse scrub are largely the result of overgrazing in ancient times.

However, if their numbers were not too great, migrating flocks and herds could have changed the landscape into places better suited for them to flourish. Controlled burning by shepherds could have maintained or improved the quality of grazing, by removing old or dead plant material of little nutrient value and encouraging a flush of new succulent growth. On the other hand, this management could have arrested natural succession, as clearings would normally succeed to woodland. As well as destroying seedlings by fire, the grazing animals would have also eaten them or the seeds.

It is likely that one of the primary agents for forest clearance, on any scale, was pastoral agriculture. At first, places with naturally sparse woodland may have been chosen, such as higher elevations in mountain areas. Grazing and browsing would have halted the regeneration of these woodlands, so old trees would not have been replaced when they died, gradually creating a more open landscape. The sparser vegetation could have changed further due to the reduction in rain interception by the thinner woodland canopy, the removal of nutrients from the herbs and grasses by grazing animals and by leaching causing the soil in many places to become impoverished and more acidic. In upland areas of Great Britain, the open moors are largely a result of this process, which favoured certain plants such as *Vaccinium* or other ericacious species, except in the highest mountains that lie above the natural treeline and always had an alpine or tundra vegetation.

In the Alps and other mountain areas, like the altiplano of the Andes, the practice of transhumance, the annual driving of flocks from lower valleys to high elevations in summer, has been practised for

An alpine pasture in the Italian Dolomite mountains. This landscape has been altered by grazing over the centuries. The tree cover has been reduced and the grassy vegetation altered by selective grazing. Such pastures were used, from Neolithic times, in summer to relieve the pressure from animals on cultivated or meadow land on early farms in the valleys below.

thousands of years. The treeline, where the forested slopes give way to open mountain tops, has been exploited and significantly altered over the centuries. The krummholz zone has only survived browsing in extremely inaccessible places and a simpler and lower elevation margin between forest and mountain top has developed. Some clearance of trees for firewood and hut construction has also taken place. Distinct patterns occur where the vegetation has become dominated by grasses and herbaceous plants; many species are non-native to the sites, having been brought in by animals. Amongst the fresh, lush vegetation, different kinds of wild flowers flourish in different places, such as damper hollows or drier ridges. This results in a detailed mosaic of semi-natural vegetation closely related to micosite diversity.

The alpine pastures developed most successfully where the forest was already sparse, the grass grew better and the snow melted earliest. These are the south and west facing slopes which are also prone to avalanche, because they are more open and can warm up quickly. In Switzerland, this led to early protection of forests on such slopes to reduce avalanche danger. Thus there is a direct relationship between the location of the pastures and the landform and climate. The result is a landscape mosaic of original vegetation and pasture.

In other places, animals were grazed in the forest in such a way that the wooded character survived and developed a particular pattern. In the vicinity of villages in mediaeval Europe, wood pastures were used for grazing and foraging by domestic animals. Pigs were let into the forest to feed on acorns and beech mast (seed) in the autumn. Cattle and horses also spent much time foraging there, to allow haymaking to take place on grassland. Grazing in the forest was regulated by the landlord and by those who had the rights to let certain numbers of their animals graze at particular times. The landscape that developed was dominated by a semi-open canopy of mature, branchy trees at variable, but usually quite wide spacing. Beneath this might be some undergrowth of plants capable of withstanding browsing, such as holly and grasses. If the area was managed for tree regeneration, parts of the wood pasture might be fenced off to allow seedlings to grow. Once tall enough to be out of reach from browsing animals, these enclosures were opened and new areas enclosed for regeneration. These compartments were managed in cycles over long periods.

When the main animals kept in the area were deer, especially fallow deer introduced into Great Britain by the Normans, a variation on the wood pasture landscape developed. Deer parks were large expanses of wood pasture, enclosed by a hedge, ditch or bank and fence of palings. The landscape of irregular clumps, groups and single trees that developed later had a significant influence on early landscape design and is often considered an especially attractive one. This may be because it has echoes of the savannah landscapes of ancestral human development alluded to earlier, or because it contains a powerful combination of coherence, complexity and mystery. The part open/part enclosed character allows us to understand the landscape, whilst we are only able to see part of it at a time.

Other patterns characteristic of wood pasture included pollarding, that is cutting branches off trees some 10 feet/3 metres above the ground to allow new shoots to grow quickly and to provide the small diameter wood so useful to early societies for huts, hurdles, causeways and palisades. The height of the cuts ensured that the deer or cattle could not reach to browse the tender shoots. This is an example of early *silvo-pastoral* management, where early woodland management and animal husbandry (and later hunting for sport rather than survival) were practised together, creating a landscape primarily for its utility that later became appreciated for its beauty in the interplay of mass and space and the diverse forms of the open grown trees.

There are surviving examples of these early wood pastures, such as Hatfield Forest in Essex, England, occupying key locations in the

A traditional wood pasture landscape at Hatfield Forest, Essex, England. The large trees spaced across the scene were pollarded (cut above the height of browsing animals) to produce wood products whilst wild or domestic animals grazed beneath. This example has been continuously managed by traditional methods for centuries.

geography of mediaeval villages; many wood pastures were later cleared and converted to arable farming when the common rights enjoyed by the villagers were extinguished.

Other landscapes that are the result of pastoral agriculture are the steppes of central Asia, the pampas of South America and the semi-desert regions of the USA. Native peoples used the local herbivores to exploit these, wandering from place to place with the seasons, the available fodder and access to water. Recent increases in population have put pressure on some of these vulnerable landscapes, as has the over-commercialization of ranching in some places; here the long established balance with natural processes has broken down and problems like soil erosion or the increase in unpalatable plants, reducing the grazing value, has occurred. In parts of the USA cattle ranching replaced the bison herds, but overgrazing with too much stock has caused the proportion of sagebrush and creosote bush to increase, whilst native prairie grasses and herbs have been eliminated. The process of over grazing has changed the pattern of the landscape. This has implications for the future management of these lands. The patterns of grazed, pastoral landscapes tend to be less diverse, simpler mosaics. They are less likely to be aesthetically attractive, because of the reduction in diversity, particularly at the small scale. The link with ideas of ecological aesthetics is significant (see the reference to Aldo Leopold in Chapter Three).

Early Cultivated Landscapes

Pastoral agriculture has a long history and has played a major role in human development and consequent exploitation and change to the landscape. However, these changes are relatively light when compared with the effects of cultivating crops. From its origins with the domestication of cereals such as wheat, rye, barley and oats in Europe, rice in Asia and maize in the Americas during the Neolithic period, the spread of crop husbandry changed culture and landscape. It also affected the relationship of people with the land, constraining them at crucial times of year like seed sowing and harvest, but also freeing people from the need to live on the margins of survival, by hunting and gathering or from following and tending flocks. Farming made civilization possible and great cultural achievements attainable due to rising populations and surplus labour.

Farming spread slowly from the centres of early development in the Middle East and it took between three and four thousand years to reach the most western and northern extremities of Europe. Early farming was largely dependent on the clearance of forest to yield land for cultivation. Some of the first attempts would probably have been of the shifting cultivation type still practised today in some remote places and only finally relinquished in Europe in the early years of the 20th century. The practice of cutting and burning patches of forest gives open soil, fertility in the form of ash, whilst the blackened surface heats up quickly in the spring. Seeds can be planted and crops harvested, but without manure, the fertility can reduce drastically in a few years, forcing the farmers to repeat the process elsewhere. The forest grows back over the cleared areas and eventually replenishes the nutrients.

In many respects this process of shifting cultivation and forest regrowth is not dissimilar to the results of natural disturbance by fire described in Chapter Six. People are likely to have observed the lusher growth and warmer soil following natural fires and began first, to rely on the natural plant colonizers for food as well as attracting game, and only later collected roots and seeds for planting. This was more like horticulture than agriculture. However, the landscape continued to be a dynamic, patchy pattern of different successional stages of forest. The patchiness may have been on a smaller scale than that resulting from natural disturbance, since the clearance was limited to the ability of people to cut and burn an area with limited manpower and primitive tools. In the Neolithic period, improved flint axes could be surprisingly efficient for cutting trees, whilst by the Bronze and Iron Ages, metal axes were available, enabling clearances to be larger. The landscape of shifting cultivation or swidden could be seen in Finland until the 20th century.

Abandoned clearings gave a more diverse pattern to the landscape, with more birch (a pioneer woodland species), more edge and as a result they probably attracted higher populations of deer and their associated predators.

Sedentary agriculture of crop raising and possibly mixed farming with livestock, led to the gradual development of rural landscapes that have persisted, often little altered, to the present day. There are wide variations in appearance between different areas, depending on the landscape being used and the crops being grown. Where no livestock was involved, few enclosures, walls, hedges or fences were needed or made, resulting in open landscapes of large fields. Irrigation created other patterns for distributing water and often needed long term communal organization.

The Pattern of Agricultural Development

Let us consider a hypothetical case of colonization by early Neolithic settlers into a western European country like Great Britain. Parties of colonizers may have penetrated inland along rivers in dug out canoes and looked for suitable places to start a settlement. They may have been in family groups or small clans intending to develop a communal farmstead settlement, bringing seed, livestock and tools with them.

Using their experience to find a site with fertile soil and where the forest was sparser and reasonably easy to clear, they would start by hewing out a few small fields and constructing their first houses. These irregularly shaped fields would be big enough to cultivate by the

This sketch sequence shows how a landscape could have developed as Neolithic farmers colonized the British countryside. a) Before farmers arrive, hunter-gathering people only have small scale effects on the landscape which is covered in deciduous forest. b) Family groups of farmers arrive and carve fields from woodland around settlement sites chosen for aspect, crop growing potential and access. Some clearance of hill tops is also undertaken. There are no signs of protection around settlements. c) As time goes on settlements grow and coalesce. Clearance expands on hilltops but some of the podzolic soils are showing signs of loss of fertility. At this Bronze Age period some fortification is needed around the settlements. d) By early mediaeval times the process of clearance and creation of field patterns is almost complete. The woodland remains in inaccessible places or where it is needed to produce wood products for the community.

available labour and probably produced a crop during the first season. As time progressed the settlers would clear more fields from the woodland, probably looking for level sites and avoiding steep banks or valley sides which were difficult to cultivate. The trees at the edge of newly cut woodland would develop into sturdy individuals and become densely branched so at the next clearance they might have been left as a useful barrier to stock. These eventually became the thick, irregular hedges containing a wide variety of species so typical of such landscapes today.

At the same time the settlers probably let their animals graze in parts of the woods, thus developing wood pasture as well as more open areas on any higher hills in the locality. After a while, if the settlement was successful, expansion in the population and further woodland clearance would lead to several family or clan settlements coalescing to form a continuous expanse of farmland. Some woodland of useful species capable of being coppiced, that is being cut to the ground and sprouting again, would be set aside to provide firewood and supplies of round timber needed for domestic use.

It would seem the Neolithic period of settlement was a relatively peaceful one, as few signs of fortifications or settlement protection have been found. In stony places, the fields were gradually cleared of stones

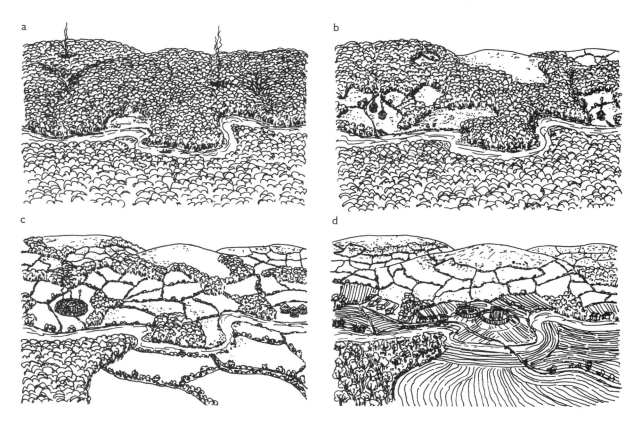

and the hedges became earth and stone banks or walls. Where the land was very open after clearance, with few hedges, these walls would have been used for stock control. Trackways wound their way amongst the fields linking settlements, giving access to the fields and forming trade routes and drove roads to move herds to and from upland pastures. Major tracks also followed the open high ground, as ridgeways.

The pattern thus formed was a self-organized landscape. The fabric was similar across large expanses of country, because each family group had to carry out the same tasks, using the same tools on the same type of land and under the same climatic conditions. The early farmers had no means of overcoming unfavourable ground, so they either avoided it or failed in the attempt to farm it. The fields carved from the woodland did not need to be geometric in shape and it would have been more efficient to follow natural site variations, based on landform and drainage. Field sizes were dictated by the area that could be cultivated. Thus a strongly unified pattern of irregular fields and winding lanes interspersed with farmsteads or hamlets evolved over time.

The patterns are mosaic landscapes combining patches with corridors as described in Chapter One. This characteristic helps us understand why they are frequently also rich in wildlife as well as being perceived as attractive.

At the margins of cultivatable ground, in the upland valleys of the Pennines, Lake District or Welsh borders, the climate and soil were more difficult than the lowlands and favourable counties of Kent or Surrey. The upper slopes quickly became cleared of woodland, but the heavier rainfall and acid soil soon led to the development of heather moorland and some peat formation. On the mid slopes some woodland remained, possibly receiving some management, whilst in the valley bottoms farmsteads were built and fields cleared. As populations rose, additional ground was needed for crops and fields expanded up the

A scene in the Llanthony Valley in the Black Mountains of Wales. Here the fields were carved out of woodland: the hedges extend from it and the pattern is strongly interlocking. The bracken areas dotted with scrub are probably former woodland only cleared in the last hundred years. A reduction in sheep numbers on the moorland or cessation of grazing or cropping in the fields could easily lead to woodland recolonization.

An area of agricultural land where the irregularly shaped fields and thick, mixed hedgerows suggest ancient countryside. The present fields are bigger than the original ones; banks in some of them show former hedge lines. This pattern dates back some thousands of years when farmers originally cleared the woods. Near Crickhowell, Wales.

slopes, whilst extra animals pushed the grazing on the hill tops downwards, squeezing the woodland in between. If bad weather persisted, starvation loomed or pestilence occurred to reduce the population levels, these pressures would relax allowing woodland to recolonize marginal fields and moorland. This ebb and flow of farming and woodland regrowth has continued in many of these areas up to the present day.

There is increasing evidence that many of the Neolithic patterns of settlement and fields have survived virtually intact to this day. These are what Oliver Rackham, the British landscape and woodland historian, called 'ancient countryside or landscapes', although there may be several variants of them. In many cases, the irregular outlines of fields are bounded by walls, dykes or hedge banks, which can be proven to date back by up to 5000 years. In other cases, the field patterns show more regularity, leading some people to the premature conclusion that they were planned and laid out as a highly organized act in a short space of time.

This plan shows the characteristic pattern of lowland English ancient countryside with winding lanes, irregular fields, nucleated settlement and relict broadleaved woodlands with irregular boundaries.

A fascinating example from Co. Mayo in Ireland was discovered in the 1930s following peat cutting on the slopes above Ballycastle. These 'Ceide fields' are a layout of stone walls preserved beneath peat up to 5 metres deep. It is believed that 5000 years ago Neolithic people arrived and started clearing the woodland. The moist climate was ideal for grass growing (as it is today) and cattle rearing was the main form of farming. The field layout has the semblance of being laid out all at once, such is the high level of order of fields covering a large area. However, it is possible, as more land was cleared over the years, that the walls were continued up the slopes perpendicular to the contour and parallel with each other, in order to keep agreed territories in place. It seems unlikely that all the land could have been cleared simultaneously and the fields arranged to a master plan handed down by some form of higher authority or community agreement.

The key characteristic about many of these patterns was the way they fitted into the landscape; people also understood how to maximize the use of available resources. Topographical effects can be very striking, like aspect in mountain areas. In the Dolomite Mountains in the north of Italy, there is a very marked pattern, where south or west facing slopes of valleys have been cleared of forest, whilst north and east slopes remain densely forested. In climates where animal fodder must be preserved as hay for use in winter, those sites where hay drying can be almost guaranteed will be cleared and maintained whilst shady, damp sites will be avoided. The steepest slopes will also be eschewed, whilst house sites and access roads and tracks must use naturally level places where possible. Thus a constant, well defined pattern emerges as the result of thousands of individual or collective decisions, all hingeing on the limitations or opportunities presented by the interaction of climate and topography.

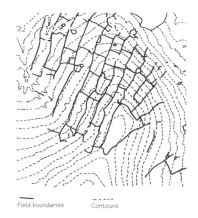

Field boundaries   Contours

A plan of the Ceide Fields of County Mayo, Ireland. They show parallel systems of walls running up hill with subdivisions across the slopes, farmstead sites and other smaller enclosures. (After Caulfield, 1978)

This scene in the Italian Dolomites shows a settlement pattern which is highly dependent on the aspect of slopes. The south and west facing slopes have been cleared for fields. Hay can be dried and stored in the small wooden barns. The houses receive warmth and are all sited along the access road. North and east facing slopes are maintained as forest.

Other locations favoured for meadow land included flood plains. Normally wooded, early settlers may have noticed how deposits of silt were related to early flushes of grasses and herbs. Clearance of the woods enabled grassy areas to grow early in the spring, which was advantageous for hay making and later grazing. Water meadows and flood plain meadows were also readily accessible by boat. However, flooding was dangerous for habitation and so houses were built on river terraces and other higher landforms, where more fields could also be made. The meandering pattern of the original vegetation may have persisted where strips of woodland were retained on natural levees, helping to tie the agricultural pattern visually into the landscape.

Alluvial fans were also chosen, because fresh deposits of fertile material and more level sites were rare commodities in steep, mountainous territory, even if the risk of flooding was great. Lakeshores were also accessible by boat, an important early means of transport. Houses and access tracks were probably sited on the natural levees, following the branching patterns of streamlets on the more complex deltas.

Like the way some natural vegetation patterns are most obvious in marginal or transitional landscapes, so are cultural patterns easier to see in remoter, more difficult surroundings. The choice of sites and the survival of the most favourable, the last successful colonization before cultivation was impossible and the need to conserve the best land can all be seen in a wide variety of examples.

In Finland, clearance of the forest for agriculture has taken place in the last few centuries unlike several millennia ago in many other countries. As it is a mainly forested country in a difficult climate, the pattern of farms takes careful account of the landform, soils, drainage, sunlight and communication. The landform is all glacial in origin with many eskers, kettle holes and drumlins interspersed with rocky ridges. Frequently, villages and farmland are located on former lake terraces, between the lakes or boglands in the depressions, and below the

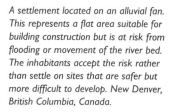

A settlement located on an alluvial fan. This represents a flat area suitable for building construction but is at risk from flooding or movement of the river bed. The inhabitants accept the risk rather than settle on sites that are safer but more difficult to develop. New Denver, British Columbia, Canada.

An aerial view of a settlement pattern in central Finland. An irregular, interlocking layout of fields has been carved from the forest which is retained on the most rocky, hilly or swampy terrain. Houses are set into the edges of the forest or on rocky knolls. Farmland is precious and must be conserved.

forested ridges. Linking roads often wind their way through these mid slopes with farms arranged along either side. The fields have been cleared of forest to different degrees in different places.

The farmsteads are normally sited on higher ground, often on rocky knolls protruding through the glacial gravels. This ensures that no valuable soil is built on. The cleared areas form interlocking patterns with the forest in the hinterland and their size depends on the complexity of the local landform. The pattern frequently shows meandering edges where the fields and roads follow the undulating

A view of farmland in southern Finland. The position of the farmsteads tucked into the forest edge on rising ground can be seen. The forest is a constant presence, enclosing and defining space throughout the landscape.

Isolated farmsteads in Iceland. The massive, steeply sloping mountains rise a short way inland from the coast, leaving a gentle plain capable of growing grass. Here the topography is a severely limiting factor on the pattern and intensity of the agricultural settlement.

topography and gradient changes. As the landscape provides few open views, the experience of travelling through it provides the key ingredients of coherence, complexity and mystery. Management to protect these qualities in the best of these cultural landscapes is under consideration.

In countries such as Norway or Iceland, the steep fjords or cliffs limit the pattern of human habitation to a narrow band between the sea and upper slopes, which are too steep and rocky to cultivate. Property lines run perpendicular to the shore and contours, as it is a universal arrangement to equalize access to the shore and quality of land amongst the community. On the west coast of Norway, the need for shelter dictates the settlement layout. Although west facing slopes would normally be chosen, where these are the most exposed to storms sheltered parts are preferred, often facing east or northeast. The population of some of these remote places was often higher in the past than it is now, since the harsh living conditions prompted many poorer people to emigrate.

In Ireland, the ancient pattern of the Ceide fields was long abandoned to the bog and elsewhere empty valleys were once highly populated. The introduction of the potato as the staple food in the 17th century allowed the population to increase. People had to extend cultivation onto steep slopes high up on hillsides. If the soil was sparse it was laboriously augmented with seaweed or shell sand and formed into parallel beds, often inappropriately named 'lazy beds'. After the potato famine of the 1840s large numbers of people emigrated and once populous valleys emptied. The patterns of the lazy beds can still be seen, a testament to human persistence and also the continuing story of attempted colonization and later abandonment. The patterns show varied alignments of the lazy beds according to landform and slope, expressing the character of the topography.

European types of self-organized patterns can also be seen in the New World, where settlers had to clear forests and establish farmsteads. Often the settlers treated North America like Europe, and took a long time to learn the ways of the native vegetation, wildlife and

A fossilized landscape of 'lazy beds' in Ireland abandoned during the potato famine of the 1840s. They show the extent to which increasing population forced people to spread out and colonize extremely marginal areas. Doolough Valley, County Mayo.

climate. For example, parts of the Ozark Mountains in Arkansas in the USA closely resemble landscapes in England or Wales, the countries of origin of many of the original settlers. However, the colonization pattern soon became more organized and planned, forming a different lineage of pattern creation to the self-organized system so far examined.

The settlement patterns, that is the distribution of farmsteads, of hamlets, villages and towns and their layouts, developed later in many areas, long after the initial clearances had been completed. In Great Britain, the ancient patterns persisted into the mediaeval periods, with a typical, dispersed settlement of houses and farms scattered across the landscape, compared with nucleated settlements, where most of the houses are in villages. Studies of these patterns in England have shown

In the Ozark Mountains of northern Arkansas, USA where fields carved from the forest by the English settlers leave woody hedges behind and recreate a pattern very reminiscent of the ancient countryside of England.

there are two distinct zones, corresponding to ancient landscapes, with dispersed settlement, and a central zone, relating to 'planned' landscapes with nucleated settlements. These zones can be identified by, amongst other means, analysing place names containing allusions to woodland or woodland clearings, which denote ancient landscapes. These patterns also follow the main geological, topographical and agricultural regional variations of the country. Such distinct patterns have originated from all the influences mentioned so far plus the pattern that has arisen as a result of 'planning'.

In areas where water is scarce, irrigation has been practised for millennia. Many of the earliest civilizations, dating back over 5000 years, developed where irrigation, using river floodwaters, enabled large populations to build up and surplus labour to be available for monumental building programmes. The Tigris and Euphrates in Mesopotamia, the Nile in Egypt, the Indus in what is now Pakistan and the Yangtze in China are all prime examples of this. Some of the earliest, highly organized societies with strong central control developed in these places and exhibit the first evidence of planned and, later, designed landscapes. The characteristics of planning and design contrast with those of self-organization and will be discussed in the next section. However, other irrigation systems also belong to the self-organized class of landscapes.

In the Mediterranean, after the deforestation of ancient times much soil was washed away. Only by careful management could soil be kept, allowing plants such as vines or olives to thrive. Steep terrain in these semi-arid landscapes was irrigated, using precious water usually occurring as rainfall in winter; this was collected in cisterns and then carefully rationed over a drier growing season. Individual farmers built cisterns to store water and made terraces on hillsides to provide level

The landscape of the Peloponnese, Greece. This once forested landscape was cleared some thousands of years ago and suffered soil erosion in antiquity. This may have been a contributor to the demise of the Bronze Age civilization of which the city of Mycenae, whose ruins lie in the foreground, was prominent. Modern terraces and olive cultivation conserve the vestiges of the once deep soil.

These rice terraces in Sri Lanka are another example of a self-organized pattern where topography and careful control of water flow, together with soil conservation have been the determining factors. Terraces are a common feature in many landscapes produced by different cultures.

planting beds that prevented soil erosion and held water as it was released and flowed downhill. These terraces and irrigation systems have remained in use for many centuries. As each farmer and his descendants constructed and maintained the systems, the landscape of an area achieves a sense of continuity and harmony, because all terraces have to be constructed in the same way, even though individuals or small communities work independently from each other.

In the Far East, seedlings of rice, the staple diet, are grown in flooded fields or paddies. On flatter areas the fields are flooded in a regular pattern of canals and ditches, evenly distributed for an equal supply of water. In steep areas, terraces are used and again act to control erosion and soil loss, to hold water and facilitate its distribution. The key to the layout of terraces is to follow the contours precisely since the horizontal surface of the water has to be maintained to prevent it from flowing away. Thus, step-like terraces create a strongly defined series of linear, meandering patterns across often exceptionally steep slopes. When filled with water and edged with bright green grasses or herbs, these landscapes make an unforgettable sight. The terrace system can start small and gradually be extended up and along a slope. Major breaks in the slope can result in a larger scale pattern, whilst intricate or complex landforms produce a finer result.

Once again we see evidence of self-organized landscapes, where many people operating over long periods of time and frequently independently of each other, have produced a continuous, coherent landscape that fits together so perfectly with outstanding aesthetic quality. There is diversity across the landscape, where local site variations were taken into account and yet there is also great similarity.

A sketch of part of the English Lake District showing how the overall pattern of settlement is strongly related to the topography. Cultivation is pushed upwards as far as it is worthwhile and reflects the character of the landform in the irregular boundary between field and mountain. Woodland is sometimes fitted in between the two. The irregular pattern to the fields suggests that it conforms to the criteria of ancient countryside.

The ancient countryside landscapes are excellent examples of places where full sensory engagement can be achieved. They developed in situations where people walked around them, so experiencing the topography, the winding lanes, the scents and sounds as well as the sights. The intimate hedged landscapes also contain a sense of mystery that invites us to explore them, as described in Chapter Three.

The self-organized cultural landscapes also contain massiveness and intensity proper (in Whitehead's terms). This leads to a sense of strength that is frequently increased, where the cultural landscape is set within a more natural one such as the moorland margin in Wales, the mountains of the Dolomites, the Finnish forest or the desert surrounding irrigation patterns. This strength is more powerful, because the self-organized, cultural patterns relate strongly to landform, soil and climate.

This aesthetic unity has often been damaged by recent activities that are not reliant on the nuances of slope, aspect, soil, shelter and so on provided by the landform and original vegetation. Such disharmony has often been the result of technological developments, often with disastrous physical and aesthetic results.

As well as the self-organized aspect, there are also fractal qualities to be seen in all the examples discussed so far. The major distribution of land use, clearance from woodland, alpine pasture zones, cultivation terraces or extensive, ancient field patterns are repeated in the smaller scale, finer aspects of layout, field shape, woodland edge, crop distribution or terrace structure.

The irregular, interlocking shapes also have a fractal dimension which can be measured and shows very well, the differences between self-organized and planned layouts.

The probabilistic models, discussed for patterns of natural plant colonization in Chapter Six, also have application to the cultural patterns, particularly at the margins of cultivation. It is more probable that harvests will succeed on good soils, on favourable aspects and low elevations than on poorer soils, unfavourable aspects and high elevations. Thus, when fluctuations in climate occur (following probabilistic patterns and cycles) the unfortunate people living in the least favourable areas are the first to starve or be forced to abandon their land, as happened in Ireland during the potato famine. Economic fluctuations also play a part, especially in more recent times. Thus chaos theory (discussed in Chapter One) comes into play, even when its subjects are ostensibly governed by human decisions based on rationale.

These unplanned landscapes also followed the same influences on their patterns as did the preceeding natural vegetation, responding to the interaction and controls on ecosystem processes exerted by the landform. Climatic fluctuations, elevation, aspect, shelter, water flows, animal movement, all presented constraints and opportunities experienced by the farmers who cleared the forests and tilled the land over the millennia. They were part of the ecosystem, although they did not act harmoniously with it in every case.

Forest destruction, causing catastrophic soil erosion and damage to hydrology, is not a recent phenomenon. However, in general, the more successful, self-organized, cultural landscapes have a closer relationship to their environments than many other human processes of pattern creation.

Planned Landscapes

The next set of cultural patterns derive their unity, continuity and similarity, mostly from preconceived planning, often directed by higher authorities like the state. The term 'planned landscape' was introduced by Oliver Rackham in Great Britain, to contrast with the ancient, self-organized landscapes discussed in the last section. However, planning of landscapes has been practised for many centuries, if not millennia, in numerous places alongside self-organization, as one of the various layers of effects that have created the current landscape.

Planned landscapes imply that the organization of land tenure, the subdivision of agricultural land into fields and also the governmental organization of regions is carried out according to a set of rules, a master plan or a standard template. We can include early irrigation systems, Roman and Greek engineering and land organization, the planned enclosure of open field systems and modern highway construction amongst examples of planned landscapes.

In order to plan and lay out an area for any of these examples, some principles of land survey and rudimentary map making were needed, including importantly, a working knowledge of geometry. The word means 'to measure the earth' and so it is clear that the science of geometry and the principles defined by Euclid and Plato were introduced, primarily, to divide up land and to organize its layout.

The Sumerians and Egyptians developed their civilizations during the third millennium BC around highly organized irrigation systems to collect floodwater and hold it amongst the fields, using systems of canals. The equal distribution of water and its even flow needed precise calculations of areas, gradients and volumes. Egyptian surveyors used sighting rods much like surveyors use today. Such instruments allow preplanned straight lines to be laid out, together with right angles and other easily constructed geometric shapes derived from simple mathematical calculations. Pharaoh was a god and in charge of nature, of the annual inundation and the assurance of fertility. It is no wonder that some of the early pharaonic tombs were the pyramids; these simple, yet powerful geometric polyhedrons, perfect in their symmetry and elegance, offered sharp contrast with the irregularity of nature. Geometric shapes have, since that time, been associated with power over nature, the power of higher authority and the separation of people from nature.

The science of surveying and of measurement acquired a significance in the careful recording of dimensions of buildings like Solomon's temple during the second millennium BC, of statues erected by Persian kings or the Israelite tabernacle recorded in the Bible. Measurements assumed great importance in societies who were keen on formal organization The planned layout of irrigation was also easy to control and monitor, because it could be divided into sections and problems could be quickly spotted and repaired. This aspect, of easy control and allocation to individuals, either to maintain or settle, is another important strength of planned landscapes.

The Greeks and Romans developed surveying into a science. The Roman army engineers, in particular, are renowned for the precision of their road alignments to obtain the shortest and fastest distance between two points. The layout of their camps and cities was also highly planned. Where they colonized a landscape, it was customary to award retiring legionary soldiers a piece of land. These awards were of standard size and laid out as part of new towns, villas, roads and water supply systems in lands where such things did not occur until the Romans arrived. This system of subdivision was known as a *centuriation*. Romanization meant not merely the adoption of Roman customs, but also recreating Roman landscapes and territorial organization. Tax collection was also made easier when land units were standardized.

We have questioned whether the Irish Ceide fields are indicators of early planned land organization. Some people argue that organic shapes imply no planning, whilst only geometric shapes arise from planning. Perhaps there was also a hybrid of unplanned, gradual field clearance with occasional planned setting out of field boundaries. Building walls needs some preplanning, whereas leaving hedges, as land is cleared from forest, requires more gradual adjustment to take advantage of the right trees or shrubs as these occur.

Planned landscapes in Great Britain began with the development of the feudal system. After the Norman Conquest in 1066, an hierarchical structure of land holding developed, based on allegiance to one's overlord and the guarantee of providing him with troops as required. At the bottom of the social hierarchy were the *villeins* or serfs, peasants tied to the land and required to work a set number of days for the lord of the manor and the rest for themselves. The archetypal landscape usually associated with this social structure is an open field system. This was concentrated down the middle NE-SW zone of England, between the two ancient landscape zones. It may also have coincided with the land best suited at that time, to grain growing on a large scale or where population pressure had already caused a reorganization of the ancient landscapes that preceded the open fields.

The classic layout of such a village was the strip system and this implies the landscape had to have been planned in order to be

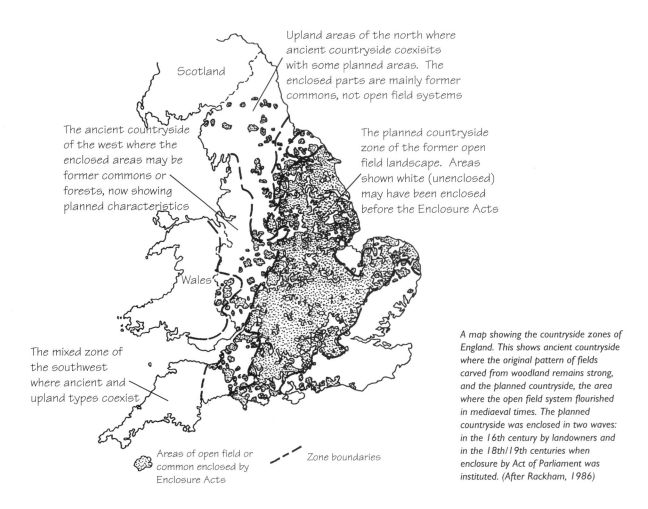

Upland areas of the north where ancient countryside coexisits with some planned areas. The enclosed parts are mainly former commons, not open field systems

The ancient countryside of the west where the enclosed areas may be former commons or forests, now showing planned characteristics

The planned countryside zone of the former open field landscape. Areas shown white (unenclosed) may have been enclosed before the Enclosure Acts

Scotland

Wales

The mixed zone of the southwest where ancient and upland types coexist

Areas of open field or common enclosed by Enclosure Acts

Zone boundaries

A map showing the countryside zones of England. This shows ancient countryside where the original pattern of fields carved from woodland remains strong, and the planned countryside, the area where the open field system flourished in mediaeval times. The planned countryside was enclosed in two waves: in the 16th century by landowners and in the 18th/19th centuries when enclosure by Act of Parliament was instituted. (After Rackham, 1986)

A plan of a typical English mediaeval open field system showing the strips allocated to different tenants and the nucleated village. This example is at Admington in Warwickshire, England. It developed from the nucleation of once scattered farms so that grain production could be maximized. (After Soul, 1997)

Village

regulated. Three large fields were communally cultivated, each villein having a strip or number of strips (a *selion*). The fields were cultivated according to a rudimentary crop rotation system to allow periodic manuring from cattle. Coppice woods provided fuel, timber and other woodland produce; they were also regulated into equal sized 'cants', each felled according to a cycle of around 15 to 20 years. Wood pasture, open pastureland, water meadows and moorlands provided communal grazing for cattle, sheep and pigs depending on the location. Deer parks, hunting forests and monastery land were also present. In Scotland, a similar system called 'run-rig' was used. In the Highlands, it persisted until the clearances (forced eviction of the people) of the 18th and 19th centuries. Such landscapes would have presented a sense of order that contrasted with wilder areas. It could have been appreciated by the lord of the manor as a sign of his power and perhaps been endowed with religious significance. There may have been an aesthetic dimension to this, a satisfaction in the sight of a well ordered world where life followed the seasons.

The feudal organization was also interested in taxation. William the Conqueror started a tax assessment of most of England soon after he became king. This 'Domesday Survey' recorded every animal, plot of land, plough, mill and most other taxable items. The methods of land measurement were not sophisticated, being based on the amount of land a team of oxen could plough in a day, which presumably varied to some extent according to soil and terrain; nevertheless, the fields were measured according to standard acres, furlongs, perches and other units.

The open field system was suited to the midlands of England, where plains or gently rolling terrain could carry large fields. Elsewhere, the preponderance of animal husbandry and the landform, soils, existing woodland and climate, probably precluded its development and favoured the continuance of the ancient countryside.

The decay of the feudal system started after the ravages of the Black Death plague in the 14th century. About one third of the population is estimated to have died during the epidemic and labour for arable farming became scarce. Villeins were able to leave the land and take up better paid work elsewhere. Sheep husbandry needed less labour and became more common. In some places whole villages and their field systems disappeared. During the 16th century, the monasteries were dissolved and their land given or sold to old or new gentry and aristocracy. There was also a demise in the hunting forests, as population recovery after the plague increased the demand for land.

During the 18th century agricultural improvements took place. The development of crop rotations to improve yield and maintain soil fertility, better breeding of animals and the beginnings of mechanical husbandry, prompted many large landowners to plan and remodel their estates. The old open fields and many of the common grazings were enclosed to allow better control of animals, to facilitate crop rotation and to establish a new system of tenant farmers. Remnants of hunting forests were cleared, whilst heaths were 'reclaimed' by use of lime to improve the soil and bogs, fens and marshes were cleared and drained.

This vogue for improvement was both economic and aesthetic. The new parks that were laid out around the houses of the landowners were simultaneously better for food production and represented scenes reminiscent of paintings of idealized Classical landscapes. Beauty was followed by the sublime in the styles adopted over time and naturalistic

An aerial view of a parliamentary enclosure landscape. The regular straight field boundaries, roads and dispersed farmsteads are typical. Lincolnshire, England.

A diagrammatic plan of a typical parliamentary enclosure landscape showing the pattern of straight, rectilinear field boundaries, straight roads and isolated farmsteads (built as part of the improvements).

layouts superceded geometric ones. While the fields remained utilitarian in their geometry, the landscapes of pleasure demanded naturalness. It was at this time that the first landscape gardeners worked, and philosophers like Edmund Burke and Immanuel Kant considered beauty and the sublime (see Chapters Three and Four).

Some landowners so completely remodelled their estates that roads were realigned, new farmsteads built amongst the newly enclosed land and villages reconstructed in new locations. The countryside, so recently open and treeless, became enclosed by hedges or stone walls, each with trees planted along them at intervals. The layouts of these landscapes were set out by land surveyors, who used ranging rods and chains to measure out precise areas in a consistent geometric fashion.

The hedges were mainly planted in single rows of quickthorn (hawthorn), with oaks, elm, and ash trees planted in them, rather than the thick mixed woodland hedges in the ancient landscapes. Hedgebanks were absent, but ditches were needed to improve drainage in some places. As these landscapes matured, and were battered over the years by the elements and farming practices, the effects became superficially similar to the ancient, self-organized landscapes that were described earlier. However, the plan view shows the different provenance and its geometry often lies less easily on the land than the older patterns.

Colonization and Planned Landscapes in Eastern Europe

Where early colonizing people in Neolithic times developed the ancient, self-organized landscapes, the colonizers of the mediaeval period onwards were subject to more control over their land and the way it was colonized. Frequently, conquered or newly discovered territory was granted to the nobility or the church, who in turn used the feudal or tenant systems to apportion their lands to settlers.

In the 13th and 14th centuries, there were crusades by the Teutonic Order of Knights, from what was then Germany, into areas mainly lying east of the River Elbe, inhabited by pagan tribes such as Prussians, Lithuanians and Wends. The conquered lands called the *Ostsiedlung*, already carried settlements and villages, albeit of a low density and unsophisticated agriculture, but this did not stop the new masters from colonizing them. Robert Bartlett, a British historian, has demonstrated how they laid out new estates, new villages and created carefully planned, regular and geometric layouts. They also invited or recruited settlers from western Europe to take over land, using entrepreneurial agents called *locatores*. For example, whole villages of people of Flemish origin were established, as well as Gascons, Germans, Franks and others. The colonizers were given special allowances, tax exemptions and civil liberties in order to entice them to the newly conquered eastern areas. Villages were named by their originators, sometimes recalling their founders' or *locators*' name. The areas were granted in lots of *mansi*, a unit of land measurement of about 40 acres or 16.6 hectares in the case of a Flemish *mansus* or 60 acres (25 hectares) for a Frankish one.

The new settlements were often carved out of woodland (still extensive in these territories compared with western Europe). The first task was to establish and demonstrate the granted areas on the ground. In wooded land this was difficult. Methods of survey included smoke signals in wooded valleys or sightings from hilltops. Marks were made on trees and then the land was subdivided. Measurement was usually made very carefully so that future remeasurements might not mean increased assessments for taxes. Where possible, measuring rods and measuring lines were used, which resulted, predictably, in rectilinear layouts. A book was written on ensuring that fields were laid out precisely.

As well as a new field layout the settlers in eastern Europe introduced bigger and better ploughs and more cereal cultivation, so that the new landscape pattern resembled the more open fields of other grain producing areas than the old mixed farming of patches cut from the forest. In addition there is a sense, in the descriptions written at the time (the 14th century), that the settlers were consciously taming the wilderness and converting primitive, unsophisticated and inefficient landscapes into well ordered, modern and efficient ones - efficient at raising taxes if nothing else. Today the pattern of German settlement east of the Elbe is striking. One example is the village type called a *Waldhufendorfer*, where the present farmsteads are aligned along a

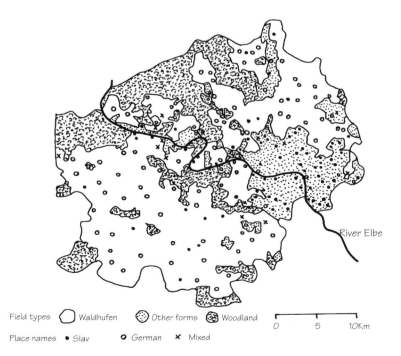

A map showing the place names and field types for an area of the Ostsiedlung, the mediaeval colonization of Eastern Europe. This area, called Kreis Pirna, originally settled by Slavic people, north of Dresden in Germany was analysed by Herbert Hellbig.

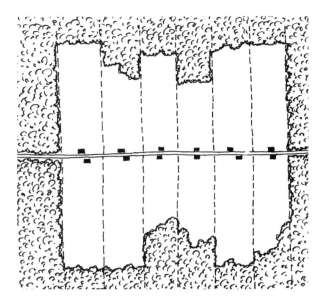

The layout of a settlement based on the mansus, the unit of measurement used by settlers in the Ostsiedlung. Each farmstead is located along a road and the mansus extends back a set length. The degree of clearance of each mansus depended on the quality of the site and the vigour of the settler and his family.

street at regular intervals. Their holdings take the form of a broad strip of land stretching from the rear of the farmstead. This type of village was first developed for wooded areas where the farmer could keep adding to his land by gradually extending the clearance along his strip. The strips are each of a *mansus*, being around 300 feet (92 m) wide and over a mile (1.6 km) long.

The landscape must have presented interesting contrasts between the self-organized earlier patterns and the more recent planned ones. The settlers probably considered their ordered landscape superior to that of the pagans, representing the authority and correctness of the christian religion and its placing of people in relation to the world. There may not have been much more of an aesthetic component than this, a sense of comfort in order amid the pagan wilderness.

Planned Landscapes of North America

In the early colonization of North America, by English settlers in the 17th century, the native population was small, scattered and not very advanced in terms of agriculture and settled landscapes. The native Indians were mobile and moved from place to place to hunt, gather and practice shifting cultivation. Accordingly, they were not deemed to be landowners in European legal terms and hence were easily dispossessed or had their lands bought from them cheaply. Thus, the land was largely unfettered by settlement patterns and could be divided up any way the settlers wished.

William Cronon, the American historian, has documented the development of the early pattern of land use in New England. The English king, as feudal overlord, granted land to individual nobles or companies, who, in turn, could give it to settlers. The conditions of the grants were often vague about dividing up the land to early settlers and so they had to devise their own means. Early attempts to grant land to individuals were eschewed in favour of groups of people joined up as 'towns' and land was granted to these as a body, each receiving an area of around 6 square miles.

The land was purchased from the Indians and held in common, that is owned by the founders of the town as a group. They then divided up the land according to the social status and needs of each person, thus preserving something of the social hierarchy to which they were accustomed in England. House sites and fields for cultivation were first selected followed by pasture and woodland, marshlands for hay and so on.

In the early transactions, land was described topographically and perceived as landscapes with particular characteristics; as time went on and the recording of land grants became more precise, the parcels were treated less as real landscapes and more as abstract areas that only became real when settlers found, marked and subdivided them. Soon a system of laying out units on a geometrical grid was developed, mostly based on lines of latitude that could be fixed on the ground using a sextant; in many cases these related to the main land grant of the colonies. For example, Massachusetts was an area granted to the Massachusetts Bay Company that lay between latitudes 40 and 48 degrees north. The land was then laid out on a master plan for a particular area and subdivided into townships, sections and so on. The townships and individual owners had to mark their boundaries by blazes on trees, a practice legally required to be maintained in a number of states in the USA to this day.

An aerial view of part of the state of Maine in the USA. This diverse landscape was cleared by settlers in the 17th or 18th centuries but may have become reforested during the early/mid 20th century. The pattern is based on land division into 'townships' and then into standard farm units laid out to a grid. Land clearance and maintenance depended on the owner and the suitability of the terrain.

The early settlers chose lands already altered and in some cases cleared by the native Indians, but later they also had to clear much of the forest. Here the classic interaction between land clearance constrained by ecological factors leading to a self-organized landscape, occurred within the planned geometric surveyed pattern. The settlers soon learned how to identify the best land from the tree species. Trees that gave moist forest conditions and preferred damper sites such as maples, ashes, hickories and beeches developed rich black humus greatly sought after by farmers, who looked for European parallels in land quality. Oak and chestnut produced drier soils with lower nutrients, due to more frequent fires, and also had denser undergrowth that was more difficult to clear. They also needed more work to develop good agricultural conditions. The acidic, sandy soils beneath conifers (podzolic conditions), moist in the case of spruce and hemlock and dry under pine, were avoided.

The soil released from the forest contained a store of nutrients that quickly diminished (the reason the Indians practised shifting cultivation) and so required the same amount of manuring, to keep it in good condition, as was needed in Europe. The initial landscape pattern that developed was of a field and settlement layout very similar to that of Europe within the highly planned tenure system. Arguably, the settlers also sought to make it reminiscent of the landscapes they had been used to in Europe and felt comfortable with.

We can infer that the settlers, often living in remote locations, far away from the landscapes of their original homes, subconsciously sought to recreate familiar surroundings. This is an aesthetic response, where the sense of comfort is increased in places where people instinctively know their way around. It is consistent with the idea of perception where we seek affordances in the environment. In order to cope with a strange scene it is a natural response to try to alter it to fit our preconceived expectations. It fits the theory of the aesthetic of engagement.

An interesting pattern of land ownership can be seen in the area of New England, where Vermont, New Hampshire and Quebec, Canada meet. The major boundary is international, partly following the Connecticut River and then following the line of the 50th parallel (line of latitude). The Vermont/New Hampshire border follows the river with the land in each state divided up into towns and then into square or rectilinear lots. Most ownership boundaries follow variants of the lot lines and thus have a geometric outline. There is a curiosity in the boundary of the town of Canaan, Vermont, which lies at an angle to the others resulting in a number of triangular lots where the towns meet. The landform of the area is very diverse, with a well defined river valley containing an active flood plain used as hay meadow, river terraces, steep slopes and major landforms including Monadnock Mountain, a dome shaped, igneous intrusion with a distinctly radial pattern of ridges and valleys. Thus, a strange visual interaction occurs

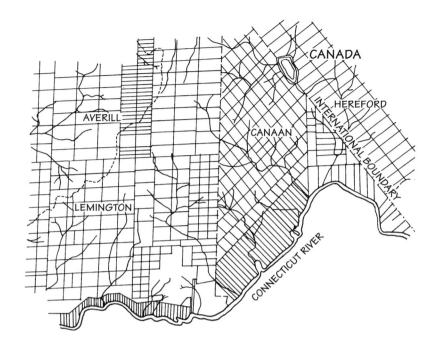

An example of an unusual land survey pattern of townships in northern Vermont, USA. The Canadian border, the Connecticut River and different town layouts have produced a complex legal pattern which ignores the underlying hilly topography.

between the geometric property lines and the landform, ecological forest patterns and drainage systems. This is particularly noticeable where one landowner has cut his forest up to a lot line, so that the geometric shapes stand out awkwardly in contrast to tree species patterns that are related to the landform and aspect, as described in Chapter Six.

The planned geometric landscape became dominant in the Midwest of the USA and expanded westwards. Where the prairie landscapes of the plains began, its subdivision by visual survey, using ranging rods, prismatic compasses and other instruments, was very straightforward. It is also a land with few landmarks and enormous size. In 1803, President Thomas Jefferson negotiated the acquisition from France of the Louisiana Purchase, a huge chunk of land through the middle of what is now the USA, and started the colonization by farmers of the lands west of the Missouri and Mississippi Rivers. This 'Jeffersonian Grid' is relentless in its Cartesian regularity (except where longitude corrections are needed) and gave complete organization to the landscape. Whole state boundaries were aligned on the grid, counties, cities, townships, farm house sites and streets all followed it. The basic division was the section, 1 mile by 1 mile, then the 1/4 mile section and the lot.

As well as its simplicity of survey, the grid made it easy to allocate land to settlers. It was also inherently fair in that each settler was allocated the same amount of land (160 acres), although land quality was not always the same.

While there was not a specific aesthetic component to the land survey, the fact that it commenced at a time when Cartesian views of the world and the place of people within it were important cannot be overlooked. The principle of 'Manifest Destiny', where it was believed that the USA had the right to expand across the continent to the Pacific Ocean, meant that the sense of establishing civilization, taming the wilderness and arranging the land so that individual freedom was encouraged also became an aesthetic goal that persists to this day. The sense of imposing order on unruly nature has always had an aesthetic dimension, while the strictly functional landscape is the result of individual freedom enshrined in the US constitution in a way not found in Europe or other colonial settlements.

In many states in the USA, the entire land that was not built on is now cultivated except for sloughs (wet hollows) and watercourses. In other places, the pattern had to be fitted into the landform, drainage and vegetation structure. In Canada, where the grid was used similarly, the prairie provinces resemble those of mid western USA. Ontario, by way of contrast, is mainly naturally wooded. There are sandy soils, bogs and lakes, rocky places and other areas that were not worth clearing. The common pattern here is often of farmsteads set out along a road aligned to the grid, with rectilinear farm boundaries at precise intervals. The land was then cleared progressively back from the road and house until the limits of what was worth clearing were reached.

The sequence of development of a landscape typical of Ontario, Canada. a) The original landscape pattern of forest, river, lake and bog relating to topography, geomorphology and drainage. b) The grid survey pattern laid out and granted to settlers. c) The pattern of land use where each settler has cleared what the site and his energies can provide as crop land. The rest is managed as woodland.

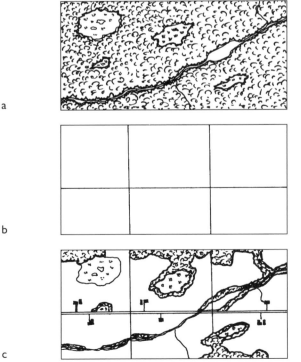

a

b

c

This varied according to the available labour, energy and tenaciousness of the settlers, so that land was cleared further back on some holdings. This pattern, seen from the air, is the dominant formality of the grid and the cleared and settled landscape ceasing at lines, defined partly by the grid and partly by nature, with natural irregular patterns beyond. It is symbolic of the tension between man and nature, civilization and wilderness in a recently colonized land of difficult climate.

Settlement Patterns

So far the study of cultural patterns has concentrated on land use and its character. Mention has been made of some aspects of settlements in relation to the divide between ancient and planned countryside. Rackham notes the prevalence of nucleated settlements, principally villages, in the planned zone, whilst dispersed settlement is more typical in the ancient zone. This is because the open field system of arable farming also depended on houses for peasants being sited together. There was no point in the peasants living near the fields, because their allotments of land were located in different parts of the area. By contrast, in the ancient landscapes, each farm represented the clearance of wildwood and each farmer had a set amount of land conveniently situated around the farmstead.

The layout of villages varied. Three main types of farming villages (as opposed to later specialized villages for industrial or fishing purposes) can be found in England. There are villages laid out around an open grassy area or 'green', those aligned along a single street and/or irregular clusters of houses perhaps with several clusters (polyfocal). It is not certain why they should exist in this way but there are some theories.

The diagram illustrates the three basic village types: a) A street village. b) A village green. c) An irregular, polyfocal village.

a

b

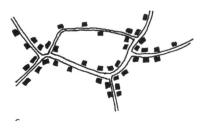

c

An example of a polyfocal nucleated village from the Cotswolds, Gloucestershire, England. The village nestles amongst the landform, connected by a pattern of lanes. Each focal part of the village may have developed at different times.

For many people the village green epitomizes the character of an English village, with a well or pond, a church, a maypole (used in May Day celebrations) and an inn. Most may have been originally laid out for defence. Many of this type can be found in northeastern England, where Viking raids occurred in the 9th and 10th centuries. There may have been palisades around the exterior perimeter. Sometimes the roads leading in were set at right angles so that attackers could not charge straight into the village and its entrances could be more easily defended. One theory is that the green could be used to harbour livestock against attack and possibly to keep wolves away at night. This might be one of the earliest types of village layout.

The street village developed in various places once the road system had become established; it is thought generally that this may be a later type of settlement.

The irregular village may have arisen from individuals claiming land for themselves rather than an organized founding. Buildings are grouped rather than dispersed and several groups may form the village.

The Process of Village Development

The nucleated villages of England, which occupy the central swath of planned landscape, were rarely in existence before 1000 A.D. Previously, there was either no settlement or occupation of a very different type. This contradicts a common interpretation of the Domesday Book, William the Conqueror's assessment of the country, compiled in 1086. The misconception is based on an assumption that each parcel of land described in the book is synonymous with a village. This was not the case. In the highland areas of England, especially the Pennines, the Domesday landscape comprised isolated farmsteads and small groups of cottages. This was also true of the Welsh Marches and heathland areas in central and southern England.

Villages could have developed anywhere, but were limited by the territorial boundaries of the land available for the subsistence of their inhabitants. These boundary lines are often of great antiquity, many arising from late Roman times. They frequently became parishes and thus had to support the local church by payment of tithes (a tax of 10 per cent on produce payable to the church by each parishioner household). Where the parishes were larger, as in the north of England, these might have contained several villages or clusters of hamlets.

Whilst the possible reasons for the origins of some nucleated designs or forms have been postulated, there are four basic ways in which these villages could have evolved:

- growth from a single place;
- the agglomeration of several single places close enough to merge;
- the collapse of a pattern of dispersed settlements into one of nucleated villages;
- deliberate planning.

The first process of development, by steady growth from a single farmstead could have occurred when a family expanded and land was subdivided amongst the next generation. The resulting form might be loose and amorphous if there were no features such as a road or road junctions along which to arrange the houses.

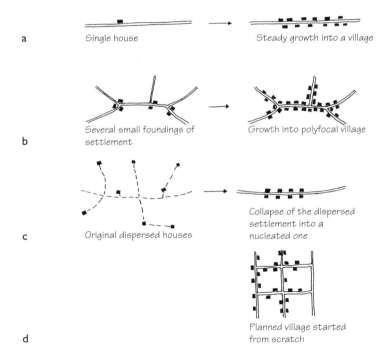

a

Single house   Steady growth into a village

b

Several small foundings of settlement   Growth into polyfocal village

c

Original dispersed houses   Collapse of the dispersed settlement into a nucleated one

d

Planned village started from scratch

Diagrammatic examples of how villages grew and developed:

a) Steady growth from a single farmstead.

b) Agglomeration of several centres.

c) Collapse of a dispersed settlement into a planned one.

d) Conscious planning as a new foundation.

The second process, by agglomeration of several centres could have led to composite or polyfocal layouts. The junctions of several roads or a number of large farmstead settlements near one another and expanding gradually would both produce this form. This is an example of a self-organized pattern and may have had a better sense of fit into the landscape than some of the others.

The collapse of a dispersed settlement, by people abandoning their houses and reforming the village into a nucleated layout, is the third process. The reason for this decision might have been changes to farming and land reorganization (for example, from ancient to planned strip field), defensive needs or economic changes of some sort.

The conscious planning of a village is often considered a recent phenomenon associated with the 18th and 19th centuries, agricultural improvement and ornamental parks. There are a number of well known examples of this, but others go back, probably, to the late Saxon/early Mediaeval periods. The great concentration of nucleated villages in Northumberland, Durham and North Yorkshire appear to have been planned soon after 1070, following periods of devastation by Vikings in 1066 and William the Conqueror's 'Harrying of the North' in 1069-70. Land was given out to new lords and large scale rebuilding was required. Other instances of planned villages are linked to castle building.

Thus the layouts may also reflect how the villages were founded. Many place names suggest that a single person led a community in establishing a village so that there might have been an element of planning. Many of these were Anglo-Saxon and later Viking in origin, suggesting how the colonization of the Romano-British landscape by Anglo-Saxons and of parts of the Anglo-Saxon landscape by Vikings took place. Layout patterns native to the home country could also have been used.

The distribution of settlement names can also reveal some distinct patterns that tell something of the colonization history. An example from the Cleveland Hills of North Yorkshire in northeast England reveals such a pattern. The Cleveland Hills are the northern escarpment of the North York Moors and rise steeply out of the Stokesley Plain. The land is good quality on the plain, but the steeper, north facing slopes are wooded or rough grazings, with heather moorland on the summits. Strung along the foot of the escarpment are a line of villages each separated by only a few miles. For the main part alternate villages have either an Anglo-Saxon or a Danish name. Presumably, the Anglo-Saxons founded a number of villages and a few hundred years later there was enough room to fit a second founding in between, perhaps using underutilized land along the boundary areas of existing villages. The parishes for each village, conforming to the estates of the original Lord of the Manor, tend to run up and down slopes and some of the farms at the hill foot have rights to graze sheep on the moors above, reflecting the old land tenure patterns.

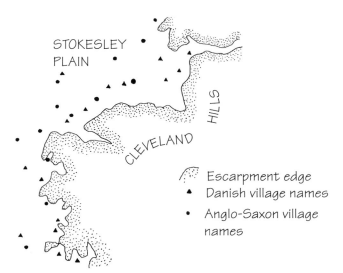

STOKESLEY PLAIN

CLEVELAND HILLS

Escarpment edge
▲ Danish village names
• Anglo-Saxon village names

A map showing the distribution of Anglo-Saxon and Danish village names in relation to the escarpment of the Cleveland Hills in North Yorkshire, England. The pattern suggests the interposition of later Danish villages into a pre-existing Anglo-Saxon settlement.

In the case of the *Ostsiedlung*, the mediaeval colonization east of the Elbe, there have been attempts to plot village layouts according to Slavic or German origins, but the distinction is not always so clear. The *Waldhufendorf* layout mentioned previously, of spaced farmsteads along a street, is a known German type. Another is the *sackdorf* or 'cul-de-sac' village and yet another is the rundling where the houses are shaped in a horse shoe pattern for defence. Both of these are more common across central Europe. Place names can be more useful determinants. In places the German names correspond to *Waldhufendorfer* and were probably cut from woodland that contained no settlement, whilst Slav or mixed areas had irregular field patterns and were derived from the original agricultural pattern.

Slavic village layouts can still be seen in Russia. A single wide road or street usually has wooden houses of traditional construction arranged along either side. Garden strips run back from the houses. These originated on private estates before the Russian Revolution. They were collectivized by the Communist regime during the 1920s and 1930s, but still retain much of their original character.

In Norway the quality of the land is so variable in most places that each farm has its house, but each landholding is quite small. In some areas, the fertile land is so limited that all the houses appear to cluster into a village because this was the only way to conserve the good land. In Iceland, the same is true in some places, but in others the land is so poor that individual farms have to be large in order to be viable. Many areas of Finland have dispersed settlements, often described as villages, but not recognizably so in the English sense of the word. There is usually a strong sense that the settlements fit into the landscape, because of the need to respond to site and microclimate. This gives a sense of unity to the scene and helps its coherence.

An aerial view of a modern Russian village from Ryazan Province, east of Moscow. The wooden houses are arranged in a linear fashion along either side of a wide, unpaved street. The width allows animals to be driven to and from each house. Gardens and fields run in strips back from the houses. Although recently released from collectivization this village probably closely resembles the typical planned village of much of eastern Europe.

In Sweden, before the 18th-19th centuries, most settlements were in villages or hamlets. A *toft* was the hamlet site where several farm houses and their buildings were located, surrounded by enclosed fields and meadows (divided into individually owned strips) and by common pasture and forest land. The landowners met periodically to agree the way the land was managed. Villages would appear to have arisen during the mediaeval period when scattered farms combined to permit the use of two field and three field cultivation systems (similar to the development of nucleated villages in England following the introduction of the open field system). Villages also arose as isolated farms were subdivided through inheritance (as also postulated for England).

Village layouts differed around the country. Those with churches developed and became locally important with a range of special buildings such as vicarages, almshouses and schools. Village locations were closely related to the terrain and its limitations. Around the high coast (see Chapter Five) south facing, sloping locations predominate, either on poor rocky land or valley sides next to clay soils. In flatter areas of boulder clay and till deposits such as in Skane, the large villages lay in the wider valleys surrounded by the fields. Above the high coast, settlements were positioned on fine grained glacial deposits on hilltops. In the north, frost free locations were chosen, either on high slopes where cold air did not collect, or by the sea or lake shores where the water ameliorated the temperatures.

As well as the siting and layout already described, there were planned features such as sack shaped enclosures around which houses were arranged (rather like the *sackdorf* of Germany), often with a pound for the cattle.

There were also planned villages laid out as single or double rows of farms. Land was distributed according to various provincial laws under the 'sunwise' system. Here the width of the house plots had to reflect the size of the farms and the sequence of the farms also had to be reflected in the sequence of strips in the village fields (hence each was arranged in similar fashion so that the sun rose and set in the same way on both farmstead and land).

Unlike in parts of Great Britain, in Sweden the pattern of these original villages has now almost vanished. This is due to various land reforms during the 19th century which resulted in radical changes to farm sizes and layout and to the settlements that accompanied them. The land was separated into individual farms replacing the old strips and the original farmsteads were relocated. This resembled the English planned landscapes that replaced the open field system. Hence, the current farmhouses are 19th century in design. Some villages of the old type survive and some modern farms remain on former village sites.

Settlement patterns everywhere have been as prone to fluctuation over the centuries as the natural patterns described in the previous chapter or the upper limits to agriculture discussed in this. Some English and German villages grew into towns, acquired charters to hold fairs and markets and generally prospered, whilst many others decayed or vanished. Some disappeared following the Black Death plague, others succumbed later. In some places, isolated farms record the locations of once extensive villages.

In New England in the USA, the landscape of the early colonization has decayed in many areas. Townships, once almost completely agricultural with farmsteads and villages similar to those in Great Britain, were abandoned from the 1920s and 1930s onwards, their wooden houses rotting leaving stone built cellars and chimney stacks to record their passing. The forest has quickly recolonized the abandoned fields so that landscapes which were largely open at the turn of the 20th century have returned to forest now.

Settlements were sometimes founded as semi-speculative ventures. Land was subdivided into plots and the founders advertised for tenants. Inducements such as a market charter or exemption from taxes were offered. Sometimes this was successful, whether for a colony in America, New France, Upper Canada or a new village or town in England. Others failed completely. All of these are noted for their gridded layouts.

The Pattern of Buildings

The structure and style of the buildings constructed in the landscape developed in a similar way to the field or village patterns arising from the interaction of people's activities with the landform, ecosystem and climate.

Well wooded countries usually made ubiquitous use of timber for building construction. This was the case in countries now using other materials when wood was still plentiful. The earliest forms of timber buildings, still seen in parts of Africa, were circular in plan with conical roofs. Later, more rectangular forms developed which became the precursors for the stone or brick versions of today. Many countries still use wooden construction, though industrially produced components may be prevalent. In countries like Great Britain, where wood ran out and other materials were locally available, the pattern of buildings reflects a greater diversity of style and method of construction.

Patterns of Vernacular Buildings and Villages in Sweden

Sweden, a heavily forested country, shows quite distinctive patterns of building construction and layout, using wood almost completely. Timber buildings can be modified easily compared with brick or stone, but do not last as long, so there is less of a legacy compared with Great Britain. Details in the building construction can also be changed; for example, where peasants followed the styles adopted by the gentry for their houses.

Timber construction is one of the oldest and most persistent building methods. It has used logs in the round or squared and shaped with dovetailed corners for walling. It produced the traditional log cabin and was used until the early 20th century. Buildings constructed using this method tended to be small, limited by the length of the logs (which were not usually joined lengthwise); hence, farmsteads over most of Sweden had a multi-building layout, where there was one building for each function arranged in a rough square.

An example of an old log house from Norway that is identical to the vernacular type found in the north of Sweden.

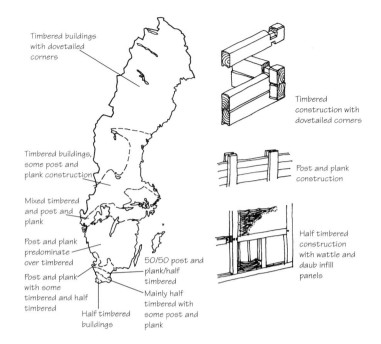

Timbered buildings with dovetailed corners

Timbered construction with dovetailed corners

Timbered buildings, some post and plank construction

Post and plank construction

Mixed timbered and post and plank

Half timbered construction with wattle and daub infill panels

Post and plank predominate over timbered

Post and plank with some timbered and half timbered

50/50 post and plank/half timbered

Mainly half timbered with some post and plank

Half timbered buildings

The pattern of vernacular buildings once prevalent in Sweden. Being built of wood such houses are not as durable as the stone and brick of Great Britain. (After Selinge, 1994)

The second construction method used was post and plank, especially where oak was in good supply in the south, but also in pine areas further north. Staves (vertical planks side by side) were also used in the west of the country for wall construction. Larger buildings can be constructed using these methods, especially where durable timber is available.

Half timbering, using a wooden frame construction infilled with wattle (woven twigs) and daub (clay mixed with straw) or, later, brick, is the third method, mainly found in the south. This construction is also common in Denmark, Germany, Holland and England. These two methods could produce large buildings with several uses such as house/barn combinations. Brick and stone were used in some places, sometimes in combinations with timber construction.

Initially, all the methods of construction relied on hand tools - axes, adzes, and hand saws - until water or steam powered sawmills started to produce large quantities of sawn planks. Plank construction, in combination with the other methods, became more common and produced a greater similarity in the appearance of buldings in many parts of Sweden. Log buildings were often faced with vertical boarding that hid their original construction.

Another feature of rural Swedish buildings is the use of red paint, which came into use in the mid 18th century. This is still produced today, together with yellow ochre, by the Stora Copperberget mine at Falun in Dalarna. It preserves the timber, as well as giving it a warm appearance. In some places, the house was painted yellow to contrast with the rest of the farm buildings.

Farm layouts were usually based on a multi-building system. This gave rise to local variations depending on what buildings were needed and how they were arranged. For example, in places like Skane, in the far south, half timbered houses were linked to stone outbuildings arranged around three sides of a square.

Regional Building Variations in Great Britain

The buildings that give the pattern and sense of place to the British landscape are small manor houses, farmhouses and cottages, barns, stables, cow houses and cart sheds, mills, kilns, workshops and chapels. The types of building reflected the needs of the type of farming or industry taking place. Farms in arable areas needed barns for grain rather than cow byres or sheep folds; sheep farmers needed stores of fodder distributed around the farm for winter use; dairy enterprises needed milking sheds, dairies and haybarns. Farmsteads in nucleated villages drew their labour from the village cottages; farms in dispersed areas may have needed cottages or bothies to house tied workers.

These buildings gave local distinctiveness to an area mainly by virtue of two things: the style, form or layout of the buildings and the materials from which they were constructed. To some degree the two were linked, because in many cases, the materials partly dictated the way the building was constructed and the form it took.

The main variations of vernacular buildings across Great Britain can be correlated with landform, geology and land use. If a series of overlays is constructed relating landform to the upland/lowland zone, the land use into arable/mixed/pastoral and the geology into building stone of various kinds or alternative materials in its absence a distinctive map emerges, dividing neatly into definite areas.

The landform, whether mountainous, lowland vale, moderate hills, plain or plateau can be related to land use type, population density and degree of remoteness. Remoter areas in the harsher climates of mountainous regions were less prosperous and so buildings tended to be smaller, simpler and lacking in decorative detail. They also made greater use of local materials because transport was difficult and expensive. Well populated lowland valleys tended to be more prosperous and produced more, larger buildings with decorations. Such places often lacked some materials, but could afford to import them from elsewhere. This trend increased as better communications developed such as canals and railways in the 18th and 19th centuries. From this point on buildings began to lose their vernacular distinctiveness in such areas.

In Great Britain the pattern of building can be illustrated by examining the interaction of these factors within a selection of its regions.

The Cotswold Hills and the oolitic limestone belt (extending from Dorset and Wiltshire, Gloucestershire, Northamptonshire and north

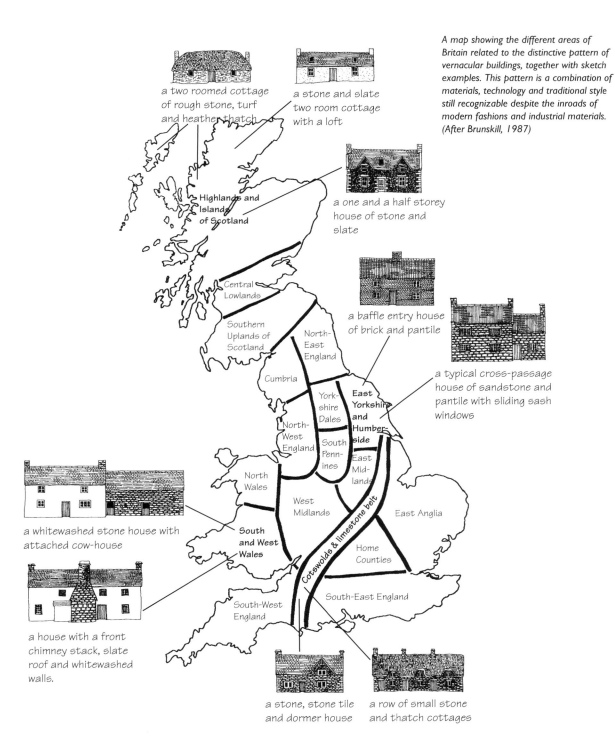

a two roomed cottage of rough stone, turf and heather thatch

a stone and slate two room cottage with a loft

A map showing the different areas of Britain related to the distinctive pattern of vernacular buildings, together with sketch examples. This pattern is a combination of materials, technology and traditional style still recognizable despite the inroads of modern fashions and industrial materials. (After Brunskill, 1987)

a one and a half storey house of stone and slate

Highlands and Islands of Scotland

a baffle entry house of brick and pantile

a typical cross-passage house of sandstone and pantile with sliding sash windows

Central Lowlands

Southern Uplands of Scotland

North-East England

Cumbria

York-shire Dales

East Yorkshire and Humber-side

North-West England

South Penn-ines

East Mid-lands

a whitewashed stone house with attached cow-house

North Wales

West Midlands

Cotswolds & limestone belt

East Anglia

South and West Wales

Home Counties

a house with a front chimney stack, slate roof and whitewashed walls.

South-West England

South-East England

a stone, stone tile and dormer house

a row of small stone and thatch cottages

eastwards into Lincolnshire) provided a very distinctive character, most noticeable in Gloucestershire, where the belt of rock is widest. The golden, yellow stone was used for walls, roofs and field walls. The stone is easily dressed and carved into details, such as mullions used to divide windows. House layouts varied with the cross-passage type appearing. This evolved from a mediaeval layout, where the passage leads from front to rear of the house and the main fireplace backs onto the passage. Tall stone barns were also characteristic. These buildings, since their walls and roofs are both made of stone, seem to have grown out of the landscape. They weather to a colour that blends into their surroundings, enhanced by the growth of lichens on the stone. Thus a strong unity is established.

South and West Wales mainly used stone and occasionally clay for walls. Originally many roofs were thatched, but later these were replaced with slate, leaving steep pitches intact. Painting the exterior of rough stone houses was common. Where houses and barns adjoined, the barn would be left unpainted to distinguish it from the house. Cross-passage houses were used in the southeast whilst in the west (Pembrokeshire) a rare layout called the front chimney was built. Brick dressings to the rough stone walls were used in later examples in the more industrial areas of the Welsh Valleys. Dormer windows were often added to make rooms in the roof spaces. As in the Cotswold example, the rough stone blends into the landscape very well. However, the whitewashed houses stand out in contrast, adding focal points to the scene. These houses usually nestle among the soft landforms for shelter and are not obvious except from close quarters. The sudden discovery of a farmstead when travelling along a winding lane enhances the sense of mystery in the landscape.

East Yorkshire and Humberside yield sandstone or limestone that are both readily available and easily dressed. Houses were predominantly cross-passage of stone (sometimes brick) construction and once thatched roofs were mainly replaced with pantiles (originally imported from Holland). The cross-passage layout in this area derived from mediaeval plans, with an open hall in the centre, a parlour at one end and the kitchen or scullery at the other end, across the passage. Farm buildings tended to be separate from the houses. Although the land use ranges from arable vales, to upland and open wolds and moorland valleys, the house styles remain very similar throughout the region. The red pantile roofs provide a colour contrast in the landscape, complementing the natural greens of the vegetation. The warm colours help to make the houses inviting.

The Highlands and Islands of Scotland have a different history to most of the rest of Great Britain. Their population, who until the late 18th/early 19th centuries, lived a life of pastoral agriculture based on the black cattle economy, were forcibly removed by landlords to be replaced by sheep. The resettlement of many people into coastal villages meant much new building of many cottages, based on a simple

A vernacular house from a village in North Yorkshire, England. The use of local stone, clay pantiles for the roof and the layout plan are all traditional to the area. This is a 'cross passage' house where there is a passage running from the front door seen here to the back of the house. A kitchen was traditionally to the left with a hall and parlour to the right.

one storey plan. In the northwest and the Hebridean Islands a special form of land tenure was established called crofting. This evolved a dispersed settlement pattern of small strip fields, common grazing and only part-time work on the land. Two-room cottages were occupied by people (at one end) and animals (at the other). Rough stone and turf with heather thatch for roofs, were the main, easily acquired materials. Wood for roof trusses was very limited and came from driftwood, the few forest areas remaining, or had to be imported. These farmhouses, though crude in appearance, were robust and provided effective shelter for people and their animals in a severe climate. Better cottages retained the same basic plan, but were constructed of mortared stone with slate roofs.

Highland farmhouses, usually built in the 19th century, are typically of one and a half storeys, stone with slate and possibly rendered outer walls. They incorporated more modern details like sash windows, but retained traditional construction methods and proportions.

The aesthetic result in the Highlands and Islands is different from other areas. The harsher climate, the bleaker locations and the small sizes of the cottages give a sense of human survival under difficult conditions. There is more of a contrast between settled and wild areas than elsewhere. The open landscapes permit the settlement pattern to be more easily seen, as a widely spaced scatter across the scene.

It is important to recognize that the traditional buildings seen in Britain today are those that have survived, being substantially constructed and well maintained. Generally, these represented rebuilding in the landscape when stone, brick, slate and tile replaced the wattle, daub and thatch of former centuries. This 'Great Rebuilding' happened in several phases: the minor gentry and those of manorial status undertook it during the 13th to 16th centuries, the ordinary farmers carried it out during the 16th to 18th centuries, whilst the poor cottagers had to wait until the mid 18th century onwards. The rebuilding was latest in the far west and north of Great Britain. The buildings can all be described as 'vernacular', meaning they were built for permanence by the local people, using local materials constructed according to local traditions, although subject to gradual innovations. Hence, particular vernacular characteristics belonged to definite regions of the country. They differed from designed buildings, whose builders followed design rules developed by professors in academia and built according to the latest styles using materials that might have been transported over long distances.

Towns and Cities

In most countries the pattern of agriculture, hamlets and villages of rural areas provided food and services to a dispersed population that sought to utilize the land as best it could, within the ecological and aesthetic awareness and technological limits of the time. We have noted some of the various population, climatic and economic fluctuations that have affected countryside patterns over the centuries. This rural landscape not only provided for its own subsistence but also supplied food and other products to towns and cities outside the locality, in exchange for craft or industrial products. Local trade expanded regionally and internationally and gave rise to distribution systems and communication networks. Overlying this was the politics of power, economics, defence, law and the church. Towns and cities are above hamlets and villages in a settlement hierarchy; the former provided goods and services such as protection in return for food and services from the latter.

Town and City Location Patterns

The location of towns and their distribution pattern, depended on their function and the size and productivity of their hinterland and its population. Towns often arose in association with places of defence (from large Iron Age fortified hilltop settlements called *oppida* to mediaeval castles), control of trade (bridges or ferries over rivers or traffic along roads or rivers) and for exchange of goods and services. We have already noted that many villages began as fair or market places and those that succeeded became market towns. Their distribution had to be convenient for the exchange of goods and services. Cattle, sheep, geese and other livestock had to be driven to them from the surrounding farms. In the Welsh Marches it has been observed that the market towns are, on average, 14 miles apart. This gives a maximum of 7 or so miles for driving livestock, possibly an optimum distance, as well as yielding sufficient quantities to keep the market going and traders in business. In country districts the market

The pattern of small market towns in Wales. The average distance between them is related to the amount and type of farming, the topography and the ability of cattle or sheep to be driven or transported to a market and back in a day.

Main upland areas of Wales

A hill top town in Italy. The castle crowns the summit whilst the town crowds around it, protected by walls. The town can command the plain around it and provide refuge for the populace in times of trouble.

town remains an important trading centre, used for selling livestock and for supplying farm equipment, as well as other goods and services.

In many lands, towns were mainly related to defensive positions. In much of Italy, hilltop towns with defensive walls arranged around a castle, present a definite pattern. The same pattern is common in France, Germany and Spain and it reflects the prevalence of wars throughout the centuries.

With the development of industry, specialized towns (and villages) arose in association with sources of power or raw materials. In the mediaeval period in Great Britain, once the Black Death plague had completed its first outbreak, there was an increase in sheep husbandry, leading to the development of a woollen cloth weaving industry. A rich class of merchants arose, as did towns based on the commerce of wool. Ports connected with this trade also boomed when wealth increased and merchants exported high value products and imported luxury goods.

Water power was important to the nascent industry of mechanized cotton and wool spinning and weaving during the 17th and 18th centuries. Hence, centres of manufacture arose in Great Britain and elsewhere where swift flowing streams could be harnessed, raw materials obtained and finished goods moved easily to markets. This began a pattern of settlement based on different criteria to agriculture, although dependent on the landscape for raw materials and power.

With the development of steam power in the 18th century, the iron and steel industry, potteries and shipbuilding, new patterns emerged, first in Great Britain and then in other countries. These industrial patterns were not connected with the cultural patterns of preceding centuries and they also owed nothing to the patterns of agricultural settlement or the ecology of the area. The pattern of industry and industrial settlement is related not to surface structures, but to the geology of coal, iron ore, china clay or limestone; most of these materials were mined from deep underground. Together with this very swift town and city growth, a new mesh of communication systems of canals and railways developed. This overlaid and often bore little relationship to the old patterns of roads and tracks that served the agrarian and cottage industry economy.

As the transport system developed in Great Britain, it became easier and cheaper to move heavy and cumbersome materials around the country. This enabled bricks, slates, tiles and other materials to be used anywhere. The use of local materials, which often proved less durable or needed high maintenance, was diluted by their substitutes. Thatched roofs disappeared to be replaced by clay tiles or Welsh slates. Brick replaced expensive stone or wood of low durability. The rural landscape of remoter parts not served by railways or canals changed more slowly than the Midlands or the north of England, where growth was greatest.

Industrialization occurred in other countries, although often not to the same extent. Northern France, Belgium, the Ruhr of Germany, parts of Pennsylvania and the Midwest of the USA developed in similar ways. Other countries in Europe were less industrialized and so retained more of their traditional, agricultural settlement patterns until much later in the 19th or 20th centuries.

Town and City Layout

The main consequence of industrialization in most countries was to move the patterns and processes of landscape away from a self-organized pattern, evolving in concert with nature's limitations and technological constraints, towards fast changing, planned or chaotic layouts, using industrial techniques and technology that could ignore the landscape, climate, drainage and soil. For the first time, people began to have power to move mountains, to change rivers, and to alter extensive areas completely, so that no vestiges of nature remained. This significant shift can be observed in the evolution of the layout of towns and cities.

The older cities (with the exception of a few planned examples at a relatively small scale) had arisen and developed gradually to no prearranged plan. They were organic, self-organized and reflected a human scale of space and mass, walking pace and social intercourse. Winding streets grew from winding lanes through fields. Public spaces, ranging from civic and ceremonial squares to market places, to neighbourhood squares or plazas, gave a hierarchy of structure that continued into the courtyards and gardens of private properties. However, such cities were not always salubrious places to live, with no drainage or sewers and overcrowding in the poorest quarters.

A visit to an old city, especially one that has survived intact without war damage, has few motor cars on its streets and has avoided significant modernization, presents a character and atmosphere that is distinct and unique. The irregular, organic structure leads the explorer ever deeper into its different quarters. Narrow lanes lead at right angles from wider streets into complex labyrinths, now branching again, now reconnecting with a small square or wider street. This pattern shows all the characteristics of self-organized fractal structures like branching angle variation depending on the sizes of the streets or lanes. In many ways, it is not dissimilar to some of the naturally evolved forms of distribution of energy or water such as stream systems or the structure of the blood supply to the body.

In any country, those towns or cities constructed on hills had to develop their layout to conform with the topography. Winding streets climb gently along the contours, allowing carts to make their way through the town, whilst series of narrow steps permit shorter, although more exacting, journeys for pedestrians. Strangers to such towns may initially lose their bearings, as they are led back and forth along the winding streets yet, at the same time feel that by following any of the lanes, they could end up in a square, church or main street. The inherent quality of the layout and its hierarchy of streets and distribution of open spaces is easily read and understood; there is a self-organized, fractal quality that enables us to understand the whole by knowing a part. Such towns and cities provide many opportunities for aesthetic engagement as described in Chapter Three.

Prague in the Czech Republic is an interesting example of an almost intact old city that developed in an organic fashion from early mediaeval origins. Classical buildings were inserted in the 18th century and later, but the street layout and many of the buildings convey a great unity through the use of similar materials and construction techniques that provide a vernacular character, for example, the use of steeply pitched

The old city of Prague, a fine example of a self-organized pattern of winding streets and a matrix of vernacular architecture into which grander public buildings have been inserted over the years. The apparent confusion of roofs belies the efficient street pattern and array of spaces that give the city its unique character.

roofs clad in terracotta tiles produces a strong visual sense of unity when seen from high places. The major influences on the city are the River Voltava and the high valley sides that confine the city to the flatter flood plain. The Castle of Hradcany, sited on the heights, dominates the city, exercising spiritual and temporal power. The city is a complex, yet understandable maze of streets and open spaces much as described above. The layouts of cities like Prague contain the qualities of coherence, complexity and mystery that lead to such strong and pleasurable aesthetic experiences, not only for visitors but also for residents.

By contrast, the planned city layouts of the 19th and 20th centuries, as well as those dating back to ancient times in many countries, are almost all laid out on geometric principles, especially rectilinear grids. These are one of the significant human patterns described in Chapter One. Streets laid out at right angles and defined by the facades of hollow blocks, or insulae, of buildings are characteristic. The means of achieving these can be two fold. Firstly, the land is all owned by one person who can control the layout, in the form of a master plan, and has the financial resources to put in some infrastructure. Some planned towns were erected to house workers at large industrial plants or coal mines. The control of street layout extended to building styles, creating a great uniformity and anonymity of the streets. This method was used in many places in Great Britain, where increasing populations in cities, due to a rising birth rate and immigration of people from rural areas, led to large developments. Some of these towns were poorly built with cramped, airless houses and inadequate sanitation; others were more generous with space and amenities.

In the United States of America, the gridiron form of towns was mainly developed from the planned layout of the landscape (the Jeffersonian grid). The sections of land within the grid could be owned by a single owner and subdivided on strict area principles for dwellings. House lots could be of varying sizes depending on the anticipated class of occupant; hence the spatial hierarchy often reflected the social one. There was also the use of the idealized city layout, first described by the Roman architect Vitruvius in the 1st century AD. Savannah, in Georgia, was cut out of the forest and built from scratch according to these principles. One advantage of the grid is that extra cells can be added in any direction.

In contrast to the complex, interdigitated structure of older, self-organized cities, where the city landscape is defined by its spaces more than its buildings, the modern metropolis is planned around the car with a series of buildings separated by wide, amorphous, unenclosed spaces. The standard block layout keeps the scale and texture of the city landscape the same, so there is little variation between the high status public domains or those of lower status or in domestic occupation. Distances must be covered in a vehicle instead of on foot and the large spaces required for their operation increases the scale further.

Often the development and growth of towns and cities at different periods reflected the prevailing influences of self-organization or planning. Frequently, there is an old core area characterized by an organic, self-organized development. This was usually mediaeval in origin. The growth may show different phases, such as the early construction of defensive city walls leading to very dense settlement within them. Then, during relatively peaceful conditions, population growth would encourage the town to spread beyond the walls. During the 19th and 20th centuries, industrial development and the interests of landowners, led to large expansion of a planned nature. These cities grew prodigiously, largely based on housing or industrial estates, built over a short space of time to a highly ordered layout and using a small range of building styles.

The city of Barcelona, in the Catalonia region of northern Spain shows many elements of growth and city form described above. The old city has a complex, irregular layout, wide pedestrian streets like the Ramblas and gracious squares such as the Plaza Real, or the square in front of the Cathedral, that are connected by a range of winding streets, lanes and alleys. Arches and gates separate the public realm from the private spaces of courtyards and gardens. There is an abrupt change when the old self-organized city form stops and the gridiron layout begins. This comprises standard width streets at regular intervals, defining city blocks whose square plan is relieved by angled corners to produce 'square like' spaces at each intersection. This layout, from the 19th century, reflects the single controlling authority that was able to dictate this development.

In many ways the grid based cities, especially the large scale North American ones laid out with cars in mind, have less potential for aesthetic engagement than the older, self-organized examples that

a) shows part of the older, more irregular layout of mediaeval Barcelona in Spain whilst b) shows the 19th century planned layout which adjoins the older portion.

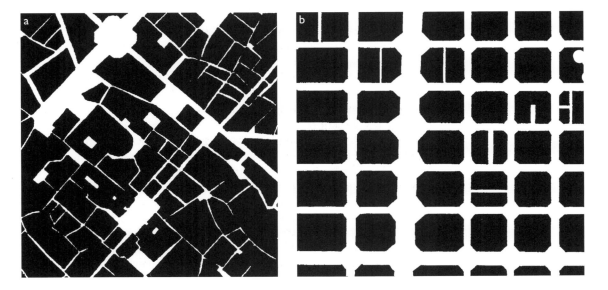

developed around pedestrian circulation. The more attractive planned cities or towns are those with a smaller, more human scale and a balance in the architectural style or use of vernacular construction between monotony and over-diversity. The monotonous, sprawling 19th century industrial city leaves the inhabitants with few opportunities for aesthetic enrichment, thereby diminishing their quality of life.

Three major themes in town and city development have emerged since the late 19th and early 20th century. The first was the desire to correct many of the social and aesthetic problems of the working class industrial city, by designing and building ideal 'garden cities', usually as suburbs to existing towns and cities. Pioneered by the English planner Ebenezer Howard, these used styles borrowed from English villages and their vernacular architecture. Their more open character has a public health objective, while the vernacular style was used to reflect an aesthetic character that was recognized as having a higher value for everyday life. This is the first instance where traditional, self-organized patterns were consciously used, instead of idealized geometric ones, in an urban plan.

The second theme is that of the new town, built in Great Britain and in Europe since the Second World War. These sought to incorporate healthy environments and good design with efficient transport. Some suffer from monotonous and unimaginative house designs or from unfashionable styles of architecture, but they usually contain plenty of green areas. They have been valuable test areas for planners, architects and landscape architects to apply lessons learned from the industrial era and to develop towns and cities appropriate to modern life. One of the lessons from them is that while the basic plans usually work very well, the lack of attention to detail and the absence of much diversity in the houses has not maximized the aesthetic possibilities. A better understanding of patterns and the use of fractal geometry would have helped produce coherence, complexity and mystery.

The third theme, in many ways the most influential in terms of the total effect on the landscape, is that of privately developed mass housing built by both private and public agencies. This has created a landscape mainly of detached or semi-detached houses set in their gardens and arranged with car access as a major factor; they contain very few public spaces. These housing estates have sometimes swamped small villages or country towns and reduced the distinctiveness of their vernacular architecture. Thus, the absence of the reference to, or development from, a basis of characteristic patterns found in the local landscape has prevented the aesthetic possibilities from being realized.

The Pre-conquest Landscape of Mexico

As a contrast to the examples presented so far, which have a European bias, it is worth examining the landscapes of farming, settlement and

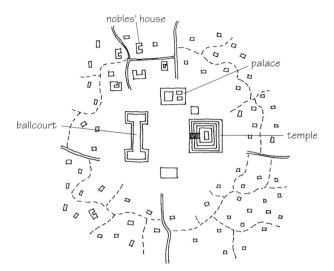

nobles' house

palace

ballcourt

temple

The layout of an Aztec city in Mexico comprised a highly formal, ceremonial part and a more self-organized, irregular pattern for residential quarters.

town produced by a very different culture, that of the various peoples of the Valley of Mexico culminating with the Aztec culture of the 15th century, just before the European conquest.

The agricultural landscape has a self-organized pattern very similar to parts of Europe. Farmers expanded the land under cultivation, so that a pattern of irregular fields, interspersed with vernacular houses, developed. In drier, hilly areas, a system of terraces was constructed to provide more level fields and to intercept and hold rainwater. This pattern was also self-organized: it was not until the development of a strong central authority that planned irrigation schemes were laid out. In wetter, marshy places raised fields, called *chinampas* were created, resulting in a complex, fractal structure of great productivity.

The towns and cities comprised carefully planned ceremonial centres, including pyramids, temples and ball courts (used for a game of religious significance), together with market places and houses for the nobility. The ceremonial-religious life of these peoples was extremely important and much effort was expended on the construction of sometimes huge temple platforms and pyramids. The rest of the inhabited city layout contained some grid-like sections but mainly exhibited the self-organized irregularity typical of many European examples, although of much lower density and interspersed with large gardens. All the houses were constructed in similar ways, to traditional plans, out of similar materials, such as adobe, or sun-dried mud bricks, so that a strong sense of unity would have been evident.

There is evidence of the Aztec field systems still being used today, whilst rural houses bear many similarities to those of the Aztec period; hence, in many respects the rural scene resembles closely the 15th century landscape. The cities have disappeared, being built over or destroyed, although some of the temple complexes have been restored in the 20th century.

The pattern of curving terraces made of rocks and defined by agave plants in this view of countryside north of Mexico City. The pattern is very similar to those produced by other cultures in response to a semi-arid climate.

From this brief discussion, we note that the propensity for self-organized landscapes is fairly universal, that strong central authorities often create highly planned ceremonial centres and urban layouts or are capable of organizing complex irrigation systems. The visual manifestation of these urban landscapes, as artistic and architectural styles developed their unique forms, tends to differ more than rural settlement patterns, which have been dictated by the landform, soils, climate and basic technology the world over.

Conclusions to the Study of Human Patterns

At the conclusion of this section there are several major themes and repeated patterns that can be observed universally. The first is the nature of self-organized human settlement related to the constraints and opportunities of landform, climate and ecological potential. The similarity of these patterns across landscapes is remarkable and leads to the conclusion that they are fundamental and archetypal patterns that emerge spontaneously. The pattern/process feedback yields these patterns and the suitability of their purpose is a product of evolution.

The second theme is the superimposition of simple Euclidean geometry upon the land wherever planned landscapes are produced. This has been the case since ancient times. The patterns are superimposed over those of nature, leading to a sense of disunity in many instances. The significance of such patterns, in terms of expressing human power over nature, is inescapable. Once again it is the ubiquity of the geometry that creates another archetype found the world over.

The persistence of these patterns arises from different causes. The self-organized patterns persist, because they best fit the landscape and continue to do so as they continue to evolve. The persistence of the planned patterns arises, because of a constant desire to simplify and control, within a social and political framework of economic activity.

Once the forces at work in the landscape are neither in harmony nor balance with those of nature, or are greater than can be controlled by a guiding hand, the landscapes often start to show a range of problems. They also tend to lack many of the characteristics that give high aesthetic value such as coherence, complexity and mystery. On the other hand, healthy and enriching landscapes are founded in a harmony of process and pattern, irrespective of whether the processes are natural, human or a mixture of both, and whether the patterns are self-organized or planned and designed with certain objectives in mind. The key to success is to plan and design from the point of view of the human inhabitant, acknowledging the fact that the quality of the landscape is important for the quality of life. The development of street layouts and multi-scaled architecture that encourage the aesthetics of engagement should be an objective in urban design.

This concludes our examination of the range of human patterns encountered in the landscape. We are now ready to study practical means of analysing them so that we can use that understanding in their planning, design and management.

Analysing Cultural Patterns

Where the landscape is mainly cultural and dominated by human activity and development, methods are needed to detect different patterns that can be related to their origins and to connections with landform, soil, hydrology and ecology.

Cultural patterns include those of land use, settlements and communications. Hence, in addition to environmental issues, we also need to assess the morphology, scale, continuity, local distinctiveness, condition, rate of change and persistence of cultural patterns.

There are several aspects to the analysis of cultural patterns. Firstly, there is the way the landscape has developed, particularly the physical characteristics of field pattern, settlement layout and village and city morphology. This analysis should seek to relate cultural patterns to the physical and ecological factors, such as landform, hydrology, soil and natural plant communities, that influenced them to different degrees in different places. This produces a description of land character as an objective, factual starting point for the second aspect, that of aesthetic factors.

The analysis of aesthetic factors relates the major characteristics of the cultural pattern to the aesthetic qualities explored in Chapter Three. The combination of the analysis of land character and aesthetic factors produces the landscape assessment that can be used directly as a basis for planning, design or management, in combination with the analyses of landform, hydrology and ecology already described in Chapters Five and Six.

Landscape Assessment

Methods of analysing these patterns at a large scale have been developed in Great Britain under the general title of landscape assessment. They are frequently prepared at a county or district level (at the scale of local government units, because the responsibility for town and country planning lies with them). They usually cover a range of landform and geological types, and seek to synthesize the interaction of surface patterns of land use, enclosure, settlement and communication with persistent major influences to derive homogenous land character types. This analysis is of rural areas and not urban or suburban ones.

A flow chart describing the interconnection of information used in a landscape character assessment. (After Warnock, 1997)

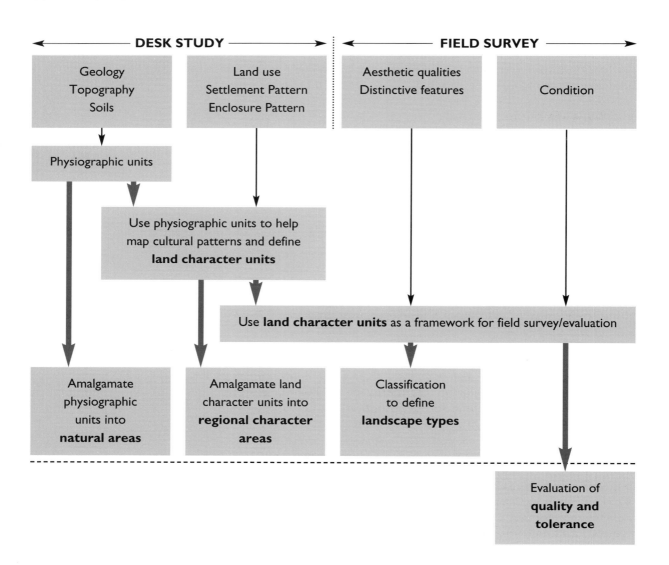

Landscape assessment can be regarded as a parallel process to landscape ecological analysis. It starts at the same point with the underlying geology, topography and soils but then becomes concerned with the dominant cultural layers, as opposed to the natural vegetation, wildlife and ecosystem processes. The processes of landscape change are included, but they are more likely to be human in origin rather than natural. There is no reason why both kinds of analysis cannot be prepared for the same area: they could provide interesting contrasts and identify many avenues for better design and management.

The purpose of landscape ecological analysis, as discussed in Chapter Six, was to reveal the pattern/process/functioning/dynamics of a predominantly natural landscape, whereas the purpose of landscape assessment is to provide an understanding of the pattern/process/history/rate of change of a cultural landscape in order that its protection, management, enhancement or controlled change can be planned and designed to a better standard. The identification of the purpose is important, so that the relevant information can be assembled at the correct scale.

Assembly of Information

There are several layers of information and analysis to be assembled. The physiographic information of geology, topography and soils are analysed in the way described in Chapter Five. These are used to give physiographic units. The soil pattern, derived from the geology, may also provide a surrogate for the long vanished natural vegetation pattern because this was usually closely related to the soils and their drainage (as described for the National Vegetation Classification in Chapter Six). These units provide the basic framework for other layers to be superimposed. They are assembled from contour, geology (solid and drift or superficial) and soils (usually from agricultural classification). The assessment recently completed for the English county of Worcestershire shows the relationship between landform, geology and soils.

The next layer comprises ecological information. This can use the NVC as mentioned above, or other ecological units. Since these are usually strongly related to the soils and landform within a climatic zone, the ecological pattern tends to reinforce the physiographic units. However, ecological information in a long settled landscape also reflects land use and management, so overlapping with the next layer, that of land use.

Land use reflects the current picture and is taken from recent aerial photographs. Arable cropland, pasture, rough grazing, moorland, woodland and some other minor categories are plotted on maps using suitable colour codings. Land use is usually related to the soils, drainage and ecology of the area. It may be that broad patterns of farming types can be identified, such as arable, pastoral, or mixed.

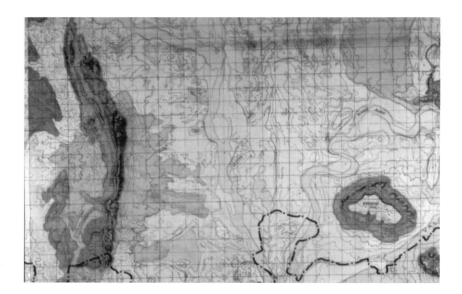

An example of physiographic units for part of the county of Worcestershire, England, based on geology and landform. (After Warnock, 1997)

These may simplify or further emphasize the physiographic or ecological units beginning to emerge.

The next layer to be added is that of cultural use. In countries with a long history of human presence, the landscape is a *palimpsest*, where the remains of numerous layers are retained in the land. Determining which of these is significant for the development of the pattern of the landscape can take much research. A good starting point is to prepare map bases showing existing field boundaries. Where the field pattern is intact aerial photographs can also be of great use. Old maps going as far back as possible (to the 16th century if available), will help to chart and date the phases of enclosure and the longevity of boundaries.

A land cover map for part of the area of the physiographic units for Worcestershire shown above.
(Reproduced with permission of the Ordnance Survey © Crown copyright MC 027257)

For example, in England, as we have seen, field patterns can be divided into planned and ancient zones, with the planned being further divided into the gradual enclosure of open fields and universal enclosure by Act of Parliament. The date of enclosure can be ascertained from maps and legal documents such as charters and the Acts of Parliament. Some of this can be time consuming and needs specialist skills.

It is possible to assemble the basic categories from examination of the field boundary morphology, looking for characteristic indicators. The assessment for Worcestershire shows several basic types of field shape of several size classes with their typical boundary characteristics. Older maps can be consulted to check the significance and permanence of the boundaries between areas of different types. The base maps can be colour coded for each variety. If the maps are viewed at arm's length, distinct patterns may be apparent. These patterns may correlate closely with the land use or farming type patterns, soil quality and landform.

In countries where settlement has been more recent, such as North America, the field pattern is likely to reflect a combination of soil types and the survey grid or township plan. The area described earlier in the chapter, at the junction of Vermont, New Hampshire and Quebec, has a pattern of land ownership and use based on township plans of different angles, which only become visible when woodland clearance or recolonization or forest management activities follow the survey lines.

The more persistent patterns have particular interest, because they demonstrate some compatibility with aspects of site and the original ecology. This sense of unity in the pattern is likely to provide a distinctive character and a commensurate aesthetic satisfaction. (See Chapters Two, Three and Four.)

In part, settlement patterns, the next layer, can also be determined by map study, particularly the distinction between dispersed and nucleated patterns. Later growth and development can be interpreted through maps produced at different times and also by site visits to

Examples of field patterns characteristic of Worcestershire, showing the ancient countryside, early enclosure of open fields and parliamentary enclosure. (After Warnock, 1997)

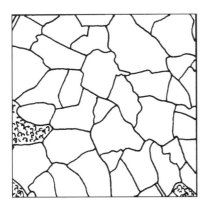

examine the style and use of materials of the buildings, the street layout, the density patterns and social standing of the original occupants. Villages, hamlets and small towns may not have changed to the same degree as larger towns. Distinct changes of character may have occurred when a rural area was quickly developed by the introduction of industry. The study of Worcestershire reveals a distinctive pattern, where the nucleated settlements coincide with the planned countryside zone of former open fields on the most fertile soils, whereas the dispersed settlements occur on ancient countryside in areas of poorer soil. In fact Worcestershire lies on the boundary between ancient and planned countryside which can be observed on small scale as well as large scale maps.

Village morphology is the next aspect to be identified. A map showing colour coded dots for each settlement type will show if there is a dominant one likely to be an indicator of a pattern. In long settled areas in Great Britain, the village names may be meaningful, although some expert knowledge is necessary to decipher their present names from original Saxon, Viking, Norman, Celtic or Gaelic words. Place name endings are usually easy to spot and a colour coded map of these will also show a pattern, especially when overlaid with a map of parish boundaries.

An example of analysis of village types in part of Worcestershire showing the pattern of their distribution.
(After Warnock, 1997)

| County boundary | Boundary between nucleated and dispersed settlement | Dispersed settlement | Nucleated settlement |

In North America, where settlers came from many countries, there may be patterns present in the place names. Settlers frequently named their settlements after the places they came from. The countries and regions of origin, together with the dates of founding, help to show how the settlements developed. This picture can be confused in places like New England where many villages were given biblical place names, although this may signify the founding religious group. Building styles may also be associated with the origin of the settlers as may their favoured types of agriculture.

The summation of the land use, enclosure pattern and settlement pattern maps are then overlaid on the physiographic units and combined to produce maps of land character units. These depict physical descriptions of areas with relatively homogeneous characteristics. They do not represent landscape character because the element of human perception has not yet been included.

The physiographic units can be amalgamated to form natural areas which relate to distinctive semi-natural vegetation types. In Great Britain these are scattered remnants, and a refinement is to add the National Vegetation Types as potential vegetation units, using the correlation between the National Vegetation Classification and ecosystem site classification.

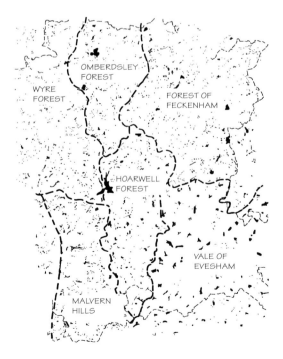

An example of land character units in Worcestershire showing the pattern related to physiographic, land cover and settlement information.
(After Warnock, 1997)

A view of the landscape of part of Dartmoor in Devon, England.

The land character units can also be amalgamated into regional character areas. These might comprise a number of different landform, soil, enclosure and settlement variations and yet exhibit a distinctive character at a larger scale. A classic example might be Dartmoor in the southwest of England. The underlying geology of granite gives the area a distinctive quality and yet there are escarpments, moorland plateaux and river valleys, which have different topography, soil, agriculture and field patterns. Nevertheless, it is Dartmoor that is the most powerful image and not the individual subdivisions.

At this point it is an optional step to include communication patterns in the analysis. There is a risk that modern patterns bear little relationship to the underlying factors determining them, because they have often been subject to drastic recent changes of greater effect.

Maps showing different character zones a) of the setting of Dartmoor; b) within the Dartmoor character area.

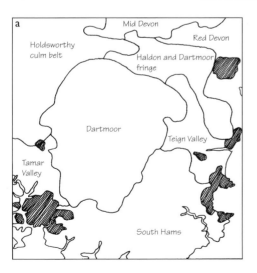

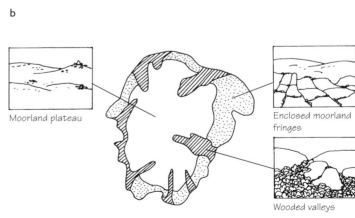

Nevertheless, they form an important part of the landscape and may be worth exploring.

Communication patterns in older, settled countries may exhibit a multi-layered complexity. Some types are fairly obvious, such as Roman roads, ridgeways or ancient sunken lanes. Roads or tracks connecting dispersed settlements may have more recent origins in planned landscapes, where their geometry may be mistaken for Roman, whilst other roads are derived from tracks that ran amongst the large open fields. A chronicle of how systems developed can be obtained from a comparative study of old and new maps; this can identify phases of importance of different elements and the extent to which these are persistent or ephemeral, such as abandoned canals and railways or the frequently changing hierarchy of roads.

In peasant societies, before the introduction of motor vehicles, most people walked, whilst some used horses and carts. A network of footpaths and tracks would develop whose use might be regarded traditional, although some routes may not always be readily discernible on the ground. Their pattern reflects agrarian times when the countryside was more populated. In Great Britain, their recreation value is increasingly recognized and many are now legally protected as statutory rights of way. These are shown on maps and add to the overall pattern of communication.

In places where peasant societies persist or where hunting and gathering is still practical, there is likely to be an established pattern of trails linking settlements to outlying fields, hunting and gathering areas, ceremonial routes or sites for rituals. Colour coded maps showing these can reveal the rich web of interconnection of such people's lives with the landscape.

A recurring pattern may be easier to identify in recently settled areas where there have been fewer changes, because of the shorter time involved. In areas where the land has been abandoned over the last sixty or seventy years, such as parts of New England, the communication patterns may have disappeared over large areas, because roads and tracks were not needed, and the woods can easily grow over gravel roads. Some isolated places, like northern British Columbia, have no roads, and those that are constructed have a specific purpose, such as logging access, so these patterns will reflect a different rationale to those of settled areas.

Field survey should follow the data collection and overlays that led to the basic land character type definition in order to check that the pattern is identifiable. Boundaries can be clarified and photographs taken of each type to help the assessment of vernacular building patterns and to identify the current condition of the landscape.

At this stage the analysis examines our perception of the landscape in terms of its distinctive features, aesthetic qualities (which may be positive or negative) and its current condition including an assessment of its sensitivity and robustness to change.

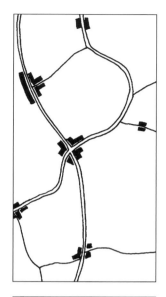

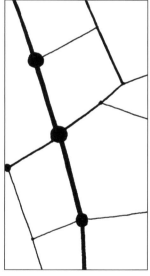

An example of a communication pattern based on a hierarchy of routes and junctions where they are connected.

Landscape character analysis, following the methods described in Chapter Four, changes the assessment from that of land character, solely based on the understanding of physical, ecological and cultural patterns, into something more useful for planning, design and management. This part of the assessment should be as rational and descriptive as the rest and avoid subjective descriptions which may be biased by the backgrounds and attitudes of the surveyors. Each land character area that emerges from the assessment will have its own special characteristics that define it as a locally distinctive landscape. Names should be chosen for them that reflect these key features.

Another use of the field survey is to assess the condition of the landscape. Some ancient or planned enclosure patterns may be largely intact and well maintained. Others may be partly removed, unmanaged or decaying. Buildings, villages and other features may also vary in their condition. This provides information about the degree of persistence of the patterns and is also useful in forming planning, design and management policies and guidelines for a particular area. The tolerance to change of each character type can also be described.

Following the assessment by experts, there is scope to conduct surveys and studies of the public (both residents and visitors), to elicit their perspectives and preferences about the different landscape types. This places their aesthetic responses in a framework that is geographically relevant and relates preferences or attitudes to particular qualities, patterns, conditions and the sense of unity, diversity and *Genius loci* of particular places. Such a basis is vital for sound, sustainable land use decisions and the design and scale of any new developments.

Analysing City Morphology

City morphology is frequently a complex interweaving of many different functions, systems and spaces. A city is composed of buildings that define external spaces. The interface of buildings and their various functions with external spaces having different functions is an important issue to consider. In the village or town and especially in the city, building edges define the transition from space to space, function to function and private to public domain. In our discussion on ecological patterns, we also noted that edges and ecotones were important determinants of pattern types and their aesthetic qualities. Kevin Lynch, the American planner, categorized cities into the following components, each of which can be linked to one of the types of patterns found in nature as described in Chapter One:

- Districts (sites, places, spaces; contributing to city mosaics).
- Edges (lines of life, lines of contrast; defining the mosaic).
- Paths (meanders and branches).
- Nodes (enclosures, foci, monuments, individual city architecture; related to graph theory patterns).

Sometimes city buildings give clear signals about the nature of the space, its function, position in the spectrum of private to public domain and the type of person admitted. Entrances of huge scale, beyond comfortable, human proportions, display power and solidity. The doorways to banks, government buildings, military structures, museums, educational establishments and churches typify this. These edifices are often associated with large public spaces so that their majestic proportions can be displayed and their scale adjusted to fit into that of the city.

This is especially true of self-organized cities with complex, fractal structures. The fractal dimension and space filling characteristics of all the streets, lanes, squares, alleys, courtyards, parks and gardens is very large and the total amount of edge correspondingly great (see analysis of Venice below). The character of edges is also very varied. Sometimes the transition from street to building interior is abrupt, with a door leading straight into a room. More often there is some kind of transition. Gateways, steps, porches, small gardens or courtyards, approached through narrow openings, all separate the various spaces, physically and psychologically.

A city can also be analysed as a network of various communication systems such as: people move between home, work, shops, entertainments, churches and parks; goods move in and out; services of water, electricity, gas, sewage and refuse keep the city supplied and clean; communication by cables also intersect and connect the structure of the city. Network analysis and hierarchies of communication patterns will demonstrate where separation, integration, dispersion, concentration, efficient or inefficient characteristics are present. These also show how the process of city life operates: it is an analysis not unlike the interaction of flows and structures examined in the section on landscape ecological analysis in Chapter Six.

Communication corridors are used by different forms of transport. Whether in city, town, village or countryside, there is often a distinct relationship between the route, its importance, the transport type most likely to use it and its speed. An analysis of this in relation to the urban pattern can explain why some places have particular problems.

In order to see how analysis of city form can tell us about the relationships between origin, function and aesthetics, we will now examine two examples.

Venice, a Fractal City

Venice displays a self-organized layout for a city at its most fully developed. One of the world's most beautiful cities, we admire its uniqueness as an island in a lagoon accessed by water or on foot. The uniqueness of the city helps to focus on fractal geometry, a fascinating characteristic of self-organized landscapes.

Venice was founded shortly after the fall of the western Roman Empire in 476 AD, by people who escaped to the mudbanks and islands

A view to the main part of Venice seen from a church tower. The occurrence of churches and other public buildings hints at the inner structure of spaces but there is no apparent order to the layout.

in the lagoon formed by the deltas of the many rivers that flow into the northern Adriatic. These mudbanks were probably very similar to those usually found in river deltas described in Chapter Five. The movement of water - river flow and tidal movements - created a complex pattern of islets and channels, both wide and narrow. The earliest inhabitants built houses on wooden posts (piles) to keep them from sinking into the mud and used shallow bottomed boats for communication. One particular cluster of mudbanks and a larger island, separated by the deep channel or Rivus Altus (Rialto), became quite populous so that over time the settlement coalesced into a single city. The channels between the islets and mudbanks were retained, extended and gradually firmed up creating the present day canals.

Protected by the waters of the Lagoon and positioned to take advantage of trading opportunities between Europe and Asia, the city became wealthy with a substantial colonial empire. The wealth was invested in palaces, churches and art. Thus, a diverse architecture was created, based on the pattern originally determined by the mudbanks and water channels. We tend to concentrate on the unique qualities of the canals, the gondolas, the palaces and art and yet without the underlying delta pattern and processes the city would not be as it is today.

The fractal quality of the city is expressed in two ways. One is the pattern of canals that interpenetrates the built form, the other is the pedestrian street network that winds from one side of the city to the other. From the main Grand Canal, which dissects the city and the surrounding lagoon, extends an arterial pattern of secondary canals. These wind into the various neighbourhoods. From there, a finer, narrower set penetrates like alleyways into the urban fabric. Like the blood system of the body they facilitate the transport of people and goods into the heart of the city in a most efficient way. There is a similarity of canal layout at a range of scales from the larger, deeper channels, serving main traffic and providing the main flushing of dirt, to the smallest, serving lighter traffic and local flushing needs. The accessibility of the original channels was enhanced, where necessary, by digging extra canals, so that the efficiency of distribution was maintained. Thus, this fractal pattern also conforms to the branching patterns described in Chapter One.

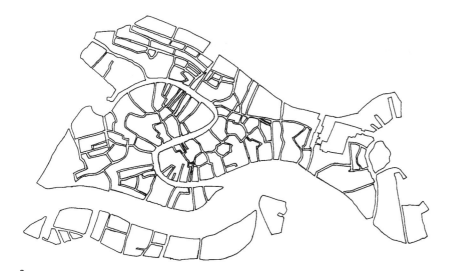

a

a) A plan of the city layout showing how the canal system interpenetrates its structure. This shows how the city layout was based on the transformation of mud-flats. b) The interconnection of canal and terrestrial circulation together with the hierarchy of spaces in a portion of the city; this yields the strongly fractal, self-organized pattern of the city.

canals
buildings

b

The pedestrian circulation system links the canals with other parts of the city. The main public space, Piazza San Marco, is well known to the tourists who flock to Venice and is one of the great city spaces. From there, a main thoroughfare leads across the Rialto through the city. The many churches that serve each neighbourhood normally have a square in front, linked by lanes and streets of varying sizes. In its way this system mirrors that of the canals, extending the porosity of the city and in many places complementing it.

One of the features of such a layout is the amount of edge or building facade created, not dissimilar to the phenomenon of scale of measurement of a fractal coastline described in Chapter One. This structure of edge, related to different spaces and different degrees of public to private space, is a key element in the functional and territorial character of Venice as well as its aesthetic qualities.

In Venice the city is exemplified by the Piazza San Marco with the original symbols of power in St Mark's Cathedral and the Doge's Palace. However, throughout the city, there are local areas each with a square, a church and some cafes or restaurants. The narrow streets and lanes intersecting the city lead deeper into the residential areas where gates or doors lead off into courtyards and enclosed gardens. These enclosed, private spaces are shut off from the street life. The transition is marked by an entrance, passage, gate, threshold, porch or stairs.

Edinburgh, Old and New Towns

The old and new towns of Edinburgh, Scotland, showing the contrast between the self-organized town on the volcanic rock and the classical, geometric layout of the planned one. (Courtesy Patricia and Angus MacDonald).

Edinburgh, the capital city of Scotland, is clearly divided between the Old Town and the New Town. This distinction illustrates with absolute clarity the contrast in layout, process of development, aesthetic and spatial characteristics that make the city one of the most dramatic and beautiful anywhere. The Old Town was sited for defensive reasons on the ridge between Edinburgh Castle and the Palace of Holyroodhouse. The street that connects the two is the famous Royal Mile. This layout arose due to the geology and the

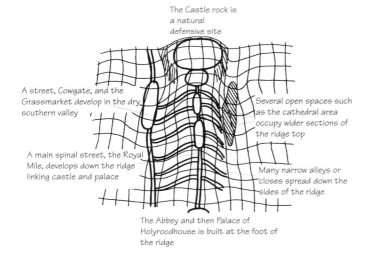

The Castle rock is a natural defensive site

A street, Cowgate, and the Grassmarket develop in the dry southern valley

A main spinal street, the Royal Mile, develops down the ridge linking castle and palace

Several open spaces such as the cathedral area occupy wider sections of the ridge top

Many narrow alleys or closes spread down the sides of the ridge

The Abbey and then Palace of Holyroodhouse is built at the foot of the ridge

a

a) A plan of the old town of Edinburgh, Scotland, showing how the streets and 'closes' (narrow alleys) relate to the underlying topography; b) a plan of the new town showing the proportions and symmetry of the planned layout.

Charlotte Square terminates the axis and creates a space

Gardens occupy the drained valley

The railway is located in the valley bottom

The former dump is used as public space and to connect the Old and New Towns

High level bridges link Old and New Towns over the valley

GEORGE STREET

Gardens use the sloping ground to the north

Streets continue the lines northwards

Small lanes service the main streets

Princes Street edges the southern side of the town

St Andrew's Square forms a space of elegant proportions giving spatial contrast to the streets

Queen Street edges the northen side of the town

b

landform that underlies this part of the city. Castle Rock is an ancient volcanic plug dating from the time, some 300 million years ago, when the area was a volcano. During the ice ages, this plug resisted the west to east flow of ice that gouged out two deeper valleys to the north and south, whilst leaving the ridge uneroded. This crag and tail feature provided a perfect defensive site and a place where a town could develop to take advantage of the protection afforded by the castle. The tail became the Royal Mile at the foot of which lies the Palace, a former monastery, and the Holyrood Park, based on the other volcanic remains of Arthur's Seat and Salisbury Crags.

The Royal Mile became a backbone from which steep streets and 'closes' developed down to the southern valley, occupied by the market places of the Grassmarket and the Cowgate, whilst to the north there was a lake (the Norloch) in the valley. Due to the steepness of the slopes and the change in level from valley to ridge, tall, many storied buildings developed, extending up and down from the Royal Mile level. These tenements were very densely populated and the city became renowned for its filth and smoky atmosphere since all the houses had coal fires and everybody threw their rubbish and excreta into the streets. Walls encircled the foot of the city, extending the protection from the castle. The Old Town is a good example of a self-organized layout, strongly influenced by the landform. The streets lead to closes that penetrate deep into the tenements giving a most efficient distribution of access, air and light; however, due to the height of the buildings, many are permanently shaded.

The New Town of Edinburgh presents a clear contrast. It is acknowledged as an elegant, classical city, whose aesthetic appearance is unrivalled. It is a planned and designed layout based on classical principles dating from mid-1700s in the case of the First New Town; it has developed, by a series of separate estate housing developments until the present day. The original New Town, designed by James Craig, is a series of rectilinear streets defined by two squares at the east and west ends. The town adjoins the Norloch near the Old Town and was laid out on a greenfield site, so there were no existing roads to incorporate. The houses conformed to the rules of proportion of the classical revival, a major architectural movement of the later 18th century, based on Greek style and design. Many of the blocks were designed to present the balanced facade of a single building, even though there were several houses or tenements within each. The use of a yellow grey sandstone, careful details and carvings all contribute to the elegant, restrained unity of the whole.

The later phases continued the theme. Some incorporated circles and crescents in their layouts, gardens and parks for the private use of the householders, churches and other buildings. The styles developed from Georgian to Regency, Victorian, Edwardian and into 20th century forms.

The aesthetic qualities found in the city of Edinburgh derive partly from the characteristics of massiveness and strength (in Whiteheadian terms), coherence, complexity and mystery, and also demonstrate unity, diversity and a strong sense of place as defined in Chapter Three. The two contrasting city forms encourage a deep engagement for the pedestrian explorer of the streets.

Designing with Cultural Patterns

The cultural end of the landscape continuum presents several possibilities for designers: to be radical, ignoring the existing setting and producing a new and idealized landscape, to work in a more conservative fashion within long established, multi-layered landscape patterns, or to choose a middle path of creativity set in a more conservative context. What is appropriate depends on the design objectives, the strength of character of the existing landscape and the value already attached to its aesthetic qualities. There is also a role for restoration of cultural landscapes but this presents some complications which will be explored later.

Designing New Cultural Landscapes

The completely creative approach is occasionally able to start with a newly formed land base as the result of demolition, reclamation of disturbed land or drainage of the sea; under such circumstances, the designer has free rein within the local physical and climatic conditions. However, the creative process may be more difficult, because there is no framework, few constraints and few cues for a designer. Instead, the design objectives, the purpose of the landscape to be created and its functional requirements may be invoked to devise the conceptual space.

In addition, an understanding of patterns could provide the inspiration for the designer. Many of the natural patterns described in Chapter One can be appreciated as aesthetic symbols. Richard Dubé, an American landscape architect, has recently identified a number of specific patterns which he believes can be associated with certain meanings, to invoke particular aesthetic responses by people using his designs. This technique has been used for centuries by the Chinese and Japanese and to some extent during the picturesque vogue in Europe and North America. Dubé has formalized the method and it must be interpreted carefully, lest it be used to create 'landscapes by numbers'.

In his method Dubé defines each pattern form by a number of features. For example, he identifies a delta as a pattern form. Its *category* is: large scale, reduced scale and texture, its *origin* being erosion and deposition. He also refers to the *normal viewing perspective*, in this case oblique. He then lists its *defining attributes* which, for the delta are: undulating, flat plane, network of forking and divergent planes; increase in quantity of planes as distance is increased from the source; in river form, planes are defined by slightly elevated adjacent planes and bulky masses rising behind. Following this Dube specifies the main *aesthetic attributes* as the transition from one to many. The *emotional response* evoked by this pattern may be curiosity: many choices, many paths to follow or climbing many limbs to different destinies. He then suggests a range of *applications*, such as walkways, ramps, three-sided wall, orchard, arboretum, water, stairs. This is meant as a source of inspiration: perhaps a path from the entrance of a garden branches like a delta, opening many possibilities, depending on which are followed, all having to be retraced to the origin before choosing another.

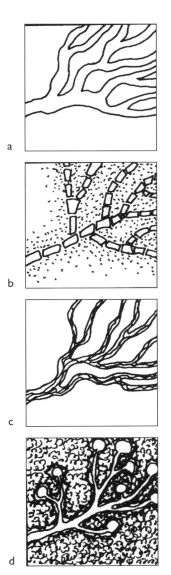

a

b

c

d

An example of the use of natural patterns, in this case the delta, to evoke aesthetic responses (from Dube, 1997) a) the delta pattern; b) path layout; c) streams; d) small spaces in woods.

In larger scale designs of new housing, new towns and the like, there is what the British planner J.D. Porteous has described as 'quaintscape': the layout of new housing by recreating winding passages, courtyards, and continuity of indoor and outdoor spaces reminiscent of older self-organized patterns. He calls this inauthentic, because it is designed to look as if it is self-organized, but it actually works, partly because the layouts relate to our perception and thus to the aesthetics of engagement. Care is needed to avoid this approach turning into the superficial application of pastiche ornamentation. It is the conscious use of spatial patterns reflecting how we best use and perceive urban spaces that is important (p. 239, Fig. 15).

Designing Within Prominent Cultural Patterns

In those rural landscapes where long and continuous settlement has resulted in a persistent, self-organized pattern, the management of landscape change and insertion of new features is a challenge. There are plenty of unfortunate examples, such as widespread use of modern bungalows in Ireland (built to standard sets of plans, unrelated to vernacular styles, taken from Fitsimmons' 1993 book *Bungalow Bliss*), to show how this valuable character can be compromised. In such cases more conservative approaches are likely to be appropriate.

A good starting point is the type of landscape assessment described earlier. The detailed understanding of landscape, provided by such assessments, will identify the most significant contributors to character. From this, various types of landscape planning guidance for a range of activities can be developed. These allow changes to happen in ways and at time scales that respect the inherent character rather than destroy it. The English county of Staffordshire has produced a two-tiered landscape assessment comprising a regional framework, within which local character areas were defined. This enables the various branches of local government administration, responsible for

An Irish bungalow located in a prominent position not found in the case of vernacular examples. The design is not based on vernacular traditions but introduces a note of suburbia into a rural scene.

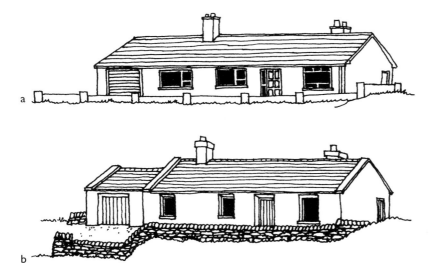

An example of how to design a new house which respects and fits into the long established pattern of the landscape and the vernacular traditions of Ireland. a) is the originally proposed building that exhibits no respect for form, proportion or material, while b) shows how the same functions could be better designed. (After Bord Failte)

planning strategies for housing, forestry, minerals and highways to make use of this assessment and associated guidance in an integrated way, thus ensuring that the various strategies are compatible with landscape character.

For specific subjects like housing, it may be desirable to produce more detailed design advice. The cultural and aesthetic value of vernacular architecture was noted earlier, when samples of the range exhibited in Great Britain were illustrated. It is important to avoid too much pastiche of vernacular form; it is also essential to permit vernacular traditions to evolve. However, when vernacular traditions have disappeared, new and creative solutions are needed. Some useful publications describe and define the typical and significant characteristics of vernacular architecture in various places in Europe: proportions, roof pitches, window types, materials and so forth. This sets a guiding framework for new designs that can be accomodated without pastiche and avoiding the blandness of standard types. Such a book exists in Ireland, but because it gives only guiding principles and does not supply plans ready for construction, it has been eclipsed by the infamous *Bungalow Bliss*. The Scottish Office has also produced useful guidance for Scotland.

In many areas of countryside and urban fringe in both Europe and North America, the problem is not only individual houses, but a more general spread of blandness or sprawl. In Europe, despite reasonably strong development planning regulations, low density housing, urbanization of rural areas by the introduction of features such as street lights and pavements, commercial buildings and advertisement signs have had a serious affect on landscape character. In North America, particularly the USA, development planning barely exists. The commercial landscape of strip malls extending out of small towns blurs the distinction between town and country.

While many parts of the USA continue to suffer the effects of sprawl, some people are attempting to plan for development. At the large scale, there have been some influential regional landscape planning processes carried out in the upper mid west states of Illinois, Wisconsin and Michigan. These have used an approach not dissimilar to landscape assessment, though using sieve mapping after the McHargian model (following the approach promoted by Ian McHarg in his influential book *Design with Nature*). There is an element of pattern analysis here, as published by the American landscape planner Philip H. Lewis. The approach uses patterns as form determinants, especially landforms, drainage and so on. These patterns are similar to, but not so sophisticated in their analysis as the methods presented here, although this may be appropriate at the regional level of plan. Within the regional planning structures there are smaller scale models, based on communities, including revitalization of towns and residential areas.

Another example of settlement design that tries to avoid the worst economically driven development has been carried out in New England by landscape planner R. Arendt. This uses design based on small town character to help the growth of settlements in a way that respects the landscape. Sketches are used to demonstrate the different alternatives.

Designing for Landscape Restoration

Restoration or preservation may be an objective where prominent patterns of field boundaries (hedges, walls), trees and woods occur in ancient and planned countryside, because of their powerful aesthetic appeal. In such circumstances restoration may not be able to reconstruct the original pattern, because it may be impractical or uneconomic in terms of land use. However, where funds permit, it is appropriate to restore the *character* of such areas.

In Europe, woodlands are nowadays frequently planted on land not needed for agriculture. Here an evolution of the existing pattern is usually the best option. The pattern of existing woods can be analysed using techniques described in Chapter Six and the design developed by 'growing' new woods from it, in an interlocking fashion, using the cues provided by landform, soil, drainage, and other land use constraints. In this way, the ebb and flow of agriculture at its margins can be included in the desired landscape development and bureaucratic solutions, derived from rules, avoided (such as standard sized areas or a model layout). This approach has been adopted in many of the areas covered by landscape character assessments. It gives freedom to individual landowners, within the range of possibilities suggested by the landscape pattern.

Landscape restoration can also be applied to villages, small towns and other landscapes, where decaying buildings can be rebuilt, inappropriate recent additions removed and vernacular details replaced. This helps achieve at least the minor form of beauty, in Whiteheadian terms, regardless of whether any more change takes place.

A wooded landscape in the south of England in part of the ancient countryside zone.

A sequence of concept sketches to show how woodland could be expanded whilst respecting the character of the landscape. a) An analysis of the landscape character. b) New woodland 'growing the pattern'.

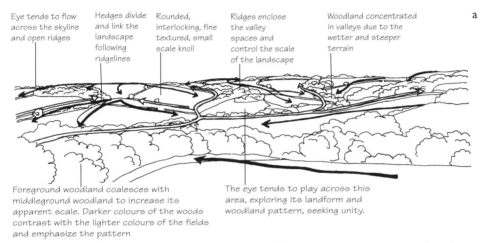

Eye tends to flow across the skyline and open ridges

Hedges divide and link the landscape following ridgelines

Rounded, interlocking, fine textured, small scale knoll

Ridges enclose the valley spaces and control the scale of the landscape

Woodland concentrated in valleys due to the wetter and steeper terrain

a

Foreground woodland coalesces with middleground woodland to increase its apparent scale. Darker colours of the woods contrast with the lighter colours of the fields and emphasize the pattern

The eye tends to play across this area, exploring its landform and woodland pattern, seeking unity.

A medium to small scale landscape with a coherent pattern of predominantly open summits and patches of woodland linked to hedges and set in valleys and hollows. The lines of visual force are quite strong, helping to reinforce the unity of the pattern. The scene is moderately diverse and contains some complexity. There is a sense of mystery, drawing us to explore the scene and to learn more about it.

b

Extra woodland 'grows' the pattern to strengthen the sense of enclosure and interlock without taking away the character. The pattern of open tops and wooded valleys reinforces the unity of the landscape. The sense of coherence is increased, diversity and complexity enhanced and mystery maintained. Thus the character is retained and built on while the landscape is allowed to change. The design uses the major structural characteristics of the landscape in order to achieve its unity.

The Challenge of Urban Landscapes

Tensions between development and conservation occur in some fast developing countries. In Mexico, many states are experiencing rapid growth and old colonial cities, whose centres contain extremely beautiful, partly planned and partly self-organized structures, are under pressure of adverse change. The scope for urban sprawl is very great, because of the lack of planning systems and development zoning regulations compared with Europe. In one or two instances, whole towns have been strictly preserved, such as San Miguel de Allende and Guanajuato. This is only partly successful, because it tends to fossilize them. This makes them ideal for tourism and other uses, such as universities or colleges, but impedes the development of economic diversity, which may become a problem over time (p. 240, Fig. 16).

Therefore, the need for creative urban planning is not solely a phenomenon of the most affluent countries. It needs vision to assess how the key ingredients of the character of Venice, Edinburgh, Prague or Guanajuato could be protected, enhanced or repeated in every city or town. These cities have special conditions to help them, such as a unique geological position, an outstanding example of urban design, geographical isolation by water, absence of war or the past glories of silver mining. Some also have special problems. The main one is traffic, particularly cars. Edinburgh and Prague have huge traffic flow that their narrow streets were not designed to accommodate. Guanajuato has some car free areas and a unique system of tunnels that take traffic beneath much of the city. Venice alone is completely car-free and so can be used by pedestrians today as it always has been.

In my view, for most people, urban living is only conducted efficiently on foot and at walking pace in the various neighbourhoods. The aesthetic qualities of life need the well known, ordinary, comfortable and safe haven of the home; the semi-public, semi-private landscape of neighbours, local shops, and the places frequented every day for work and recreation. This includes local parks or other green spaces, open markets, small squares and occasional places to meet, pass the time of day and engage in social activities.

At the larger scale of civic life, there are the public spaces that define the city or town, such as main streets, grand squares, large parks, providing opportunities for cultural events, and major transport nodes. The fractal dimensions can involve changes in urban character from the difference between the organic, vernacular neighbourhoods, with maximum edge for individual, family and social interaction, to the carefully planned and grandly designed public realm of fine architectural monuments that may define the region or state. Added to these urban, aesthetic qualities are the commercial and industrial domains where the pace of change, constant demolition and rebuilding can contribute to the vibrancy of the urban experience. Large metropolises also need efficient mass transit to move people between neighbourhoods and allow them to retain pedestrian scale.

Cliff Moughtin, a British urban planner, has recently suggested that urban design should take two sets of factors into account. The first is the spatial structure of streets, squares and street blocks or insulae that form the boundaries of public space. He suggests that the street block should be of mixed use and no more than four storeys high. This reinforces what has been observed above. The second set of factors is the importance of ornament and decoration, something lost in the era of Modern architecture. This detail should be applied to facades (where massiveness, in Whiteheadian terms provides the major form of beauty, as exemplified by the buildings of the Spanish architect Antonio Gaudí), corners (lending mystery to the layout), skylines and roofscapes (helping to provide coherence), the city floor (paving, where more detail gives coherence with complexity and contributes to massiveness), landmarks, sculpture and furniture.

In these circumstances, there is much scope for creative design. Firstly, at the community level, there is the architecture or landscape architecture that seeks to work with local people in their own neighbourhoods. This might involve the evolution and development of new vernacular housing, local parks and wildlife areas, traffic management and means of making communities feel safe. Continuation or creation of a distinctive structure for such places will ensure their aesthetic quality. The use of spaces of different shape and size, defining their edges and private/public interface, and using textural qualities, colours, details and ornament that give *Genius loci*, are all aspects of design worthy of special attention.

The major public spaces reflect a town's status and identity on behalf of the community. They need to be almost permanent in their purpose, not only as buildings and spaces to accommodate institutions or cultural events but also as the anchors of the city form and identity. Examples are the castles of Edinburgh and Prague, the churches of Venice and Guanajuato, the public squares such as Piazza San Marco or Staromesti Namesti or the Jardin de la Union in Venice, Prague and Guanajuato respectively; the main streets such as the Grand Canal or Princes Street in Venice and Edinburgh. These were established or laid out with a confidence and a purpose that is not always seen today because of commercial pressures or an unwillingness to invest in such prestigious projects. These places are what gives each city its essential character. They can be categorized as, for example, skylines (Edinburgh, Prague and Venice), where the distinctive silhouettes also provide unity. There can also be the spaces, especially the primary and secondary ones found in Venice, where identity with both the city as a whole and with neighbourhoods is important. The same occurs with streets such as in Edinburgh.

The economic life of the town or city takes place in shops, offices, factories, warehouses and transport corridors. Such places can be vibrant with the economic pace and pulse of production. They are also

The City of Prague, dominated by the castle and the cathedral on the hill, providing dramatic displays of temporal and secular power. The place of public buildings and the way in which they provide a sense of identity in a city should not be overlooked. There is also a hierarchy - national, regional, local, neighbourhood - to be considered.

places where people pass much of their time. Unfortunately, many of these buildings are of little aesthetic merit and cumulatively create a discordance, which can be depressing to people living and working there. Aesthetic considerations may not be a priority for most owners, but the quality of environment at work is an important part of the setting of everyday life and should motivate rather than dishearten. The places employees use and the associated landscape structure need creative thought. Factories could be designed to reflect the drama of the powerful processes they use, as could commercial buildings echo their diverse influences.

Nevertheless, the large size of many factory or warehouse buildings and the simplicity and cheapness of their construction often mean that they are not related to a human scale. Vast areas of cladding, huge doors and wide yards can oppress the people, unless design techniques are used to break down these proportions. Conversely, *Hi-tech* architecture, as used in many high technology factory buildings, can express this technology with interesting and varied construction details.

Unity could be achieved by designing the settings and communication corridors to integrate with existing features such as river valleys, wetlands, woodlands and other buildings. This has been used in the concepts of some science or business parks for high status, high-tech factories and offices but it could be used more widely. Frequently such developments represent missed opportunities for the creation of good aesthetics in terms of their layout, architectural and landscape composition.

It is rare that there is an opportunity to put the best urban design theory into practice for a completely new town or city. A recent example is the town of Seaside in Georgia in the USA. Here, instead of a layout based on the usual North American grid, a layout of streets and public spaces was designed that incorporated variations in scale and proportion as well as shape. This framework is gradually being filled with houses built to high standards of design. There are design guidelines in place for sections of the town so that, while each house can be individual, there is sufficient similarity in form, materials, details or colours to achieve a sense of unity. The town also has public spaces and buildings that help to give it identity and character. The result is a semi-planned, semi-organic development as the town gradually grows and a kind of modern vernacular develops, within the preordained framework. Thus a balance is achieved between the fulfillment of the needs of the whole community and those of the individuals who live there. The scale and pattern manage to combine efficient functioning with an urbane, diverse aesthetic experience.

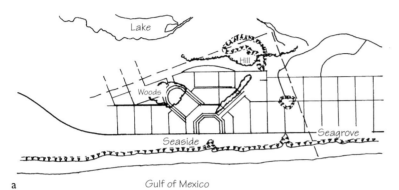

a

These diagrams illustrate the layout of the town of Seaside in Georgia, USA. a) shows the general plan and context, including the shore, woods and water; b) shows the layout of the public areas and buildings which anchor the design and give the town its identity; c) shows the plots for private building development set within the larger structure. (After Mahoney and Easterling, 1991)

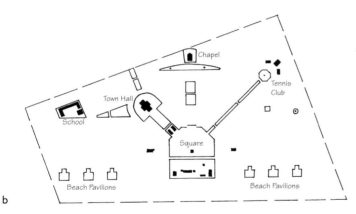

b

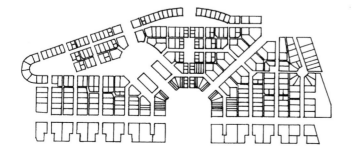

c

Summary and Conclusions

In this chapter we have traced aspects of the evolution of human landscape over the millennia, noting the early relationships between settlement, landform and ecology. As time passed, parts of this relationship remained important, while technology and economic forces encouraged other patterns to develop. In some places the ancient, self-organized patterns of early settlement have proved to be robust, lasting to the present time. They have given a strong character to the landscape that is frequently associated with a high aesthetic value, partly because of the sense of coherence, complexity and mystery found there and partly due to the opportunities for engagement with them.

We also encountered a different set of patterns that arose as a result of planning. Here, the pattern could either blend with the underlying natural landscape patterns or it could override and conflict with them. Some grid layouts, such as those found in North America, have a certain relentlessness to them, where their geometry conflicts with strong topography or ecological patterns to produce disharmony.

Patterns of towns and villages were also examined, their distribution, origins, layout and building materials. We found the same division into self-organized and planned patterns, further reinforcing the contrast between those that appear to have grown out of the landscape and those imposed on it. Planned settlements are not devoid of aesthetic merit and in some instances their orderly layout is appealing to the senses. However, most people find the irregular, more mysterious villages and towns more aesthetically pleasing than the somewhat predictable planned ones.

Cities behave in the same way. The self-organized pattern of old cities stimulates an intimate aesthetic engagement of all the senses, and a kind of visceral experience. The stylish elegance of planned cities provides a more intellectual aesthetic appreciation. Both have their place, but many people might choose the intimate, fractal qualities of self-organized cities, because they have evolved as people have used them, rather than being laid out with less concern for the way they function.

We looked at ways of analysing human patterns. There is the procedure of landscape assessment for rural landscapes where their character emerges as the product of all the influences, both natural and cultural. There are ways in which we can describe the pattern of a city layout and the ways in which the inhabitants use it.

Finally, we considered some of the creative opportunities for design, while recognizing that there are also instances when the strength of character of a pattern should be allowed to dictate what should be done. While it is perhaps more obvious that we should follow the guidance of the positive influences of pattern and process in more natural landscapes, this is also relevant in the human ones considered here, where most people live and where the opportunities for aesthetic engagement are greatest.

CHAPTER EIGHT

RECLAIMING THE LANDSCAPE

Introduction

As the tensions between continued use of the world's resources and protection of the environment increase, solutions become more complex. Thus I felt it helpful to write a book whose main purpose is to provide a deeper, more creative insight for design solutions in the landscape through a better understanding of natural patterns and processes, linked with perception and aesthetics. International obligations to protect the environment and the need for local communities to have more involvement in managing their landscapes is requiring most of the scientific and professional disciplines, concerned with landscape and environment, to combine their expertise and work at a wide range of scales and for a number of different clients.

So far the book, whilst assembling aspects relating to a wide range of disciplines and landscapes, has not addressed the ways in which the connection between international obligations, local communities and specialist knowledge can be integrated so as to achieve better, more effective and realistic solutions. In this chapter I hope to offer a way forward, using the understanding of pattern, perception and process as the key. In particular I will address the following issues, which are ones that appear important to me:

1. How can current political and legislative initiatives for protecting

the environment be translated into more effective action using limited resources?

2. How can relationships between communities and landscapes be revitalized and how can people in these communities become more involved in developing their own sustainable solutions to the problems they face?

3. How can scientific and professional landscape and environmental disciplines be better integrated so that truly holistic, sustainable solutions are achieved?

4. Where should the understanding of pattern and process based planning and design be applied?

The answers to these issues could lead towards a vision for better ways in which the landscape might be planned, designed and managed by the year 2020. This 2020 vision is evolutionary rather than revolutionary; it is also a personal vision, and as such, selective and partial. Nevertheless, I hope it may stimulate some readers to take holistic and creative approaches to sustainable development further forward.

1. How can current political and legislative initiatives for protecting the environment be translated into more effective action using limited resources?

There are a plethora of international, national, regional and local initiatives aimed at reducing pollution, environmental degradation, damage to the ozone layer or global warming. There are others designed to deliver sustainable development, better forest management, city development, habitat and species protection and soil conservation.

The United Nations Conference on Environment and Development (the Earth Summit) seeks consensus among all the nations of the world on a wide range of issues. These suffer from tensions amongst the different ambitions, priorities and resources available to different countries, ranging from the affluent, such as the USA, to the impoverished, such as Burkhina Faso.

Each nation has prepared action plans on sustainable development. For example the United Kingdom is committed to the actions outlined in *Sustainable Development: The UK Strategy*. This is further defined in relation to aspects such as biodiversity and forestry, with action plans linked to other international accords. For example, forestry is promoted through *Sustainable Forestry: The UK Programme*, which is drawn from the Earth Summit and the Ministerial Conference on the Protection of European Forests, Helsinki 1993 (the Helsinki Accords). These link to guidelines, standards and monitoring programmes.

Biodiversity is an important issue, especially where Biodiversity Action Plans complement those for sustainable development. Many of these concentrate on the protection of rare and endangered species and habitats. Many of these also fall within other conventions such as the Ramsar Convention or, in Europe, within the scope of European Union Directives.

Pollution or carbon dioxide emission reduction targets have proved to be difficult to agree worldwide, despite their global benefits. The desire by nations to maintain or reach a desirable standard of living for their people is slowing down the achievement of longer term, more altruistic objectives.

Once environmental treaties, protocols, accords, action plans, regulations, codes of practice and guidelines have been agreed, enacted and set in place, delivery mechanisms are needed. Establishment of protected areas is usually the responsibility of government agencies, though is not always easy to achieve. In Great Britain, for example, full consultation with owners and stakeholders is carried out individually (for Natura 2000 sites). This is very time consuming and resource demanding, and tends to lead to an imbalance of resource allocation, as more is given to nature conservation than landscape. This is a problem with limited resources. However, most other environmental requirements fall to a range of non-governmental organizations, businesses and individual citizens to comply with, regulated by government agencies. It is this implementation that presents a major challenge; for example, it is often viewed as laying an unwanted burden on industry.

One of the areas where this challenge is being met is in forest resource management. In Canada, the Province of British Columbia has enacted a Forest Practices Code. This is intended to meet the requirements of sustainable forest management whilst allowing the forest industry to flourish. The Code comprises the Forest Practices Act 1995 and regulations suggested by a number of Guidebooks. These cover a very wide field of activities, presented as a series of individual topics. Their application scale can vary from large landscapes, in the case of a Biodiversity Guidebook, to the pruning of individual trees in the Pruning Guidebook. Thus, a forest manager, prescribing the correct silvicultural operations for felling and reforesting a site of around 40 hectares, has to apply all of these in some detail. This is a complex, time consuming and expensive task.

It is becoming accepted that delivery of the Forest Practices Code cannot be achieved efficiently, by applying every regulation in separate sequences of action. Instead, the application of broader, integrated planning and design, commencing with a large area of forest and working down through succeeding levels to the basic management unit, is a more cost effective way of achieving a better result. Not only can large scale issues be dealt with at the large scale level, and smaller details at the smaller scale, but a truly integrated process can be followed. This has been amply demonstrated at the Hazelton Mountain and West Arm Demonstration Forest examples described in Chapter

Six. The key is an understanding of pattern and process. This means applying creative design to move from the existing forest to its desired future condition for a range of purposes. This approach uses design skills, visual thinking and a direct link to aesthetics, all based on the objective analysis and practical detail needed to develop creative solutions.

In principle, this holistic approach should not require that special areas are protected or set aside, avoiding the situation where, often, limited resources are concentrated on small areas of land. Good landscape management everywhere should obviate the need to preserve special areas, because nowhere is at risk of careless development. Furthermore, the reliance on protected areas has the effect of putting development pressure on non-protected landscapes, which are perceived as having low or no value. These may degrade faster, so that protected areas can become isolated and vulnerable. Thus, the implementation of treaty obligations for sustainable development should be applied more widely across all landscapes rather than an over reliance on a system of protected areas, to safeguard the environment (see issue four, below)

My first vision is that the principles of landscape planning and design, based on the understanding of pattern and process, will be used as the chief means of meeting goals set out in international, national, regional and local treaties, protocols, codes and guidelines for sustainable development and environmental protection everywhere.

2. How can relationships between communities and landscapes be revitalized and how can people in these communities become more involved in developing their own sustainable solutions to the problems they face?

In Chapter Three on aesthetics, the value and importance of everyday engagement with the landscape was explained and emphasized. For many people, the aesthetic pleasure landscape provides, as part of everyday life, has become unavailable, due to the deteriorating quality of some landscapes and the way many of us allow our access to landscape to become filtered by car windows or television screens.

Many people in the developed world do not become actively involved in their own landscapes, yet profess themselves concerned about the fate of remote rain forests, coral reefs or polar ice caps. Such is the power of the media and popular interest in natural history, that many people probably know more about endangered animals in far off places than about their own local landscape. In developing countries, the pressures for survival mean that many people are unable to consider the well being of their landscape, even though they depend on it for food, fuel, grazing and water. At both extremes, people are missing opportunities for fruitful aesthetic engagement with their own habitat and chances to take responsibility for it.

Most of us live in places, whether city, town or country, with their own history and sense of identity. The amount of public involvement, or opportunity for it, in local decision making, depends on the political system, land use planning regulations, bureaucratic structures and degree of direct effect on people's lives of any decisions. For many people, the local environment may only become relevant or important when something in it is threatened, perhaps an historic feature or wildlife habitat. Then the single issue can galvanize local opinion and develop into a popular movement to save the feature. Most of the time, the majority of people in many countries are content to let elected representatives or professional specialists act on their behalf.

While professional, scientific or academic disciplines have the technical expertise to understand issues and develop planning, design and management solutions, it may not be appropriate to leave the entire process to them. Their values may not be the same as those of local communities, while the solution they propose may be difficult to achieve, because of a lack of local support. Increasingly, the best and most achievable solutions, whether for soil conservation in the Sahel region of Africa, forest management in Canada or urban development in Great Britain, are developed with the active participation of local communities throughout projects, right from their initiation.

Community involvement should not be viewed as a means of legitimizing actions already proposed by technical specialists or elected representatives. Instead, the specialists should act as consultants to the community. They should provide technical assistance to help the community convert their aspirations and values into practical, high quality solutions.

For this approach to be successful, new processes of involvement are needed. These should go well beyond consensus building and negotiation, although this is important at the early stages, when issues and values associated with the landscape are being explored. If people adopt a fixed position on an issue before the full facts and alternative positions are known, unfettered, creative approaches at solution generation will be impossible. Facilitators, trained in skills of involving people and in the planning and design process, can guide the community towards solutions. The vocabulary of pattern and process can be introduced and used as a common currency between community members and technical specialists. It should stimulate and raise the quality of discussion and exchange of information.

The model presented here includes stages where the community and technical specialists work together and separately. The facilitator helps the community identify and describe the values they place on the landscape. The technical specialists help to describe the patterns and processes giving rise to these values, often using local knowledge to refine their analysis. Part of the identification and discussion of values will involve perceptual and aesthetic issues that can be related to the pattern/process analysis. The technical specialists may then develop a range of planning, management and design options that meet the values and objectives defined by the community, within the framework of the constraints and opportunities presented by the landscape. The community evaluate and criticize the proposals and move towards an acceptable solution that is worked up into a design or management plan by the technical specialists. The community, where possible, become the decision makers. They need to develop skills as buyers of professional services, in critique and in the planning, design and management processes in order to participate fully in their role.

The success of this approach extends beyond the way a project is set up and the protocol by which it operates. It also depends on the understanding of the vocabulary of pattern, process and perception. The aesthetics of engagement is at the heart of reawakening the relationships between people and place. Thus a literacy of the landscape is necessary, a subject not presently taught in schools. Some knowledge will be gained through subjects like biology, geography or social history. Environmental education could be expanded to give school students a grounding in how to apply knowledge of patterns, processes and associated aesthetic issues. It could be part of a programme to develop good citizenship skills in children.

A good example of following this approach to planning, design and management is the way in which the analysis for the Hazelton Mountain area of British Columbia in Canada, as described in Chapter Six, was developed. It was perhaps easier to apply the process there, because the majority of the land is in public ownership and the community is heavily dependent on it for their livelihood. A group of 19 people came together, at the invitation of the local forestry managers (advertised in the local press) over two days to analyse the 40 thousand hectare area. I facilitated the meeting which was sponsored by the Ministry of Forests. Participants included technical specialists in forestry, ecology, landscape, silviculture, engineering and so on, provided by the Ministry of Forests. Local people, including representatives of the Gitxsan native band, also participated. Landscape maps were available and an ecological 'primer' was prepared to explain terminology to the lay members of the group. The whole group then participated in the analysis and produced a series of values and objectives related to areas of distinct landscape character. The results were made into a visual report, full of photographs and maps, and a design completed for half of the area. This was considered by the group as a means of meeting the objectives within the carrying capacity of the landscape and the legal requirements of the Forest Practices Code.

My second vision is that communities are encouraged to participate fully in decisions that affect their local landscapes, using professional specialists as their consultants, basing their achievements on an understanding of landscape patterns and processes that is part of an education received by all children.

3. How can scientific and professional landscape and environmental disciplines be better integrated so that truly holistic, sustainable solutions are achieved?

In the introduction to the book, I listed the range of disciplines involved in land management, planning and development. This included a range of natural science disciplines such as geologists, geomorphologists, biologists, ecologists and hydrologists, who can explain the workings of natural processes; cultural geographers, archaeologists and landscape historians, who can explain the development of the human landscape; landscape architects, civil engineers, land managers, foresters, land use planners and recreation planners, who develop and implement land use strategies, management plans and designs. This is a long, but not exhaustive list. What is clear is that each discipline, while partly overlapping some others, may only be involved with a relatively narrow, though detailed, aspect of the landscape.

Not all of the disciplines are integrated by nature or training, nor are they expected to produce plans, designs or management proposals. Whilst there are some overlaps, there is no common vocabulary enabling each discipline to communicate effectively and work with others. On the contrary, many have specific terminologies that may be almost incomprehensible to others. The problem of interdisciplinary communications is also mirrored between professional specialist and lay person.

The integrative disciplines tend to be those who develop and apply land and resource management planning and problem solving, often in the context of competing objectives. These include land agents/ chartered surveyors/land managers (terms vary in different countries), land use planners, landscape architects, urban development planners and (in part) civil engineers and architects.

In order to improve cross-discipline integration, there needs to be an efficient means of increasing everyone's awareness and understanding of the wide range of landscape issues. The pattern/perception/process theme could provide this. It should, alongside the aesthetic theory and application that links it to design, become a key component of the training of students in all the disciplines listed above, and be added to syllabuses for continuing professional education.

The more people become used to considering their own expertise in the wider context explored in this book, the better multi-disciplinary integration will be facilitated. This argues for the extension of team work, where the leaders of projects are not necessarily those with the biggest budgets, but those who have specific integrative training and experience. It follows that developing techniques for integrated working and decision making in the education of these disciplines is also important.

My third vision is that the vocabulary of pattern, perception and process will become the common medium of exchange amongst all landscape and environmental based professional disciplines, whether in research, planning, design or management.

4. Where should the understanding of pattern and process based planning and design be applied?

The potential field of application of the approach advocated here is a wide one: it could be the entire world. However, the imperative for its application is greatest where landscape change is fastest, where major changes to land management practices are occuring or where the landscape is under severe development pressure. How far and how sophisticated the application can be will depend on the available resources of skills and finance. Three important circumstances can be identified, where the approach could provide the greatest benefits.

a) The developed landscapes of Europe, the USA, Canada, Australia, New Zealand, Japan and in nations rapidly developing their industries, such as Mexico, Malaysia or South Africa. Here the main forces of landscape change are economic. The trends are for industrialization, intensive land use, urban growth and infrastructure development. These activities pay little or no heed to natural or cultural patterns, except the most constraining. The environmental movement is active in many of these countries, although not all, and most try to encorporate in their economic development some kind of natural and cultural protection, through the creation of national parks, nature reserves, protected cultural heritage sites and the like (see issue one, above). The result can be a dichotomy between protected, sometimes preserved areas, where expertise and resources for conservation are often focused, and the rest of the landscape. There may be some form of development or land use planning control to temper the economics driven landscape changes. It may be assumed by developers, because there is a network of protected areas, that the rest of the landscape is unimportant and freely available for economic development. This tends to place the landscape under more pressure. However, such areas are where most people live and spend most of their time. For example, 85% of the British population live in 'ordinary landscapes' where the aesthetic quality may be quite low.

If the pattern/process approach is adopted and applied to everyday landscapes outside protected areas, there should be greater scope for achieving sustainable development. The ecological functioning of much more of the landscape could be enhanced, as could its aesthetic value, thus raising the quality of people's lives. Moreover, the pressure to protect more areas could be relaxed because there could be fewer threats.

A typical scene of urban sprawl in the USA driven by economic forces and laissez faire planning policies. This is one important area where the design approach advocated in this book could have beneficial effects both functionally and environmentally.

The character of the interface between forest and farmland could be designed to reflect natural patterns

Analysis of hydrological patterns and processes could be used before natural drainages are altered

Natural patterns and processes could be allowed to continue in natural areas

Forest management activities, such as logging could be based on ecosystem patterns and processes.

A sketch of a landscape in North America showing the opportunities to apply the different design and management techniques described in this book, ranging from natural resource planning to urban development.

Analysis of the soils and drainage patterns and processes could be undertaken before irrigation and use of intensive farming is developed further

Flood control by engineered structures on the river could be reviewed so that some degree of natural function is restored

Sprawling settlement development could be avoided by better planning and design of urban patterns and use of local architecture

Ecological functioning could be restored in intensively farmed areas by developing a habitat network

Town planning, could use an analysis of patterns and processes to maintain both good functioning and good aesthetics.

Landscape character analysis could help with siting of new development in the countryside

Management of semi-natural landscapes could make use of a combination of landscape ecology and landscape character to direct landscape change

A sketch depicting a European landscape with the type of issues that present opportunities to use the methods described in this book.

Restoration of natural hydrology and river ecology could help many aspects of landscape functioning

Intensively farmed areas could be improved or restored using landscape ecology and landscape character analysis

Rural settlement and communications could be managed and enhanced using landscape character analysis

b) The countries of the former Soviet Union and eastern Europe, where central planning has now largely disappeared, are in need of updated forms of landscape planning. Many countries have few resources for this and their expertise may be strong in some areas, but weak in others. For example, there are few landscape architects in the former Soviet Union, because none were trained between 1957 and the 1990s. A recent priority has been to catch up with other countries in the designation of protected areas to meet the obligations of international treaties. Pollution from old industries is another problem to be given high priority. In many of these countries, there is no history of community participation or of non-government organizations or pressure groups. However, economic activity has also slowed down in some countries so there is less pressure on resources at the moment.

This means that new and up to date models of landscape based planning need to be introduced. The lack of resources does not

A view across the city of Vladimir in Middle Russia. This area is suffering from the results of the Soviet system and its collapse. Infrastructure has decayed and old industrial practices left a legacy of pollution. There is a major opportunity to use modern planning and design methods as these places become modernized.

permit sophisticated methods to be adopted yet but would not prevent community participation to be developed and plans to be put in place to help sustainable development of natural resources when the economies are revitalized. The high levels of education in these countries should enable local people to play full roles and counterbalance the shortage of cash funding.

c) Developing countries. Here the problems are related to forest clearance, population pressure, soil erosion, urbanization and desertification. Expertise available in these countries varies, with a significant amount provided by aid agencies for development projects. Financial support is usually low, so that low cost, low technology solutions are needed. In the past, much aid was concentrated on expensive, large projects such as dams for irrigation. The trend is away from this to community based projects. Here there is considerable scope for using the pattern/process model at a community level, facilitated by trained people, perhaps provided by aid agencies. Agricultural development, forest management, reforestation, settlement planning and soil conservation could be integrated into a sustainable plan for a local community (perhaps based around territories of indigenous peoples). Any plan must be based on an understanding of patterns and processes so as not to overload systems that may be very fragile, because of human and grazing pressures (p. 240, Fig. 17).

The common thread, connecting all these examples of application, is the need for an holistic approach, based on the landscape scale. This is not only the scale at which patterns and processes often operate, but may also be the extent of the perceived landscape belonging to a community. Thus, the practical level of planning can equate with the home landscape and the pattern/process understanding can be directly related to the aesthetic engagement of the community.

All land use issues must be dealt with together. Agricultural development affects hydrology, forests and settlements, so that none should be considered separately. This can save time and produce more effective solutions that present fewer constraints to development, because management can become the tool used to maintain a healthy landscape, whilst at the same time requiring fewer resources for implementation.

My fourth vision is that the pattern, perception and process approach will be taken up in landscapes of all conditions, developed and modified to suit the circumstances, scale, resources and political climate of each county or region.

2020 Vision

In order to assess where these visions might lead, I believe there should be some aims to achieve by the year 2020. These should be:

1. The pattern process approach will have become the common vocabulary of the land-based professions and technical specialists.

2. The pattern/process language will be taught in all schools, colleges and universities; the 3 Ps of landscape literacy (Patterns, Perception, Process) to complement the 3 Rs of general literacy (Reading, wRiting and aRithmetic). It could be used to enhance environmental education currently practised in combination with aesthetic awareness.

3. Every country, as part of its continuing commitment to sustainability, will develop demonstration areas, where the method of pattern/process based planning, design and management will be applied and tested, so that it can be evaluated and refined to fit local circumstances.

BIBLIOGRAPHY

Alexander, C., Neis, M., Anninon, A. and King, L. (1987) *A New Theory of Urban Design,* Oxford University Press, Oxford.

Anon (1976) *Landscape Valuation*, University of Manchester, Manchester.

Anon (1987) *Our Common Future (The Brundtland Report): Report of the 1987 World Commission on Environment and Development*, Oxford University Press, Oxford.

Anon (1992) Biogeoclimatic Zones of British Columbia Research Branch, Ministry of Forests, Victoria, BC, Canada.

Anon (1992) *Earth Summit '92*, The Regency Press Corporation, London.

Anon (1994) Sustainable Development: The UK Strategy, CM2426, HMSO, London.

Anon (1994) Sustainable Forestry: The UK Programme, CM2429, HMSO, London.

Appleton, J. (1996) *The Experience of Landscape* (Revised Edition), John Wiley and Sons, Chichester.

Arendt, R. (1994) *Rural by Design: Maintaining Small Town Character,* American Planning Association, Chicago.

Arieti, S. (1976) *Creativity: The Magic Synthesis,* Basic Books, New York.

Arnheim, R. (1969) *Visual Thinking*, University of California Press, Berkeley.

Arno, S. F. and Hammerly, R. P. (1984) *Treelines*, The Mountaineers, Seattle.

Bacon, E. N. (1974) *Design of Cities* (Revised Edition), Thames and Hudson, London.

Barrie, T. (1998) *Spiritual Paths, Secret Places,* Shambola Publications, Boston.

Bartlett, R. (1993) *The Making of Europe*, Penguin Books, London.

Baskent, E. Z. and Jordan, E. A. (1995) Characterizing Spatial Structure of Forest Landscapes, in *Canadian Journal of Forest Research 25*, pp 1830-1849.

Bell, S. (1993) *Elements of Visual Design in the Landscape*, E & FN Spon, London.

Bell, S. (1995) New Woodlands in the Landscape, in Ferris-Kaan, R. (Ed) *The Ecology of Woodland Creation*, John Wiley and Sons Ltd, Chichester.

Bell, S. (1997) The Importance of Landscape Design, in The After-Use of Disturbed Land, in Moffat, A. J. (Ed) *Recycling Land for Forestry,* Forestry Commission Technical Paper 22, Forestry Commission, Edinburgh.

Berleant, A. (1924) *The Aesthetics of Environment,* Temple University Press, Philadelphia.

Boden, M. A. (1994) What is Creativity? in Boden, M. A. (Ed) *Dimensions of Creativity,* MIT Press, Cambridge, Massachusetts.

Bord Failte (undated) *Building Sensitively In Ireland's Landscapes*, Bord Failte, Dublin.

Botkin, D. B. (1990) *Discordant Harmonies*, Oxford University Press, Oxford.

Brennan. A. (1988) *Thinking About Nature*, Routledge, London.

Briggs, J. (1992) *Fractals, The Patterns of Chaos*, Thames and Hudson, London.

Bruce, V., Green, P. R., Georgeson, M. A. (1994) *Visual Perception: Physiology, Psychology and Ecology* (3rd Edition), Psychology Press, Hove.

Brunskill, R. W. (1981) *Traditional Buildings in Britain,* Victor Gollancz, London.

Brunskill, R.W. (1987) *Illustrated Handbook of Vernacular Architecture,* Faber and Faber, London.

Budiensky, S. (1995), Chaos in Eden in *New Scientist 148.*

Burke, E. (1958) *A Philosophical Enquiry into the Origin of Our Ideas of the Sublime and the Beautiful,* (Boulton, J.T. Ed), Routledge and Kegan Paul, London.

Cambridgeshire County Council (1991) *Cambridgeshire Landscape Guidelines: A Manual for Management and Change in the Rural Landscape*, Cambridgeshire County Council and Granta Editions, Cambridge.

Carlson, A. and Sadler, B. (1982) *Environmental Aesthetics: Essays in Interpretation*, University of Victoria.

Caulfield, S. (1978) Neolithic Fields: The Irish Evidence, in H. C. Bowen and P.J. Fowler (Eds) *Early Land Allotment in the British Isles,* pp 137-143, Oxford, British Archaeological Reports: British Series 48.

Clifton-Taylor, A. (1987) *The Pattern of English Building* (4th Edition) Faber & Faber, London.

Connely, W. (1960) *Louis Sullivan: The Shaping of American Architecture*, Horizon Press, New York.

Corner, J. (1996) The Obscene (American) Landscape, in Spens, M. (Ed) *Landscape Transformed*, Academy Editions, London.

Countryside Commission (1994) *The New Map of England: A Celebration of the South Western Landscape,* Countryside Commission, Cheltenham.

BIBLIOGRAPHY

Cronon, W. (1983) *Changes in the Land*, Hill and Wang, New York.

Crowe, Dame S. and Mitchell, M. (1988) *The Pattern of Landscape*, Packard Publishing, Chichester.

Dasman, R. F. (1976) *Environmental Conservation* (4th Edition), John Wiley and Sons, New York.

Department of Environment (1992) *Landform Replication as a Technique for the Reclamation of Limestone Quarries*, HMSO, London.

Diaz, N. and Bell, S. (1997) Landscape Analysis and Design, in *Creating a Forestry for the 21st Century*, Kohn, K.A. Franklin, J.F., Island Press, Washington DC.

Dubé, R. L. (1997) *Natural Pattern Forms: A Practical Sourcebook for Landscape Designers*, Van Nostrand Reinhold, New York.

Duff, J. (1994) *West Arm Demonstration Forest Workshop Report*, B.C. Ministry of Forests, Nelson, British Columbia.

Elia, M. M. (1996) *Louis Henry Sullivan*, Princeton Architectural Press, Princeton.

Erickson, J. (1992) *Plate Tectonics*, Facts on File, New York.

Exploratorium, The (1993) *By Nature's Design*, Chronicle Books, San Francisco.

Eysenck, H. S. (1994) The Measurement of Creativity, in Boden, M. A. (Ed) *Dimensions of Creativity*, MIT Press, Cambridge, Massachusetts.

Fairnie, A. (1998) *Principles and Methods in Landscape Ecology*, Chapman & Hall, London.

Fines, K. D. (1968) Landscape Evaluation in East Sussex, in *Regional Studies*.

Fitsimmons, J. (1993) *Bungalow Bliss* (Tenth Edition), Kells Art Studio, Kells.

Forman, R. T. T. and Godron, M. (1986) *Landscape Ecology*, Wiley, New York.

Forman, R. T. T. (1995) *Land Mosaics*, Cambridge University Press, Cambridge.

Foster, C. A. (1992) *Aesthetics and the Natural Environment* (Unpublished PhD Thesis, University of Edinburgh.)

Foster, D. R. and Boose, E.R. (1992) Patterns of Forest Damage Resulting from Catastrophic Wind in Central New England USA, in *Journal of Ecology* 80, 79-98.

Franklin, J. F. and Forman, R. T. T. (1987) Creating Landscape Patterns by Forest Cutting: Ecological Consequences and Principles, in *Landscape Ecology* 1, 5-18.

Gibson, J. J. (1966) *The Senses Considered as Perceptual Systems*, Houghton Mifflin, Boston.

Gibson, J. J. (1979) *The Ecological Approach to Visual Perception*, Houghton Mifflin, Boston.

Gleick, J. (1988) *Chaos, Making a New Science*, Heinemann, London.

Gobster, P. H. (1995) Aldo Leopold's Ecological Aesthetic: Integrating Esthetic and Biodiversity Values, in *Journal of Forestry*, Feb, pp 6-10.

Gould, P. and White, R. (1986) *Mental Maps* (2nd Edition), Routledge, London.

Gunter, P. (1996) *A Whiteheadian Aesthetics of Nature: Beauty and the Forest* (Unpublished).

Haines-Young, R. and Chopping, M. (1996) Quantifying Landscape Structure: A Review of Landscape Indices and Their Application to Forested Landscapes, in *Progress in Physical Geography*, Vol 20 No 4, Arnold, London.

Hale, J. (1994) *The Old Ways of Seeing*, Houghton Mifflin, New York.

Harris, S. L. (1980) *Fire and Ice: The Cascade Volcanoes* (Revised Edition), The Mountaineers, Seattle.

Hastings, H. M. and Sugihara, G. (1993) *Fractals: A User's Guide for the Natural Sciences*, Oxford University Press, Oxford.

Hibbert, C. (1988) *Venice: The Biography of a City*, Grafton Books, London.

Hill, M. O. (1979) *TWINSPAN - A FORTRAN Program for Arranging Multivariate Data in an Ordered Two-way Table by Classification of the Individuals and Attributes*, Section of Ecology and Systematics, Cornell University, Ithaca, New York.

Holland, S. S. (1976) *Landforms of British Columbia, A Physiographic Outline*, Bulletin 48, British Columbia Department of Mines and Petroleum Reserves, Victoria.

Hoskins, W. G. (1955) *The Making of the English Landscape*, Hodder and Stoughton, London.

Huggett, R. J. (1995) *Geoecology*, Routledge, London.

Humphrey, N. (1992) *History of the Mind*, Harper Collins.

Huston, M. A. (1994) *Biological Diversity*, Cambridge University Press, Cambridge.

Jeglum, J. K. and Fangliang, H. (1995) Pattern and Vegetation Environment Relationships in a Boreal Forested Wetland in Northeastern Ontario, in *Canadian Journal of Botany* 73, pp 629-637.

Jellicoe, G. and Jellicoe, S. (1995) *The Landscape of Man* (Revised Edition), Thames and Hudson, London.

Johnson, A. (1995) The Good, The Bad and the Ugly: Science, Aesthetics and Environmental Assessment, in *Biodiversity and Conservation* 4 pp 758 - 766.

Johnson, C. A. (1998) *Geographic Information Systems in Ecology*, Blackwell, Oxford.

Kant, I. (translated by J. H. Bernard) (1981) *The Critique of Judgement*, MacMillan, London.

Kaplan, S. (1988) Perception and Landscape: Conception and Misconception, in Nasar, J.L. (Ed) *Environmental Aesthetics,* Cambridge University Press, Cambridge.

Kaufman, W. (1993) How Nature Really Works, in *American Forests*, March/April 1993, pp 17-19 and 59-61.

Kohler, W. (1947) *Gestalt Psychology: An Introduction to Modern Concepts in Psychology*, Liveright Publishing Corporation, New York.

Landscape Institute/Institute of Environmental Assessment (1995) *Guidelines for Visual Impact Assessment*, E & FN Spon, London.

Lee, T. R. (1991) *Forests, Woods and People's Preferences.* Unpublished report to the Forestry Commission, Ediburgh.

Leopold, A. (1981, first published 1949) *A Sand County Almanac,* Oxford University Press, New York.

Lewin, R. (1993) *Complexity: Life at the Edge of Chaos,* Dent, London.

Lewis, P. H. (Jr) (1996) *Tomorrow by Design*, John Wiley and Sons, New York.

Lhina, R. R. (Ed) (1988) *The Biology of the Brain: From Neurons to Networks*, Freeman and Co, Oxford.

Lugo, A. E. (1995) Reconstructing Hurricane Passages Over Forests: A Tool for Understanding Multiple Scale Responses to Disturbance, in *Tree* Vol 10, No 3.

Lynch, K. (1960) *Image of the City*, MIT Press, Cambridge, Massachusetts.

Mabbutt, J.A. (1977) *Desert Landforms*, MIT Press, Cambridge, Massachusetts.

Mahoney, D. and Easterling, K. (Eds) (1991) *Seaside: Making a Town in America*, Princeton Architectural Press Inc, New York.

Marr, D. (1982) *Vision: A Computational Investigation into the Human Representation and Processing of Visual Information*, Freeman, San Francisco.

Maser, C. (1990) *The Redesigned Forest*, Stoddart Publishing Co. Ltd, Toronto.

McAulay, I. (1989) *CONVEX: A Computer Program for Analysing the Degree of Convexity or Concavity of Landform*, Turnbull Jeffrey Partnership, Edinburgh.

McHarg, I. (1969) *Design with Nature*, Natural History Press, New York.

Mills, J., Box, J. and Coppin, N. (1995) Natural Legacies, in *Landscape Design* 238.

Ministry of Forests of British Columbia (1997) *Landscape Analysis to Guide Landscape Planning, Design and Management : Unpublished Report of Proceedings of McCully Creek Workshop*, Hazelton, British Columbia.

Moffat, A. J. (1997) *Recycling Land for Forestry*, Forestry Commission Technical Paper 22, Forestry Commission, Edinburgh.

Moughtin, C. (1996) *Urban Design, Green Dimension*, Butterworth, London.

Moughtin, C. , Oc, T. and Tisdell, S. (1995) *Urban Design: Ornament and Decoration*, Butterworth, London.

Muir, P.S. (1993) Disturbance Effects on Structure and Tree Species Composition of Pinus Contorta Forests in Western Montana, in *Canadian Journal of Forest Research* Vol 23, No 8, pp 1617-1625.

Murphy, P. *By Nature's Design,* Chronicle Books, San Francisco.

Naismith, R.J. (1985) *Buildings in the Scottish Countryside*, Victor Gollancz, London.

O'Connell, J. W. and Korff, A. (Eds) (1991) *The Book of the Burren*, Tir Eolas, Newtownlynch Kinvara, Ireland.

Oliver, C. D. and Larson, B. C. (1996) *Forest Stand Dynamics: Updated Edition*, John Wiley and Sons, New York.

Perkins, D. N. (1994) Creativity: Beyond the Darwinian Paradigm, in Boden, M.A. (Ed) *Dimensions of Creativity*, MIT Press, Cambridge, Massachusetts.

Perry, D. A. (1994) *Forest Ecosystems*, John Hopkins University Press, Baltimore.

Pojar, J., Klinka, K. and Meindinger, D.V. (1987) Biogeoclimatic Ecosystem Classification in British Columbia, in *Forest Ecology and Management* 22, pp 119-154.

Porter, E. V. and Gleick, J. (1990) *Nature's Chaos*, Cardinal Books, London.

Porteus, J. D. (1996) *Environmental Aesthetics*, Routledge, London.

Price, L. W. (1981) *Mountains and Man*, University of California Press, Berkeley and Los Angeles.

Pyatt, D. G. and Suarez, J. C. (1997) *An Ecological Site Classification for Forestry in Great Britain*, Forestry Commission Technical Paper 20, Forestry Commission, Edinburgh.

Pyne, S. J. (1982) *Fire in America*, Princeton University Press, Princeton.

Rackham, O. (1986) *The History of the Countryside*, Dent, London.

Roberts, B. K. (1977) *Rural Settlement in Britain*, Hutchinson, London.

Roberts, B. K. (1987) *The Making of the English Village*, Longman, London.

Robertson, A. (1994) Directionality, Fractals and Chaos in Wind Shaped Forests, in *Agriculture and Forest Meteorology* 72, pp 133-166.

Rodwell, J. S. (1991) *British Plant Communities 1: Woodland Communities*, Cambridge University Press, Cambridge.

Rose, M. C. (1976) Nature as Aesthetic Object: An Essay in Meta-Aesthetics, in *British Journal of Aesthetics* 16 (1).

Saito, Y. (1984) Is There a Correct Aesthetic Appreciation of Nature?, in *Journal of Aesthetic Education*, 18 (4).

Scharma, S. (1995) *Landscape and Memory*, Harper Collins, London.

Schopenhauer, A. (1969) (Translated by E.F.J. Payne) *The World as Will and Representation*, Dover Publications.

Schwenk, T. (1996) *Sensitive Chaos* (Revised Edition), Rudolf Steiner Press, London.

Selinge, K-G., (Ed) (1994) *National Atlas of Sweden: Cultural Heritage and Preservation*, SNA Publicity, Stockholm.

Sharp, R. P. (1988) *Living Ice*, Cambridge University Press, Cambridge.

Sircello, G. (1975) *A New Theory of Beauty*, Princeton University Press, Princeton.

Smith, M. E. (1996) *The Aztecs*, Blackwell, Cambridge, Massachusetts.

Snyder, G. (1995) *A Place in Space*, Counterpoint, Washington DC.

Soul, N. (Ed) (1997) *The Oxford Illustrated History of Mediaeval England*, Oxford University Press, Oxford.

Sparshott, F. E. (1963) *The Structure of Aesthetics*, University of Toronto Press, Toronto.

Sternberg, R. J. (Ed) (1988) *The Nature of Creativity*, Cambridge University Press, Cambridge.

Stevens, P. S. (1974) *Patterns in Nature*, Penguin Books, London.

Stewart, I. (1995) *Nature's Numbers*, Weidenfield and Nicholson, London.

Storr, A. (1972) *The Dynamics of Creation*, Penguin Books, London.

Strahler, A. and Strahler, A., (1998) *Introducing Physical Geography* (2nd Edition), John Wiley and Sons, New York.

Stronhal, E. (1992) *Life in Ancient Egypt*, Cambridge University Press, Cambridge.

Swanson, F. J., Kratz, T.K., Caine, N. and Woodmansee, R.G. (1988) Landform Effects of Ecosystem Patterns and Processes, in *BioScience* Vol 38 No 2, pp 92-98.

Taylor, C. (1975) *Fields in the English Landscape*, J. M. Dent & Sons, London.

Taylor, C. (1983) *Village and Farmstead*, George Phillips, London.

Tuan, Yi-Fu (1993) *Passing Strange and Wonderful: Aesthetics, Nature and Culture*, Island Press, Washington DC.

Turner, M. G. (1989) Landscape Ecology: The Effect of Pattern on Process, in *Annual Review of Ecological Systems* 20, pp 171-97.

Van der Ryn, S. and Cowan, S. (1996) *Ecological Design*, Island Press, Washington DC.

Vitruvius (Translated by M. H. Morgan) (1960) *The Ten Books of Architecture*, Dover Publications, New York.

Warnock, M. (1976) *Imagination,* Faber & Faber, London.

Whitehead, A.N. (1955) *The Concept of Nature*, Cambridge University Press, Cambridge.

Whitehead, A.N. (1960) *Adventures of Ideas*, Mentor Books, New York.

Willard, D. (1980) On Preserving Nature's Aesthetic Feature, in *Environmental Ethics*, 2 (4).

Wilson, E. (1994) *8000 Years of Ornament*, British Museum Press, London.

Wood, E.S. (1995) *Historical Britain*, The Harvill Press, London.

Wyckoff, J. (1970) *Rock, Time and Landform*, Harper and Row, New York.

INDEX

INDEX